Agricultural Development

Agricultural Development:
An International Perspective

Yujiro Hayami and Vernon W. Ruttan

THE JOHNS HOPKINS PRESS
Baltimore and London

The Johns Hopkins Press, Baltimore, Maryland 21218
The Johns Hopkins Press Ltd., London

Library of Congress Catalog Card Number 76–150663
International Standard Book Number 0–8018–1259–3(c)

TO
KAZUSHI OHKAWA AND THEODORE W. SCHULTZ

Contents

vii

PART IV
Can Growth Be Transferred?

PART V
Retrospect and Prospect

APPENDICES

TABLES

Tables (continued)

FIGURES

Figures (continued)

Preface

This book is the outgrowth of a relatively limited initial search for regularities in the variations in agricultural production and resource use among countries. The search was then extended to see if the intercountry regularities were also reflected in the historical experiences of selected countries.

Our efforts to interpret the observed regularities among countries and over time have resulted in considerable dissatisfaction with the existing theories of agricultural and economic development. The dissatisfaction is primarily concerned with the conventional treatment of technical and institutional change. We have also been concerned that much theoretical discussion has focused on the role or contribution of the agricultural sector in the total development process, while providing little insight into the agricultural development process. The theory of agricultural development has largely been ignored.

We identify the capacity to develop technology consistent with environmental and economic conditions as the single most important variable which explains the growth of agricultural productivity of nations. Yet the process of technical change has typically been treated as exogenous to the economic development process.

For the past two decades there have been increasingly sophisticated attempts to "measure technical change" and to "account for growth." However, the process by which technical change is induced by economic forces has received only limited attention. The "theory of induced innovation," while suggestive, is of limited value because it has been formulated entirely within the framework of the theory of firm. The innovative behavior of the public sector has been neglected. This defect is particularly critical in agriculture, because public sector research in science and technology represents a major source of progress in agriculture.

Our investigation into the process by which public sector research responds to economic and social forces has led us to a consideration of the process by which institutions evolve in response to economic and technical opportunities. The institutions which govern the processes by which scientific and technical knowledge is created, such as experiment stations and patent laws, are of central importance. So are the institutions, such as market and tenure institutions, which facilitate the introduction and use of new technology in agricultural production or internalize the gains from the use of new technical opportunities.

xiii

In order to proceed with our investigation of agricultural development, we were impelled to develop a model in which technical and institutional changes are induced by economic forces which reflect product demand, original resource endowments, and resource accumulation associated with the historical processes of economic development. The model we have developed does not possess formal elegance. It is partial, in that it is primarily concerned with production and productivity. Relatively little attention is given to the role of consumption and demand. Yet the model has added significantly to our power to interpret the process of agricultural development in both the advanced and less developed countries.

The research on which this book is based was supported by the Rockefeller Foundation, the Minnesota Agricultural Experiment Station, and the Economic Development Center of the University of Minnesota. It draws on earlier research by the authors extending back almost two decades. It also draws on works by their colleagues, particularly Robert E. Evenson, Kinuyo Inagi, Barbara B. Miller, William W. Wade, Saburo Yamada, and Sachiko Yamashita.

Dana G. Dalrymple, Kenzo Hemmi, Kazushi Ohkawa, and Theodore W. Schultz have read an earlier manuscript and have given us invaluable comments. We have also benefited from comments and suggestions at the various stages of research from Dale W. Adams, Martin E. Abel, Randolph Barker, Lucas Calpouzos, Colin Clark, K. William Easter, Walter P. Falcon, Darrell F. Fienup, Zvi Griliches, Earl O. Heady, James P. Houck, Sam C. Hsieh, Shigeru Ishikawa, D. Gale Johnson, Bruce F. Johnston, Charles E. Kellogg, Simon Kuznets, Theodore Morgan, Albert H. Moseman, Arthur T. Mosher, James I. Nakamura, Richard R. Nelson, Takashi Negishi, J. Frank O'Connor, Willis L. Peterson, Malcolm J. Purvis, Gustav Ranis, Wayne D. Rasmussen, Philip M. Raup, Nathan Rosenberg, Mathew D. Shane, Anthony M. Tang, C. Peter Timmer, Mataji Umemura, and Sterling Wortman. Lester R. Brown, Donald D. Durost, Charles H. Gibbons, Austin S. Fox, Hideo Kobayashi, Toshihiro Kojima, Akira Matsuzaki, William N. Parker, William Paddock, Yoshikiyo Saegusa, Shujiro Sawada, P. E. Stryg, Hugh Wooten, and Saburo Yamada assisted us in providing relevant information and data. We quote with permission from numerous publications which are acknowledged in the text. Without the unflagging efforts of Mrs. Barbara Miller in technical and editorial assistance this book could hardly have been completed. For all these benefits we express the deepest gratitude.

This book is dedicated to Kazushi Ohkawa and Theodore W. Schultz. Their work has exerted a pervasive impact on development thought and policy in both the East and West, and we have found it impossible in writing this book to escape the impact of their thought or to fully acknowledge our debt to them.

Agricultural Development

CHAPTER ONE

Introduction

In the first two decades following World War II the productivity gap between the developed and developing countries widened sharply. The developed nations which had been, on balance, net importers of food grains prior to World War II became net exporters of food grains to the low income countries. Much of this grain was moved to the developing countries in the form of food aid or was sold on concessional terms.

During the late 1960's a series of technical breakthroughs has created a new potential for rapid increases in grain production in the less developed countries of the tropics and subtropics. A major issue facing policymakers and planners in many developing nations today is whether the potential agricultural surpluses can be converted into a viable basis for sustained economic growth.

Economic doctrine with respect to the relative contribution of agricultural and industrial development to national economic growth has experienced a sharp transition during the last several decades. Economists who a decade ago were emphasizing the critical contribution of urban industrial growth to agricultural development are now equally impressed with the importance of an agricultural surplus for economic development. Analysts, who were skeptical at the willingness of peasant producers in poor countries to adopt new technology, are now disturbed by the price and income distribution effects of rapid growth in food grain production. These shifts in opinion have been reflected by shifts in agricultural and industrial development perspectives and policies adopted by the policymakers and planners of the developing countries.

In part this change in emphasis is a product of the new range of development problems with which economists have begun to concern themselves. Western economies are characterized by rapid technical progress in agriculture, relatively modest rates of population growth, and a declining response in the demand for farm products to income growth. Rapid urban industrial development has been perceived as clearly essential if the rural labor, made redundant by the rapid gains in labor productivity in agriculture, is to escape from low productivity employment in the rural sector and make an important contribution to national economic growth. This has been particularly true in the less industrialized regions of major national economies, such as the Southeastern United States, and the less industrialized nations of multinational economic systems, such as the Southern European members or associate members of the European Common Market (EEC).

During the last several decades the attention of economists has increasingly shifted to a concern with the problem of economic development in low income national economies that had not yet solved the problem of how to transform traditional agriculture into a viable source of sustained growth in food production.

This shift in orientation reflects an increasing need for analysis of the agricultural development problems of nations characterized by static agricultural technology, rapid increases in the demand for farm products in response to population and income growth, and the "pathological" growth of urban centers. It also represents a pragmatic response to the lack of success of much of the development effort and development assistance that has been attempted by both national and international agencies in areas outside of the Western economic system—in Asia, Africa, and Latin America.

No clear-cut system of "new development economics" has yet emerged to dominate the fields of economic development theory and policy as completely as the "new economics," based on John Maynard Keynes's work, dominated income and employment theory after 1936. However, a new consensus seems to have emerged that an effective economic development strategy, particularly during the early stages of economic growth, depends critically on the achievement of rapid technical change, leading to productivity growth in agriculture.

This consensus has not yet been accompanied by comparable agreement regarding the processes by which rapid productivity and output growth can be achieved in the agricultural sector. Theodore W. Schultz has suggested that significant growth in productivity cannot be brought about by the reallocation of resources in traditional agricultural systems. Significant opportunities for growth will become available only through changes in technology—new husbandry techniques, better seed varieties, more efficient sources of power, and cheaper plant nutrients.[1] Investment in such activities as agricultural research, leading to the supply of new inputs, and in the education of the farm people who are to use the new inputs will provide the basis for technical change and productivity growth in agriculture.

The Schultz theory is incomplete, however. It does not fully incorporate resource allocation to, and in, the sector which produces and supplies the new

[1] Theodore W. Schultz, *Transforming Traditional Agriculture* (New Haven: Yale University Press, 1964).

inputs.[2] This sector consists of the suppliers of the new inputs, such as innovative farmers, public research institutions, and agricultural supply firms, and it competes with other sectors of the economy in the use of scarce resources. The issue of how a society allocates resources to this new input sector and how the resources are allocated among different activities within the sector is fundamental to the agricultural development process. Some of the products of this sector (for example, new husbandry techniques) are not traded through the market. This raises the question of how the information concerning product demand and factor endowments can be effectively conveyed to the suppliers of new inputs.

There is also the more difficult question of the relationship between technological, institutional, and economic changes. By what processes are economic institutions transformed to enable society to capture the economic gains implicit in new technical alternatives? An operationally meaningful theory of technical change and productivity growth in agriculture must answer such questions. A meaningful theory of agricultural development must incorporate the economic behavior of public and private sector suppliers of knowledge and new inputs and the economic response of institutions to new economic opportunities as a component of the economic system rather than treat technical and institutional change as exogenous to the system.

In this book we attempt to show how a model, in which technical and institutional changes are treated as endogenous factors, responding to economic forces, can aid in the historical analysis of agricultural growth, particularly in Japan and the United States. We believe this model represents a significant advance in the foundations upon which a more complete theory of economic development can be built.

Our main concern then, is to identify the necessary conditions for agricultural growth. We accept as fundamental that growth in agricultural output is, in most societies, essential to the development process and that the contribution of agricultural growth to the development process is positively related to the rate of productivity growth in the agricultural sector. Furthermore, we regard the new methods, materials, and opportunities associated with technical advance as a fundamental source of institutional change in modernizing societies.

It is not a major purpose of this book to investigate the conditions under which productivity growth in agriculture will be translated into national economic growth. The resources made available to society by productivity growth in the agricultural sector create an opportunity for the growth of material welfare. We look to others to provide an understanding of the con-

---

[2] In a recent publication Schultz does view research "entrepreneurs" as responding to economic opportunities. See Theodore W. Schultz, "The Allocation of Resources to Research," *Resource Allocation in Agricultural Research*, ed. Walter L. Fishel (Minneapolis: University of Minnesota Press, forthcoming, 1971).

ditions under which these opportunities for over-all economic growth are fully realized. This will require more careful analysis of the conditions under which the potential dividends of agricultural productivity growth remain unrealized because of failures in social, political, and economic organization, and of the forces which lead to the dissipation of the potential for growth in a pursuit of the symbols rather than the reality of national development.

HYPOTHESIS

Our basic hypothesis is that a common basis for success in achieving rapid growth in agricultural productivity is the capacity to generate an ecologically adapted and economically viable agricultural technology in each country or development region. Successful achievement of continued productivity growth over time involves a dynamic process of adjustment to original resource endowments and to resource accumulation during the process of historical development. It also involves an adaptive response on the part of cultural, political, and economic institutions, in order to realize the growth potential opened up by new technical alternatives. We have outlined this hypothesis more formally in an "induced development model." The model attempts to make more explicit the process by which technical and institutional changes are induced through the responses of farmers, agribusiness entrepreneurs, scientists, and public administrators to resource endowments and to changes in the supply and demand of factors and products.

The state of relative endowments and accumulation of the two primary resources, land and labor, is a critical element in determining a viable pattern of technical change in agriculture. Agriculture is characterized by much stronger constraints of land on production than most other sectors of the economy. Agricultural growth may be viewed as a process of easing the constraints on production imposed by inelastic supplies of land and of labor. Depending on the relative scarcity of land and labor, technical change embodied in new and more productive inputs may be induced primarily either (a) to save labor or (b) to save land.

The nonagriculture sector plays an important role in this process. It is a supplier of the modern technical inputs which can be substituted for land and labor in agricultural production. We hypothesize that the high agricultural productivity of the developed countries is based on (a) the development of a nonagriculture sector capable of transmitting increased productivity to agriculture in the form of cheaper sources of power and plant nutrients (for example, tractors and chemical fertilizers), and (b) the capacity of society to generate a continuous sequence of technical innovations in agriculture which increases the demand for the inputs supplied by the industrial sector. A continuous stream of new technical knowledge and a flow of industrial inputs in which the new knowledge is embodied represents a necessary condition for modern agricultural development. This stream of new technical inputs must be complemented by investments in general education and in production education for farmers and by efforts to transform institutions to be consistent with the new growth potentials if the full productive potential of the new knowledge and the new inputs is to be realized.

The critical element in this process is an effective system of market and nonmarket information linkages among farmers, public research institutions, private agricultural supply firms, and the markets for factors and products. It is hypothesized that the proper functioning of such interactions is a key to success in the generation of the unique pattern of technical change necessary for agricultural development in any developing economy.

APPROACH

The tests of the induced development hypothesis presented in this book are based on international time-series and cross-sectional comparisons of the levels of production, productivity, and inputs in agriculture. It is only through such comparisons that the patterns of technical change and growth in agriculture evidenced in the experiences of various countries can be generalized. The international comparisons also offer an opportunity to test the induced development hypothesis over a much broader range of variation in variables, especially factor proportions, than would be possible within any single economy.

The first test of the hypothesis regarding the interaction among resource endowments and technical change is obtained from an intercountry cross-section comparison of agricultural production. The hypothesis is subjected to a further test based on time-series data for the United States and Japan. Both the United States and Japan have been successful in achieving growth in agricultural output and productivity for at least a century, despite enormous differences in resource endowments, institutions, and cultures. The analysis is further extended to include the processes by which the scientific and technical capacity to generate an ecologically adapted and economically viable agricultural technology is transferred from the developed to the less developed countries. The historical experiences of Japan, Taiwan, and Korea are compared to those of the tropical countries which are currently experiencing a "green revolution" in grain production.

PLAN OF THE BOOK

This book consists of five major parts. In Part I (Chapters 2 and 3) we develop the theoretical framework in some detail. In Chapter 2 we review theories of economic development leading to a consensus on the critical role played by agriculture in the over-all development process. In Chapter 3 we specify elements required for the construction of a relevant theory of agricultural development, including technical change as an endogenous component of the total system.

In Part II (Chapters 4 and 5) we explore in greater detail the nature of the agricultural productivity gap among countries and the sources of the productivity gap as revealed through intercountry analysis during the post World War II period. The impact of industrial development and the implication of resource endowments and accumulation on the choice of technology are inferred from the intercountry cross-section analysis.

In Part III (Chapters 6 and 7) we present a quantitative historical analysis of the agricultural development experience of Japan and the United States since 1880, with particular attention to the forces which induced the distinct pattern of technical change throughout most of the period and which are now bringing about convergence of agricultural development patterns in the two countries.

In Part IV (Chapters 8, 9, and 10) we explore the conditions for successful transmission of agricultural technology among countries. Transfer of scientific knowledge through the development of experiment station capacity, in contrast to specific designs, materials, or techniques, is shown to be essential in this transfer process in our world. The economic forces conducive to the transfer of a particular technology are examined. The experience of the transfer of rice production technology from Japan to Taiwan and Korea during the interwar period is analyzed as a case, and its implications for the recent advances in grain production technology in Asia are discussed.

In Part V (Chapters 11 and 12) we utilize the previous analysis to identify causes of success and failure in agricultural development among countries. In Chapter 11 particular emphasis is given to the failure to achieve effective sequencing of institutional reform, factor accumulation, and technical change in much of the agricultural development effort of the 1950's and 1960's. In Chapter 12 we explore, from the perspective suggested by the induced development model, the policy implications of the new potentials for growth opened up by the technical innovations in grain production of the late 1960's.

Part I Problems and Theory

CHAPTER TWO

Agriculture in Economic
Development Theories[1]

There has been a sharp transition in economic doctrine with respect to the relative contribution of agricultural and industrial development to national economic growth during recent decades. There has been a shift away from an earlier "industrial fundamentalism" to an emphasis on the significance of growth in agricultural production and productivity for the total development process. As economists have become involved in the analysis of development problems in nations characterized by static agricultural technology and rapid growth in demand for agricultural products, attention has increasingly shifted to a concern with the conditions under which an agricultural surplus can occur and be sustained.

In this chapter the literature on the role of agriculture in economic development is reviewed in order to show the significance of the problem to be treated in this book for development theory and policy.[2] Particular attention will be given to the more recent "growth stage" and "dual economy" literature.

As already noted, no clear-cut system of "new development economics" has emerged to dominate the field of economic development theory as completely as the "new economics," based on Keynes's work, dominated income, employment, and growth theory after 1936. Two approaches have been used

---

[1] The material in this section draws heavily on Vernon W. Ruttan, "Growth Stage Theories and Agricultural Development Policy," *Australian Journal of Agricultural Economics* 9 (June 1965): 17–32; Vernon W. Ruttan, *Growth Stage Theories, Dual Economy Models and Agricultural Development Policy*, Department of Agricultural Economics, University of Guelph, Pub. No. AE 1968/2; and Vernon W. Ruttan, "Two Sector Models and Development Policy," *Subsistance Agriculture and Economic Development*, ed. Clifton R. Wharton, Jr. (Chicago: Aldine, 1969), pp. 353–60.

[2] The reader may want to supplement the material presented in this chapter with the very comprehensive "review of the literature relating to agriculture's role in the economic development" by Bruce F. Johnston, "Agriculture and Structural Transformation in Developing Countries: A Survey of Research," *Journal of Economic Literature* 8 (June 1970): 369–404. For a more detailed treatment see John W. Mellor, *The Economics of Agricultural Development* (Ithaca: Cornell University Press, 1966).

frequently in attempts to stake out the boundaries of a "new development economics." One of these approaches is the "growth stage" or leading sector approach which, in recent literature, is identified with W. W. Rostow.[3] The other is the dual economy approach along lines set forth in the work of Dale W. Jorgenson[4] and of John C. H. Fei and Gustav Ranis.[5]

It seems useful, therefore, to review the evolution of thought with respect to the relative contribution of industrial and agricultural development to the process of economic growth within the framework of these two approaches.

GROWTH STAGE THEORIES

Efforts to systematize the process of economic growth within a framework of sequential stages, with general application across national and cultural boundaries, represent a persistent tendency in economic thought. The earlier growth-stage literature was primarily a product of the nineteenth-century German economic historians.[6] It was not a coincidence that the growth-stage approach emerged originally in Germany in the nineteenth century, because Germany was then a late-comer to industrialization (relative to Britain), and the promotion of industrialization and economic growth were regarded as major goals of German nationalism. With the rebirth of interest in economic growth during the last several decades, economists and historians have joined in the effort to satisfy the demand for a general development theory by dividing economic history into discrete linear segments.[7]

The German Tradition (Marx and List)

There are two major traditions in the nineteenth-century German literature of growth-stage theories: (a) Karl Marx and the Marxists and (b) Friedrich

[3] W. W. Rostow, "The Take-Off Into Self-Sustained Growth," *Economic Journal* 66 (March 1956): 25–48; *The Stages of Economic Growth; a Non-Communist Manifesto* (Cambridge: Cambridge University Press, 1960).

[4] Dale W. Jorgenson, "The Development of a Dual Economy," *Economic Journal* 71 (June 1961): 309–34; "Testing Alternative Theories of the Development of a Dual Economy," *The Theory and Design of Economic Development*, ed. Irma Adelman and Erik Thorbecke (Baltimore: The Johns Hopkins Press, 1966), pp. 45–60; "Surplus Agricultural Labour and the Development of a Dual Economy," *Oxford Economic Papers* 19 (November 1967): 288–312; "The Role of Agriculture in Economic Development: Classical versus Neoclassical Models of Growth," ed. Wharton, *Subsistence Agriculture*, pp. 320–48.

[5] Gustav Ranis and J. C. H. Fei, "A Theory of Economic Development," *American Economic Review* 51 (September 1961): 533–65; John C. H. Fei and Gustav Ranis, *Development of the Labor Surplus Economy: Theory and Policy* (Homewood, Ill.: Irwin, 1964); "Agrarianism, Dualism, and Economic Development," ed. Adelman and Thorbecke, *Theory and Design of Economic Development*, pp. 3–41.

[6] Bert F. Hoselitz, "Theories of Stages of Economic Growth," *Theories of Economic Growth*, ed. Bert F. Hoselitz (Glencoe, Illinois: Free Press, 1960), pp. 193–238.

[7] Political scientists have also not been immune to the penchant for development "staging." See Robert T. Holt and John E. Turner, *The Political Basis of Economic Development; An Exploration in Comparative Political Analysis* (Princeton: D. Van Nostrand, 1966), pp. 39–50.

List and the German Historical School. Both Marx and List emphasized five stages in the development process. Their stages were, however, based on entirely different principles.

Marx based his stage classification on changes in production technology and associated changes in the system of property rights and ideology. His stages include primitive communism, ancient slavery, medieval feudalism, industrial capitalism, and socialism. In the Marxian system, economies evolve through these stages, driven by the forces generated by struggles between two classes, one controlling the means of production to combine with labor and the other possessing no means of production but labor. The class struggle reflects the continuing contradiction between the evolution of economic institutions and progress in production technology.[8]

In spite of the unrealistic assumption that society is organized in two socioeconomic classes with mutually inconsistent interests engaged in a continuous struggle over the division of income, the "Marxist analysis is the only genuinely evolutionary economic theory that the period produced."[9] Apart from ideological considerations, the work of Marx is of contemporary significance because of the major importance which he gave to the role of technical change in shaping economic institutions. In the Marxian system, changes in the "mode" or the technology of production represent the dynamic source of changes in social organization.[10] Marx considered growth of agricultural productivity as a "precondition" to the emergence of industrial capitalism.[11] He was impressed by the efficiency of large-scale farming in England and regarded structural changes leading to the elimination of peasant farming as an essential step in agricultural development.

List based his stage classifications on shifts in occupational distribution. His five stages include savage, pastoral, agricultural, agricultural-manufacturing, and agricultural-manufacturing-commercial. Both the List stages and the numerous other stage schema developed by the German Historical School (Bruno Hildebrand, Karl Bucher, Gustav Schmoller) are little more than "a simple expository device for impressing upon beginners (or the public) the lesson that economic policy has to do with changing economic structures."[12]

---

[8] This perspective is expressed in a number of Marx's works, typically Karl Marx, *A Contribution to the Critique of Political Economy*, trans. N. I. Stone (Chicago: Charles H. Kerr, 1918). For a review of the Marxian historical perspective see Mandell Morton Bober, *Karl Marx's Interpretation of History* (Cambridge: Harvard University Press, 2nd ed. rev., 1948).

[9] Joseph A. Schumpeter, *History of Economic Analysis* (New York: Oxford University Press, 1954), p. 441.

[10] Karl Marx, *Capital, A Critique of Political Economy*, ed. Frederick Engels (New York: The Modern Library, copyright, 1906, by Charles H. Kerr and Company). According to Marx, "Technology discloses man's mode of dealing with Nature, the process of production by which he sustains his life, and thereby also lays bare the mode of formation of his social relations, and of the mental conceptions that flow from them," p. 406n. For a review of the Marxian perspective on the role of technical change see Bober, *Interpretation of History*.

[11] Marx, "The So-called Primitive Accumulation," pp. 784–848.

[12] Schumpeter, *History of Economic Analysis*, p. 442.

Yet the work of List is also of contemporary interest because of his emphasis on nationalist industrial and commercial policies in achieving a transition from an agricultural to an industrial economy. In List's view, progress in agriculture could only occur under the stimulus of export demand or through the impact of domestic industrial development. Of these two sources, because of the double impact of the increased demand for farm products from an expanding nonfarm sector and of the development of more efficient methods of production resulting from the application of science and technology, List regarded domestic industrial development as the most important generator of agricultural progress.[13] His policy prescription for the developing economies of the nineteenth century was to encourage industrialization through commercial policies designed to promote the growth of both import substitutes and industrial exports.[14] These prescriptions continue to have great intuitive appeal to the industrial entrepreneurs and political leadership of developing countries.[15]

Structural Transformation (Fisher–Clark)

The "resemblance between List's three last stages and the concept of primary, secondary and tertiary production, developed in the 1930's by Allan G. B. Fisher and propagated further by Colin Clark" has been emphasized by Bert F. Hoselitz.[16] Fisher emphasized the "steady shift of employment and investment from the essential 'primary' activities . . . to secondary activities of all kinds, and to a still greater extent into tertiary production" which ac-

[13] Friedrich List, *The National System of Political Economy* (London: Longmans, Green and Company, 1885; reprinted by Augustus M. Kelley, New York, 1966). For a review of the significance of List's work see K. William Kapp, "Friedrich List's Contribution to the Theory of Economic Development," *Hindu Culture, Economic Development and Economic Planning in India*, ed. D. William Kapp (New York: Asia Publishing House, 1963), pp. 165–70; and Hoselitz, "Theories of Stages of Economic Growth."

[14] List did not regard protectionism as an end in itself, but rather as a means to achieve the greatest development of national productive power. In the introductory essay to the 1904 English edition, J. S. Nicholson pointed out that List held that "nations must modify their systems according to the measure of their own progress. In the first stage they must adopt free trade with the more advanced nations as a means of raising themselves from a state of barbarism and of making advances in agriculture. In his second stage they must resort to commercial restrictions to promote the growth of manufactures, fisheries, navigation, and foreign trade. In the last stage, 'after reaching the highest degree of wealth and power,' they must gradually revert to the principle of free trade and of unrestricted competition in the home as well as in foreign markets, so that their agriculturists, manufacturers, and merchants may be preserved from indolence and stimulated to retain the supremacy which they have acquired." List, *National System of Political Economy* (reprinted without page numbers following p. 444).

[15] Harry G. Johnson, "The Ideology of Economic Policy in the New States," *Economic Nationalism in Old and New States*, ed. Harry G. Johnson (Chicago: University of Chicago Press, 1967), pp. 131–32.

[16] Hoselitz, "Theories of Stages of Economic Growth," pp. 202–3.

companies economic progress.[17] In Clark's formulation the economic growth which accompanies this transformation is achieved, first, by increases in output per worker in any sector and, second, by the transfer of labor from sectors with low output per worker to sectors with higher output per worker.[18]

Fisher, as did List, held that such a transition was closely associated with the advance of science and technology. But an intense empiricism inhibited Clark from attempting an adequate theoretical foundation for his transition generalization. Nor did he provide any significant policy guidance for the problem of how a predominantly agricultural society might proceed to achieve a successful transition to a modern industrial society.

The important impact of the Fisher–Clark generalizations on economic thought and on economic policy during the decade immediately following World War II must be attributed to three factors: (a) the weight of empirical evidence generated by Clark's massive scholarship; (b) a felicitous choice of a value-loaded terminology; and (c) the equating of economic progress with industrialization by the planners and policymakers of countries which were attempting to emerge from economic and/or political colonization.

By the mid-1950's the analytical validity and statistical evidence, as well as the policy implications of the Fisher–Clark generalizations, were being questioned.[19] Analytical criticisms were directed toward the arbitrariness of the distinctions and lack of uniformity of income elasticity of demand among products classed within each of the three categories. A number of critics pointed to the tendency of official statistics to conceal the high proportion of time spent by the rural population in secondary (handicraft, etc.) and tertiary (transport, trading, personal service, etc.) activities in economies in which occupational specialization is limited.

Leading Sectors (Rostow)

The decline of professional interest in the Fisher–Clark stages during the last decade is due, at least in part, to the emergence of Rostow's "leading sector" growth-stage approach.[20] Rostow identifies five stages in the transition

---

[17] Allan G. B. Fisher, *Economic Progress and Social Security* (London: Macmillan, 1945), p. 6. For Fisher's earlier works, see *The Clash of Progress and Security* (London: Macmillan, 1935), pp. 25–43; and "Production, Primary, Secondary, and Tertiary," *Economic Record* 15 (March 1939): 24–38.

[18] The best exposition of Clark's approach is found in Colin Clark, "The Morphology of Economic Growth," Chapter X, *The Conditions of Economic Progress*, ed. Colin Clark (London: Macmillan, 1940), pp. 337–73. This chapter has been omitted in later editions.

[19] P. T. Bauer and B. S. Yamey, "Economic Progress and Occupational Distribution," *Economic Journal* 61 (December 1951): 741–55; and "Further Notes on Economic Progress and Occupational Distribution," ibid. 64 (March 1954): 98–106; Simon Rottenberg, "Notes on 'Economic Progress and Occupational Distribution,'" *Review of Economics and Statistics* 35 (May 1953): 168–70; S. G. Triantis, "Economic Progress, Occupational Redistribution and International Terms of Trade," *Economic Journal* 63 (September 1953): 627–37.

[20] Rostow, "The Take-off into Self-sustained Growth," and *Stages of Economic Growth*.

from a primitive to a modern economy: the traditional society, the preconditions for take-off, the take-off, the drive to maturity, and the age of high mass consumption. These stages are, except for the first and last, transition stages rather than a succession of equilibrium positions.

Rostow's objective in identifying "the five major stages-of-growth and . . . the dynamic theory of production which is their bone-structure" was much more ambitious than any of the earlier growth-stage approaches, except that of Marx. Rostow was primarily concerned with the process by which a society moves from one stage to another, and his historical analysis was conducted with the objective of providing policy guidance to the leaders of the developing countries, since "it is useful, as well as roughly accurate, to regard the process of development now going forward in Asia, the Middle East, Africa, and Latin America as analogous to the stages of preconditions and take-off of other societies, in the late eighteenth, nineteenth, and twentieth centuries."[21]

Rostow's approach starts from the empirical premise that "deceleration is the normal optimum path of a sector, due to a variety of factors operating on it, from the side of both supply and demand."[22] The problem of transition and hence of growth, therefore, becomes how to offset the tendency for deceleration in individual sectors to achieve growth in the total economy.

On the supply side, Rostow introduces the concept of a sequence of leading sectors which succeed each other as the basic generators of growth. On the demand side, declining price and income elasticities of demand are introduced as technical factors dampening the growth rate of leading sectors and transforming them to sustaining or declining sectors. Technology plays an important role in both the emergence of new leading sectors and in the elimination of older sectors.

All three growth-stage theories reviewed here treat the transition from an agricultural to an industrial society as the major problem of development policy. Rostow's system, like that of Marx, clearly specifies a dynamic role for the agricultural sector in the transition process. In an open economy, primary sector industries may act as leading sectors and, at a particular time, carry the burden of accelerating growth. In addition, agriculture must provide food for a rapidly increasing population, provide a mass market for the products of the emerging industrial sectors, and generate the capital investment and labor force for new leading sectors outside of agriculture.[23]

Rostow, as well as the other growth stage proponents, has not escaped criticism. Most of the papers presented at the 1960 conference of the International Economic Association on "The Economics of the Take-Off into Sustained Growth" rejected either Rostow's dating of the take-off for pres-

[21] Ibid. (1960), p. 3.
[22] Ibid., p. 13.
[23] This is roughly equivalent to the role which Marx assigned to agriculture, in the original accumulation of capital, a precondition for the emergence of industrial capitalism.

ently advanced countries or the concept of the take-off itself.[24] Cairncross and Kuznets have vigorously attacked the analytical criteria employed to identify successive stages, the leading sector hypothesis, and the historical validity of Rostow's empirical generalizations concerning the take-off stage for the presently developed countries.[25]

Students from less developed countries have found even greater difficulty in identifying their experience with any particular stage. One article reached the rather startling conclusion that "after entering into the 'take-off' stage in 1957, the [Philippine] economy immediately slipped back into the 'preconditions' . . . stage."[26] Furthermore, the approach contains no mechanism to explain why countries such as Argentina, Chile, Ceylon, Burma, and India, all of which experienced very rapid growth during the latter years of the nineteenth century, failed to achieve a successful take-off.

Rostow's recognition of the critical importance of rapid growth in agricultural output during the early stages of economic development has led to a rapid "diffusion" of the leading sector model among students of agricultural development. A sequence of three agricultural development stages, which roughly parallels the precondition, take-off, and drive-to-maturity states in the Rostow model, have been presented in papers by Maurice Perkins and Lawrence Witt,[27] Bruce F. Johnston and John W. Mellor,[28] and Forrest F. Hill and Arthur T. Mosher.[29] A synthesis of these approaches, constructed by Clifton R. Wharton, Jr., is presented in Table 2–1.[30]

Perkins and Witt have followed Rostow in emphasizing the importance of leading commercial sectors within agriculture, in contrast to the more static

[24] W. W. Rostow, ed., *The Economics of Take-Off into Sustained Growth* (London: Macmillan, 1964). See also the review of the volume by W. Paul Strassmann, *American Economic Review* 54 (September 1964): 785–90.

[25] A. K. Cairncross, "Essays in Bibliography and Criticism XLV: The Stages of Economic Growth," *Economic History Review*, second series, 13 (April 1961): 450–58; Simon Kuznets, "Notes on the Take-Off," ed. Rostow, *The Economics of Take-Off*, pp. 22–43.

[26] Gabriel Y. Itchon, "Philippines: Necessary Condition for 'Take-Off,'" *Philippine Economic Journal* 1 (First Semester, 1962): 30.

[27] Maurice Perkins and Lawrence Witt, "Capital Formation: Past and Present," *Journal of Farm Economics* 43 (May 1961): 333–43.

[28] Bruce F. Johnston and John W. Mellor, "The Role of Agriculture in Economic Development," *American Economic Review* 51 (September 1961): 566–93. The Johnston–Mellor approach has been elaborated in a series of articles by J. W. Mellor, "Increasing Agricultural Production in Early Stages of Economic Development: Relationships, Problems and Prospects," *Indian Journal of Agricultural Economics* 17 (April–June 1962): 29–46; and "The Process of Agricultural Development in Low-income Countries," *Journal of Farm Economics* 44 (August 1962): 700–16.

[29] Forrest F. Hill and Arthur T. Mosher, "Organizing for Agricultural Development," in *Science, Technology and Development*, vol. 3, *Agriculture*, United States papers prepared for the United Nations Conference on the Application of Science and Technology for the Benefit of the Less Developed Areas (Washington: U.S. Government Printing Office, 1962), pp. 1–11.

[30] Clifton R. Wharton, Jr., "Research on Agricultural Development in Southeast Asia," *Journal of Farm Economics* 45 (December 1963): 1161–74.

Table 2–1. Summary of ten major characteristics of agricultural development from Stage I through Stage II and into Stage III*

General character	Stage I (Static)	→ Stage II (Transitional) →	Stage III (Dynamic)
1. General values, attitudes, motivations	Negative or resistant		Positive or receptive
2. Goals of production	Family consumption and survival		Income and net profit
3. Nature of decisionmaking process	A-rational or traditional		Rational or "choice-making"
4. Technology or state of arts	Static or traditional with no or slow innovation		Dynamic or rapid innovation
5. Degree of commercialization of farm production	Subsistence or semi-subsistence		Commercial
6. Degree of commercialization of farm inputs	Family labor and farm produced		Commercial
7. Factor proportions and rates of return	High labor/capital ratio; low labor return		Low labor/capital ratio; high labor return
8. Institutions affecting or serving agriculture and rural areas	Deficient and imperfect		Efficient and well developed
9. Availability of unused agricultural resources	Available		Unavailable
10. Share of agricultural sector in total economy	Large		Small

* This table is an attempt to synthesize the Perkins–Witt, Johnston–Mellor, and Hill–Mosher stage classifications.

Source: Clifton R. Wharton, Jr., "Research on Agricultural Development in Southeast Asia," Journal of Farm Economics 45 (December 1963): 1162.

subsistence sectors, in the adoption of technological innovations and as a source of much of the increase in the output of food and export commodities. Johnston and Mellor, using Japan and Taiwan as models, emphasize the possibilities of transforming the subsistence sector into a small-scale commercial sector. The difficulty of resolving this issue, within the framework of growth-stage analysis, is symptomatic of the difficulty faced by stage approaches in generating useful guides to agricultural development policies at any particular time in economic history. W. David Hopper has made a similar point in his comment that "every developing country . . . fits each of the stages."[31]

DUAL ECONOMY MODELS

The dual economy approach emerged out of an attempt to understand the relationship (or lack of relationship) between a lagging traditional sector and a growing modern sector within nonwestern societies affected by the economic, political, and military intrusions of western colonialism. The static dual economy models emphasized the limited interaction between the traditional and modern sectors. The newer dynamic dual economy models identify agriculture as the traditional sector and industry as the modern sector and attempt to trace the increasing interaction between the two sectors in the process of development.

Static Dualism

Two distinct variations of static dualism can be identified in the literature: (a) a "sociological dualism" which stresses cultural differences leading to distinct "western" and "nonwestern" concepts of economic organization and rationality; (b) an "enclave dualism" which emphasizes the perverse behavior of labor, capital, and product markets through which the modern industrial nations of the west interact with traditional societies in other parts of the world.[32] Both variants are important to an understanding of the assumptions about the structure and economic behavior of developing economies that have been incorporated into modern dual economy models.

Sociological dualism was primarily the product of inquiry by the Dutch economist J. H. Boeke into the reasons for the failure of Dutch colonial policy

---

[31] W. David Hopper, "Discussion: The Role of Agriculture in the World Economy," ibid. 43 (May 1961): 347.

[32] We are indebted to Richard Hooley, "The Concept of Dualism in the Theory of Development" (National Planning Association Center for Development Planning, M-9285, March 1968, mimeo.) for clarification of this distinction.

in Indonesia.[33] The failure of the liberal economic policies adopted in 1870 to reverse the "diminishing welfare" of the Indonesian masses, particularly in Java, led to an intensive re-evaluation of colonial policy. Beginning with his doctoral thesis in 1910, Boeke argued that western economic thought was not applicable to tropical-colonial conditions and posited the need for a separate theoretical approach to the problems of such economies. "Where . . . there is a sharp, deep, broad cleavage dividing the society into two segments, many social and economic issues take on a quite different appearance and western economic theories lose their relation to reality—and hence their value."[34] Boeke thus assumes, as a precondition for his dualism, the coexistence of two social systems which interact only marginally through very limited contact in the product and labor markets.

The central tenet of Boeke's thesis is a fundamental distinction between the objectives of economic activity in western and eastern society. He argued that while economic activity in the west, and in the western enclaves in the east, is based on the stimulus of economic need, the Indonesian is guided primarily by social needs. He is particularly critical of attempts to explain the allocation of resources or the distribution of income in terms of neoclassical marginal productivity theory, mainly because of the great immobility of resources in eastern society.

The major policy implication of the Boeke analysis is the futility of attempting to introduce western technology and western institutions into Indonesian, and, by inference, other Asian economic systems. The only effect of efforts to bring about technological change in traditional agriculture through the introduction of new inputs from outside the agricultural sector is an acceleration in the rate of population growth.

Boeke's static dualism has been strongly criticized by a number of Dutch economists, almost from its first appearance.[35] More recently Benjamin Higgins has questioned the accuracy of Boeke's empirical observations and has suggested specific examples of the usefulness of western economic analysis to counter the examples he presented.[36] Indeed, he suggests that Boeke's criticisms of western thought stem in part from his unfamiliarity with western thought since Marshall and Schumpeter.

Academic criticism of the Boeke thesis has not prevented it from exerting a substantial impact on economic policy. In spite of its "colonialist" origin it

[33] J. H. Boeke, *Economics and Economic Policy of Dual Societies as Exemplified by Indonesia* (New York: Institute of Pacific Relations, 1953). For an excellent summary of Boeke's work see *Indonesian Economics: The Concept of Dualism in Theory and Policy*, vol. 6 of *Selected Studies of Indonesia* by Dutch Scholars (The Hague: W. Van Hoeve Publishers Ltd., 1961). In addition to Boeke's classic article, "Dualistic Economics," the book contains several of his other articles, as well as a critical review of his work by other Dutch scholars.

[34] Dutch Scholars, ibid., p. 170.

[35] Ibid.

[36] Benjamin Higgins, "The 'Dualistic Theory' of Underdeveloped Areas," *Economic Development and Cultural Change* 4 (1955–56): 99–115.

has been widely accepted, either explicitly or implicitly, among members of the intellectual elite and the bureaucracy in the economic policy and planning agencies in many new nations. It provides an intellectual rationalization for an industrialization policy which avoids investment in fertilizer, agricultural chemicals, and farm equipment industries in favor of other heavy industry and import substitutes. And Boeke's "backward bending supply curve" provides a rationalization for failure to achieve productivity gains in agriculture, in spite of (a) failure to invest in agricultural research, education, irrigation, and manufactured inputs and (b) the adoption of price policies which provide only minimal incentives to utilize available technology.

Enclave dualism, as a variant of static dualism, reflects very heavily the efforts of a number of trade theorists to explain "the spectacle of . . .: a high productivity sector producing for export coexisting with a low productivity sector producing for the domestic market" (p. 474).[37] Higgins,[38] explicitly rejecting the sociological dualism of Boeke, traces the origin of dualism to differences in technology between the modern and subsistence sectors.[39] In his view, the modern sector concentrates heavily on the production of primary commodities in mining and on plantations. It imports its technology from abroad. The imported technology employed in the modern sector is basically labor-saving, with relatively high and fixed capital coefficients. This is in contrast to the technology employed in the traditional sector, which is characterized by wide substitution possibilities between capital and labor and the use of labor-intensive production methods. Expansion of the modern sector is primarily in response to demand in foreign markets, and its growth has relatively little impact on the local economy. Expansion of the traditional sector is limited by shortages of savings.

H. Myint goes beyond Higgins in emphasizing the significance of the capital market as a basis for enclave dualism.[40] In his system the access of the modern commercial, industrial, and agricultural sectors to modern financial markets makes capital available to it at a fraction of the cost of capital to the traditional sectors, thus leading to the adoption of more capital-intensive technology and higher levels of labor productivity. He also suggests that the enclave financial sector tends to produce a net inflow of capital from the subsistence sector and a net outflow to international financial centers. The impact of the modern enclave on local economic development is thus limited by both its low demand for labor and its failure to channel investment into the local economy.

[37] H. W. Singer, "The Distribution of Gains between Investing and Borrowing Countries," *American Economic Review* (Proceedings) 40 (May 1950): 473–85.

[38] Higgins, "The 'Dualistic Theory' of Underdeveloped Areas."

[39] Benjamin Higgins, *Economic Development: Principles, Problems, and Policies* (New York: Norton, 1959), pp. 325–33, 424–31.

[40] H. Myint, *The Economics of the Developing Countries* (London: Hutchinson University Library, 1964), pp. 69–84.

Dynamic Dualism (Jorgenson and Fei–Ranis)

Although recent interest in dynamic dualism focuses very heavily on the work of Jorgenson[41] and of Fei and Ranis,[42] the now classical article by W. Arthur Lewis on "Economic Development with Unlimited Supplies of Labor"[43] represents the intellectual "take-off" for the Jorgenson, Fei and Ranis, and most other recent dual economy literature.[44] Indeed, Lewis's work can be regarded as the bridge between static and dynamic dualism.

The dynamic dual economy models accept the static typology of "sociological" and "enclave" dualism as essentially valid for a broad class of under-developed economies, particularly the postcolonial economies of South and Southeast Asia and Africa, and the Latin American economies with large indigenous populations. According to Fei and Ranis, these economies "are characterized by the coexistence of two sectors: a relatively large and over-whelmingly stagnant subsistence agricultural sector in which institutional forces determine the wage rate, and a relatively small but growing commercialized industrial sector in which competitive conditions obtain in the input markets."[45]

The main thrust of the dynamic dual economy models has been to explore the formal relationships which would permit an escape (a) from the Malthusian trap which Boeke regards as the inevitable consequence of attempting to introduce new technology into the native agriculture and (b) from the lack of effective labor and capital market relationships between the modern enclave and the traditional economy. Indeed, productivity increases in agriculture become, in the dynamic models, the mechanism which permits a continuous reallocation of labor from the agricultural to the industrial sector.

In the Fei–Ranis model (which Jorgenson terms classical) the subsistence sector is characterized by (a) disguised unemployment and underemployment; (b) zero marginal productivity of labor; (c) a positive "institutionally determined" wage rate for agricultural labor, which approximates the average

[41] Jorgenson, "The Development of a Dual Economy"; "Testing Alternative Theories"; "Surplus Agricultural Labour"; and "The Role of Agriculture in Economic Development."

[42] Ranis and Fei, "A Theory of Economic Development"; Fei and Ranis, *Development of the Labor Surplus Economy;* and "Agrarianism, Dualism, and Economic Development."

[43] W. Arthur Lewis, "Economic Development with Unlimited Supplies of Labour," *Manchester School of Economics and Social Studies* 22 (May 1954): 139–91; "Unlimited Labour: Further Notes," ibid. 26 (January 1958): 1–32.

[44] Three major contributions to the dual economy literature which appear to owe little intellectual debt to Lewis's earlier work are Anne O. Krueger, "Interrelationships between Industry and Agriculture in a Dual Economy," *Indian Economic Journal* 10 (July 1962): 2–13; William H. Nicholls, "An 'Agricultural Surplus' as a Factor in Economic Development," *Journal of Political Economy* 71 (February 1963): 1–29; and G. S. Tolley and S. Smidt, "Agriculture and the Secular Position of the U.S. Economy," *Econometrica* 32 (October 1964): 554–75. Krueger refers to previous work by Sayre P. Schatz, "A Dual-Economy Model of an Underdeveloped Country," *Social Research* 23 (Winter 1956): 419–32, which discusses some of the features of an economy characterized by enclave dualism.

[45] Fei and Ranis, *Development of the Labor Surplus Economy*, p. 3.

productivity of labor in the subsistence sector; and (d) fixed land inputs. Under these conditions Fei and Ranis argue that it is possible to transfer labor from the subsistence sector to the commercial-industrial sector without reducing agricultural output and without increasing the supply price of labor to the industrial sector during the early stages of development. Indeed, the transfer of one worker from the subsistence to the nonsubsistence sector results in an agricultural surplus which then becomes available as an investment fund for the development of the industrial sector. Fei and Ranis also envisage additional agricultural surpluses as a result of productivity increases from labor-intensive capital improvements. Agriculture, in this system, contributes both workers and surplus production in the form of a "wage fund" for the expansion of the industrial sector. In such a system the major functions of public policy are (a) to design institutions which transfer the ownership of such surpluses from the agricultural sector to the government or to the entrepreneurs in the commercial-industrial sector and (b) to avoid dissipation of the potential surplus through higher consumption in the rural sector.

A critical point in the development of the dual economy, within the context of the Fei–Ranis model, occurs at the time when the marginal value product of agricultural labor begins to rise above zero. At this point, the transfer of one worker from the subsistence to the commercial-industrial sector does not release a sufficiently large "wage fund" to support his consumption in the commercial-industrial sector. This results in a "worsening of the terms of trade" for the industrial sector, which can only be offset by some combination of productivity growth and decline in the rate of population growth in the commercial-industrial sector.

Another critical point occurs when the marginal value product of labor exceeds the "institutionally determined" wage rate in the agricultural sector. At this point, a rise in the industrial wage rate is required if the industrial-commercial sector is to compete effectively with the subsistence sector for labor. If, at this stage, rapid productivity growth in the agricultural sector is achieved, the "dualistic" features of the economy atrophy and agriculture increasingly takes on the role of an appendage of the one-sector economy taken as a whole.

In the Jorgenson dual economy model, the assumptions of (a) zero marginal productivity of labor and (b) an institutionally determined wage rate in the subsistence sector are dropped. Wage rates are determined in an intersector labor market even during the initial stages of development. As a result labor is never available to the industrial sector without sacrificing agricultural output, and the terms of trade move against the industrial sector continuously throughout the development process rather than after substantial development in the commercial-industrial sector.

In Jorgenson's system, an economy's ability to generate an agricultural surplus depends only on three parameters: (a) the rate of technical progress in agriculture; (b) the rate of population growth; and (c) the elasticity of output in the agricultural sector with respect to changes in the agricultural labor force. For an economy caught in a low level equilibrium trap, an escape is possible through: (a) changes in the rate of introduction of new technology in agricultural production and (b) changes in medical knowledge and practices which lower the birth rate more rapidly than the death rate. Note that in the Jorgenson model, technological change must be introduced into the agricultural sector from the very beginning of the growth process.

The Jorgenson model has moved somewhat closer to operational relevance than the Fei–Ranis model. The Fei–Ranis assumption of zero marginal productivity of labor and an "institutionally determined wage rate" in the subsistence sector, giving rise to a horizontal labor supply curve to the industrial sector which persists until agricultural employment begins to decline absolutely, is difficult to defend in view of recent work on labor productivity in subsistence agriculture.[46]

This weakness in their formal model does not imply that Ranis and Fei are unaware of the critical importance of agricultural productivity growth in the early economic development process. On the contrary they insist "any underdeveloped economy which attempts to force the pace of industrialization while disregarding the need for a priori—or at least simultaneous—revolution in its agricultural sector will . . . find the going most difficult. We are thus keenly aware of the fact that any success criterion which concentrates only on the industrial sector's ability to absorb labor is merely an index which implicitly summarizes the simultaneous capacity of the agricultural sector to release labor."[47] The zero marginal labor productivity assumption of Ranis and Fei represents a convenient but misleading pedagogical device. This assumption should be relaxed or replaced by more realistic assumptions with respect to intersector labor market behavior in drawing policy implications from their model.

The major weakness of the Jorgenson model, relative to the Fei–Ranis model, involves the Malthusian population response mechanism and a zero income elasticity of demand for food.[48] The assumption that population

---

[46] Charles H. C. Kao, Kurt R. Anschel, and Carl K. Eicher, "Disguised Unemployment in Agriculture: A Survey," *Agriculture in Economic Development*, ed. Carl Eicher and Lawrence Witt (New York: McGraw-Hill, 1964), pp. 129–44; Theodore W. Schultz, *Transforming Traditional Agriculture* (New Haven: Yale University Press, 1964); W. David Hopper, "Allocative Efficiency in a Traditional Indian Agriculture," *Journal of Farm Economics* 47 (August 1965): 611–24; Morton Paglin, "Surplus Agricultural Labor and Development: Facts and Theories," *American Economic Review* 55 (September 1965): 815–34. For a reaction to the criticism by Schultz and others see Fei and Ranis, "Agrarianism, Dualism, and Economic Development," p. 9.

[47] Fei and Ranis, *Development of the Labor Surplus Economy*, pp. 121, 151–99.

[48] The implications of adopting a more general set of assumptions have been explored by R. Ramanathan, "Jorgenson's Model of a Dual Economy—An Extension," *Economic Journal* 77 (June 1967): 322–27.

growth is a direct function of per capita consumption is clearly not consistent with recent demographic experience. Neither is the assumption of a zero income elasticity of demand for food.

Both the Fei-Ranis and the Jorgenson dual economy models have the significance of confirming, in formal terms, the intuitive judgment (a) that a shift in the domestic terms of trade toward agriculture signals a breakdown in the economic transformation leading to sustained growth and (b) that this can only be offset by some combination of a more rapid rate of technological change in agriculture and/or dampening of the rate of population growth. It would appear, however, that the simplicity of both models could lead to substantial underestimation of the difficulty of achieving such a transformation.[49]

Perhaps the most serious limitation in both models stems from the treatment of productivity gains in agriculture as a factor which shifts the production function without imposing any demand on resource inputs other than labor-intensive capital improvements such as land reclamation and development. The production of technical change in agriculture is itself, however, a relatively capital-intensive activity, particularly when one considers the human investment involved. Furthermore, it frequently requires a relatively long gestation period and has highly uncertain returns. The short-run supply of new technical knowledge appears to be relatively inelastic with respect to increases in expenditure on research personnel in both developed and less developed countries. Technical change is one of the more difficult products for a country in the early stages of economic development to produce. And when it does become available, it is typically channeled into the agricultural sector embodied in the form of inputs, such as fertilizer and insecticides, which are purchased from the nonagricultural sector. Failure to include a term in the subsistence sector production function which permits resource flows into the agricultural sector represents an unnecessary restriction on the use of technical changes embodied in inputs purchased from the modern sector.[50] It is entirely possible, in an open dual economy model, that it would appear appropriate in some situations to have a net flow of savings into the agricultural sector.[51,52]

A second major limitation is that both models ignore the problem of re-

[49] For further discussion of these limitations see Ruttan, *Growth Stage Theories.*

[50] Alvin L. Marty, "Professor Jorgenson's Model of a Dual Economy," *Indian Economic Journal* 12 (April–June 1965): 437–41.

[51] Shigeru Ishikawa, *Economic Development in Asian Perspective* (Tokyo: Kinokuniya Bookstore, 1967), pp. 290–356.

[52] Recently Fei and Ranis have presented a model of the "open agrarian economy." John C. H. Fei and Gustav Ranis, "Agriculture in the Open Economy," *The Role of Agriculture in Economic Development*, ed. Erik Thorbecke (New York: Columbia University Press, 1969), pp. 129–59. They suggest a series of "growth" stages running from closed agrarianism to open agrarianism and finally dynamic dualism.

source use in the intersector commodity markets. Markets are treated as disembodied communications systems through which resources and commodities are transferred between the modern and traditional sectors without absorbing either capital or labor in the process. The transfer of labor from the farm to the nonfarm sector is viewed as the source of a "wages fund" which then becomes available to support development in the nonagricultural sector. In most underdeveloped countries, substantial labor and capital resources are absorbed in the storage, transportation, and trading activities involved in making the marketable surpluses produced by the agricultural sector available to urban consumers. Thus, a shift of workers from a rural or village location to an urban location associated with growth in employment in the nonsubsistence sector typically requires a substantial increase in labor and capital inputs allocated to the marketing sector.[53] As development occurs, a higher and higher portion of food flows through wholesale and retail channels. For countries starting out with a relatively low ratio of food passing through wholesale and retail channels, the rate of increase in resources devoted to marketing can be explosive, as the share of the population residing in urban centers rises and even modest gains in per capita income levels are achieved. These very substantial "leakages" of agricultural surpluses into the marketing process imply more severe constraints on the potential for growth resulting from the simple transfer of labor resources from the subsistence to the modern sector than implied by the modern dual economy models.

A Micro-Economic Perspective

We have, in this chapter, identified a number of significant insights into the process of economic development that have been contributed by economists working within the growth stage and dual economy traditions. We have also outlined several of the specific limitations of the historical generalizations, development theories, and growth models which have emerged from these two traditions. Our most fundamental criticism, however, is directed at the macroeconomic approach to development theory and policy.

Clearly the dual economy models have contributed important insights into the development process. They represented a significant advance over the completely aggregative post-Keynesian one-sector, one-input models of the Harrod–Domar–Mahalanobis type. As the dual economy models have evolved, they have become more sophisticated and realistic.[54] They have con-

---

[53] Robert D. Stevens, *Elasticity of Food Consumption Associated with Changes in Income in Developing Countries* (Washington: U.S. Department of Agriculture, Economic Research Service, FAER No. 23, March 1965); Vernon W. Ruttan, "Agricultural Product and Factor Markets in Southeast Asia," *Economic Development and Cultural Change* 17 (July 1969): 501–19.

[54] See, for example, Jan Sandee, "A Programming Model for a Dual Economy," ed. Thorbecke, *Role of Agriculture in Economic Development*, pp. 219–30.

tributed to the interpretation of economic history and to the evolution of growth-stage concepts that are more firmly grounded analytically than the earlier generalization. As a result, it is increasingly recognized that "the functions which the agricultural and industrial sectors must perform in order for growth to occur are totally interdependent."[55] This is clearly an important contribution to economic "doctrine" when contrasted with the naïve industrialization-first doctrines of the 1950's.

In our judgment, the major advances in the understanding of economic development processes and in the design of development policies must be more solidly based on an understanding of microeconomic processes and behavior. Since World War II, development theory, research, and policy have been excessively focused at the macroeconomic level. Attention has been focused on the strategic role of demand and of fixed capital investment, to the neglect of the accumulation of labor and managerial skills and of scientific and technical knowledge. This has been a direct consequence of the powerful impact which Keynes's intellectual achievements, and of those who have followed him, have had on the capacity to deal effectively with the key problems of income and employment, inflation and deflation, and the international monetary system.[56]

The economic policies necessary to achieve economic development must, in contrast, be based on more effective resource allocation by households, firms, and public agencies among sectors and over time. The process of simplification and abstraction that has been so powerful in the development of the macro models must be reversed. Methods of analysis capable of utilizing more precise information with respect to consumption, production, and supply relationships must be employed.

This book represents an attempt to employ the theory and method of microeconomics to advance the understanding of the process of agricultural development.

[55] Erik Thorbecke, "Introduction," ibid., p. 4.

[56] Harry G. Johnson, "The Economic Approach to Social Questions," *Economica* (New Series) 35 (February 1968): 1–21; Harry G. Johnson, "Ideology of Economic Policy," p. 135. Also Theodore Morgan, "Investment *versus* Economic Growth," *Economic Development and Cultural Change* 17 (April 1969): 392–414.

CHAPTER THREE

Toward a Theory of Agricultural Development

The review of development economics literature in the previous chapter indicates that a new consensus has emerged to the effect that agricultural growth is critical (if not a precondition) for industrialization and general economic growth. Nevertheless, the process of agricultural growth itself has remained outside the concern of most development economists. Both technical change and institutional evolution have been treated as exogenous to their systems.

The central focus of this book is the complex set of interactions among resource endowments and economic entities (farms, public institutions, private industries) leading to technical change and productivity growth in agriculture. In our opinion, technical change represents an essential element in the growth of agricultural production and productivity from the very beginning of the development process. The process of technical change in agriculture can best be understood as a dynamic response to the resource endowments and economic environment in which a country finds itself at the beginning of the modernization process. The design of a successful agricultural development strategy involves a unique pattern of technical change and productivity growth in response to the particular set of factor prices which reflect the economic implications of resource endowments and accumulation in each society. It may also involve complex patterns of institutional evolution in order to create an economic and social environment conducive to an effective response by firms and individuals to the new technical opportunities.

In this chapter, we present a detailed exposition of this central theme. First, we review the theories of agricultural development that are reflected, both explicitly and implicitly, in the literature on agricultural and economic development. We then explore the nature and generation of technical changes in agriculture. Explicit attention is given to the forces that influence the rate and direction of technical change. These include the fundamental nature of biological and mechanical processes in agriculture, the significance of factor endowments, and the interactions between factor endowments and the broader economic environment through the price system.

THEORIES OF AGRICULTURAL DEVELOPMENT

A first step in any attempt to evolve a meaningful perspective on the process of agricultural development is to abandon the view of agriculture in pre-modern or traditional societies as essentially static.[1] Sustained rates of growth in agricultural output in the range of 1.0 percent per year were feasible in many preindustrial societies. With the advent of industrialization, potentials for the growth of agricultural output shifted upward to the range of 1.5–2.5 percent per year. Following the Industrial Revolution, rates of growth in this range occurred over relatively long periods in Western Europe, North America, and Japan. Since the middle of the twentieth century, the growth potential of agricultural production has apparently again shifted upward to annual growth rates of over 4.0 percent. Sustained growth rates in this range have been observed primarily in newly developing economies such as Mexico, Taiwan, and Israel, rather than in the older industrial economies.[2]

Viewed in a historical context, the problem of agricultural development is not that of transforming a static agricultural sector into a modern dynamic sector, but of accelerating the rate of growth of agricultural output and productivity, consistent with the growth of other sectors of a modernizing economy. Similarly, a theory of agricultural development should provide insight into the dynamics of agricultural growth—into the changing sources of growth—in economies ranging from those in which output is growing at a rate of 1.0 percent or less to those in which agricultural output is growing at an annual rate of 4.0 percent or more.

[1] Even in pre-modern times, agriculture was characterized by the continuous, though relatively slow, development of agricultural tools, machines, plants, animals, and husbandry practices. The rate of development was influenced by long-run patterns of population growth and price fluctuations. For Western Europe see S. H. Slicher van Bath, *The Agrarian History of Western Europe, A.D. 500–1850* (London: Edward Arnold, 1963). Comparable historical detail is not available for Asia. However, the view expressed here is consistent with the material presented by Shigeru Ishikawa, *Economic Development in Asian Perspective* (Tokyo: Kinokuniya Bookstore Co., 1967). See also Ester Boserup, *The Conditions of Agricultural Growth: The Economics of Agrarian Change Under Population Pressure* (Chicago: Aldine, 1965); Clifford Geertz, *Agricultural Involution: The Process of Ecological Change in Indonesia* (Berkeley: University of California Press, 1966); and Thomas C. Smith, *The Agrarian Origins of Modern Japan* (Stanford: Stanford University Press, 1959).

[2] U.S. Department of Agriculture, *Economic Progress of Agriculture in Developing Nations, 1958–1968* (Washington: Economic Research Service, May 1970). During the 1950–68 period "developing countries, as a group, boosted farm production as fast as the developed countries . . .—about 2.8 percent per year. . . . Agricultural output growth rates differ widely for the 54 developing countries studied. In 34 of the 54 countries, agricultural output expanded 3 percent or more per year; 17 of these countries had growth rates of 4 percent and above" (p. xiii).

It seems possible to characterize the literature on agricultural development into four general approaches: (a) the conservation; (b) the urban industrial impact; (c) the diffusion; and (d) the high pay-off input models.

The Conservation Model

The conservation model of agricultural development evolved from the advances in crop and livestock husbandry associated with the English agricultural revolution and the concepts of soil exhaustion suggested by the early German soil scientists. This theory was reinforced by the concept of diminishing returns to labor and capital applied to land in the English classical school of economics and the traditions of ethical, aesthetic, and philosophical naturalism of the American conservation movement.

The English agricultural revolution consisted of the evolution of an intensive, integrated, crop-livestock husbandry system.[3] In the process, the Norfolk-crop-rotation system replaced the open-three-field system in which arable land was allocated between permanent cropland and permanent pasture. This involved the introduction and more intensive use of new forage and green manure crops and an increase in the availability and use of animal manures. This "new husbandry" permitted the intensification of crop-livestock production through the recycling of plant nutrients, in the form of animal manures, to maintain soil fertility. The advances in technology were accompanied by the consolidation and enclosure of farms and by investments in land development. The net effect was a substantial growth in both total agricultural output and output per acre. The inputs used in this conservation system of farming were largely supplied by the agricultural sector itself. This system, which had evolved over several centuries, was popularized in the late eighteenth and early nineteenth centuries by Arthur Young and other exponents of agricultural science. Its diffusion provided the technical basis for English "high farming" as it evolved in 1850–70, following the repeal of the Corn Laws.[4]

---

[3] In recent years agricultural historians have stressed the "evolutionary" in contrast to the "revolutionary" aspects of these changes. ". . . the increase in agricultural output does not appear to have been due primarily to the discovery of new ways of doing things. The improved methods were the result of the accumulation of a very large number of small adaptations, and while a few of them do sum up to methods which can legitimately be regarded as new (the advances in cattle breeding, for example), the substitution of turnips and grass crops for fallow, the technique responsible for the most revolutionary changes, was already known. That is to say, the increase in output, where it was not merely the result of the employment of more men and land, arose from the spread of the best existing techniques rather than from the invention of new ones." H. J. Habakkuk, "Economic Functions of English Landowners in the Seventeenth and Eighteenth Centuries," *Essays in Agrarian History*, vol. I, ed. W. E. Minchinton (New York: Augustus M. Kelley, 1968), p. 190 (first published in *Exploration in Entrepreneurial History*, vol. 6, 1953).

[4] For further discussion see Lord Ernle, *English Farming, Past and Present* (6th ed.; London: Heinemann, 1961); G. E. Mingay, "The Agricultural Revolution in English History: A Reconsideration," in Minchinton, *Essays in Agrarian History*, vol. II, pp. 11–27 (reprinted from *Agricultural History* 37 [July 1963]); C. Peter Timmer, "The Turnip, the New Husbandry, and the English Agricultural Revolution," *Quarterly Journal of Economics* 83 (August 1969): 375–95.

The British doctrine of "new husbandry" was transplanted to Germany by its ardent advocates, Albrecht Thaer and his followers. Their investigations of the nature and principles of soil and plant nutrition led to a doctrine of soil exhaustion.[5] This doctrine held that the danger of soil exhaustion was so great that any permanent system of agriculture must provide for the complete restoration to the soil of all the elements removed by a crop. According to Abbott P. Usher, "the doctrine of soil exhaustion first took shape in the latter part of the eighteenth century, when the humus theory of plant-nutrition was dominant. It was then supposed that plants derived their food from the organic matter in the soil, collectively designated as humus."[6] This led to a presumption that good farming practice should maintain the organic content of the soil at a definite level, usually the level natural to the particular soil.

With the demonstration of the relation of soil minerals to plant growth by Justus von Liebig and others during the second quarter of the nineteenth century, the soil exhaustion doctrine was extended to include the maintenance of the mineral content of the soil.[7] The investigations of German soil scientists thus appeared to provide a scientific basis for the hypothetical calculations by the English classical economists, from Malthus and Ricardo to Mill, of diminishing returns to labor and capital applied to agricultural production.

The tradition of naturalism, which represented in many respects a reaction to the mechanistic conception of nature associated with the scientific revolution, was compatible with the experience of the English agricultural revolution, the classical theory of diminishing returns, and the growing body of natural resource literature.[8] The synthesis led to the formulation of a more sophisticated doctrine of natural resource scarcity.[9] Summarized in economic

---

[5] See Abbott Payson Usher, "Soil Fertility, Soil Exhaustion, and Their Historical Significance," ibid. 37 (May 1923): 385–411.

[6] Ibid., p. 386.

[7] "Liebig's explanation of plant growth rested upon four propositions: (1) that the nitrogen needed by plants was derived from the air; (2) that the plants utilized the mineral elements in inorganic forms; (3) that the amounts of minerals required by plants could be ascertained by analysis of the ash; (4) that plant growth would be directly proportioned to the supply of the mineral least abundantly furnished by the soil. . . . The new theory seemed not only to make the fertility of soils minutely calculable, but also to indicate a relatively brief period of productivity for most soils. Soil exhaustion thus became a corollary of the mineral theory as well as of the humus theory, and Liebig judged all agricultural practices in terms of their relation to the maintenance of the mineral content of the soil." Ibid., p. 389.

[8] Liebig attributed the decline of classical civilization to soil exhaustion. This view of the relationship between soil exhaustion and the decline of civilization has remained a persistent threat in the "underworld" of conservation literature. For several more recent restatements see Fairfield Osborn, *Our Plundered Planet* (Boston: Little, Brown, and Co., 1948); William Vogt, *Road to Survival* (New York: William Sloane and Associates, Inc., 1948); Tom Dale and Vernon Gill Carter, *Topsoil and Civilization* (Norman: Oklahoma University Press, 1955). For a discussion of some of the doctrines about soils, see Charles E. Kellogg, "Conflicting Doctrines about Soils," *Scientific Monthly* 66 (June 1968): 475–87.

[9] The two major contributions to the evolution of doctrine during the last half of the nineteenth century were Darwin and Marsh. According to Barnett and Morse, "Darwin, with a social impact perhaps even larger than Malthus' original impact, generalized as a law of nature the concept of the 'struggle for food.' And, although Malthus, no less than Darwin,

terms the doctrine asserts: that natural resources are scarce, that the scarcity increases with the progress of time, and that resource scarcity threatens to impair levels of living and economic growth.[10]

In recent years the scarcity doctrine has been subject to substantial re-examination and revision. The re-examination has proceeded at three levels. First, there has been a re-examination of the possibilities of agricultural growth under the conditions of the preindustrial technology assumed by the classical economists. Second, there has been an attempt at the hands of land and resource economists to "rationalize" the theory of conservation. Finally, there is the attempt, of which this book is an example, to examine the implications of industrialization for advances in mechanical, chemical, and biological technology for the long-term growth of agricultural output.

The classical view is now regarded as based on an inadequate understanding of the history of agricultural development, even in England and Western Europe.[11] Its major deficiency, even for a preindustrial society, stemmed from an oversimplified view of the role of land in agricultural development. The history of land use, both in temperate and tropical regions, indicates that the supply of land services has been much more elastic than implied by the static

---

claimed to be stating natural law, there was the added force of Darwin's greater prominence and the fact that his contribution emanated from a practicing scientist and many of the leaders of the Conservation Movement were natural scientists themselves. Second, and more important perhaps, the Darwinian contribution played a central role in the development and propagation of the popularized version of naturalistic philosophy that was so strong in the Conservation philosophy." Harold J. Barnett and Chandler Morse, *Scarcity and Growth, the Economics of Natural Resource Availability* (Baltimore: The Johns Hopkins Press, 1963), p. 88. In reviewing the work of George P. Marsh, *Man and Nature: Physical Geography as Modified by Human Action* (New York: Charles Schribner, 1864, [rev. ed., 1874]; and Cambridge: Harvard University Press, 1965) Barnett and Morse comment that "there are, in Marsh's view, such extensive possibilities of modification of the balance of man and nature—favorable and unfavorable—that the scarcity doctrines of Malthus and Ricardo presumably could not for him be natural laws. Since scarcity is no longer an ineluctable force, its effects are no longer inescapable. Before Marsh, and in the eyes of the classical economists, there was no question that scarcity was always operative. . . . After Marsh, if his lessons are believed, the question became empirical since man and his environment are so susceptible to change," Barnett and Morse, *Scarcity and Growth*, p. 93.

[10] Ibid., p. 49. For a formal statement and analysis of the scarcity model see pp. 101–47.

[11] The classical view did not go without challenge even in its initial statement, "The American economist, H. C. Carey, . . . asserted that the real law of agricultural expansion is the very reverse of that stated by Ricardo and affirmed by Mill. He argued that agricultural land was not used in the order of best quality first. Rather cultivation begins with poorer lands, and later extends to more fertile ones. The result is that expansion of agricultural output is carried on under conditions of increasing returns. The reason that settlers in a new country do not use the lands of greatest quality first is that river lowlands are unhealthy, or require considerable prior investment in clearance and drainage. Settlement, therefore, commences on lands that are high and less fertile. Only as population increases and wealth accumulates are the more fertile lands eventually brought into use." Barnett and Morse, ibid., p. 67. For a recent clarification of the Ricardo–Carey controversy see Ralph Turvey, "A Finnish Contribution to Rent Theory," *Economic Journal* 65 (June 1955): 346–48.

view of land as either the "original and indestructible powers of the soil" or as a "natural" agent of production.[12]

The most extreme challenge to the classical position has been suggested by Ester Boserup.[13] In a survey of historical patterns of land use under pre-industrial conditions in both temperate and tropical regions, Boserup suggests a pattern of continuous development from more extensive to intensive systems. The sharp distinction between cultivated and uncultivated land, implied by the concepts of the intensive and extensive margin, is replaced by a concept of increasing frequency of cropping and by changes ranging from forest and bush fallow to multicropping systems in which the same plot bears two or more crops each year. In this view, soil fertility is a dependent variable, responding to the intensity of land use, rather than a determinant of the intensity of land use.

Both the classicals and their critics do, however, share the perspective of agriculture as a relatively self-contained system. The inputs used in agricultural production were, by and large, supplied by the agricultural sector itself. Industrial inputs were not viewed as playing a significant role at either the extensive or intensive margin. Increased land productivity was achieved, as during the English agricultural revolution, primarily through labor-intensive methods of fertility enhancement (such as green manuring and forage livestock systems), land development (such as drainage and irrigation), and capital formation in the form of livestock and fruit- and nut-bearing trees.

The movement by economic historians and land and resource economists to "rationalize" the theory of conservation began in the mid-1920's with an attempt to explore the economic importance of conservation principles, particularly in the field of fertility maintenance, as a guide to agricultural practice.[14] By the early 1950's a new body of literature embracing both tech-

---

[12] "The use of soils in agricultural production commonly means a change in the environment from that in which the soils were formed. Man clears the forest and plows the prairie. He drains extra water out of some soils and adds extra water to others through irrigation. In extreme cases, he may rearrange soils entirely, as has been done in rice paddies of Japan and with peats and dune sands in Holland. More changes are usually made in chemical than in physical properties. Furthermore, the changes tend to reduce differences among soils as they are used for agricultural purposes." Roy W. Simonson, "Changing Place of Soils in Agricultural Production," *Scientific Monthly* 81 (October 1955): 173–82. ". . . a particular parcel of land suitable for farming is a complex physical structure in which there is embedded, as one approaches the surface, an intricate biological mechanism. How much or how little of it is natural or original or indestructible has little or no meaningful relation to its productivity." Theodore W. Schultz, *The Economic Organization of Agriculture* (New York: McGraw-Hill, 1953), p. 140.

[13] Boserup, *Conditions of Agricultural Growth.*

[14] Abbott Payson Usher, "Soil Fertility, Soil Exhaustion, and their Historical Significance," *Quarterly Journal of Economics* 37 (May 1923): 385–411. According to Usher, "it is steadily becoming clearer that science affords no basis for the static concept of the fertility program. The calculation of the minerals removed by the crop does not furnish a certain or adequate guide to fertilization. For high farming it may be necessary to add much more of some elements than is removed: low farming may be justified in limiting its fertility program

nical (soils, plant nutrition, agronomic, engineering) and economic considerations was leading to a more rational view of both the farm management and public policy aspects of soil fertility and of the role of land in agricultural development.[15]

In the United States this attempt at rationalization was under continuous pressure, however, as a result of the stagnation in the national economy during the 1930's,[16] the resource drains resulting from World War II, and a neo-Malthusian perspective generated by the postwar population explosion.[17,18]

In retrospect, a fundamental limitation of both the "conservation fundamentalists" and the early attempts to "rationalize" the conservation principles was the failure to recognize the full impact of technical change on resource use and productivity in agriculture. In the United States the period between 1900 and 1925 was a period of relative stagnation in agricultural productivity. The impact of the stagnation was reflected in higher food prices during the first two decades of this century. Even after 1925 the growth in productivity was obscured by the depression and by World War II. As a result, it was not unreasonable for postwar resource assessment studies to

---

to the maintenance of nitrogen and organic matter. The modern farmer, too, is not primarily concerned with maintenance of the 'original' powers of the soil; his problem is to modify the natural soil in accordance with his needs" (pp. 410–11). See also John Ise, "The Theory of Value as Applied to Natural Resources," *American Economic Review* 15 (June 1925): 284–91; Siegfried von Ciriacy-Wantrup, "Soil Conservation in European Farm Management," *Journal of Farm Economics* 20 (February 1938): 86–101.

[15] Much of the work is summarized in Arthur C. Bunce, *The Economics of Soil Conservation* (Ames: The Iowa State College Press, 1942); Siegfried von Ciriacy-Wantrup, *Resource Conservation; Economics and Policies* (Berkeley: University of California Press, 1952); and R. Burnell Held and Marion Clawson, *Soil Conservation in Perspective* (Baltimore: The Johns Hopkins Press, 1965).

[16] It was claimed that the solution to the depressed conditions in agriculture was to be found in an agrarian philosophy of subsistence and conservation. "How many of our farm families, in difficult financial circumstances today, would be better off tomorrow under an altered agriculture that placed subsistence above market cash, and substituted scientific methods for habit in the use of land?" H. H. Bennett, *The Land We Defend*, U.S. Department of Agriculture, Soil Conservation Service (Washington: U.S. Government Printing Office, July 1940), pp. 13–14.

[17] For an excellent historical perspective see M. K. Bennett, "Population and Food Supply: The Current Scare," *Scientific Monthly* 68 (January 1949): 17–26. According to Bennett, the English speaking world has experienced three waves of pessimism about food supply since the first one touched off by Malthus. The second came in the 1890's, the third a few years after World War I, and the fourth after World War II. If Bennett were writing in 1969 instead of 1949 he would have identified a fifth wave in the mid-1960's.

[18] The concern led to a series of postwar appraisals of the resource needs of the American economy. These include (a) U.S. Department of Agriculture, Bureau of Agricultural Economics, *Agriculture's Capacity to Produce, Possibilities under Specified Conditions* (Washington: U.S. Department of Agriculture, Agriculture Information Bulletin No. 88, June 1952); (b) President's Materials Policy (Paley) Commission, *Resources for Freedom* (Washington: U.S. Government Printing Office, June 1952); (c) President's Water Resources (Cooke) Policy Commission, *A Water Policy for the American People* (Washington: U.S. Government Printing Office, 1952).

reflect a scarcity perspective.[19] It was not until the mid-1950's that the new perspective on the relationship between technical change and resource availability and output growth became widely accepted, even in economics literature.[20]

With this new perspective it has been possible to analyze and test the resource-scarcity doctrine more rigorously than in the past. In their definitive study of *Scarcity and Growth*,[21] Harold J. Barnett and Chandler Morse first analyze the implications of the scarcity doctrine under the classical assumption of a parametrically invariant world and then in a world characterized by technical progress. They conclude that "the conditions which must exist if there is to be a clear presumption of diminishing returns in a parametrically invariant world are far more restrictive than is commonly realized. . . . The plain fact is, however, that the acceleration of sociotechnical change has now become the dominant influence on economic growth. Parametrically constrained models thus . . . cannot be made to represent twentieth century reality."[22,23]

This review of the evolution of the conservation model of agricultural development, the criticism of it, and its refinements should not be taken as complete rejection of it as an approach to agricultural development. Within the framework of a low-food-drain, preindustrial economy, a modern version of the conservation model—drawing on the insights of Young on the English

[19] The President's Water Resources Policy Commission concluded that "present food surpluses are transitory. The real agricultural problem is how to assure sufficient production to meet the requirements of an expanding population," (Report of President's Water Resource Policy Commission, p. 159). The report of the President's Material Policy Commission projected a 1975 index of land inputs of 111 (1950 = 100). As a result of increased land productivity, the cropland index actually declined, standing at ninety (1950 = 100) in 1968; *Changes in Farm Production and Efficiency; A Summary Report, 1970* (Washington: U.S. Department of Agriculture Statistical Bulletin No. 233, June 1970).

[20] Schultz had pointed out, as early as 1932, that agriculture in Iowa seemed to be characterized by increasing returns stemming from technological advance. Theodore W. Schultz, "Diminishing Returns in View of Progress in Agricultural Production," *Journal of Farm Economics* 14 (October 1932): 640–49. For references to more recent literature see Theodore W. Schultz, "A Framework for Land Economics—The Long View," ibid. 33 (May 1951): 204–15; Schultz, *Economic Organization of Agriculture*, pp. 146–51; Vernon W. Ruttan, "The Contribution of Technological Progress to Farm Output: 1950–75; "*Review of Economics and Statistics* 38 (February 1956): 61–69: Theodore W. Schultz, "Connections Between Natural Resources and Economic Growth," *Natural Resources and Economic Growth*, ed. J. J. Spengler (Washington: The Johns Hopkins Press, 1961), pp. 1–9.

[21] Barnett and Morse, *Scarcity and Growth*.

[22] Ibid., p. 147.

[23] In their empirical analysis Barnett and Morse test what they refer to as "strong" and "weak" versions of the scarcity hypothesis. The strong scarcity hypothesis implies that the economic quality of resources has declined in spite of technological progress. A decline in the real cost of the products of extractive industries would lead to rejection of the "strong" scarcity hypothesis. The weak hypothesis implies that the unit costs of extractive goods will rise relative to the unit costs of nonextractive goods. The empirical tests result in rejection of both scarcity hypotheses for the total extractive sector and for the agricultural sector alone. Barnett and Morse, *Scarcity and Growth*, pp. 7–11, 151–216.

agricultural revolution and incorporating the more recent perspectives of resource economists such as Barnett and Morse, and of agricultural historians such as S. H. Slicher van Bath and Boserup—has both great explanatory and prescriptive value.

The conservation approach to agricultural development—emphasizing the evolution of a sequence of increasingly complex land and labor-intensive cropping systems, the production and use of organic manures, and physical facilities to more effectively utilize land and water resources—clearly was capable, in many areas of the world, of sustaining reasonably high rates of growth in agricultural production, in the range of 1.0 percent per year, over relatively long periods of time. Agricultural growth rates in this range are not compatible, however, with the requirements of less developed countries today for modernization and economic development under conditions of explosive population growth and rising per capita incomes.

The Urban Industrial Impact Model

In the conservation model, locational divergencies in agricultural development were related primarily to differences in environmental factors. Developments in the nonagricultural sectors were not brought, explicitly, into the agricultural development process. The conservation model stands in sharp contrast to models in which geographic differences in the level and rate of economic development are primarily associated with urban industrial development. Initially, the urban industrial impact model was formulated to explain geographic variations in the intensity of farming and in the productivity of agricultural labor in an industrializing economy. Efforts in this direction draw their primary intellectual inspiration from the early efforts of Johann Heinrich von Thünen (1783–1850) to determine both the optimal intensity of cultivation and the optimal farm organization or combination of "enterprises."[24] Von Thünen generalized the Ricardian theory of rent to show how urbanization determines the location of production of agricultural commodities and influences the techniques and intensity of cultivation.[25]

In the United States the implications of the location of urban industrial development for agricultural development were outlined by Schultz in 1953: "(1) Economic development occurs in a specific locational matrix. . . . (2) These locational matrices are primarily industrial-urban in composition. . . . (3) The existing economic organization works best at or near the center of a particular matrix of economic development and it also works best in

[24] See Joosep Nõu, *Studies in the Development of Agricultural Economics in Europe* (Uppsala: Almqvist and Wiksells, 1967), pp. 184–230, for a history of the impact of von Thünen's work on economic thought. Von Thünen, like Arthur Young and other founders of agricultural science, viewed agricultural economics as part of an integrated science of agriculture.

[25] H. D. Dickinson, "Von Thünen's Economics," *Economic Journal* 79 (December 1969): 894–902.

those parts of agriculture which are situated favorably in relation to such a center."[26]

In formulating his hypothesis, Schultz drew both on the Fisher–Clark structural transformation model of general economic development and on the von Thünen tradition of land economics. He was particularly concerned with the development of a hypothesis that would explain the failure of agricultural production and price policy to remove the substantial regional disparities in the rate and level of development in American agriculture. Schultz presented a rationale for the urban industrial impact hypothesis in terms of more efficient functioning of factor and product markets in areas of rapid urban industrial development than in areas where the urban economy had not made a transition to the industrial stage. Major attention was placed on structural imperfections in labor and capital markets. The role of the urban industrial sector as a source of new and more productive inputs was not stressed.

Formulation of the urban industrial impact hypothesis generated a series of empirical studies designed to test both the validity of (a) the empirical generalizations and (b) the factor and product market rationale.[27] Results of these studies have generally sustained the validity of Schultz's empirical generalizations with respect to the impact of urban industrial growth on geographic differentials in per capita or per worker farm income. The tests of the factor and product market rationale, however, have been much less conclusive.

The policy implications of the urban industrial impact model appear to be most relevant for the less developed regions of the highly industrialized countries. In these areas, agricultural development can be accelerated by either increased industrial decentralization or migration of surplus agricultural workers to more distant urban industrial centers.

The only significant test, with which we are familiar, of the urban industrial impact hypothesis in a less developed country is an intensive analysis by William H. Nicholls for the state of São Paulo (Brazil) for 1940–50.[28] Prior to

[26] Schultz, "A Framework for Land Economics"; Schultz, *Economic Organization of Agriculture*, p. 147.

[27] Vernon W. Ruttan, "The Impact of Urban-Industrial Development on Agriculture in the Tennessee Valley and the Southeast," *Journal of Farm Economics* 37 (February 1955): 38–56; Daniel G. Sisler, "Regional Differences in the Impact of Urban-Industrial Development on Farm and Nonfarm Income," ibid. 41 (December 1959): 1100–1112; Anthony M. Tang, *Economic Development in the Southern Piedmont, 1860–1950: Its Impact on Agriculture* (Chapel Hill: University of North Carolina Press, 1958); William H. Nicholls, "Industrialization, Factor Markets, and Agricultural Development," *Journal of Political Economy* 69 (August 1961): 319–40; Dale E. Hathaway, "Urban-Industrial Development and Income Differentials between Occupations," *Journal of Farm Economics* 46 (February 1964): 56–66; Dale E. Hathaway, J. Allen Beegle, and W. Keith Bryant, *People of Rural America* (A 1960 Census Monograph) (Washington: U.S. Government Printing Office, 1968).

[28] William H. Nicholls, "The Transformation of Agriculture in a Semi-Industrialized Country: The Case of Brazil," *The Role of Agriculture in Economic Development*, ed. Erik Thorbecke (New York: Columbia University Press, 1969), pp. 311–78. See also G. Edward Schuh, "Comment," Ibid., pp. 379–85.

1940, economic development in Brazil had occurred primarily in response to a series of export-based commodity booms along lines suggested by the "staple" or "vent for surplus" models of trade and development.[29] The growth of São Paulo was closely associated with the coffee boom that extended from 1840 to 1940. After 1940 there were clear indications that urban industrial development was beginning to exert a differential impact on labor productivity in agriculture by facilitating the flow of capital into and the flow of labor out of agriculture. The urban industrial impact was limited, however, due to the locational impact of resource-based opportunities for development and by the failure of the Brazilian government to invest in the research capacity and the agricultural services necessary to permit the agricultural sector to respond to growth in the urban industrial sector.

Agricultural development policies based on the urban industrial impact model of agricultural development appear to have limited scope in most of the less developed countries where (a) a major problem is that of achieving a satisfactory rate of economic growth in the nonfarm economy rather than the geographic distribution of economic activity; (b) the technological prerequisites for rapid agricultural growth in the face of a constant or expanding agricultural labor force are frequently not available; or (c) the "pathological" growth of urban centers resulting from population pressures in rural areas frequently runs ahead of growth in the demand for nonfarm workers.[30]

The Diffusion Model

The diffusion of better husbandry practices and of crop and livestock varieties has been a major source of productivity growth in agriculture. The classical studies by Carl O. Sauer[31] and N. I. Vavilov[32] and the more recent cytogenetic studies of plant origins have forced a recognition of the extensive diffusion of cultivated plants and domestic animals in prehistory and in the classical civilizations.[33] Such diffusion must have been an important element

[29] The staple theory is based primarily on a generalization of the Canadian experience. See Melville H. Watkins, "A Staple Theory of Economic Growth," *Canadian Journal of Economics and Political Science* 29 (May 1963): 141–58; also, Richard E. Caves, " 'Vent for Surplus' Models of Trade and Growth," *Economics of Trade and Development,* ed. James D. Theberge (New York: John Wiley and Sons, Inc., 1968), pp. 211–30.

[30] For a model of the rural-urban labor migration process in economics characterized by chronic unemployment and underemployment of a high proportion of the urban labor force, see Michael P. Todaro, "A Model of Labor Migration and Urban Unemployment in Less Developed Countries," *American Economic Review* 59 (March 1969): 138–48.

[31] Carl O. Sauer, *Agricultural Origins and Dispersals; The Domestication of Animals and Foodstuffs* (2nd. ed.; Cambridge: Massachusetts Institute of Technology Press, 1969), pp. 113–34.

[32] N. I. Vavilov, *The Origin, Variation, Immunity and Breeding of Cultivated Plants,* trans. K. Starr Chester, vol. 13, nos. 1–6, of *Chronica Botanica,* 1949–50.

[33] For an engaging nontechnical account of advances in the study of plant origins and diffusion see Edgar Anderson, *Plants, Man and Life* (Berkeley: University of California Press, 1967). For useful references to livestock adaptation and diffusion see Ralph W.

in the evolution of preindustrial labor and land-intensive conservation systems.

The diffusion approach to agricultural development rests on the empirical observation of substantial differences in land and/or labor productivity among farmers in any agricultural region, from the most advanced to the more backward. The route to agricultural development is, in this view, through more effective dissemination of technical knowledge and a narrowing of dispersion in productivity among individual farmers and among regions.

The men whose researches contributed to the evolution of the agricultural sciences were impressed with the innovations in methods of cultivation made by farmers themselves. Young, the ideologue of the English Agricultural Revolution in the eighteenth century, regarded such knowledge as the only foundation on which scientific farming could be based.[34] Liberty Hyde Bailey, writing a century later insisted, "at the present time, every intelligent farmer is an experimenter. . . . this cumulative body of experience of the best farmers is capable of yielding better results than similar work which might be undertaken at an experiment station. . . . An experiment station, which is necessarily constituted for scientific research, cannot touch many of the most vital problems of farming."[35]

Even in nations with well-developed agricultural experiment station systems, a significant portion of the total effort, until as late as the 1930's or 1940's, was devoted to the testing and refinement of farmer innovations and to the testing and adaptation of exotic crop varieties and animal species. It seems likely that even in the most advanced agricultural nations this activity contributed more to the growth of agricultural productivity than the more scientific work carried on by the experiment stations until at least the middle of this century.[36]

The diffusion model of agricultural development has provided the major intellectual foundation for much of the research and extension effort in farm management and production economics since the emergence, in the last half of the nineteenth century, of agricultural economics as a separate subdiscipline linking the agricultural sciences and economics. The developments that led to the establishment of active programs of farm management research and extension occurred at a time when experiment station research was making only a modest contribution to agricultural productivity growth. This led to a heavy emphasis on the economic analysis and diffusion of farmer innovations. A stimulus for refinement in survey methods, accounting techniques, and statistical methods developed by farm management economists was the desire to

---

Phillips, *Breeding Livestock Adapted to Unfavorable Environments* (Washington: FAO Agricultural Studies No. 1, January 1948).

[34] Nõu, *Development of Agricultural Economics*, pp. 85–107.

[35] L. H. Bailey, "Extension Work in Horticulture" (Ithaca: Cornell University Agricultural Experiment Station, January 1896), Bulletin 110, pp. 130–31.

[36] For a specific example see Martin L. Mosher, *Early Iowa Corn Yield Tests and Related Later Programs* (Ames: Iowa State University Press, 1962).

determine with greater precision the sources of productivity and income differentials among farmers.[37]

The theoretical and empirical basis for farm management research was subject to intensive review following the advances in the theory of the firm which was developed by John R. Hicks and others in the late 1930's. These conceptual advances were complemented by simultaneous advances in quantitative methods and data-processing techniques. A synthesis of the theoretical implications of the neoclassical theory of the firm and the utilization of modern quantitative techniques in the analysis of farm management and production economics was achieved by the modern production economists by the early 1950's.[38,39] With this new synthesis, the interest of agricultural economists centered even less around the problem of choice of technology than that of the farm management economists, whose methodology the production economists rejected. The problem of economic growth, both of the individual firm and of the agricultural sector, was cast firmly within the context of reorganizing production inputs to achieve increases in output per unit of input by improving the efficiency with which the existing inputs are allocated.

A further contribution to the effective diffusion of known technology was provided by the research of rural sociologists on the diffusion process. Models were developed emphasizing the relationship between diffusion rates and the personality characteristics and educational accomplishments of farm operators.[40] The insights into the dynamics of the diffusion process contributed to the effectiveness of the agricultural extension service and strengthened the confidence of agricultural administrators and policymakers in the validity of the diffusion model. The pervasive acceptance of its validity, when coupled with the observation of wide agricultural productivity gaps among developed and less developed countries and with the firm presumption of inefficient resource allocation among "irrational tradition-bound" peasants, produced

[37] For a review of these developments in the United States see Henry C. Taylor and Anne Dewees Taylor, *The Story of Agricultural Economics in the United States, 1840–1932* (Ames: Iowa State University Press, 1952), pp. 326–446.

[38] The landmark in this initial synthesis was the publication by Earl O. Heady, *Economics of Agricultural Production and Resource Use* (Englewood Cliffs, N.J.: Prentice-Hall Inc., 1952). See also Earl O. Heady and John I. Dillon, *Agricultural Production Functions* (Ames: Iowa State University Press, 1961).

[39] For a critical review of these developments see Glenn L. Johnston, "Stress on Production Economics," *Australian Journal of Agricultural Economics* 7 (June 1963): 12–26. See also V. W. Ruttan, "Production Economics for Agricultural Development," *Indian Journal of Agricultural Economics* 23 (June–April 1968): 1–14; John W. Mellor, "Production Economics and the Modernization of Traditional Agricultures," *Australian Journal of Agricultural Economics* 13 (June 1969): 25–34.

[40] For a review of diffusion research by rural sociologists see Everett M. Rogers, *Diffusion of Innovations* (New York: The Free Press of Glencoe, 1962); Everett M. Rogers, "Motivations, Values, and Attitudes of Subsistence Farmers: Toward a Subculture of Peasantry," *Subsistence Agriculture and Economic Development*, ed. Clifton R. Wharton, Jr. (Chicago: Aldine, 1969), pp. 111–35. For a more complete discussion of the international transmission of technology see Chapter 9.

an extension bias in the choice of agricultural development strategy during the 1950's.[41] These programs were expected to transform tradition-bound peasants into "economic men" who would respond more rationally to the technical opportunities that were available to them and who would reallocate resources more efficiently in response to economic incentives.

The limitations of the diffusion model as a foundation for the design of agricultural development policies became increasingly apparent as technical assistance and community development programs, based explicitly or implicitly on the diffusion model, failed to generate either rapid modernization of traditional farms or rapid growth in agricultural output.

The High-Pay-off Input Model

The inadequacy of policies based on the diffusion model led, in the 1960's, to a re-examination of the assumptions regarding the availability of a body of agricultural technology that could be readily diffused from the high-productivity to the low-productivity countries and the existence of significant disequilibrium in the allocation of resources among progressive and lagging farmers in the developing economies.

The result has been the emergence of a new perspective that agricultural technology is highly "location specific" and that techniques developed in advanced countries are not, in most cases, directly transferable to less developed countries with different climates and different resource endowments. Evidence has also been accumulated to the effect there are only limited productivity gains to be had by the reallocation of resources in traditional peasant agriculture.[42] This iconoclastic perspective was developed most vigorously by Schultz in his book, *Transforming Traditional Agriculture.*[43] He insisted that

[41] According to Moseman this extension bias was partially based on the successful experience of transfer of hybrid corn technology from the U.S. to Western Europe under the Marshall Plan. This transfer was successful because climate in Western Europe is reasonably close to that in corn producing areas in the U.S., and there was indigenous human capital, in the form of agricultural scientists and technicians in Europe, to conduct adaptive research. Albert H. Moseman, *Building Agricultural Research Systems in the Developing Nations* (New York: Agricultural Development Council, Inc., 1970), pp. 66–67.

[42] W. David Hopper, "Allocation Efficiency in a Traditional Indian Agriculture," *Journal of Farm Economics* 47 (August 1965): 611–24; Benton F. Massell, "Farm Management in Peasant Agriculture: An Empirical Study," *Food Research Institute Studies*, vol. 7, no. 2 (1967): 205–15. Pan A. Yotopoulos, *Allocative Efficiency in Economic Development; A Cross Section Analysis of Epirus Farming* (Athens: Center of Planning and Economics Research, 1968); Pan A. Yotopoulos, "On the Efficiency of Resource Utilization in Subsistence Agriculture," *Food Research Institute Studies*, vol. 8, no. 2 (1968): 125–35. See also the review of studies of supply response in traditional agriculture by Raj Krishna, "Agricultural Price Policy and Economic Development," *Agricultural Development and Economic Growth*, ed. Herman M. Southworth and Bruce F. Johnson (Ithaca: Cornell University Press, 1967), pp. 497–540.

[43] Theodore W. Schultz, *Transforming Traditional Agriculture* (New Haven: Yale University Press, 1964).

peasants in traditional agriculture are rational, efficient, resource allocators and that they remain poor because in most poor countries there are only limited technical and economic opportunities to which they can respond.

In Schultz's opinion, the key to transforming a traditional agricultural sector into a productive source of economic growth is investment to make modern high-pay-off inputs available to farmers in poor countries. We may call this view the high-pay-off input model, and according to Schultz:

> Economic growth from the agricultural sector of a poor country depends predominantly upon the availability and price of modern (nontraditional) agricultural factors. . . . The principal sources of high productivity in modern agriculture are reproducible sources. They consist of particular material inputs and of skills and other capabilities required to use such inputs successfully. . . . But these modern material inputs are seldom ready-made. They can rarely be taken over and introduced into farming in a typically poor community in their present form. . . . There are very few reproducible agricultural factors in technically advanced countries that are ready-made for most poor communities. In general, what is available is a body of useful knowledge which has made it possible for the advanced countries to produce for their own use factors that are technically superior to those employed elsewhere. This body of knowledge can be used to develop similar, and as a rule superior, new factors appropriate to the biological and other conditions that are specific to the agriculture of poor communities.[44]

This implies three types of relatively high productivity investments for agricultural development: (a) in the capacity of agricultural experiment stations to produce new technical knowledge; (b) in the capacity of the industrial sector to develop, produce, and market new technical inputs; and (c) in the capacity of farmers to use modern agricultural factors effectively. High private and social returns to investment in education and research have been demonstrated by a series of studies (Table 3–1).[45]

The enthusiasm with which the "high-pay-off input" model has been accepted and translated into an economic doctrine has been due in substantial part to the success of efforts to develop new high-productivity grain varieties suitable for the tropics.[46] New high-yielding wheat and corn varieties were developed in Mexico, beginning in the 1950's, and new high-yielding rice

[44] Ibid., pp. 145–47.

[45] Also see, for the estimation of contribution of education to agricultural output, Zvi Griliches, "Research Expenditures, Education, and the Aggregate Agricultural Production Function," *Economic Review* 54 (December 1964): 961–74; and A. M. Tang, "Research and Education in Japanese Agricultural Development, 1880–1938," *Economic Studies Quarterly* 13 (February–May 1963): 27–41 and 91–99. Tang's estimate is for the return to investment in education and research combined. It is, however, more appropriate to regard it as the estimate of return to education because the weight of educational expenditure is dominant in the total education and research expenditure.

[46] E. C. Stakman, Richard Bradfield, and Paul C. Mangelsdorf, *Campaigns Against Hunger* (Cambridge: Harvard University Press, 1967); Lester R. Brown, *Seeds of Change* (New York: Praeger, 1970); Moseman, *Building Agricultural Research Systems*.

Table 3–1. Estimates of social returns to investment in agricultural research

	Annual rate of returns		
	Internal rate[a]	External rate[b]	Benefit-cost ratio[c]
United States			
Aggregates			
Research and extension, 1949, 1954, and 1960[d]	53		
Research and extension, 1938 to 1963[e]	48		
Individual commodities			
Hybrid corn research, as of 1955[f]	37	690	69
Hybrid sorghum research, as of 1957[f]		360	36
Poultry research (public research only), as of 1960[g]	21	140	14
Mexico			
Aggregates, 1943 to 1963[h]		290	29
Individual commodities			
Wheat research, 1943 to 1963[h]		750	75
Corn research, 1943 to 1963[h]		300	30

[a] Discount rate which equates earnings from the outcome of research to costs on research.

[b] Percentage of annual earnings from the outcome of research to total past cost, assuming 10 percent interest rate.

[c] Benefit-cost ratio $= \dfrac{\text{Annual rate of return}}{100 \times \text{interest rate}}$

[d] Zvi Griliches, "Research Expenditures, Education and the Aggregate Agricultural Production Function," *American Economic Review* 54 (December 1964): 967–68. Adjusted for private research by assuming the magnitude of private research expenditures equal to public research. Griliches estimated the marginal product of research expenditure, but he himself did not estimate the annual rate of returns. The above cited figure is the estimate by Peterson based on the Griliches study. See Willis L. Peterson, "The Returns to Investment in Agricultural Research in the United States," *Resource Allocation in Agricultural Research*, ed. Walter L. Fishel (Minneapolis: University of Minnesota Press, forthcoming, 1971).

[e] Robert E. Evenson, *The Contribution of Agricultural Research and Extension to Agricultural Production* (Ph.D. dissertation, University of Chicago, 1968). Adjusted for private research expenditure.

[f] Zvi Griliches, "Research Costs and Social Returns: Hybrid Corn and Related Innovations," *Journal of Political Economy* 66 (October 1958): 419–31.

[g] Willis L. Peterson, *Returns to Poultry Research in the United States* (Ph.D. dissertation, University of Chicago, 1966).

[h] L. Ardito Barletta, *Costs and Social Returns of Agricultural Research in Mexico* (Ph.D. dissertation, University of Chicago, 1967). Reproduced from T. W. Schultz, *Economic Growth and Agriculture* (New York: McGraw-Hill, 1968), p. 85.

varieties in the Philippines in the 1960's. These varieties were highly responsive to industrial inputs, such as fertilizer and other chemicals, and to more effective soil and water management. The high returns associated with the adaption of the new varieties and the associated technical inputs and management practices has led to rapid diffusion of the new varieties among farmers in several countries in Asia, Africa, and Latin America. The impact on farm production and income has been sufficiently dramatic to be heralded as a "green revolution."[47] The significance of the high-pay-off input model is that policies based on the model appear capable of generating a sufficiently high rate of agricultural growth to provide a basis for over-all economic development consistent with modern population and income growth requirements.

As interpreted generally, the model is sufficiently inclusive to embrace the central concepts of the conservation, urban industrial impact, and diffusion models of agricultural development. Advances in conservation systems of agriculture, as, for example, the Norfolk crop rotation as propagated in England in the eighteenth century, represented a new high-pay-off input in that period. The rate of diffusion of agricultural technology can be viewed as a function of the profitability of the new inputs or techniques. The impact of urban industrial development changes the relative profitability of alternative techniques through the growth of demand and the capacity to supply the new technical inputs. The unique implications of the model for agricultural development policy are the emphasis placed on accelerating the process of development and propagation of new inputs or techniques through public investment in scientific research and education.

The high-pay-off input model, as developed by Schultz in *Transforming Traditional Agriculture*, remains incomplete as a theory of agricultural development, however. Typically, education and research are public goods, not traded through the market place. The mechanism by which resources are allocated among education, research, and other alternative public and private sector economic activities is not fully incorporated into the Schultz model.[48] The model does treat investment in research as the source of new high-pay-off techniques. It does not explain how economic conditions induce the development and adaption of an efficient set of technologies for a particular society.

---

[47] Although the term "green revolution" is used at a number of points in this study to refer to the impact of the new cereals technology, our view is essentially similar to that of Dovring. "Evidently there is no general consensus on the meaning of the term 'revolution.' This term has been over used to the point of losing any distinctive meaning." Folke Dovring, "Eighteenth Century Changes in European Agriculture: A Comment," *Agricultural History* 63 (January 1969): 181–86. The use of the term "green revolution" to describe the new high-yielding cereals technology represents an interesting footnote in the history of the international diffusion of terminology. The term was first suggested by the administrator of US AID, William Gaud, in 1968. William S. Gaud, "The Green Revolution: Accomplishments and Apprehensions," address before the Society for International Development, Washington, 1968. Later the term became widely used in popular press accounts and in the professional literature. In the interwar period the term "green revolution" was used to refer to the radical peasant political movements in Eastern Europe. See David Mitrany, *Marx Against the Peasant* (Chapel Hill: University of North Carolina Press, 1951) pp. 118–45.

[48] In his more recent paper Schultz stressed the need to direct research toward the analysis of this process. Theodore W. Schultz, "The Allocation of Resources to Research," *Resource Allocation in Agricultural Research*, ed. Walter L. Fishel (Minneapolis: University of Minnesota Press, forthcoming, 1971).

Nor does it attempt to specify the process by which factor and product price relationships induce investment in research in a particular direction.

In the last section of this chapter, we incorporate the high-pay-off input model, along with the conservation, urban industrial impact and diffusion models, into an induced development model. Before doing so it is necessary to examine in detail some of the characteristics of agricultural technology that are of particular significance in the induced development model.

ALTERNATIVE PATHS OF TECHNOLOGICAL DEVELOPMENT

The attempt to develop a model of agricultural development in which technical change is treated as endogenous to the development process, rather than as an exogenous factor that operates independently of other development processes, must start with the recognition that there are multiple paths of technological development. Technology can be so developed as to facilitate the substitution of relatively abundant (hence cheap) factors for relatively scarce (hence expensive) factors in the economy.

For example, high-yielding crop varieties are essentially an input designed to facilitate the substitution of fertilizer for land. For purposes of illustration we compare, in Table 3–2, the yield response to nitrogen of indigenous rice varieties in East Pakistan and improved varieties in Japan. The comparison shows that the yields of the indigenous varieties are as high as the improved varieties at the low level of fertilization, but that they respond negatively, or

Table 3–2. Yield response to nitrogen input by rice varieties

	Yield (lb./acre) at the levels of N				Marginal product of N	
	(1) 95 lb./acre		(2) 150 lb./acre		(2)–(1) 55	
Variety	Paddy	Straw	Paddy	Straw	Paddy	Straw
Habiganj[a]	4,785	7,948	4,372	10,478	−7.5	46.0
Batak[a]	5,445	9,488	5,875	11,743	7.8	41.0
Kamenoo[b]	5,417	5,500	6,077	7,617	12.0	38.5
Norin 1[c]	6,352	7,205	7,700	8,225	24.5	18.5
Norin 87[c]	5,118	6,352	6,517	7,892	25.4	28.0
Rikuu 232[c]	5,802	6,902	7,425	8,553	29.5	30.0

[a] Indigenous varieties in East Pakistan.

[b] A variety selected by a veteran farmer, the use of which became prevalent in Japan from 1905–25.

[c] Varieties selected through hybridization by agricultural experiment stations in Japan after the nationwide co-ordinated experiment system called "Assigned Experiment System" was established in 1926–27.

Source: Institute of Asian Economic Affairs, *Ajia no Inasaku* (Rice Farming in Asia) (Tokyo, 1961), p. 14.

only modestly, to higher levels of fertilizer application. The lack of response of the indigenous varieties to higher levels of fertilization represents a particularly serious constraint on growth of agricultural output in economies characterized by high population densities and an inelastic supply of land. Increases in output depend on the development of an agricultural technology, including fertilizer-responsive crop varieties, that can release the constraints on growth imposed by the inelastic supply of land.

Likewise, in an economy characterized by a relative scarcity of labor, substitution of land and capital for labor would be made possible primarily by improving agricultural implements and machinery. For example, for farmers using horses for plowing, the substitution of additional land and power (horses) for labor is limited by the technical limits of "horse mechanization." Introduction of tractors facilitated further substitution by making it easier for a worker to command more power and to cultivate a larger land area.

An important consideration is that new techniques, such as new husbandry practices or new seeds, are not substitutes for labor or land by themselves; but they are the inputs which behave as catalysts to facilitate the substitution of the relatively scarce factors for the less scarce factors. It seems reasonable, according to the convention of economics (Hicksian), to call techniques designed to facilitate the substitution of other inputs for labor, "labor-saving," and ones designed to facilitate the substitution of other inputs for land, "land-saving."

In agriculture, two kinds of technology generally correspond to this taxonomy: mechanical technology to "labor-saving" and biological and chemical technology to "land-saving."[49] The former is designed to facilitate the substitution of power and machinery for labor. Typically this involves the substitution of land for labor, because higher output per worker through mechanization usually requires a larger land area cultivated per worker. The latter, which we will hereafter identify as biological technology, is designed to facilitate the substitution of labor and/or industrial inputs for land. This may occur through increased recycling of soil fertility by more labor-intensive conservation systems; through use of chemical fertilizers; and through husbandry practices, management systems, and inputs (i.e., insecticides) which permit an optimum yield response.

We recognize, of course, that the distinction between mechanical and bio-

---

[49] The distinction made here between "mechanical" and "biological" technology has also been employed by Earl O. Heady, "Basic Economic and Welfare Aspects of Farm Technological Advance," *Journal of Farm Economics* 31 (May 1949): 293–316. It is similar to the distinction between "laboresque" and "landesque" capital employed by Sen. See A. K. Sen, "The Choice of Agricultural Techniques in Underdeveloped Countries," *Economic Development and Cultural Change* 7 (April 1959): 279–85. In a more recent article Hiromitsu Kaneda employs the terms mechanical-engineering and biological-chemical. See Hiromitsu Kaneda, "Economic Implications of the 'Green Revolution' and the Strategy of Agricultural Development in West Pakistan," *Pakistan Development Review* 9 (Summer 1969): 111–43.

logical technology utilized in this study may be overdrawn for expositional purposes. All mechanical innovations are not necessarily motivated by incentives to save labor, nor are all biological innovations necessarily motivated by incentives to save land. For example, in Japan, horse plowing was developed as a device to cultivate more deeply, so as to increase yield per hectare.

In the United States in recent years attempts have been made to develop crop varieties more suitable for mechanical harvesting. For example, tomatoes have been developed which have a sturdier skin and ripen at the same time, in order to facilitate mechanical harvesting. This research illustrates that the development of mechanical technology may be land-saving, and the development of biological technology may be labor-saving. Yet, historically, the dominant factor for saving labor has been the progress of mechanization; and the dominant factor for saving land has been the biological innovations.

At the most sophisticated level, technological progress depends on a series of simultaneous advances in both biological and mechanical sciences and techniques. In the case of the mechanization of tomato harvesting, the plant-breeding research and the engineering research were conducted co-operatively in order to invent new machines capable of harvesting the tomatoes specifically bred for mechanical handling.[50]

Mechanical Processes

The mechanization of farming in Great Britain, and to an even greater degree in the United States, has been intimately associated with the Industrial Revolution. The precise interrelationship between the industrial and agricultural revolutions of the eighteenth century is still a matter of debate among economic historians. It is generally agreed, however, that the relative scarcity of labor represented an inducement to adopt more capital-intensive methods in both the industrial and agricultural sectors in the United States than in Britain.[51]

[50] Wayne D. Rasmussen, "Advances in American Agriculture: The Mechanical Tomato Harvester as a Case Study," *Technology and Culture* 9 (October 1968): 531–43; and Andrew Schmitz and David Seckler, "Mechanized Agriculture and Social Welfare: The Case of the Tomato Harvester," *American Journal of Agricultural Economics* 52 (November 1970): 569–77.

[51] H. J. Habakkuk, *American and British Technology in the Nineteenth Century; The Search for Labour Saving Inventions* (Cambridge: Cambridge University Press, 1962), p. 14. Habakkuk argues that "the course of agricultural technology in the early decades of the nineteenth century may well have accentuated the disparity between the terms on which labour was available to industry in the U.S.A. and England. In America improvements in agriculture took the form primarily of increasing output per head and the increase initially was probably more rapid than in industry; in England on the other hand, agricultural improvement was devoted primarily to increasing yields per acre and, even where there was an increase in output per head, the abundance of labour made it difficult for the labourer to enjoy the increase. In America agricultural improvements raised, and in England prevented, a rise in the terms on which labour was available to industry."

Although progress of agricultural and industrial mechanization represents a response to the same set of fundamental economic forces, the mechanization of agriculture cannot be treated as simply the adaptation of industrial methods of production to agriculture. The spatial nature of agricultural production results in significant differences between agriculture and industry in the pattern of machinery use. It imposes severe constraints on the efficiency of large-scale production in agriculture.[52]

In the industrial sector, the replacement of handcraft methods of production with machine methods forced a factory system of organization in which the individual worker becomes specialized in one particular operation or function. In farming, the sequence of operations from preplanting to post-harvesting remains as widely separated by time intervals after mechanization as before. The spatial dimension of crop production requires that the machines suitable for agricultural mechanization must be mobile—they must move across or through materials that are immobile, in contrast to moving materials through stationary machines, as in most industrial processes. The seasonal or time characteristic of agricultural production requires a series of specialized machines—for land preparation, planting, weed control, and harvesting—specifically designed for sequential operations, each of which is carried out only a few days or weeks in each season. This also means that it is no more feasible for workers to specialize in one operation in mechanized agriculture than in premechanized agriculture. In addition, it means that in a "fully mechanized" agricultural system, because of the mobility and specialization characteristics, investment per worker is frequently higher than in industry.[53] The mobility characteristic means that the machine must not only have the power to perform the specific operation but must be able to

[52] John M. Brewster, "The Machine Process in Agriculture and Industry," *Journal of Farm Economics* 32 (February 1950): 69–81. "In pre-machine times, farming and manufacturing were alike in that operations in both cases were normally done sequentially, one after another; usually by the same individual or family. The rise of the machine process has forced agriculture and industry to become progressively different in respect to the sequence in which men once performed both farm and industrial operations. For in substituting machine for hand power and manipulations in agriculture, individuals in no wise disturb their pre-machine habit of doing their production steps one after another whereas in making the same substitution in industry men thereby force themselves to acquire increasingly the new habit of performing simultaneously the many operations in a production process. As a consequence, the 'Industrial Revolution' in agriculture is merely a spectacular change in the implements of production whereas in industry it is a further revolution in the sequence (order) in which men use their implements" (pp. 69–70). See also Nicholas Georgescu-Roegen, "Process in Farming versus Process in Manufacturing: A Problem of Balanced Development," *Economic Problems of Agriculture in Industrial Societies*, ed. Ugo Papi and Charles Nunn (London: Macmillan and New York: St. Martin's Press, 1969), pp. 497–528.

[53] Data presented by Paul Zarembka, "Manufacturing and Agricultural Production Functions and International Trade: United States and Northern Europe," *Journal of Farm Economics* 48 (November 1966): 952–66; Allen G. Smith, "Comparative Investment per Worker in Agriculture and Manufacturing Sectors of the Economy," *American Journal of Agricultural Economics* 53 (February 1971): 101–2.

move itself across frequently unfavorable terrain while performing the operation. The specialization characteristic means that machines employed in agriculture must be adapted to perform operations that require their use for only a short time each year.

It is clear, regardless of the impact of the economic organization of agriculture, that the major economic force leading to the greater use of mechanical equipment in agriculture is the drive to reduce labor costs. The major consequence is a rise in labor productivity—output per worker or per man-hour. In economies where the price of labor—of man—is low and where the price of material goods—of machinery—is high, there is little economic incentive for mechanization of field operations. As the value of labor rises, either as a result of rising demand for labor in the urban industrial sector or as a result of greater domestic or international demand for agricultural commodities, mechanization is typically adopted first for those activities in which stationary power sources can be used—for pumping water and threshing grain, for example. Mechanization of motive power for machines which must move across the landscape typically represents a later stage in farm mechanization.[54]

The implications of progress in mechanical technology on labor productivity is illustrated by many examples from the historical experiences of the United States, Canada, England, and other western economies. The impact of the evolution of harvesting machinery in the United States during the nineteenth century, as calculated from documentation by Leo Rogin, is illustrated in Figure 3–1.[55]

The usual method of harvesting wheat, before the adoption of horse-drawn machinery, was to reap it with a hand sickle. With the sickle, a worker could harvest between one-third and one-half an acre per day. The cradle, a scythe with a frame composed of tapering wooden fingers attached alongside the blade to permit simultaneous cutting and "bunching" of the grain, was introduced toward the end of the colonial period, and its use permitted an approximate doubling of the acres harvested per day per worker. The cradle represented an answer to the relative labor scarcity in North America when

[54] This has been the general sequence of mechanization, historically. The stationary and mobile power sources may, however be adopted by some developing countries concurrently, rather than in sequence, because the progress of farm mechanization has made a more complete set of farm mechanization devices available. In other countries, the adoption sequence may be considerably shortened. Even where tractor power is introduced fairly early in the development process, however, it tends to be used first in those areas, such as land preparation, where its advantage relative to animal power or hand methods is greatest. See W. J. Chancellor, "Mechanization of Small Farms in Thailand and Malaysia by Tractor Hire Services," paper presented at the 1970 Annual Meeting of American Society of Agricultural Engineers, Minneapolis, 1970 (St. Joseph, Michigan: American Society of Agricultural Engineers, 1970).

[55] Leo Rogin, *The Introduction of Farm Machinery in Its Relation to the Productivity of Labor in the Agriculture of the United States during the Nineteenth Century* (Berkeley: University of California Press, 1931). See also Slicher van Bath, *Agrarian History of Western Europe*.

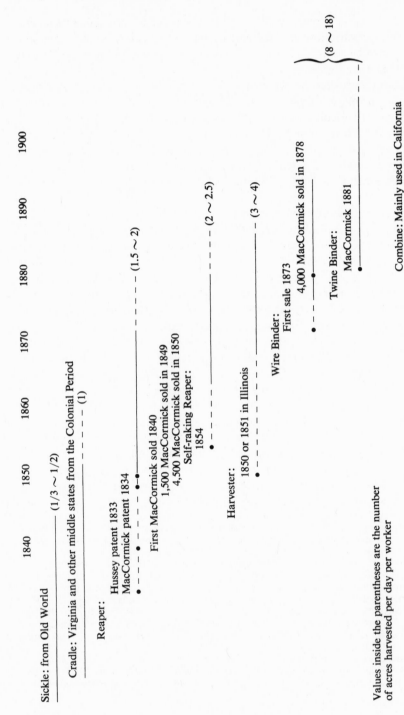

Sickle: from Old World

———— (1/3 ~ 1/2)

Cradle: Virginia and other middle states from the Colonial Period
———— – – – – (1)

Reaper:
Hussey patent 1833
MacCormick patent 1834
First MacCormick sold 1840 – – – – – – (1.5 ~ 2)
1,500 MacCormick sold in 1849
4,500 MacCormick sold in 1850
Self-raking Reaper:
1854 – – – – – (2 ~ 2.5)

Harvester:
1850 or 1851 in Illinois – – – – – (3 ~ 4)

Wire Binder:
First sale 1873
4,000 MacCormick sold in 1878

Twine Binder:
MacCormick 1881 } (8 ~ 18)

Combine: Mainly used in California

1840   1850   1860   1870   1880   1890   1900

Values inside the parentheses are the number
of acres harvested per day per worker

FIGURE 3–1. Evolution of harvesting machinery in the United States during the nineteenth century.

Note: Man-labor requirements for harvesting small grains (reaping, binding and shocking):

		Acres/day/worker
Sickle	1/3 ~ 1/2 acres/day/worker	1/3 ~ 1/2
Cradle	2 acres/day/2 workers (one cutter plus one binder)	1
Reaper	10 ~ 12 acres/day/6 ~ 7 workers (1 driver plus 1 raker plus 4 ~ 5 binders)	1.5 ~ 2
Self-raking Reaper	10 ~ 12 acres/day/5 ~ 6 workers (1 driver plus 4 ~ 5 binders)	2 ~ 2.5
Harvester	10 ~ 12 acres/day/3 workers (1 driver plus 2 binders)	3 ~ 4
Self-binder		
2 horse case	8 acres/day/worker	8
3 horse case	10 ~ 12 acres/day/worker	10 ~ 12
4 horse case	18 acres/day/worker	18

(*Source:* Leo Rogin, *The Introduction of Farm Machinery* [Berkeley: University of California Press, 1931].)

settlement was still concentrated east of the Appalachian Mountains. The first horse-drawn reapers, which permitted a second doubling of acreage harvested per worker per day, were patented in the 1830's and were in widespread use by 1850. This innovation corresponded to the dramatic expansion in cultivable land area relative to labor after the opening up of the Midwest. A series of improvements followed, permitting a further doubling of labor productivity during the 1860's. The next major advance came with the invention of wire and twine binders, which replaced the self-rake reaper and the hand-binding harvester. The incorporation of automatic binding equipment, together with other improvements in size and efficiency of operation, permitted a doubling or tripling of labor productivity in grain harvesting. The ultimate step in the evolution of harvesting methods began with the introduction of the combine—a combined harvester and thresher. Except for limited adoption in the extensive wheat growing areas of California and the Red River Valley of the north, the advantage of using a combine was not great, relative to the twine binder, until after the development of machinery having more efficient motive power than the large steam tractors available at the turn of the century.

The entire significance of this sequence of innovations in grain harvesting was to increase labor productivity. To the extent that any impact on land productivity was involved, it was a factor contributing to the extension of grain production into the drier areas of the Great Plains, where grain yields were lower than in the eastern grain producing regions.

From this discussion, it seems reasonable to hypothesize an agricultural production function in which mechanical equipment is viewed primarily as a substitute for labor; and evolution of the mechanical equipment is designed to bring about larger output per worker by increasing the land area which can be operated per worker. Furthermore, it seems apparent that the production functions which described the individual grain harvesting technologies, from the sickle to the combine, were induced by changes in relative factor costs, reflecting the rising resource scarcity of labor relative to other inputs.

Biological and Chemical Processes

In agriculture, biological and chemical technology and processes are more fundamental than mechanization or machine processes.[56] The implications

---

[56] Arthur T. Mosher, *Getting Agriculture Moving: Essentials for Development and Modernization* (New York: Praeger, 1966). "Plants are the primary factories of agriculture. They take in carbon dioxide from the air through their leaves. They take in moisture and chemical substances from the soil through their roots. Out of these, using the energy of sunlight, they make seeds, fruits, fibers and oils that man can use. Livestock are important secondary factories of agriculture. Depending on plants for their food, they can eat many parts of plants that man does not, such as the stems and leaves of grasses. They transform plant materials into still other products of use to man: meat, hides, wool, eggs and milk" (p. 15).

of these biological and chemical processes for the economic development and organization of agriculture are generally not well understood by social scientists, planners, and political leaders. The treatment of biological and chemical innovations in a typical treatise on economic development is passed over with a quick reference to the need for "new seeds and improved methods of cultivation," with little apparent insight into the significance of this terminology. The technical changes associated with mechanization seem to imply a sharp break with the past and the prospect of "instant modernization." Advances in biological and chemical technology typically pose neither the threat nor the promise of a radical reorganization of the agricultural production systems which have characterized the mechanization of motive power in agriculture.

Advances in biological and chemical technology have been induced primarily by a desire to increase crop output per unit of land area or to improve the yield of animal products per unit of feed. In crop production, these advances have typically involved one or more of the following three elements: (a) land and water resource development to provide a more satisfactory environment for plant growth; (b) modification of the environment by the addition of organic and inorganic sources of plant nutrients to the soil to stimulate plant growth and the use of biological and chemical means to protect plants from pests and disease; and (c) selection and design of new biologically efficient crop varieties specifically adapted to respond to those elements in the environment that are subject to man's control. Similar processes can be observed in advances in livestock agriculture.

The implications of biological and chemical innovations can be illustrated from English, United States, Japanese, Taiwanese, and other historical experiences. Two examples, one from the English and one from the Taiwanese experience, are particularly instructive.

The English agricultural revolution of the eighteenth century is regarded by economic historians as a critical complement of the Industrial Revolution.[57,58] As explained in the previous section, the agricultural revolution consisted of the development of an integrated crop-livestock system of husbandry. Rotation of arable cropland and pasture replaced the traditional fertility depleting open-field system. In most areas, the use of the turnip, for both green forage and winter fodder, was the key innovation in the new system, although in some areas new grasses and legumes played a critical role.

[57] Both the nature of the English agricultural revolution of the eighteenth century and its relationship to the industrial revolution have been the subject of considerable historical debate in recent years. For an excellent evaluation see Timmer, "English Agricultural Revolution."

[58] "English farming was technically the most advanced in Europe during the 18th century. As from the middle of that century, England was regarded by the countries of Europe as a school of agriculture. . . . Among the technical innovations and improvements . . . mention may be made of new methods of tillage . . ., new crops . . ., new farming systems . . ., new breeds of animals . . . and new methods of drainage." Joosep Nõu, *Development of Agricultural Economics*, p. 87.

This new system increased the livestock-carrying capacity of the land. The increase in livestock population produced the dung necessary to improve soil fertility and raise the yield of grain crops. The marketed value of both crops and livestock per unit of land area was substantially increased. On the better managed operations, increases in the marketable value of crops and livestock in the neighborhood of 50 percent were entirely feasible.

The increase of net returns to labor was considerably less dramatic. The new system was much more labor-intensive than the traditional system. Turnips were a labor-intensive crop, and labor requirements increased almost as much as output. Labor requirements were, however, distributed more evenly throughout the year, thus contributing to a rise in the number of days worked, that is, in labor input per agricultural laborer.

The primary impact of the English agricultural revolution of the eighteenth century was to increase land, not labor, productivity. According to C. Peter Timmer, "the agrarian revolution did not supply surplus labor for an industrial army of workers. It did provide food for the rapidly rising population from which both an increased agricultural and industrial labor force were recruited."[59]

Taiwan represents a particularly useful case in which to examine the utilization of the several technological and institutional elements associated with rapid agricultural development.[60] All of the three elements which we have identified with biological technology have been involved in the transformation of Taiwanese agriculture. Furthermore, the rapid development of agriculture in Taiwan has been "induced" rather than "autonomous." Taiwan has been the recipient of extensive development assistance for over two-thirds of a century—first from the Japanese colonial administration, from the beginning of the twentieth century until World War II, and then by the United States, from shortly after the end of World War II until the mid-1960's.

By the mid-1920's, under Japanese administration, Taiwan had acquired a number of the essential elements needed for rapid development of its rice economy: (a) the development of improved rice varieties, initially through selection of the best local varieties and later through a program of plant breeding designed to develop locally adapted fertilizer-responsive varieties;

---

[59] Timmer, "English Agricultural Revolution," p. 384.

[60] For a more detailed discussion of the material on Taiwan summarized in this section, see S. C. Hsieh and T. H. Lee, *Agricultural Development and Its Contribution to Economic Growth in Taiwan: Input-Output and Productivity Analysis of Taiwan Agricultural Development* (Taipei: Chinese–American Joint Commission on Rural Reconstruction, Economic Digest Series no. 17, April 1966); S. C. Hsieh and V. W. Ruttan, "Environmental, Technological and Institutional Factors in the Growth of Rice Production: Philippines, Thailand, and Taiwan," *Food Research Institute Studies*, vol. 7, no. 3 (1967): 307–41; Raymond P. Christensen, *Taiwan's Agricultural Development: Its Relevance for Developing Countries Today* (Washington: U.S. Department of Agriculture, Foreign Agriculture Economics Report 39, April 1968); and T. H. Lee, "Intersectoral Capital Flows in the Economic Development of Taiwan, 1895–1960," *Journal of Agricultural Economics* (Taiwan) 7 (June 1969): 69–97.

(b) the availability of irrigation systems capable of delivering water to much of the rice land throughout the year; and (c) the availability of technical inputs, such as chemical fertilizers, through an economic integration with the Japanese economy. In addition, economic integration also resulted in rapid development of the local transportation and marketing systems, opening up the Japanese market and creating incentives to increase the marketable surplus of rice in Taiwan.

The varieties developed by Japanese breeders in Taiwan are referred to as Ponlai varieties. The first Ponlai variety was introduced commercially in 1922 on 400 hectares of land. By 1940 Ponlai varieties were planted on half of the total rice area. The development of the new Ponlai varieties and the development of irrigation systems were intimately related to rapid growth in the use of commercial fertilizer in rice production after the mid-1920's. An essential element in the breeding strategy for the development of the Ponlai varieties was the incorporation of the genetic capacity to respond to higher levels of fertilization. The introduction of the Ponlai varieties, with a complementary improvement in cultural practices and investment in irrigation, resulted in rapid increases in yield per hectare, over 2 percent per year until 1938, when the Japanese military efforts began to direct resources away from development objectives.

In contrast to the English agricultural revolution, in Taiwan labor productivity and the labor earnings of individual cultivators rose concurrently with the rise in land productivity which resulted from the introduction of modern biological technology in Taiwanese agriculture. Major factors in the rise in output per worker were the changes that permitted an approximate doubling of labor inputs per worker.[61]

From this discussion, it seems reasonable to consider that the new husbandry techniques or the new seeds in which new biological and chemical technologies are embodied can be viewed primarily as the inputs which facilitate the substitution for land of artificial sources of plant nutrients, either purchased or produced by more labor-intensive conservation systems.

AN INDUCED DEVELOPMENT MODEL

It seems clear, from the previous discussion, that there are multiple paths of technical change in agriculture available to a society. The constraints imposed on agricultural development by an inelastic supply of land may be offset by

61	Number of agricultural workers	Multiple cropping index	Labor input in man days worked	Labor productivity per farm worker
1911–15	100	116	100	100
1921–25	98	121	118	118
1956–60	149	180	198	226

Source: Hsieh and Lee, *Agricultural Development*, pp. 24, 41.

advances in biological technology. The constraints imposed by an inelastic supply of labor may be offset by advances in mechanical technology. The ability of a country to achieve rapid growth in agricultural productivity and output seems to hinge on its ability to make an efficient choice among the alternative paths. Failure to choose a path which effectively loosens the constraints imposed by resource endowments can depress the whole process of agricultural and economic development. The construction of an induced development model involves, in addition to the elements considered in the models discussed earlier in this chapter, an explanation of the mechanism by which a society chooses an optimum path of technological change in agriculture.

There is a substantial body of literature on the "theory of induced innovation." Much of this literature focuses on the choice of available technology by the individual firm. There is, also, a substantial body of literature on how changes in factor prices over time or differences in factor prices among countries influence the nature of invention. This discussion has been conducted entirely within the framework of the theory of the firm. A major controversy has centered around the issue of the existence of a mechanism by which changes or differences in factor prices affect the inventive activity or the innovative behavior of firms.

The "induced innovation" models available in the literature offer little insight into the mechanism through which differences in resource endowments affect resource allocation in public sector research. In most economies which have achieved a high rate of growth in agricultural production and productivity, public sector research has represented an important component of the total resources devoted to agricultural research. Substantial resources have also been devoted by the public sector to educational and infrastructure investments in support of technical change in agriculture. In this section we extend the "induced innovation" model to include the process by which the public sector investment in agricultural research, in the adaptation and diffusion of agricultural technology and in the institutional infrastructure that is supportive of agricultural development, is directed toward releasing the constraints on agricultural production imposed by the factors characterized by a relatively inelastic supply.

The induced development model we advance here embraces as critical elements for agricultural and economic development the mechanisms of (a) induced innovation in the private sector; (b) induced innovation in the public sector; (c) interaction between technical change and institutional development; and (d) dynamic sequences of technical change and economic growth.

The term "innovation" employed here embraces the entire range of processes resulting in the emergence of novelty in science, technology, industrial management, and economic organization rather than the narrow Schumpeterian definition, which relates innovation to the activities of private business entrepreneurs. Joseph A. Schumpeter insisted that innovation was economically and sociologically distinct from invention and scientific discovery. He rejected the idea that innovation is dependent on invention or advances in science. This distinction has become increasingly artificial.[62] When greater precision in terminology is required, we will call the Schumpeterian innovation "entrepreneurial innovation," as distinct from "technical innovation" and "scientific innovation." In this framework, invention becomes a subset of technical innovations on which patents can be obtained.

Induced Innovation in the Private Sector

It had generally been accepted, at least since the publication of *Theory of Wages* by Hicks, that changes or differences in the relative prices of factors of production could influence the direction of invention or innovation.[63] There have also been arguments raised by W. E. G. Salter and others against Hicks's theory of induced innovation.[64] The arguments run somewhat as follows: Firms are motivated to save total cost for a given output; at competitive equilibrium, each factor is being paid its marginal value product; therefore, all factors are equally expensive to firms; hence there is no incentive for competitive firms to search for techniques to save a particular factor.

The difference between our perspective and Salter's is partly due to a difference in the definition of the production function. Salter defined the production function to embrace all possible designs conceivable by existing scientific knowledge and called the choice among these designs "factor substitution" instead of "technical change."[65] Salter admits, however, that "relative factor prices are the nature of signal posts representing broad influences that de-

[62] See, for example, Carolyn Shaw Solo, "Innovation in the Capitalist Process: A Critique of the Schumpeterian Theory," *Quarterly Journal of Economics* 65 (August 1951): 417–28; Vernon W. Ruttan, "Usher and Schumpeter on Invention, Innovation and Technological Change," ibid. 73 (November 1959): 596–606; and Paul M. Hohenberg, *Chemicals in Western Europe: 1850–1914* (Chicago: Rand-McNally and Company, 1967). Our view is similar to that of Hohenberg. He defines technical effort as the product of purposive resource using activity directed to the production of economically useful knowledge. ". . . technical effort is a necessary part of any firm activity, and is only in part separable from production itself. Traditionally it is part of the entrepreneur's job to provide knowledge to organize the factors of production in an optimum way, to adjust to market changes, and to seek improved methods. Technical effort is thus subsumed under entrepreneurship" (p. 61).

[63] J. R. Hicks, *The Theory of Wages* (London: Macmillan 1932), pp. 124–25. See also the review of thought on this issue in Syed Ahmad, "On the Theory of Induced Invention," *Economic Journal* 76 (June 1966): 344–57.

[64] See W. E. G. Salter, *Productivity and Technical Change* (Cambridge: Cambridge University Press, 1960), pp. 43–44. For further discussion see William Fellner, "Two Propositions in the Theory of Induced Innovations," *Economic Journal* 71 (June 1961): 305–8; Charles Kennedy, "Induced Bias in Innovation and the Theory of Distribution," ibid. 74 (September 1964): 541–47; P. A. Samuelson, "A Theory of Induced Innovation Along Kennedy, Weisäcker Lines," *Review of Economics and Statistics* 47 (November 1965): 343–56; Ahmad, "On the Theory of Induced Invention."

[65] Salter, *Productivity and Technical Change*, pp. 14–16.

termine the way technological knowledge is applied to production."[66] If we accept Salter's definition, the allocation of resources to the development of high-yielding and fertilizer-responsive varieties adaptable to the ecology of Pakistan, which are comparable to the improved varieties in Japan (Table 3-1), for example, cannot be considered as a technical change. Rather, it is viewed as an application of existing technological knowledge (breeding techniques, plant-type concepts, etc.) to production.

Although we do not deny the case for Salter's definition, it is clearly not very useful in attempting to understand the process by which new technical alternatives become available. We regard technical change as any change in production coefficients resulting from the purposeful resource-using activity directed to the development of new knowledge embodied in designs, materials, or organizations.[67] In terms of this definition, it is entirely rational for competitive firms to allocate funds to develop a technology which facilitates the substitution of increasingly more expensive factors for less expensive factors.[68] Syed Ahmad clearly shows, assuming entrepreneurs conceive alternative new technical possibilities which can be developed by the same amount of research costs, that, if one factor becomes more expensive relative to another over time, the innovative efforts of entrepreneurs will be directed toward saving the factor which becomes more expensive. Similarly, in a country in which a factor is more expensive relative to another factor than it is in a second country, innovative efforts will be directed toward saving the relatively more expensive factors.

Induced Innovation in the Public Sector

Innovative behavior in the public sector has largely been ignored in the literature on induced innovation. There is no theory of induced innovation in the public sector.[69] This is a particularly critical limitation in attempting to understand the process of scientific and technical innovation in agricultural

---

[66] Ibid., p. 16.

[67] Hohenberg, *Chemicals in Western Europe*, p. 57.

[68] Ahmad, "On the Theory of Induced Invention." See also discussion by Fellner and Ahmad in William Fellner, "Comment on the Induced Bias," *Economic Journal* 77 (September 1967): 662–64; Syed Ahmad, "Reply to Professor Fellner," ibid. 77 (September 1967): 664–65; discussions by Charles Kennedy, "On the Theory of Induced Invention—A Reply," ibid. 77 (December 1967): 958–60; and Syed Ahmad, "A Rejoinder to Professor Kennedy," ibid. 77 (December 1967): 960–3.

[69] There is a growing literature on public research policy. See Richard R. Nelson, Merton J. Peck, and Edward D. Kalachek, *Technology, Economic Growth and Public Policy* (Washington: The Brookings Institute, 1967). The authors view public sector research activities as having risen from three considerations: (a) fields where the public interest is believed to transcend private incentives (as in health and aviation); (b) industries where the individual firm is too small to capture benefits from research (agriculture and housing); and (c) broad-scale support for basic research and science education (pp. 151–211). For a review of thought with respect to resource allocation in agriculture, see Fishel, ed., *Resource Allocation*.

development. In most countries which have been successful in achieving rapid rates of technical progress in agriculture, "socialization" of agricultural research has been deliberately employed as an instrument of modernization in agriculture.

Our view of the mechanism of "induced innovation" in the public sector agricultural research is similar to the Hicksian theory of induced innovation in the private sector. A major extension of the traditional argument is that we base the innovation inducement mechanism not only on the response to changes in the market prices of profit maximizing firms but also on the response by research scientists and administrators in public institutions to resource endowments and economic change.

We hypothesize that technical change is guided along an efficient path by price signals in the market, provided that the prices efficiently reflect changes in the demand and supply of products and factors and that there exists effective interaction among farmers, public research institutions, and private agricultural supply firms. If the demand for agricultural products increases, due to the growth in population and income, prices of the inputs for which the supply is inelastic will be raised relative to the prices of inputs for which the supply is elastic. Likewise, if the supply of particular inputs shifts to the right faster than others, the prices of these inputs will decline relative to the prices of other factors of production. In consequence, technical innovations that save the factors characterized by an inelastic supply, or by slower shifts in supply, become relatively more profitable for agricultural producers. Farmers are induced, by shifts in relative prices, to search for technical alternatives which save the increasingly scarce factors of production. They press the public research institutions to develop the new technology and, also, demand that agricultural supply firms supply modern technical inputs which substitute for the more scarce factors. Perceptive scientists and science administrators respond by making available new technical possibilities and new inputs that enable farmers to profitably substitute the increasingly abundant factors for increasingly scarce factors, thereby guiding the demand of farmers for unit cost reduction in a socially optimum direction.

The dialectic interaction among farmers and research scientists and administrators is likely to be most effective when farmers are organized into politically effective local and regional farm "bureaus" or farmers associations. The response of the public sector research and extension programs to farmers' demand is likely to be greatest when the agricultural research system is highly decentralized, as in the United States. In the United States, for example, each of the state agricultural experiment stations has tended to view its function, at least in part, as to maintain the competitive position of agriculture in its state relative to agriculture in other states. Similarly, national policymakers may regard investment in agricultural research as an investment designed to maintain the country's competitive position in world markets or to improve the economic viability of the agricultural sector producing import-substitutes. Given effective farmer organizations and a mission- or client-oriented experiment station system, the competitive model of firm behavior can be usefully extended to explain the response of experiment station administrators and research scientists to economic opportunities.

In this public sector induced innovation model, the response of research scientists and administrators represents the critical link in the inducement mechanism. The model does not imply that it is necessary for individual scientists or research administrators in public institutions to consciously respond to market prices, or directly to farmers' demands for research results, in the selection of research objectives. They may, in fact, be motivated primarily by a drive for professional achievement and recognition.[70] It is only necessary if there exists an effective incentive mechanism to reward the scientists or administrators, materially or by prestige, for their contributions to the solution of significant problems in the society.[71] Under these conditions, it seems reasonable to hypothesize that the scientists and administrators of public sector research programs do respond to the needs of society in an attempt to direct the results of their activity to public purpose. Furthermore, we hypothesize that secular changes in relative factor and product prices convey much of the information regarding the relative priorities which society places on the goals of research.

The response in the public research sector is not limited to the field of applied science. Scientists trying to solve practical problems often consult with or ask co-operation of those working in more basic fields. If the basic scientists respond to the requests of the applied researchers, they are in effect responding to the needs of society. It is not uncommon that major breakthroughs in basic science are created through the process of solving the problems raised by research workers in the more applied fields.[72] It appears rea-

---

[70] William A. Niskanen, "The Peculiar Economics of Bureaucracy," *American Economic Review* 58 (May 1968): 293–305.

[71] The issue of incentive is a major issue in many developing economies. In spite of limited scientific and technical manpower many countries have not succeeded in developing a system of economic and professional rewards that permits them to have access to, or make effective use of, the resources of scientific and technical manpower that are potentially available.

[72] The symbiotic relationship between basic and applied research can be illustrated by the relation between work at the International Rice Research Institute in (a) genetics and plant physiology and (b) plant breeding. The geneticist and the physiologist are involved in research designed to advance understanding of the physiological processes by which plant nutrients are transformed into grain yield and of the genetic mechanisms or processes involved in the transmission from parents to progenies of the physiological characteristics of the rice plant which affect grain yield. The rice breeders utilize this knowledge from genetics and plant physiology in the design of crosses and the selection of plants with the desired growth characteristics, agronomic traits, and nutritional value. The work in plant physiology and genetics is responsive to the need of the plant breeder for advances in knowledge related to the mission of breeding more productive varieties of rice.

sonable, therefore, to hypothesize, as a result of the interactions among the basic and applied sciences and the process by which public funds are allocated to research, that basic research tends to be directed also toward easing the limitations on agricultural production imposed by relatively scarce factors.

We do not argue, however, that technical change in agriculture is wholly of an induced character. There is a supply (an exogenous) dimension to the process as well as a demand (an endogenous) dimension. Technical change in agriculture reflects, in addition to the effects of resource endowments and growth in demand, the progress of general science and technology. Progress in general science (or scientific innovation) which lowers the "cost" of technical and entrepreneurial innovations may have influences on technical change in agriculture unrelated to changes in factor proportions and product demand.[73] Even in these cases, the rate of adoption and the impact on productivity of autonomous or exogenous changes in technology will be strongly influenced by the conditions of resource supply and product demand, as these forces are reflected through factor and product markets.

Thus, the classical problem of resource allocation, which was rejected as an adequate basis for agricultural productivity and output growth in the high-pay-off input model, is, in this context, treated as central to the agricultural development process. Under conditions of static technology, improvements in resource allocation represent a weak source of economic growth. The efficient allocation of resources to open up new sources of growth is, however, essential to the agricultural development process.

Institutional Innovation

Extension of the theory of "induced innovation" to explain the behavior of public research institutions represents an essential link in the construction of a theory of induced development. In the induced development model, advances in mechanical and biological technology respond to changing relative prices of factors, and to changes in the prices of factors relative to products, to ease the constraints on growth imposed by inelastic supplies of land or labor. Neither this process, nor its impact, is confined to the agricultural sector. Changes in relative prices in any sector of the economy act to induce innovative activity, not only by private producers but also by scientists in public institutions, in order to reduce the constraints imposed by those factors of production which are relatively scarce.

We further hypothesize that the institutions that govern the use of technology or the "mode" of production can also be induced to change in order to enable both individuals and society to take fuller advantage of new tech-

---

[73] Richard R. Nelson, "The Economics of Invention: A Survey of the Literature," *Journal of Business* 32 (April 1959): 101–27; Jacob Schmookler, *Invention and Economic Growth* (Cambridge: Harvard University Press, 1966).

nical opportunities under favorable market conditions.[74] The Second Enclosure Movement in England represents a classical illustration. The issuance of the Enclosure Bill facilitated the conversion of communal pasture and farmland into single, private farm units, thus encouraging the introduction of an integrated crop-livestock "new husbandry" system. The Enclosure Acts can be viewed as an institutional innovation designed to exploit the new technical opportunities opened up by innovations in crop rotation, utilizing the new fodder crops (turnip and clover), in response to the rising food prices.

A major source of institutional change has been an effort by society to internalize the benefits of innovative activity to provide economic incentives for productivity increase. In some cases, institutional innovations have involved the reorganization of property rights, in order to internalize the higher income streams resulting from the innovations. The modernization of land tenure relationships, involving a shift from share tenure to lease tenure and owner-operator systems of cultivation in much of western agriculture, can be explained, in part, as a shift in property rights designed to internalize the gains of entrepreneurial innovation by individual farmers.[75]

Where internalization of the gains of innovative activity are more difficult to achieve, institutional innovations involving public sector activity become essential. The socialization of much of agricultural research, particularly the research leading to advances in biological technology, represents an example of a public sector institutional innovation designed to realize for society the potential gains from advances in agricultural technology. This institutional innovation originated in Germany and was transplanted and applied on a larger scale in the United States and Japan (Chapter 7).

Both Schultz and Kazushi Ohkawa have recently argued that institutional reform is appropriately viewed as a response to the new opportunities for the productive use of resources opened up by advances in technology.[76] Our view, and the view of Ohkawa and Schultz, reduces to the hypothesis that institutional innovations occur because it appears profitable for individuals or

---

[74] At this point we share the Marxian perspective on the relationship between technological change and institutional development, though we do not accept the Marxian perspective regarding the monolithic sequences of evolution based on clear-cut class conflicts. For two recent attempts to develop broad historical generalizations regarding the relation between institutions and economic forces, see John Hicks, *A Theory of Economic History* (London: Oxford University Press, 1969); Douglass C. North and Robert Paul Thomas, "An Economic Theory of the Growth of the Western World," *Economic History Review*, vol. 23, no. 1 (second series) (1970): 1–17.

[75] For additional examples, see Lance Davis and Douglass North, "Institutional Change and American Economic Growth: A First Step Towards a Theory of Institutional Innovation," *Journal of Economic History* 30 (March 1970): 131–49.

[76] T. W. Schultz, "Institutions and the Rising Economic Value of Man," *American Journal of Agricultural Economics* 50 (December 1968): 1113–22; Kazushi Ohkawa, "Policy Implications of the Asian Agricultural Survey—Personal Notes," *Regional Seminar on Agriculture: Paper and Proceedings* (Makati, Philippines: Asian Development Bank, 1969), pp. 23–29; also North and Thomas, "An Economic Theory."

groups in society to undertake the costs. It is unlikely that institutional change will prove viable unless the benefits to society exceed the cost. Changes in market prices and technological opportunities introduce disequilibrium in existing institutional arrangements by creating profitable new opportunities for the institutional innovations.

Profitable opportunities, however, do not necessarily lead to immediate institutional innovations. Usually the gains and losses from technical and institutional change are not distributed neutrally. There are, typically, vested interests which stand to lose and which oppose change. There are limits on the extent to which group behavior can be mobilized to achieve common or group interests.[77] The process of transforming institutions in response to technical and economic opportunities generally involves time lags, social and political stress, and, in some cases, disruption of social and political order. Economic growth ultimately depends on the flexibility and efficiency of society in transforming itself in response to technical and economic opportunities.

Dynamic Sequences

In the dynamic process of development, the emergence of imbalance or disequilibrium is a critical element in inducing technical change and economic growth. Disequilibrium among the several elements in the system creates the bottlenecks which focus the attention of scientists, inventors, entrepreneurs, and public administrators on the solution of problems for attaining more efficient resource allocation.[78]

The introduction of reapers in U.S. agriculture in the mid-nineteenth century, for example, was induced as a result of an imbalance in the labor requirements between the planting and harvesting operations. In U.S. agriculture, as the frontier pushed rapidly to the west, land became progressively abundant relative to labor. In order to prevent crop spoilage the reaper was invented, in response to a compelling need to harvest wheat crops within a limited number of days. It was designed to solve the harvesting bottleneck in an

---

[77] Mancur Olson, Jr., *The Logic of Collective Action: Public Goods and the Theory of Groups* (New York: Schocken Books, 1968).

[78] Rosenberg has suggested a theory of induced technical change based on "obvious and compelling need" to overcome the constraints on growth instead of relative factor scarcity and factor relative prices. See Nathan Rosenberg, "The Direction of Technological Change: Inducement Mechanisms and Focusing Devices," *Economic Development and Cultural Change* 18 (October 1969): 1–24. The Rosenberg model is consistent with the model suggested here, since his "obvious and compelling need" is reflected in the market through relative factor prices. C. Peter Timmer has pointed out (in an October 9, 1970 letter) that in a linear programming sense the constraints which give rise to the "obvious and compelling need" for technical innovation in the Rosenberg model represent the "dual" of the factor prices used in our model. For further discussion of the relationships between Rosenberg's approach and that outlined in this section see Yujiro Hayami and V. W. Ruttan, "Professor Rosenberg and the Direction of Technical Change" (St. Paul: University of Minnesota, Department of Agricultural Economics, Paper 70–4, April 1970), mimeo.

economic environment in which the supply of land was expanding more rapidly than the supply of labor.[79] Inventive efforts were focused on solving this obvious need of farmers resulting from the relative labor scarcity in the economy.

A solution to the problems which result from one bottleneck generally creates another bottleneck. This acts as a device for transmitting technical change from one process of production to another.[80] A classical example may be seen in the English cotton industry in the early period of the Industrial Revolution: "Key's flying shuttle led to the need for speeding up spinning operations; the eventual innovations in spinning in turn created the shortage of weaving capacity which finally culminated in Cartwright's introduction of the power loom."[81]

Progress in farm mechanization is no exception to this general pattern. Original models of reapers saved cutting labor, but made raking and binding operations the bottleneck. The successive introduction of self-raking reapers and binders clearly illustrates the process of cumulative sequences in technical change (see Figure 3–1).[82] Mechanization of harvesting also created a bottleneck in threshing, calling for the introduction of power threshers. Through these cumulative sequences, the United States succeeded in developing a mechanical technology in agricultural production which facilitated the substitution of the relatively more abundant land and capital for the relatively more scarce labor (Chapters 6–7).

The cumulative sequences resulting from technical changes in agricultural production also induce changes in other sectors of the economy. Imbalance within agriculture and between agriculture and other sectors of the economy is an important source of backward and forward linkages in transmitting technical progress in agriculture to over-all economic development.[83] For example, as a result of the development of high-yielding grain varieties, rapid increases in food grain production in South and Southeast Asian countries, beginning in the late 1960's, are now creating a serious bottleneck in the

[79] This bottleneck would not have emerged unless land became more abundant relative to labor. Technically it would have been possible to prevent crop spoilage at reduced acreage while maintaining the same level of output by developing a labor-intensive technology based on scientific crop rotation and commercial fertilizers; in fact, such technology was developed in Germany and other countries in Europe in the mid-nineteenth century. U.S. farmers did not adopt such labor-intensive technology, because it was less profitable for their relative factor prices.

[80] Rosenberg's historical reconnaissance (ibid.) gives us an excellent perspective on this process.

[81] Ibid., p. 5.

[82] The process of cumulative synthesis of individual innovations in the evolution of major or strategic innovations or sequences of inventions is described in the classical study by Abbott Payson Usher, *A History of Mechanical Inventions* (Cambridge: Harvard University Press, 1954), pp. 56–83.

[83] Hirschman based his theory of economic development on this mechanism. See Hirschman, *The Strategy of Economic Development*.

marketing process (Chapter 10). This bottleneck has increased the return to investments to improve the capacity and efficiency of the marketing system.

The linkages between innovations in the nonagricultural sector with advances in agricultural technology are also critical. The secular decline in fertilizer prices, resulting from cost-reducing innovations in the fertilizer industry, served to focus attention on the limited capacity of traditional grain varieties to respond to higher levels of fertilizer. The decline in the price of fertilizer, relative to the prices of output and land, has induced efforts by experiment station researchers to overcome this bottleneck by developing more fertilizer-responsive grain varieties (Chapters 7 and 9). This effort proceeded most rapidly in countries such as Japan and the United States, where substantial experiment station capacity already existed. More recently, it has resulted in a series of institutional innovations resulting in expanded experiment station capacity in the grain-producing regions of the tropics (Chapters 8 and 9).

In this book, we attempt to elaborate and test the induced development hypothesis outlined in this section.

Part II Intercountry Comparisons

CHAPTER FOUR

The Agricultural Productivity
Gap among Countries[1]

There are great differences in agricultural productivity among nations, measured in terms of either output per worker or output per hectare. These differences became more pronounced between the mid-1950's and the mid-1960's. The existence of great differences in partial productivity ratios among countries and of divergent trends in labor and land productivity over time are consistent with the induced development model outlined in the previous chapter. Indeed, given the differences in resource endowments and relative factor prices among countries, failure to observe such differences would be clearly inconsistent with the concept of induced technical change.

Our first objective in this chapter is to establish the hypothesis that the observed differences in land and labor productivity are associated with differences in the level of biological and mechanical technology among countries and over time and to identify the significance of industrial inputs for advances in both biological and mechanical technology. In establishing this hypothesis we draw on a new set of agricultural production and productivity estimates that have been constructed to facilitate the analysis of intercountry productivity differentials.

Our second objective is to construct a more operational model, suitable for empirical testing, of the induced development process outlined in the previous chapter. The model is specifically designed to incorporate the processes by which advances in industrial technology, which reduce the costs of biological

[1] This chapter draws heavily on three earlier papers: Yujiro Hayami, "Industrialization and Agricultural Productivity: An International Comparative Study," *Developing Economies* 7 (March 1969): 3–21; Yujiro Hayami and Kinuyo Inagi, "International Comparison of Agricultural Productivities," *Farm Economist*, vol. 11, no. 10 (1969): 407–19; and Yujiro Hayami, "Resource Endowments and Technological Change in Agriculture: U.S. and Japanese Experiences in International Perspective," *American Journal of Agricultural Economics* 51 (December 1969): 1293–1303. The data used here represent a revision of the data published in the earlier papers.

and mechanical inputs to the agricultural sector, induce unique paths of technological change and productivity growth in the agricultural sector.

Our model will be used to generate a series of hypotheses that are tested in subsequent chapters. In Chapter 5 an intercountry cross-section analysis is employed to measure the relative importance of resource endowments, technology, and human capital on differences in labor productivity among nations. In Chapter 6 a time-series analysis is employed to measure the impacts of resource endowments and relative factor prices on the patterns of production and resource use in United States and Japanese agriculture from 1880 to 1960.

The data used in constructing the intercountry productivity comparisons are clearly of uneven quality. There are serious conceptual and technical problems in the collection, organization, and processing of agricultural data, even for the most advanced countries. The aggregation and index number problems are nearly insuperable. In spite of these limitations, the intercountry cross-section analysis provides useful insights. It permits us to draw on the experiences of nations with an extremely wide range of variation in the relative endowments of land and labor and in land and labor productivity. This wide range is particularly valuable in helping to clarify relationships which tend to be obscured by observations based on the experiences of an individual country or a small number of relatively homogeneous countries.

PRODUCTIVITY AND RESOURCE USE IN AGRICULTURE

In this section the two partial productivity measures, output per unit of labor and output per unit of land, are used to illustrate the wide variations in the relationship between factor endowments and agricultural output among countries and over time. The close association between variations in labor productivity and the use of mechanical inputs and of variations in land productivity and the use of biological inputs is also illustrated. At this point any interpretation of differences in the two partial productivity measures as reflecting differences in technology or efficiency is specifically avoided.[2]

A number of intercountry comparisons of agricultural production and productivity have been published since Colin Clark's pioneering work.[3] Many

---

[2] For a discussion of partial and total productivity indexes and their interpretation see Murray Brown, *On The Theory and Measurement of Technological Change* (Cambridge: Cambridge University Press, 1966), pp. 95–109. The induced development process, as outlined in chapters 4 and 6 of this study, implies a more complex interaction among resource endowments, advances in technical knowledge, changes in factor-factor and factor-product price ratios, and in partial and total factor productivity ratios than is suggested in the literature reviewed by Brown.

[3] Colin Clark, *The Conditions of Economic Progress* (1st ed.; London: Macmillan, 1940). Most previous works were surveyed by Clark in his "World Supply and Requirement of Farm Products," *Journal of the Royal Statistical Society*, vol. 117, series A, part III (1954): 263–91; and *The Conditions of Economic Progress* (3rd ed., rev.; London: Macmillan and

of these studies, including those of Clark, have become obsolete as a result of the appearance of improved data. The comparisons presented in this chapter are based on a new set of data. The detailed explanations of data sources and methods of organization are presented in Appendix A.

Intercountry Comparisons (1960)

The land and labor productivities shown in Table 4–1 were calculated as output per male worker and per hectare of agricultural land area in wheat units (one wheat unit is equivalent to one ton of wheat) for 1960 using the data explained in Appendix A. International differences in these partial productivity ratios are indeed great. Measured in wheat units, agricultural output per hectare ranged from 0.04 (Libya) to 10.24 (Taiwan), and output per male worker ranged from 2.1 (India) to 141.8 (New Zealand).

The land and labor productivity ratios for the several countries are plotted in Figure 4–1. Land productivity is measured on the vertical axis and labor productivity on the horizontal axis. Three distinct scatters or paths extending out from the origin can be observed: (a) the path indicated by the group of countries in the new continents, represented by New Zealand, Australia, Canada, and the U.S.A., where man-land ratios are particularly favorable; (b) the path indicated by countries in Asia, represented by Taiwan and Japan, where unfavorable man-land ratios prevail; and (c) the path indicated by countries in Europe, represented by The Netherlands, Belgium, and Denmark, in which the relative factor endowments are between the other two groups.

Each path seems to reflect the long-run process of agricultural growth under alternative man-land ratios. The relative availability of land and labor in the agricultural sector is a result of the original resource endowments and of the resource accumulation associated with historical growth processes of each economy. In Asia land has been the major factor limiting the increase in output. In the new continents a relatively inelastic supply of labor has represented the most significant constraint on growth of output. In order to ease the limitation set either by land or by labor, farmers try to economize in the use of the limiting factor or to substitute man-made inputs for it, e.g., fertilizer for land and tractors for labor. The growth path followed by the countries in the new continents seems to reflect a process of easing the limitation set by labor, and the one suggested by Asian countries reflects a process of easing the limitation set by land.

Such processes may be visualized by comparing Figure 4–1 and Figure 4–2.

New York: St. Martin's Press, 1957). More recently, FAO attempted to compare land and labor productivities in agriculture for 1956–60 in *The State of Food and Agriculture 1963* (Rome: Food and Agricultural Organization of the United Nations, 1963), pp. 100–20. Neither the details of the aggregation procedures nor the numerical data for aggregate output were ever published by the FAO.

Table 4-1. Estimated land and labor productivities in agriculture, 43 countries, 1960, in wheat units

Country	Output	
	per hectare (Y/A)	per male worker (Y/L)
Argentina	0.37	39.9
Australia	0.09	106.4
Austria	2.33	31.7
Belgium (and Luxemburg)	6.12	52.7
Brazil	0.60	9.4
Canada	0.58	75.8
Ceylon	2.85	3.9
Chile	0.48	12.9
Colombia	0.84	10.3
Denmark	4.60	47.4
Finland	2.02	30.9
France	2.49	35.9
Germany, Fed. Rep.	4.00	38.6
Greece	1.22	9.9
India	1.06	2.1
Ireland	1.58	21.0
Israel	1.84	28.9
Italy	3.00	16.1
Japan	7.47	10.7
Libya	0.04	n.a.
Mauritius	5.33	11.6
Mexico	0.27	5.2
Netherlands	7.21	43.1
New Zealand	1.19	141.8
Norway	3.09	31.1
Pakistan	n.a.	2.4
Paraguay	0.94	5.0
Peru	0.56	10.2
Philippines	1.88	3.8
Portugal	n.a.	7.4
South Africa	0.16	11.7
Spain	1.08	12.2
Surinam	4.46	17.1
Sweden	2.33	44.3
Switzerland	3.16	29.3
Syria	0.36	9.4
Taiwan	10.24	8.1
Turkey	0.59	7.1
U.A.R.	6.90	4.4
U.K.	1.94	44.0
U.S.A.	0.80	99.5
Venezuela	0.28	8.4
Yugoslavia	1.14	n.a.

Source: Data from Appendix Table A-5.

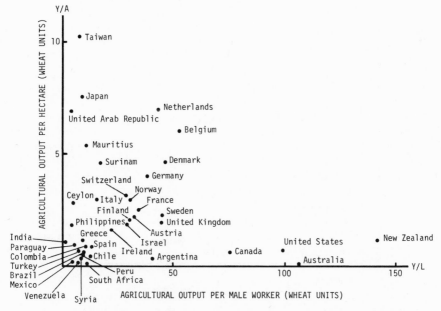

FIGURE 4–1.   International comparison of agricultural output per male worker and per hectare of agricultural land. Output data are 1957–62 averages; and labor and land data are of year closest to 1960. (Data from Table 4–1.)

In Figure 4–2 fertilizer input ($N + P_2O_5 + K_2O$) per hectare of agricultural land is plotted on the vertical axis and tractor horsepower per male worker is plotted on the horizontal axis. Fertilizer is used here as a proxy or index for the factors which substitute for land and tractor horsepower as a proxy for the factors which substitute for labor. It will be seen that the productivity ratios of the respective countries in Figure 4–1 occupy roughly the same positions as when plotted as input ratios as in Figure 4–2.

Changes in Productivity (1955 to 1965)

In Table 4–2 changes in the two productivity ratios from 1955 to 1965 are compared. The great differences in agricultural productivity between developed and less developed countries increased during this decade. Table 4–3 shows that output per male worker in thirteen developed countries (DC) increased at an annual compound rate of 4.7 percent, whereas the rate of growth of eleven less developed countries (LDC) was only 1.4 percent. The growth rates of output per hectare were of approximately equal magnitudes, but land area per male worker increased in the DC's at the annual rate of 2.6 percent, while it declined in the LDC's at the rate of 0.4 percent. In the DC's, where demand for labor in the nonagricultural sector pulled a significant amount of

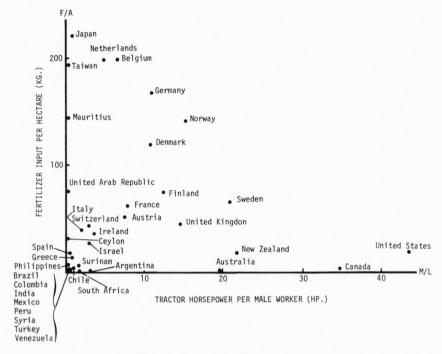

FIGURE 4–2. International comparison of tractor horsepower per male worker and of fertilizer input per hectare of agricultural land. Fertilizer data are 1957–62 averages; and labor, land, and tractor data are of years closest to 1960. (Data from Appendix Table A–5.)

labor out of agriculture, the rates of growth in labor productivity were increased by improvements in the land-labor ratio. In the LDC's where growth in the demand for labor in the nonagricultural sector was not sufficient to keep up with growth in the labor force, the decline in agricultural land area per worker depressed the growth in labor productivity.

The different patterns of productivity growth in agriculture are associated with the different patterns of inputs of factors supplied from the nonagricultural sector relative to the endowments of land and labor (compare Figure 4–3 with Figure 4–4). In the LDC's, where labor productivity growth was primarily brought about by the increase in land productivity, the input of fertilizer per hectare increased more rapidly than machinery per worker.[4] In contrast, the progress of mechanization was a primary source of growth in output per worker in the DC's.

---

[4] Probably more so than the data in Table 4–3 indicate, because a significant part of the increase in tractor horsepower represented a replacement for work animals rather than a net addition to available power in the LDC's.

Table 4–2. Estimated land and labor productivities in agriculture, 1955 and 1965

Country	Output per hectare in WU (Y/A)		Output per male worker in WU (Y/L)	
	1955	1965	1955	1965
Argentina	0.36	0.41	34.7	42.9
Australia	0.07	0.10	80.6	125.8
Austria	1.92	2.63	21.2	39.2
Belgium (and Luxemburg)	5.50	6.98	38.6	71.8
Brazil	0.48	0.63	8.1	10.4
Canada	0.59	0.75	58.7	115.2
Ceylon	2.49	3.02	3.8	4.5
Chile	0.45	0.49	11.7	13.4
Colombia	0.80	0.81	8.3	9.0
Denmark	4.00	5.02	36.9	55.7
Finland	1.73	2.29	24.7	38.2
France	2.21	2.95	25.1	45.4
Germany, Fed. Rep.	3.56	4.49	28.5	49.6
Greece	0.99	1.53	7.9	12.1
India	0.94	1.13	2.4	2.2
Ireland	1.37	1.63	16.4	24.3
Israel	2.36	2.54	14.8	38.9
Italy	2.64	3.31	10.8	20.1
Japan	7.02	7.54	7.7	13.1
Libya	0.04	0.05	n.a.	n.a.
Mauritius	n.a.	n.a.	n.a.	n.a.
Mexico	0.21	0.29	4.1	5.5
Netherlands	6.18	8.28	31.6	53.2
New Zealand	1.01	1.33	113.4	166.7
Norway	3.01	3.15	26.4	33.4
Pakistan	n.a.	n.a.	n.a.	n.a.
Paraguay	n.a.	n.a.	n.a.	n.a.
Peru	0.47	0.60	9.1	11.1
Philippines	1.63	1.39	3.7	4.1
Portugal	1.59	1.83	7.3	8.6
South Africa	0.14	0.17	9.9	12.6
Spain	1.10	1.21	8.5	12.2
Surinam	n.a.	n.a.	n.a.	n.a.
Sweden	2.23	2.69	36.7	50.1
Switzerland	2.87	3.18	23.3	31.5
Syria	0.38	0.43	9.4	11.2
Taiwan	7.85	11.92	6.7	8.1
Turkey	0.48	0.68	6.3	7.6
U.A.R.	0.56	7.75	3.7	4.6
U.K.	1.70	2.33	34.2	57.3
U.S.A.	0.74	0.87	71.2	123.5
Venezuela	0.24	0.29	6.9	10.6
Yugoslavia	0.82	1.28	n.a.	n.a.

Source: Data from Appendix Table A–5.

Table 4-3. Rates of growth in productivity and factor proportions, 1955 to 1965, annual compound rate (in percent)

Group of countries	Output per male worker (Y/L)	Output per hectare (Y/A)	Land area per male worker (A/L)	Fertilizer per hectare (F/A)	Machinery per male worker (M/L)
Developed countries	4.7	2.1	2.6	5.1	9.8
Intermediate countries	4.4	2.0	2.4	5.8	15.8
Less developed countries	1.4ᵃ	2.1ᵃ	−0.4	10.9	6.4

ᵃ Excluding Mauritius.

Developed countries: Per capita GNP higher than 700 U.S. dollars and less than 30 percent of male workers engaged in agricultural occupations: Australia, Belgium, Canada, Denmark, France, Germany, Netherlands, New Zealand, Norway, Sweden, Switzerland, U.K., U.S.A.

Less developed countries: Per capita GNP lower than 350 dollars and more than 35 percent of male workers engaged in agricultural occupations: Brazil, Ceylon, Colombia, India, Mauritius, Mexico, Peru, Philippines, Syria, Taiwan, Turkey, U.A.R.

Intermediate countries: Countries which do not belong to either of the above categories: Argentina, Austria, Chile, Finland, Greece, Ireland, Israel, Italy, Japan, Portugal, South Africa, Spain, Venezuela.

INDUSTRIALIZATION AND AGRICULTURAL PRODUCTIVITY GROWTH

Despite great differences in climate, technology, and output mix, it seems apparent that the major variations in land and labor productivity among countries are associated with differences in the levels of industrial inputs which ease the constraints imposed by the inelastic supply of the primary factors. The relations observed above are consistent with the hypothesis that growth in agricultural productivity is essentially a process of adaptation by the agricultural sector to new opportunities created by the advances in knowledge and by the progress of interindustry division of labor which has accompanied industrialization. The term "industrialization" is used here in a broader sense than simply the expansion of the manufacturing sector. It includes the coordinated growth of manufacturing, service, and related industries, including international trade and transport, that characterizes an industrial economy.

If industrialization is measured by the ratio of the number of male workers in the nonagricultural sector to the total number of male workers, the countries located close to the efficiency frontier implicit in Figure 4-1 (the efficiency frontier defined in terms of the two primary inputs, labor and land) are all highly industrialized countries, except Taiwan. The industrialization ratios, based on 1960 data, are 0.82 in New Zealand, 0.87 in Australia, 0.91 in the United States, 0.92 in Belgium, 0.88 in The Netherlands, and 0.74 in Japan.

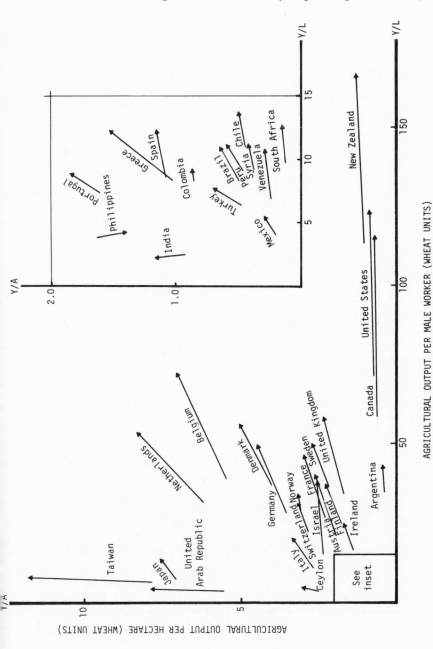

FIGURE 4–3. Intercountry cross-section comparison of changes in agricultural output per male worker and in output per hectare of agricultural land, 1955–65. (Data from Appendix Table A–5.)

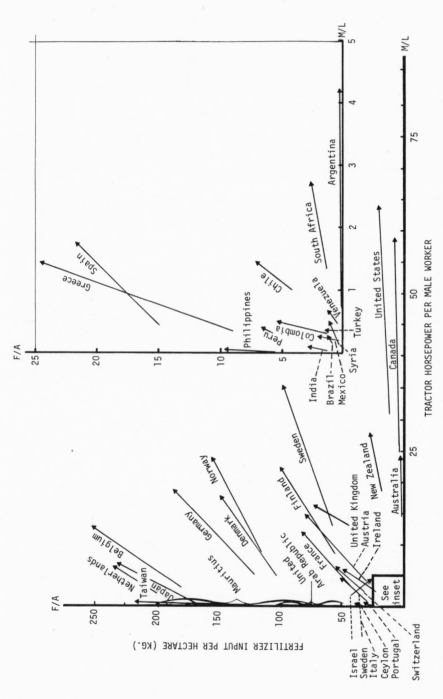

FIGURE 4-4. Intercountry cross-section comparison of changes in tractor horsepower per worker and in fertilizer input $(N + P_2O_5 + K_2O)$ per hectare of agricultural land, 1955–65.

In contrast, this ratio is very low in countries located near the origin: 0.41 in Mexico, 0.31 in Colombia, 0.47 in Syria, 0.39 in Turkey, and 0.31 in India.[5] The fact that countries such as Australia and New Zealand, which are major exporters of agricultural products and importers of industrial commodities, also rank high on the industrialization ratio seems to suggest that industrialization interacts with growth in agricultural productivity in a complex manner. The technical inputs supplied by the industrial sector represent a major source of productivity growth in agriculture. Similarly, growth in agricultural production and productivity results in a rise in the demand for the products of the industrial sector and releases the labor necessary for industrial growth.

The growth implication of the intercountry cross-section observations may be further tested by drawing on the historical experiences of five countries. Each country was selected for a specific purpose: (a) the U.S. to illustrate the growth pattern for the group of countries in the new continents, where man-land ratios are particularly favorable; (b) Japan to illustrate the growth pattern for the group of countries in Asia where unfavorable man-land ratios prevail; and (c) Denmark, France, and the U.K. to illustrate the growth pattern in the countries of Europe, where the man-land ratios are intermediate to the two groups above. In terms of the availability of data, as well as the important implications of their historical experiences on development economics, there seems to be little problem in selecting the U.S. and Japan as the representatives of the first two groups. It was difficult to choose a single country to illustrate the intermediate growth path. Among countries characterized by an intermediate growth path, Denmark, France, and the U.K. were selected to represent, respectively, the agricultural product exporting countries, the agriculturally self-sufficient countries, and the agricultural product importing countries.

The time-series paths of agricultural productivity growth in the selected countries are plotted in Figures 4–5, 4–6, and 4–7 (which are enlargements of Figure 4–1). The numbers in the parentheses indicate the percentage of male workers in nonagricultural occupations in the total number of male workers. The time-series path of the U.S. passes through the scatter of new continental countries (Figure 4–5), and the path of Japan passes through the scatter of Afro-Asian countries (Figure 4–6). The historical relationships between the level of industrialization and the level of agricultural productivity both in the U.S. and Japan are similar to the intercountry relationships.[6]

The productivity positions of European countries in 1960 are either within or on the fringe of the envelope formed by the growth paths of Denmark and

---

[5] The Taiwan case represents an example of sustained agricultural development, initially based on linkages with the nonagricultural sector of a metropolitan country (Japan) (see Chapters 10 and 11).

[6] A line which connects India, U.A.R., and Taiwan may suggest the existence of a path of agricultural growth characterized by the growth in land productivity with the development of irrigation.

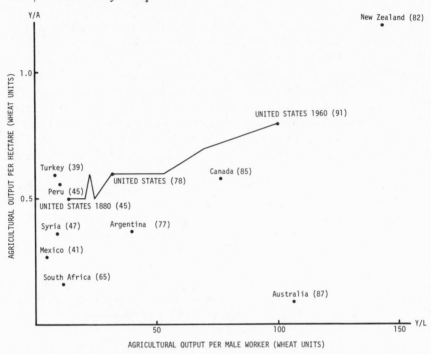

FIGURE 4-5. Historical growth path of agricultural productivity in the United States for 1880–1960, compared with intercountry cross-section observations in 1960. Values in parentheses are percent of male workers employed in nonagriculture. (Data from Appendix Table A–5 and Table B–1.)

the U.K. Denmark, which has remained relatively specialized in agriculture production among European countries, has attained a high labor productivity in agriculture by increasing the output per unit of land. In contrast, the U.K., which initiated the industrial revolution, has attained a relatively high level of agricultural efficiency mainly by enlarging agricultural land area per worker in response to the absorption of labor in nonagricultural occupations. France, which has followed an agrarian policy designed to protect the peasant family farm (la petite exploitation familiale) from external competition and internal social change, has achieved higher output per hectare than the United Kingdom but slower growth in output per worker than either the United Kingdom or Denmark. The high productivity of Danish agriculture, in spite of a relatively larger percentage of workers engaged in agriculture, has reflected its specialized role as a supplier of livestock products to the more industrialized British economy.

Industrialization can affect agriculture in many ways. Growth of the non-agricultural sector increases the demand for farm products. More favorable factor-product price ratios increase the demand for both mechanical and bio-

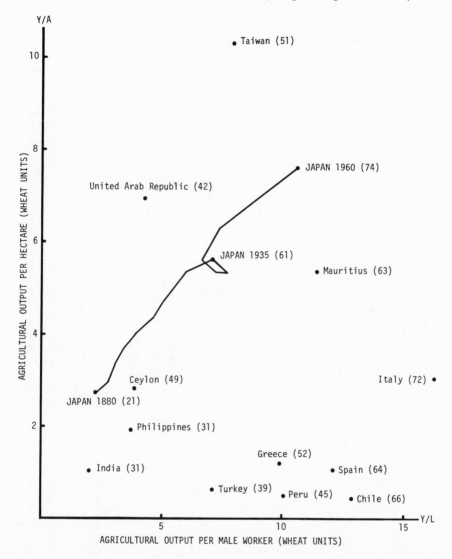

FIGURE 4–6. Historical growth path of agricultural productivity in Japan for 1880–1960, with intercountry cross-section observations in 1960. Values in parentheses are percent of male workers employed in nonagriculture. (Data from Appendix Table A–5 and Table B–2.)

logical inputs by agricultural producers. The impact of industrialization on factor markets is perhaps even more significant than the product market impact. Industrial development increases the demand for labor in the nonagricultural sector. The effect of increasing returns resulting from the progressive specialization of industry and division of labor and from the application of

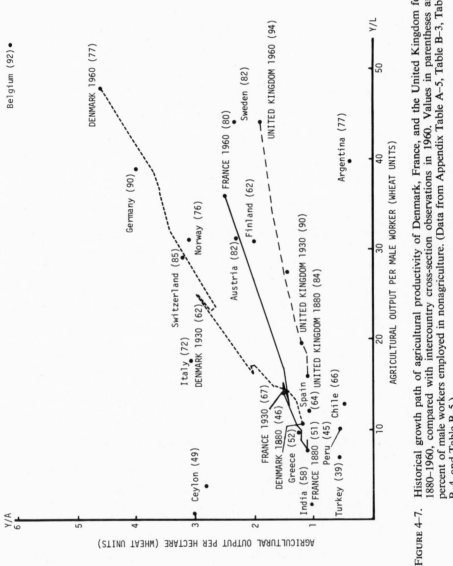

FIGURE 4-7.   Historical growth path of agricultural productivity of Denmark, France, and the United Kingdom for 1880–1960, compared with intercountry cross-section observations in 1960. Values in parentheses are percent of male workers employed in nonagriculture. (Data from Appendix Table A–5, Table B–3, Table B–4, and Table B–5.)

new knowledge is to reduce the cost of modern agricultural inputs, such as fertilizer, chemicals, and machinery, produced by the industrial sector.[7] A progressive industrial economy also contributes to growth of agricultural productivity through its greater capacity to support agricultural research; through its capacity to support both general education and production education in rural areas; through its capacity to support the development of more effective transportation and communication systems; and through the pervasive strengthening of other elements in the physical and institutional infrastructure serving rural areas.[8]

The capacity of the agricultural sector to respond to the lower prices of modern biological, chemical, and mechanical inputs relative to the prices of land and labor and relative to the prices of agricultural products is critical to the agricultural development process. The positive relationship between industrial development observed in the time-series and cross-sectional observations and elaborated above is not, however, automatic. Industrialization policies which have ignored the potential intersector factor and product market linkages, such as those followed by a number of socialist countries and a number of developing countries, have frequently failed to produce the industrial inputs necessary to release the constraints on agricultural growth imposed by inelastic supplies of land and labor. And failure to invest in agricultural research and in education and other elements of the physical and social infrastructure in rural areas has frequently limited the capacity of the agricultural sector to respond to the potential for growth associated with industrialization.

[7] Allyn A. Young, "Increasing Returns and Economic Progress," *Economic Journal* 38 (December 1928): 527–42. In his classic discussion of the sources of economic progress, Young regarded increasing returns resulting from the "enlargement of markets" and the associated "progressive division and specialization of industries" and "division of labor" as the principal source of economic progress. The "discovery of new natural resources" and "the growth of scientific knowledge" are treated as "factors which reinforce the influences which make for increasing returns." The role of market expansion, specialization, and division of function in the broad sense outlined by Young has frequently been lost sight of in recent discussions of the contribution of technical change to economic growth. Young's view that the "casual connections between the growth of industry and the progress of science run in both directions, but on which side the preponderant influence lies no one can say" (p. 535) remains valid. Current perspectives would probably place greater emphasis on advances in scientific and technical knowledge than appeared reasonable to Young writing in 1928. For a recent attempt to allocate the sources of change in efficiency in fertilizer production among sources internal and external to the fertilizer industry see Gian S. Sahota, *Fertilizer in Economic Development: An Econometric Analysis* (New York: Praeger, 1968).

[8] The high correlation between the share of nonagricultural population and the literacy rate is indicated by the United Nations Educational, Social and Cultural Organization (UNESCO), *World Illiteracy at Mid-Century* (Paris, 1957). Peterson's analysis clearly shows that in the United States nonagricultural income is a critical variable in explaining the interstate variations in public support for agricultural education, research, and extension. See Willis L. Peterson, "The Allocation of Research, Teaching, and Extension Personnel in U.S. Colleges of Agriculture," *American Journal of Agricultural Economics* 51 (February 1969): 41–56.

TECHNICAL CHANGE AND THE METAPRODUCTION
FUNCTION: A HYPOTHESIS

At this point it would seem useful to elaborate on the induced development model by formalizing, in operational terms, the process by which changes in the prices of industrial inputs are hypothesized to induce alternative paths of technical change and productivity growth in the agricultural sector of economies such as those observed in the previous section.

It seems clear that opportunities arising from industrialization do not bring about productivity growth unless they are exploited properly. A requisite for agricultural productivity growth is the capacity of the agricultural sector to adapt to a new set of factor and product prices. This adaptation involves not only the movement along a fixed production surface but also the creation of a new production surface which is optimum for the new set of prices. For example, even if fertilizer prices decline relative to the prices of land and farm products, increases in the use of fertilizer may be limited unless new crop varieties are developed which are more responsive to high levels of biological and chemical inputs than traditional varieties.

Table 3–2 in the previous chapter, which compares the yield response of several rice varieties to fertilizer application, indicated that the yields of the indigenous varieties in East Pakistan are as high as the improved varieties in Japan at the low level of fertilization, but that they are less responsive to increases in the level of nitrogen application. For illustrative purposes, the relationship between fertilizer use and yield may be drawn, as in Figure 4–8, letting u_0 and u_1 represent the fertilizer-response curves of indigenous and improved varieties, respectively. For farmers facing u_0, a decline in the fertilizer price relative to the product price from p_0 to p_1 would not be expected to result in much increase in fertilizer application or in yield. The full impact of a decline in the fertilizer price on fertilizer use and output can be fully realized only if u_1 is made available to farmers through the development of more responsive varieties.

Conceptually, it is possible to draw a curve such as U in Figure 4–8, which is the envelope of many individual response curves, each representing a rice variety characterized by a different degree of fertilizer responsiveness. We will identify this curve as a "metaproduction function" or a "potential production function." The metaproduction function can be regarded as the envelope of commonly conceived neoclassical production functions. In the *short-run*, in which substitution among inputs is circumscribed by the rigidity of existing capital and equipment, production relationships can best be described by an activity with relatively fixed factor-factor and factor-product ratios. In the *long-run*, in which the constraints exercised by existing capital disappear and are replaced by the fund of available technical knowledge, including all alternative feasible factor-factor and factor-product combinations, production

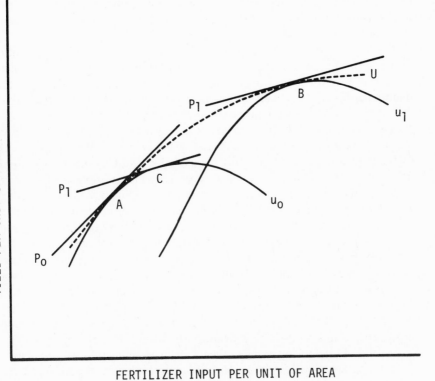

FIGURE 4–8. Shift in fertilizer response curve along the metaresponse curve.

relationships can be adequately described by the neoclassical production function. In the *secular period* of production, in which the constraints given by the available fund of technical knowledge are further relaxed to admit all potentially discoverable possibilities, production relationships can be described by a metaproduction function which describes all conceivable technical alternatives that might be discovered.[9]

We do not claim that the metaproduction function is inherent in nature or that it remains completely stable over time. The metaproduction function may shift with the accumulation of general scientific knowledge. We do consider, however, that it is operationally feasible to assume a reasonable degree of stability for a technical "epoch," the time range relevant for many empirical

[9] See Brown, *Theory and Measurement of Technological Change*, pp. 63–76 for a discussion of short-run, long-run, and secular production processes. The relationship between U and the u_i's in Fig. 4–8 is somewhat analogous to the interfirm envelope of a series of intrafirm production functions. See M. Bronfenbrenner, "Production Functions: Cobb-Douglas, Interfirm, Intrafirm," *Econometrica* 12 (January 1944): 35–44.

analyses. Shifts in the metaproduction function are much slower than adjustments along the surface, or to the surface from below, of the metaproduction function.

It is hypothesized that the adaptation of agriculture to new opportunities in the form of lower relative prices of modern inputs involves an adjustment to a more efficient point on the metaproduction function. In terms of this hypothesis it may be equally rational for farmers in Japan, where prices of fertilizer are relatively low and prices of rice relatively high, to plant varieties that are more responsive to high levels of fertilization and to fertilize more heavily than farmers in Southeast Asia, where fertilizer prices are relatively high and prices of rice are typically relatively low (see Chapter 9). In extreme cases the relative prices of land and labor may induce completely opposite paths of productivity growth. For example, in the United States, where wage rates are high relative to the price of land, it has been profitable to sacrifice yield per unit area by designing tomato plants which ripen uniformly, in order to permit mechanical harvesting. In Mexico, where wage rates are low and land is expensive, it may be more profitable to develop tomato varieties which have a more extended harvest period and are more responsive to more labor-intensive production practices in order to obtain higher yields per hectare.

From the intercountry cross-section and time-series observations, the relative endowments of land and labor at the time a nation enters into the development process apparently have a significant influence upon the optimum path to be followed in moving along the metaproduction function. Where labor is the limiting factor, the optimum for new opportunities in the form of lower prices of modern inputs is likely to be along a path characterized by a higher land-labor ratio. Movement toward an optimum position on the metaproduction function would involve development and adoption of new mechanical inputs. On the other hand, where land is the limiting factor, the new optimum is likely to be the point at which the yield per hectare is higher for the higher level of fertilizer input. Movement to this point would involve development and adoption of new biological and chemical inputs.

The partial productivity and factor input ratios presented earlier in this chapter suggest that those nations which have achieved relatively high levels of either land or labor productivity have been relatively successful in substituting industrial inputs for the constraints imposed by a relatively scarce factor, either land or labor. It seems possible to explain many of the vast differences in productivity levels and factor input ratios in agriculture among countries by hypothesizing that technical advance in agriculture occurs primarily as a result of new economic opportunities created by developments in the nonagricultural sector. The advances in mechanical and biological technology do not, however, occur without cost. Development of a more fertilizer-responsive crop variety, in response to declining prices of fertilizer, typically requires substantial expenditures on research, development, and dissemination, before it actually becomes available to farmers. Public investment in improvements in water control, land development, and other environmental modifications may also be required before it becomes profitable for farmers to adopt the newly developed varieties.

Farmers seek the new inputs and new techniques in order to move to a more efficient point on the metaproduction function in response to new factor-factor and factor-product price ratios. Only when public research institutions and private farm supply firms accurately anticipate the demands by farmers for profitable opportunities and make the new inputs or methods available to farmers is it possible to move to the optimum point on the metaproduction function. Even then, the capacity of the new variety or breed to respond to higher levels of inputs may not be fully realized until the producer fully masters the modifications in soil and water management and in other cultural practices necessary to achieve the higher yield potential of a new crop variety.[10] Production education programs by public extension services and the private sector suppliers of new inputs are frequently required to convey this information to farmers. Unless this mechanism of dialectic interaction among farmers, suppliers of new inputs, and research scientists and administrators functions properly, productivity growth in agriculture is not assured.

— Improvements in human capital in the form of educated, innovative farmers, competent scientists and technicians, and perceptive public administrators and business entrepreneurs are essential if this process is to generate continuous growth in agricultural productivity. We hypothesize that the agricultural productivity gap among countries is based on differences in the prices of modern technical inputs in agriculture and differences in the stock of human capital capable of generating a sequence of innovations which enables agriculture to move along the metaproduction function in response to changes in factor and product price relationships. The precise manner in which investment in resource accumulation, technical inputs, and human capital accounts for differences in labor productivity among countries is examined in the next chapter.

[10] This is the basis of the popular "package of practices" concept in agricultural extension. "Since success in modern farming depends on capturing the great benefits of interactions among several inputs, not simply the additive results of single improvements, the principle of interactions must be kept foremost in suggesting agricultural systems for the newly developed countries. . . . many of the local technicians and even outside advisers . . . tend to think in terms of single, slogan-like programs emphasizing one or two practices, such as improved seeds, green manures, irrigation, runoff control, pesticides, or fertilizers. Yet any one of these by itself is likely to give only low returns, whereas the right combination of practices for the local kind of soil may give truly enormous increases," pp. 81–82 of Charles E. Kellogg, "Interaction and Agricultural Research in Emerging Nations," *Agricultural Sciences for the Developing Nations*, ed. Albert H. Moseman (Washington: Publication No. 76 for the American Association for the Advancement of Science, 1964), pp. 81–91. See also Charles E. Kellogg and Arnold C. Orvedal, "Potentially Arable Soils of the World and Critical Measures for Their Use," *Advances in Agronomy*, ed. N. C. Brady (New York: Academic Press, Inc., 1969), vol. 21, pp. 109–70.

CHAPTER FIVE

Sources of Agricultural Productivity
Differences among Countries[1]

Growth in output per worker in agriculture is generally recognized as a necessary condition for economic development (Chapter 2). The great differences in agricultural labor productivity among countries have raised serious doubt among national policymakers and planners and among officials in the international aid agencies as to the possibility of substantially narrowing the gaps. Do the constraints on growth of agricultural output resulting from inelastic supplies of land in the more densely populated countries, such as India and Egypt, permanently condemn their economies to continued stagnation and the agricultural workers in such countries to low levels of productivity and income?

In this chapter we attempt to identify the sources of the differences in agricultural labor productivity among countries. Recent empirical research supports a classification of the sources of productivity differences, or of productivity growth, into three broad categories: (a) resource endowments; (b) technical inputs; and (c) human capital.[2] Resource endowments, as used in this chapter, include not only the original land resource endowments but also internal capital accumulation in the form of land reclamation and development, livestock inventories, and so forth. Technical inputs include the mechanical devices and the biological and chemical materials purchased from the industrial sector. Human capital is broadly conceived to include the

---

[1] Much of the material in this chapter has been previously published in Yujiro Hayami and V. W. Ruttan, "Agricultural Productivity Differences among Countries," *American Economic Review* 60 (December 1970): 895–911.

[2] Zvi Griliches, "Research Expenditures, Education, and the Aggregate Agricultural Production Function," ibid. 54 (December 1964): 961–74; Anne O. Krueger, "Factor Endowments and *Per Capita* Income Differences Among Countries," *Economic Journal* 78 (September 1968): 641–59; Richard R. Nelson, "A 'Diffusion Model' of International Productivity Differences in Manufacturing Industry," *American Economic Review* 58 (December 1968): 1219–48.

education, skill, knowledge, and capacity embodied in a country's population. The classification is clearly an oversimplification. Yet it does represent an advance over the earlier emphasis on single strategic factors.

Both the induced development model presented in Chapter 3 and the empirical regularities observed in Chapter 4 support the hypothesis that differences in technical inputs and human capital account for a very substantial share of the gap in labor productivity in agriculture among countries. These are the factors that permit a country to substitute relatively abundant factors for relatively scarce resources by moving out along the metaproduction function (Figure 4–8). If this is not the case, it seems unlikely that poor countries will be able to achieve substantial increases in labor productivity in agriculture or substantially narrow the agricultural productivity gap among nations.

The results of the analysis indicate that the three broad categories outlined above account for approximately 95 percent of the differences in labor productivity in agriculture between a representative group of less developed countries (LDC's) and of developed countries (DC's). In this comparison, the three factors are of roughly equal importance. When compared to the DC's of recent settlement (Australia, Canada, New Zealand, and the United States), favorable resource endowments account for somewhat more than one-third of the differences. Resource endowments represent the major factor accounting for differences in labor productivity between the DC's of recent settlement and the older DC's. Nevertheless, it seems apparent that it would be technically feasible for the LDC's, over time, to achieve labor productivity levels in agriculture well over half as high as in the more recently settled DC's, roughly comparable to the levels achieved in the older DC's. This could be achieved through increased use of technical inputs supplied from the industrial sector and improvements in the quality of the labor force, even in the absence of substantial changes in man-land ratios.

We do not, in this chapter, attempt to explore the economic and institutional factors which have led some economies to make the investments necessary to supply modern technical inputs to their farmers and to provide them with the knowledge and skill to make productive use of the new inputs. In subsequent chapters, however, we explore how Japan and the United States, two economies with extreme differences in resource endowments, have been able to follow different factor productivity growth paths as they have moved along the metaproduction function.

THE METHOD AND THE DATA

Our approach involves the estimation of an aggregate production function of the Cobb–Douglas type, employing the same set of intercountry cross-section data used in the analysis in Chapter 4, Appendix A (Table A–5).[3] Differences in agricultural output per worker are accounted for by differences in the level of conventional and nonconventional inputs per worker, classified as (a) resource endowments; (b) technical inputs; and (c) human capital.

The specific variables used in the study included labor, land, livestock, fertilizer, machinery, education, and technical manpower. In summing up the effects of resource endowments, technology, and human capital on productivity per worker, land and livestock serve as proxy variables for resource endowments; machinery and fertilizer for technical inputs; and general and technical education in agriculture for human capital.

The land actually being utilized for agricultural production can not be regarded as a mere gift of nature. It represents the result of previous investments in land clearing, reclamation, drainage, fencing, and other development measures. Similarly, livestock represents a form of internal capital accumulation. Thus, in our perspective, land and livestock represent a form of long-term capital formation embodying inputs supplied primarily from within the agricultural sector.[4] In the conservation model of agricultural development, internal capital formation of this type was almost the only source of growth in labor productivity. High inputs of both land and livestock per worker tend to be associated with high levels of labor and low levels of land per unit of output.

In contrast, as discussed in Chapter 4, fertilizer, as measured by the $N + P_2O_5 + K_2O$ in commercial fertilizers, and machinery, as measured by tractor horsepower, represent inputs supplied by the industrial sector. Technical advances stemming from both public and private sector research and development are embodied in, or complementary to, these modern industrial inputs. Advances in mechanical technology are usually associated with larger inputs of power and machinery. Biological improvements, such as the development of new high-yielding varieties, are typically associated with higher levels of fertilizer use. In this analysis, these two industrial inputs represent proxies for the whole range of inputs in which modern mechanical and biological technologies are embodied.

The proxies for human capital include measures of both the general educational level of the rural population and specialized education in the agricultural sciences and technology. Two alternative measures of the level of general education were attempted: (a) the literacy ratio and (b) the school enrollment ratio for the primary and secondary levels.[5] Both sets of data are

[3] Countries included are: Argentina, Austria, Australia, Belgium, Brazil, Canada, Ceylon, Chile, Colombia, Denmark, Finland, France, Germany, Greece, India, Ireland, Israel, Italy, Japan, Mauritius, Mexico, Netherlands, New Zealand, Norway, Peru, Philippines, South Africa, Spain, Surinam, Sweden, Switzerland, Syria, Taiwan, Turkey, U.A.R., U.K., U.S.A., and Venezuela.

[4] Perennial plants belong to the same category of inputs as livestock; but they are not included, due to the lack of data.

[5] The school enrollment ratio is regarded as a somewhat more sensitive educational index

deficient, in that they apply to the entire population and are not sensitive to differences in the quality of rural and urban education. Education in the agricultural sciences and technology was measured by the number of graduates per ten thousand farm workers from agricultural faculties at above the secondary level. These graduates represent the major source of technological and scientific personnel for agricultural research and extension.[6]

A critical assumption in this approach is that the technical possibilities available to agricultural producers in the different countries can be described by the same production function. Production function analysis, using individual countries or regions as observations, has been widely used. Aggregate agricultural production functions based on intercountry cross-section data were first estimated by Jyoti P. Bhattacharjee in 1953.[7] An aggregate agricultural production function similar to that used in this study, using states in the United States as observations, was employed by Zvi Griliches in an attempt to account for the impact of research and education on agricultural output.[8] Anne O. Krueger's recent efforts to estimate the contribution of factor endowment differentials to variations in per capita income employ the assumption that all countries are subject to a uniform production function.[9]

In a recent paper, Richard R. Nelson has argued that the assumptions of a common production function "get in the way of understanding international differences in productivity—particularly differences between advanced and underdeveloped countries."[10] Nelson's objections appear directed primarily to the empirical results obtained from use of relatively primitive two-factor production functions, as in K. J. Arrow, H. B. Chenery, B. S. Minhas, and R. M. Solow, where intercountry differences in value added per worker are related to the capital-labor ratio.[11] He insists, as a result of differential diffusion of new technology, that "at any given time one would expect to find

---

than the literacy ratio. See Mary Jean Bowman and C. Arnold Anderson, "Concerning the Role of Education in Development," *Old Societies and New States,* ed. Clifford Geertz (New York: The Free Press of Glencoe, 1963), pp. 247–79. In this article Bowman and Anderson emphasize the multidimensional nature of the relationships between education and development.

[6] We regard the index of specialized education in the agricultural sciences and technology as a superior proxy for the level of research and extension than the "state average of public expenditure on research and extension per farm" used by Griliches ("Research Expenditures"), because our variable reflects the research and extension activities in the private sector as well as in the public sector. It is also of interest that in earlier studies it has been difficult to establish a significant relationship between post primary or elite education and per capita productivity in intercountry studies. See, for example, Anderson and Bowman, ibid., pp. 257–61.

[7] Jyoti P. Bhattacharjee, "Resource Use and Productivity in World Agriculture," *Journal of Farm Economics* 37 (February 1955): 57–71.

[8] Griliches, "Research Expenditures."

[9] Krueger, "Factor Endowments."

[10] Nelson, "A 'Diffusion Model' of International Productivity," p. 1229.

[11] K. J. Arrow, H. B. Chenery, B. S. Minhas, and R. M. Solow, "Capital-Labor Substitution and Economic Efficiency," *Review of Economics and Statistics* 43 (August 1961): 225–50.

considerable variation among firms with respect to the vintage of their technology, certainly between countries, but even within a country."[12]

We share the Nelson perspective. Agricultural producers in different countries, in different regions of the same country, and on different farms in the same region are not all on the same microproduction function. This reflects differences among producers in their ability to adopt new technology. More importantly, it is also the result of differential diffusion of agricultural technology, and, to an even greater degree, of differential diffusion of the scientific and technical capacity to invent and develop new mechanical, biological, and chemical technology specifically adapted to the factor endowments and prices in a particular country or region. Furthermore, we view the generation of new technical knowledge in agriculture as endogenous. It is generated in response to changes in relative factor and product prices.

According to the hypothesis proposed in Chapter 4, technical change occurs in response to changes in relative prices along the surface of a "metaproduction function." The full range of technological alternatives described by the metaproduction function, which represents the envelope of all known and potentially available production "activities," is only partially available to individual producers in a particular country or agricultural region during any particular historical "epoch." It is, however, potentially available to agricultural scientists.

We consider the common intercountry production function which we have estimated as a metaproduction function. It is assumed that the invention and diffusion of a new "location-specific" agricultural technology through the application of the concepts of physical, biological, and chemical science and of engineering, craft, and husbandry skill, are capable of making the factor productivities implicit in the metaproduction function available to producers in less developed countries. It is also assumed that the capacity of a country to engage in the necessary research, development, and extension is measured by the two proxy variables for human capital, general education and technical education in agriculture. This effort and that of Griliches and Krueger are not inconsistent with the perspective presented by Nelson in his criticism of the empirical results obtained from two factor intercountry production functions.

ESTIMATION OF THE PRODUCTION FUNCTION*

The production function employed in this analysis is of the unrestricted Cobb–Douglas (linear in the logarithms) form. It was used mainly because of its ease of manipulation and interpretation. The coefficients of the Cobb–Douglas production function can be interpreted as indicating the elasticities of production with respect to inputs. Assuming that the factors are specified correctly,

---

[12] Nelson, "A 'Diffusion Model' of International Productivity," p. 1230.

* Readers who are impatient with the technical issues involved in production function analysis and interpretation may wish to skip this section.

the coefficients can also be interpreted as indicating the relative importance of each factor as a source of difference in output among countries.

The results of estimating the production function on intercountry cross-section data for the period centered on 1960 (1957–62) are presented in Table 5–1.[13] Each column reports the results of a regression of agricultural output on a different set of inputs. Both the production coefficients (elasticities) and the standard errors of the coefficients (in parentheses) are presented. The standard errors and the coefficients of determination, which indicate how much of the total variation in output among countries has been explained by the specified inputs, have been adjusted for the degrees of freedom.

The production functions were estimated using both the national aggregate data and the average per-farm data of outputs and inputs, in order to test the effect of any bias in the coefficients resulting from the different specifications. The results of the two sets of estimates are not sufficiently different to lead to different inferences regarding the sources of production and productivity differences among countries.

Considering the crudeness of the data, the levels of statistical significance of the estimated coefficients seem satisfactory in most cases. The coefficients for conventional inputs remain relatively stable when the proxy variables for human capital are alternately inserted or deleted from the production function. There is, of course, some instability. The coefficients for land and livestock tend to rise and the coefficients for machinery to decline when the education variables are brought into the function. The results of estimation by the method of instrumental variables (Q2–IV and Q3–IV), in which fertilizer, the only variable measured in flow terms, was lagged by using data centered on 1955, are essentially similar to the results of ordinary least-squares estimates. The test supports a conclusion that simultaneous equation bias, inherent in the ordinary least-squares procedure, is not large.

Several additional tests were conducted to test the acceptability of the methodology employed in the production function analysis. Results of tests of (a) the assumption of unitary elasticity of substitution, inherent in the Cobb–Douglas function; and (b) the stability of the production function over time, are reported in the section beginning on p. 102. An attempt to conduct a test for the existence of a common production function among countries was inconclusive.[14] Attempts were also made to include other

[13] Surinam was dropped from the sample except for Q1 and Q6 because of the lack of technical education data.

[14] The production function was estimated for different groups of countries, DC's and LDC's. The estimation was tried for various groupings for DC's and LDC's, but the results are all implausible, with most of the coefficients statistically nonsignificant or negative in sign. It seems that measurement errors in our observations (especially of nonconventional variables) are too large to make it possible to estimate the influences of variables for the groups of countries within which the ranges of data variations are relatively small. The basic assumption is, therefore, not testable on the presently available data. All we can claim is that differences in agricultural productivity among countries can be explained well with this assumption.

Table 5-1. Estimates of the intercountry cross-section production function for agriculture, 1960 (1957–62 averages)

Regression number	Per-farm basis						
	(Q1)	(Q2)	(Q3)	(Q4)	(Q5)	(Q2–IV)	(Q3–IV)
Sample size	38	37	37	37	37	37	37
Labor (L)	0.336 (0.121)	0.432 (0.114)	0.393 (0.117)			0.490 (0.110)	0.454 (0.113)
Land	0.071 (0.074)	0.108 (0.065)	0.097 (0.067)	0.117 (0.062)	0.104 (0.066)	0.108 (0.069)	0.097 (0.072)
Livestock	0.166 (0.099)	0.241 (0.089)	0.227 (0.092)	0.249 (0.086)	0.232 (0.091)	0.210 (0.094)	0.192 (0.097)
Fertilizer	0.174 (0.055)	0.124 (0.058)	0.136 (0.062)	0.121 (0.053)	0.126 (0.059)	0.096 (0.058)	0.108 (0.067)
Machinery	0.205 (0.061)	0.057 (0.067)	0.104 (0.064)	0.038 (0.053)	0.092 (0.059)	0.074 (0.068)	0.124 (0.064)
General education:							
Literacy ratio (E_1)		0.348 (0.186)	0.360 (0.247)			0.366 (0.196)	
School enrollment ratio (E_2)							0.263 (0.274)
Technical education		0.190 (0.057)	0.148 (0.055)	0.197 (0.055)	0.146 (0.054)	0.197 (0.060)	0.153 (0.056)
$L \times E_1$				0.418 (0.109)			
$L \times E_2$					0.383 (0.114)		
Coef. of det. (adj.)	0.908	0.932	0.926	0.934	0.928	0.928	0.921
S. E. of est.	0.138	0.119	0.124	0.118	0.123	0.123	0.128
Sum of conventional coefficients	0.952 (0.098)	0.962 (0.085)	0.957 (0.088)	0.943 (0.074)	0.937 (0.080)	0.978 (0.088)	0.975 (0.094)

Table 5-1—(Continued)

Regression number		National aggregate basis					
	(Q6)	(Q7)	(Q8)	(Q9)	(Q10)	(Q7-IV)	(Q8-IV)
Sample size	38	37	37	37	37	37	37
Labor (L)	0.335	0.451	0.413			0.474	0.434
	(0.064)	(0.074)	(0.075)			(0.072)	(0.074)
Land	0.056	0.088	0.076	0.097	0.080	0.092	0.080
	(0.065)	(0.062)	(0.063)	(0.061)	(0.063)	(0.065)	(0.067)
Livestock	0.191	0.247	0.235	0.263	0.243	0.219	0.205
	(0.096)	(0.089)	(0.092)	(0.086)	(0.091)	(0.093)	(0.095)
Fertilizer	0.161	0.112	0.123	0.105	0.108	0.090	0.104
	(0.053)	(0.059)	(0.063)	(0.058)	(0.061)	(0.057)	(0.064)
Machinery	0.192	0.071	0.116	0.040	0.102	0.082	0.127
	(0.056)	(0.065)	(0.060)	(0.053)	(0.058)	(0.065)	(0.061)
General education: Literacy ratio (E_1)		0.326				0.321	
		(0.187)				(0.196)	
School enrollment ratio (E_2)			0.324				0.290
			(0.248)				(0.271)
Technical education		0.182	0.142	0.195	0.139	0.182	0.142
		(0.057)	(0.055)	(0.055)	(0.054)	(0.060)	(0.056)
$L \times E_1$				0.464			
				(0.072)			
$L \times E_2$					0.432		
					(0.072)		
Coef. of det. (adj.)	0.955	0.953	0.950	0.954	0.950	0.951	0.948
S. E. of est.	0.131	0.118	0.123	0.118	0.122	0.120	0.125
Sum of conventional coefficients	0.935	0.969	0.963	0.969	0.965	0.957	0.950
	(0.035)	(0.039)	(0.040)	(0.039)	(0.040)	(0.048)	(0.040)

Note: Equations linear in logarithms are estimated by the least squares except those denoted as IV, which are estimated by the instrumental variable method. The standard errors of coefficients are in parentheses.

Source: Based on the data from Appendix A–5.

93

variables that might add to the precision of the estimates. The ratio of irrigated land to total land area was introduced, in an attempt to adjust for differences in the quality of land inputs. The coefficients for the variables employed in these attempts turned out to be either nonsignificant or to have the wrong sign.[15]

The plausibility of the production coefficients or elasticities obtained in this study may be checked by a comparison with the results from earlier aggregate production function estimates. Bhattacharjee obtained elasticities from his intercountry cross-section production functions, including only conventional variables, centered on 1950, of approximately 0.3 for labor, 0.3 to 0.4 for land, and 0.3 for fertilizer.[16] The coefficients for livestock and tractors were not significant at commonly accepted levels. The Bhattacharjee results indicate higher production elasticities for land and fertilizer than the results obtained in our study. It would appear that our model is somewhat better specified, in that we obtained statistically meaningful coefficients for livestock and machinery, as well as for the two proxy variables for human capital.

The aggregate production elasticities for U.S. agriculture were estimated by Griliches as 0.4 to 0.5 for labor; 0.1 to 0.2 for land, fertilizer, and machinery; 0.3 to 0.5 for education: and 0.04 to 0.1 for research and extension. It is rather surprising that the Griliches estimates, despite the completely different nature of the data used, are so consistent with the estimates obtained in this study.[17]

The production elasticities estimated for Japanese agriculture by Yasuhiko Yuize, in value-added terms, are in the range of 0.4 to 0.6 for labor and of 0.2 to 0.4 for land.[18] These figures are also consistent with the estimates in this study, since, according to the social account study by the Japanese Ministry of Agriculture and Forestry, the ratio of value added to gross output was around 0.7 in Japanese agriculture in the period when Yuize's study was made.[19] In the less developed countries, we do not have comparable estimates of the aggregate agricultural production function. Schultz has, however, inferred from the impact of the 1918–19 influenza epidemic that the produc-

---

[15] This does not necessarily mean that such variables have no significant influence. Studies by Hsieh and Ruttan indicate, for example, that prior to the introduction of the new rice varieties in the late 1960's, differences in yield per hectare among provinces in both the Philippines and Thailand were largely accounted for by differences in irrigation and water control. S. C. Hsieh and V. W. Ruttan, "Environmental, Technological and Institutional Factors in the Growth of Rice Production: Philippines, Thailand, and Taiwan," *Food Research Institute Studies*, vol. 7, no. 3 (1967): 307–41. The data available for intercountry analysis were apparently too crude to estimate the influence of such variables.

[16] Bhattacharjee, "Resource Use and Productivity."

[17] Griliches, "Research Expenditures."

[18] Yasuhiko Yuize, "Nogyo ni okeru Kyoshiteki Seisankansu no Keisoku (The Aggregate Production Function in Agriculture)," *Nogyo Sogo Kenkyu* 18 (October 1964): 1–54.

[19] Japan, Ministry of Agriculture and Forestry, *Nogyo oyobi Noka no Shakai Kanjo 1967* (Social Accounts of Agriculture and Farm Households) (Tokyo, 1968).

Table 5–2. Analysis of variance for testing equality of the coefficients of labor and general education

Regressions compared	Sums of squares of residues		Degrees of freedom		
	Labor and education separate S_1	Labor and education combined S_2	Labor and education separate P_1	Labor and education combined P_2	F-statistics F_c
(Q2) vs. (Q4)	0.4125	0.4156	29	30	0.22
(Q3) vs. (Q5)	0.4454	0.4502	29	30	0.31
(Q7) vs. (Q9)	0.4061	0.4152	29	30	0.65
(Q8) vs. (Q10)	0.4361	0.4477	29	30	0.77

$$F_c = \frac{S_2 - S_1}{S_1} \cdot \frac{P_1}{P_2 - P_1}$$

tion elasticity of labor in Indian agriculture was 0.4.[20] This is consistent with our estimates. Such consistency with other studies lends support to the results of estimations in this study.

Griliches found that in U.S. agriculture a percentage increase in education, which improves the quality of labor, has the same effect as a percentage increase in labor itself. In order to test whether the same assertion holds in the international dimension, we have estimated the production function by combining labor (L) and general education (E) in a multiplicative form ($L \times E$); this resulted in little change (compare Q2 with Q4, Q3 with Q5, Q7 with Q9, and Q8 with Q10). Furthermore, the analysis of variance (Table 5–2) is consistent with the inference that the coefficients of labor and general education are essentially identical. This means, given appropriate levels of other inputs, that a 1 percent increase in the level of general education per agricultural worker has essentially the same impact on agricultural output as a 1 percent increase in the agricultural labor force.[21]

Judging from the sums of coefficients of conventional inputs, compared with the standard errors of these sums (shown in parentheses below the sums of coefficients), constant returns to scale seem to prevail both at the farm firm level and at the national aggregate level. The constant returns at the farm firm level may explain the existence of farms of extremely different sizes producing the same commodities. The constant returns at the national aggregate level

[20] Theodore W. Schultz, *Transforming Traditional Agriculture* (New Haven: Yale University Press, 1964), pp. 63–70.

[21] The return to education is, of course, sensitive to the levels of other inputs. It is possible to overinvest in education relative to other inputs. See, for example, Arnold C. Harberger, "Investment in Men Versus Investment in Machines: The Case of India," *Education and Economic Development*, ed. C. Arnold Anderson and Mary Jean Bowman (Chicago: Aldine Publishing Company, 1965), pp. 11–50. For a more detailed analysis of the implications of factor endowments and rates of return to education in the United States, Chile, Mexico, and India see Marcelo Selowsky, *Education and Economic Growth: Some International Comparisons* (Chicago: University of Chicago, Department of Economics, unpublished Ph.D. Dissertation, 1967).

might be one of the distinctive characteristics of agricultural production and, if so, would have important implications for the intersectoral investment priorities for national economic development.

ACCOUNTING FOR PRODUCTIVITY DIFFERENCES

The results obtained from estimation of the agricultural production function in the previous sections will, in this section, be used to account for inter-country differences in labor productivity (output per male worker) in agriculture in 1960.

The evidence presented in the last section, and the additional tests presented in the section beginning on page 102, indicate that a common agricultural production function among countries can be approximated with reasonable accuracy by a linear homogeneous function of the Cobb–Douglas form. This means that the percentage difference in output per worker can be expressed as the sum of percentage differences in conventional and nonconventional factor inputs per worker, weighted by their respective production elasticities. Based on the results shown in Table 5–1, the following set of production elasticities was adopted: 0.40 for labor, 0.10 for land, 0.25 for livestock, 0.15 for fertilizer, 0.10 for machinery, 0.40 for education, and 0.15 for research and extension. Only the school enrollment ratio was used as the education variable in this accounting, but the results would have been essentially the same if the literacy ratio had been used.

Two alternative sets of results are presented. The first set involves group comparisons between LDC's and DC's. The second set involves individual comparisons of selected LDC's and DC's with the United States.

Group Comparisons

The sources of differences in labor productivity between eleven LDC's and thirteen DC's (Case 1); nine older DC's (Case 2); and four DC's of recent settlement are presented in Table 5–3. Each column compares for each case the percentage difference in agricultural output per worker between the LDC's and DC's with the percentage differences in input variables weighted by the specified production elasticities. The index with the output-per-worker set equal to 100 is shown in parentheses. The countries classified as LDC's, for the purposes of this comparison, all had per capita incomes of less than 350 U.S. dollars and more than 35 percent of their labor force engaged in agriculture. The countries classified as DC's had per capita incomes higher than 700 U.S. dollars and less than 30 percent of the labor force engaged in agriculture. Countries falling between these criteria are not included in the comparisons presented in Table 5–3.

Table 5–3. Accounting for difference in labor productivity in agriculture between developed countries (DC) and less developed countries (LDC) as percent of the labor productivity of DC

	Case 1 (13 DC's)		Case 2 (9 DC's)		Case 3 (4 DC's)	
Difference in output per male worker—percent	88.8 (100)*		83.5 (100)		93.6 (100)	
Percent of difference explained: Total	84.2	(95)	71.1	(85)	90.0	(96)
Resource endowments	29.2	(33)	17.5	(21)	32.6	(35)
Land	9.2	(10)	1.8	(2)	9.7	(10)
Livestock	20.0	(23)	15.7	(19)	22.9	(25)
Technical inputs:	24.3	(27)	24.3	(29)	24.5	(26)
Fertilizer	14.5	(16)	14.5	(17)	14.6	(16)
Machinery	9.8	(11)	9.8	(12)	9.9	(10)
Human capital:	30.7	(35)	29.4	(35)	32.9	(35)
General education	18.2	(21)	17.6	(21)	19.5	(21)
Technical education	12.5	(14)	11.7	(14)	13.4	(14)

* Inside of parentheses are percentages with output per worker set equal to 100.

LDC: Brazil, Ceylon, Colombia, India, Mexico, Peru, Philippines, Syria, Taiwan, Turkey, U.A.R.

DC: Australia, Belgium, Canada, Denmark, France, Germany, Netherlands, New Zealand, Norway, Sweden, Switzerland, U.K., U.S.A.

Case 1 includes all DC's; Case 2 excludes Australia, Canada, New Zealand and U.S.A from DC's; Case 3 includes only the four DC's excluded in Case 2.

Accounting formula:

$$\left(\frac{Y_d - Y_l}{Y_d}\right) = 0.10\left(\frac{a_d - a_l}{a_d}\right) + 0.25\left(\frac{s_d - s_l}{s_d}\right) + 0.15\left(\frac{f_d - f_l}{f_d}\right)$$
$$+ 0.10\left(\frac{m_d - m_l}{m_d}\right) + 0.40\left(\frac{E_d - E_l}{E_d}\right) + 0.15\left(\frac{U_d - U_l}{U_d}\right)$$

where y, a, s, f, m, are respectively output, land, livestock, fertilizer, machinery per male worker; E and U are respectively the general education (school enrollment ratio) and the technical education variable; lowercase letter d denotes DC and l denotes LDC.

The difference in average agricultural output per worker between the eleven LDC's and the thirteen DC's was 88.8 percent (case 1); the difference between the eleven LDC's and the nine older DC's was 83.5 percent (case 2); and the difference between the eleven LDC's and the four DC's of recent settlement was 93.6 percent (case 3). The six variables included in the production function accounted for 95, 85, and 96 percent of the difference in agricultural output per worker between the LDC's and the three DC groups. Intercountry differences left unexplained by resource endowments are effectively exhausted by the proxy variables for technical inputs and human capital. This is one of the most encouraging aspects of the results.

In the comparison between the eleven LDC's and the thirteen DC's (Case 1) each generalized category—resource endowments (land and livestock), technical inputs from the industrial sector (fertilizer and machinery), and human capital (general and technical education in agriculture)—accounts for approximately one-third of the explained difference in labor productivity.

The main difference between Case 1 and the other two cases is the amount of the difference explained by land. Difference in land accounts for only 2 percent of the difference in labor productivity between the LDC's and the older DC's, while it accounts for 19 percent between the LDC's and the new DC's. This implies that it should be feasible for the LDC's, even with the present land-labor ratios, to achieve levels of productivity per worker roughly equivalent to the labor productivity levels achieved by workers in the older DC's—that is, roughly four times as high as present LDC levels and well over half the level achieved by the DC's of recent settlement. The critical elements in achieving such increases in labor productivity are the supply of modern technical inputs and the investment in general education and in research and extension, which raises the capacity to develop and adopt a more productive technology.

A comparison of the Case 2 and Case 3 results does indicate, however, that limitations in resource endowments, particularly land, do represent a serious barrier to the efforts of both the LDC's and the older DC's to achieve levels of output per worker comparable to the levels currently enjoyed in the more recently settled DC's. This is the first time, to our knowledge, that the economic advantage of the favorable resource endowments in these countries has been demonstrated quantitatively.

Individual Comparisons

The individual country comparisons presented in Table 5–4 were developed in order to provide somewhat deeper insight into the sources of differences in labor productivity between different "ideal type" countries and the United States. Each row compares the percentage difference in agricultural output per worker between each country and the United States, with the linear combinations of percentage differences in input variables weighted by the specified production elasticities. The index with the output per worker difference set equal to 100 is shown in parentheses. In general, the results are consistent with the group comparisons.

In the four less developed countries—India, the Philippines, the United Arab Republic, and Colombia—resource endowments account for approximately one-third and technical inputs roughly one-fourth of the differences. Human capital accounts for more than one-third of the difference between the U.S. and India, the United Arab Republic and Colombia. In the Philippines, which has achieved a relatively high level of schooling and produces a relatively large number of agricultural college graduates, human capital explains less than one-fourth of the productivity difference. The contrast between India and the Philippines in this respect is quite striking.

Table 5–4. Accounting for labor productivity differences in agriculture of selected countries from the U.S. as percent of U.S. labor productivity, eleven selected countries

Country	Difference in output per worker from U.S. as percent of U.S.	Percentage of difference explained by			
		Total	Resource endowments (land and livestock)	Technical inputs (fertilizer and machinery)	Human capital (general and technical education)
LDC					
Asia:					
Deficit:					
India	97.8	102.1	32.7	25.0	44.4
	(100)*	(104)	(33)	(26)	(45)
Surplus:					
Philippines	96.2	82.1	33.4	24.9	23.8
	(100)	(85)	(34)	(26)	(25)
Africa:					
UAR	95.6	97.0	33.8	24.6	38.6
	(100)	(101)	(35)	(26)	(40)
Latin America:					
Colombia	89.7	89.4	25.8	24.7	38.9
	(100)	(100)	(29)	(28)	(43)
Europe					
Exporter:					
Denmark	52.3	51.0	20.4	13.2	17.4
	(100)	(97)	(39)	(25)	(33)
Netherlands	56.6	51.7	25.0	15.0	11.7
	(100)	(91)	(44)	(26)	(21)
Importer:					
United Kingdom	55.8	50.2	18.2	13.4	18.6
	(100)	(90)	(33)	(24)	(33)
Self-sufficient:					
France	63.9	64.3	26.2	16.5	21.6
	(100)	(101)	(41)	(26)	(34)
Japan	89.2	66.0	34.1	22.4	9.5
	(100)	(74)	(38)	(25)	(11)
Pastoral farming					
Less developed:					
Argentina	60.0	45.9	−4.8	24.3	26.4
	(100)	(76)	(−8)	(40)	(44)
Developed:					
New Zealand	−42.4	−49.1	−55.2	2.7	3.4
	(100)	(116)	(130)	(−6)	(−8)

* Inside of parentheses are percentages with output per worker differences set equal to 100.

In the comparisons between the countries of Europe and the United States, differences in resource endowments represent the most significant source of differences in labor productivity. The constraint of land on agricultural productivity is relatively modest for the United Kingdom, which experienced a drastic agricultural transformation after the repeal of the Corn Laws; it is strongest for France, which preserved peasant farms by protective tariffs. Increases in the use of technical inputs and improvements in the quality of human capital can bring labor productivity in the several European countries closer to the U.S. level. Nevertheless, it seems apparent that major advances in labor productivity in European agriculture toward the U.S. level, especially in countries like France, are dependent on the absorption of a higher percentage of the agricultural labor force into the nonagricultural sector. The Japanese case is similar to the European, except that Japan, characterized by stronger constraints of land, has moved further toward the exhaustion of productivity differentials associated with investments in education and research. In our judgment, the model does underestimate the significance of the land constraints in the case of the more densely populated DC's and LDC's. Without a significant increase in land area per worker, it would appear to be extremely difficult for Indian, Japanese or European agriculture to increase technical inputs per worker, especially machinery, to the U.S. level.

The two pastoral farming cases are of particular interest. In spite of low levels of technical inputs, labor productivity in Argentina is roughly comparable to that in Europe. This is due almost entirely to a favorable man-land ratio, comparable to that in the U.S. Argentina has, as a result of underinvestment in technology and human capital, failed to fully exploit its favorable man-land ratio.[22] New Zealand, in contrast, has achieved a level of labor productivity well above the U.S. level (the highest in the world) by complementing its favorable resource endowments with high levels of technical inputs and investment in human capital.

The results obtained in both the group and individual comparisons are somewhat different than those obtained by Krueger.[23] Using a different methodology, Krueger found that human capital explained more than one-half the difference in income levels between the United States and a group of less developed countries. This is in contrast to our findings, which indicate that human capital explains approximately one-third of the difference in labor productivity. Krueger's results apply to the entire economy and ours to only the agricultural sector. It seems reasonable to expect that resource endowments would be of greater relative significance in the agricultural sector than in the total economy. We see, therefore, no inconsistency between our results

---

[22] For greater detail on the Argentine case see Darrell F. Fienup, Russell H. Brannon, and Frank A. Fender, *The Agricultural Development of Argentina, A Policy and Development Perspective* (New York: Praeger, 1969).

[23] Krueger, "Factor Endowments."

and those obtained by Krueger. In general, the consistency between the results presented in Tables 5-3 and 5-4, combined with our general knowledge of the economies being studied, strengthens our confidence in the results of our analysis of the intercountry cross-section production function estimates.

IMPLICATIONS FOR AGRICULTURAL DEVELOPMENT STRATEGY

The results of the analysis in the two preceding sections are clearly consistent with the hypothesis presented at the beginning of this chapter: Differences in technical inputs and human capital do account for a very substantial share of the agricultural productivity gap among countries; and even within the resource endowments category internal capital accumulation appears to be relatively important as compared to the original endowments of land.

Nevertheless, the implications of this analysis for agricultural development strategy in the less developed countries have both encouraging and discouraging aspects. It is clear that output per worker in the several LDC's can be increased by several multiples, while land area per worker remains constant or even declines slightly. To achieve increases of this magnitude will require substantial investment in rural education and in the physical, biological, and social sciences required for the invention, development, and extension of a more efficient technology. It will also require the allocation of substantial resources to the production of the technical inputs supplied by the industrial sector.

A more discouraging aspect of this analysis is that in order to achieve levels of labor productivity comparable to the levels achieved in the DC's of recent origin, it will, at some stage, be necessary to complement those technical changes designed to increase output per unit area with technologies that reduce the labor input per unit area. Significant reductions in labor input per unit area are likely to occur, however, only in those economies in which urban industrial development is sufficiently advanced to absorb not only the growth in the rural labor force but also to permit a continuous reduction in employment in rural areas.[24] It should be noted that this has occurred in Japan only since World War II. It seems likely that most LDC's will experience large increases in the size of their agricultural labor force before growth in nonagricultural employment will be sufficient to permit an absolute decline in agricultural employment.[25]

[24] F. Dovring, "The Share of Agriculture in a Growing Population," *Monthly Bulletin of Agricultural Economics and Statistics* (FAO) 8 (August–September 1959): 1–11.

[25] "Judging by the experience of a number of developing countries, a rate of increase of nonfarm employment of 4.5 percent per year must be regarded as very rapid. But if the farm labor force initially accounts for 80 percent of the total, and the labor force is growing at

The implications for agricultural development strategy for most less developed countries seems relatively clear. An attempt must be made to close the gap in the level of modern technical inputs and in education and research. Agricultural surpluses generated by closing the gap, over and above the amount necessary to maintain the growth of agricultural productivity, must be used to finance industrial development.[26]

If successful, the effort would, over time, result in a rate of growth in the nonagricultural labor force sufficient to permit a reduction in the agricultural labor force and a rise in labor productivity toward the levels of the DC's of recent settlement.

Maintenance of the rate of growth of agricultural productivity can be expected to impose a substantial drain on the savings that can be generated from the agricultural surpluses. Initially, a substantial component of industrial capacity must be designed to provide technical inputs for the agricultural sector. Substantial investment will be needed to create the institutional infrastructure to improve general education in rural areas and to produce the technical and scientific manpower needed to bring about technical improvements in agriculture. Investment in land development, such as irrigation and drainage, will also be necessary in a number of countries in order to obtain a full return from the new biological and chemical technology.

SUPPLEMENT*

Results of tests of the unitary elasticity of substitution, inherent in the Cobb–Douglas production function, and of the stability of the estimates coefficients of the production function over time are reported in this section.

A Test of Unitary Elasticity of Substitution

In the preceding analysis in this chapter the production function was specified as being of the Cobb–Douglas type, thus assuming unitary elasticity of

---

3 percent annually, the farm labor force would increase threefold and would still account for nearly 60 percent of the total at the end of 50 years in spite of growth of nonfarm employment at a rate of 4.5 percent." Bruce F. Johnston, "Agricultural and Structural Transformation in Developing Countries: A Survey of Research," *Journal of Economic Literature* 8 (June 1970): 381.

[26] Ishikawa has suggested that achievement of national agricultural output and productivity objectives may, in some developing countries, require a net flow of savings from the nonagricultural to the agricultural sector. Shigeru Ishikawa, *Economic Development in Asian Perspective* (Tokyo: Kinokuniya Bookstore, 1967). The possibility has been such a shock to some students of development economics that they recommend a "development without agriculture" policy. See, for example, M. June Flanders, "Agriculture Versus Industry in Development Policy, The Planners' Dilemma Re-examined," *Journal of Development Studies* 5 (April 1969): 171–89.

* Readers who are not interested in technical detail may wish to skip this section.

substitution among inputs. Here we attempt to test this assumption by estimating the parameters of the CES production function developed by Arrow et al.[27]

The basic models used for estimation are

1)
$$\log (Y/L) = a + b \log W + c \log Z$$

and

2)
$$\log (V/L) = a' + b' \log W + c' \log Z$$

where Y and V are respectively gross output and value added in agriculture; L is labor; W is the wage rate (measured by output); Z is the shorthand notation for nonconventional variables which shift production function (general and technical education, in this study). It is well known that under competitive factor markets b and b' measure the elasticity of substitution (between labor and the aggregate of other conventional inputs, including current inputs, in the case of b; and between labor and capital in the case of b').

In order to be consistent with the Cobb–Douglas production function the estimated parameters of b and b' should not be significantly different from one, and the estimated parameters of c and c' should not be significantly different from zero. Such assertions are based on the following reasonings: If the underlying production function in gross output terms is the Cobb–Douglas type homogeneous of degree one:

3)
$$Y = K^{\delta}L^{1-\delta}Z^{\lambda}$$

where L and K represent respectively labor and nonlabor inputs (capital in the case of value added production functions), the equilibrium condition in the labor market produces

4)
$$\frac{\partial Y}{\partial L} = W = (1 - \delta)\left(\frac{K}{L}\right)^{\delta} Z^{\lambda}.$$

From equations (3) and (4) we have

5)
$$\frac{Y}{L} = \frac{1}{1 - \delta} W.$$

This implies that, if the underlying production function is Cobb–Douglas, output per unit of labor (likewise value added per labor unit) is a linear function of the wage rate (hence, the coefficient of the wage rate is one in the logarithmic form) and is independent of the shift variables.

The same conclusion can also be derived from the general CES production function. The CES production function which is subject to neutral shift due to Z may be written as

$$Y = \gamma[\delta K^{-\rho} + (1 - \delta)L^{-\rho}]^{-1/\rho}Z^{\lambda}.$$

[27] Arrow, Chenery, Minhas, and Solow, "Capital-Labor Substitution."

The equilibrium condition produces

$$\frac{\partial Y}{\partial L} = W = \gamma(1 - \delta)[\delta K^{-\rho} + (1 - \delta)L^{-\rho}]^{-((1+\rho)/\rho)}L^{-(1+\rho)}Z^{\lambda}.$$

From those two equations we have

$$\frac{Y}{L} = \left(\frac{\delta^{\rho}}{1 - \delta}\right)^{\sigma} W^{\sigma} Z^{\lambda\rho\sigma}$$

where $\sigma = 1/(1 + \rho)$ is the elasticity of substitution. The above relation reduces to equation (5) in the main text if $\sigma = 1$ which implies $\rho = 0$. The same relation can also be derived from the CES function subject to the labor augmentation due to Z:

$$Y = \gamma[\delta K^{-\rho} + (1 - \delta)(Z^{\lambda}L)^{-\rho}]^{-1/\rho}$$

and from the CES function subject to capital augmentation:

$$Y = \gamma[\delta Z^{\lambda}K)^{-\rho} + (1 - \delta)L^{-\rho}]^{-1/\rho}.$$

The results of estimation, based on data of twenty-two countries, are summarized in Table 5-5.[28] Two alternative sets of wage data were employed for estimation: current wage rate (W_t: 1957–62 averages) and lagged wage rate (W_{t-1}: 1952–56 averages). The lagged wage rate was tried to determine whether the adjustment might not be instantaneous. The results are quite similar, however, because there is a high correlation between current wage and lagged wage. The Koyck–Nerlove type of distributed lag model was also tried. The results were implausible, however, probably because of high intercorrelation between the wage rate and the lagged dependent variables.[29]

Both in gross output terms and in value added terms, the results of estimation are consistent with the unitary elasticity of substitution—Cobb–Douglas production function hypothesis: (a) the coefficients of wage rate are not significantly different from one and (b) the coefficients of shift variables, general and technical education, are not significantly different from zero, at conventional significance levels. There is little evidence against the use of the Cobb–Douglas production function for the intercountry cross-section analysis of agricultural production. Such a conclusion seems consistent with the ones derived from cross-regional analyses of agricultural production in the U.S.,

[28] Finland, Norway, and Sweden were dropped from the sample in the estimation of value-added production function because of the implausible estimates of value added in agriculture for those Scandinavian countries.

[29] Some of the wage coefficients became negative and some of the coefficients of the lagged dependent variables became larger than one. The serial correlation model estimated by Griliches was also tried with implausible results. Zvi Griliches, "Production Functions in Manufacturing: Some Preliminary Results," *The Theory and Empirical Analysis of Production*, NBER Studies in Income and Wealth, ed. Murray Brown (New York: Columbia University Press, 1967), vol. 31, pp. 275–322.

Table 5-5. Estimates of the elasticity of substitution function on intercountry data, 1957–62 averages

| | Wage | | General education | | | | |
| | | | Coefficients of | | | | |
Dependent variable	Current (1957–62 av.)	Lagged (1952–56 av.)	Literacy ratio	School enrollment ratio	Technical education	Coef. of det.	S.E. of estimate
(S1) Y/L	1.152 (0.094)					0.878	0.175
(S2) Y/L		1.112 (0.145)				0.736	0.258
(S3) Y/L	1.101 (0.159)		0.131 (0.331)			0.872	0.179
(S4) Y/L	1.106 (0.151)			0.162 (0.408)		0.872	0.179
(S5) Y/L	0.927 (0.196)		0.155 (0.322)		0.124 (0.085)	0.879	0.174
(S6) Y/L	0.962 (0.180)			0.107 (0.400)	0.119 (0.086)	0.878	0.175
(S7) V/L	1.047 (0.098)					0.864	0.171
(S8) V/L		1.002 (0.149)				0.709	0.250
(S9) V/L	1.039 (0.165)		0.018 (0.331)			0.855	0.176
(S10) V/L	1.039 (0.160)			0.024 (0.411)		0.855	0.176
(S11) V/L	0.886 (0.209)		0.050 (0.328)		0.102 (0.087)	0.858	0.174
(S12) V/L	0.908 (0.194)		−0.006 (0.407)		0.101 (0.087)	0.858	0.175

Notes: Equations linear in logarithms are estimated by the least squares. The standard errors of coefficients are in parentheses. Twenty-two countries are included in the sample: Austria, Belgium, Canada, Ceylon, Denmark, Finland, France, Germany, India, Ireland, Japan, Mauritius, Mexico, New Zealand, Norway, Peru, Philippines, Portugal, Sweden, Turkey, U.K., U.S.A., Finland, Norway, and Sweden are dropped from the sample for the estimation of Regression S7–S12.

Table 5-6. Estimates of agricultural production function on intercountry data, 1955 (1952–65 averages)—1960 (1957–62 averages)—1965 (1962–66 averages)*

Regression number	(Q11)	(Q12)	(Q13)	(Q14)	(Q15)	(Q16)	(Q17)
				Per capita basis			
Year	1960	1960	1955	1965	1955-60	1960-65	1955-60-65
Sample size	36	36	36	36	72	72	108
Land	0.072	0.056	0.082	0.043	0.068	0.047	0.066
	(0.061)	(0.063)	(0.061)	(0.073)	(0.042)	(0.047)	(0.038)
Livestock	0.289	0.281	0.311	0.273	0.300	0.276	0.286
	(0.092)	(0.094)	(0.093)	(0.101)	(0.064)	(0.066)	(0.055)
Fertilizer	0.105	0.107	0.124	0.142	0.126	0.125	0.137
	(0.057)	(0.063)	(0.057)	(0.083)	(0.041)	(0.049)	(0.038)
Machinery	0.076	0.125	0.061	0.152	0.090	0.144	0.106
	(0.063)	(0.059)	(0.049)	(0.063)	(0.036)	(0.041)	(0.032)
General education:							
Literacy ratio	0.362						
	(0.180)						
School enrollment ratio		0.337	0.168	0.356	0.320	0.324	0.243
		(0.243)	(0.182)	(0.336)	(0.041)	(0.189)	(0.134)
Technical education	0.182	0.137	0.194	0.099	0.168	0.113	0.122
	(0.055)	(0.053)	(0.051)	(0.050)	(0.035)	(0.034)	(0.029)
Dummy: 1960					-0.009	-0.019	-0.017
					(0.026)	(0.029)	(0.029)
1965							-0.021
							(0.030)
Coef. of det. (adj.)	0.934	0.930	0.931	0.919	0.934	0.929	0.924
S. E. of est.	0.115	0.119	0.111	0.135	0.111	0.123	0.122
Implicit coefficient of labor	0.458	0.431	0.422	0.390	0.422	0.408	0.405

Note: Equations linear in logarithms are estimated by the least squares.
The standard errors of coefficients are in parentheses.

* See data in Appendix A.

by Griliches, and in Japan, by Hiromitsu Kaneda, although their results are less conclusive, with some of the estimates of *b* being significantly different from one and some of the estimates of *c* significantly different from zero.[30]

Stability of the Production Function Over Time

In this section the stability of the agricultural production function over time is tested on the 1955, 1960, and 1965 intercountry cross-section sample. Because comparable data on the number of farms were not available for 1955 and 1965, we assumed linear homogeneity in the Cobb–Douglas production function and regressed output per capita (per male worker) on conventional inputs per capita and on nonconventional inputs per capita. The linear homogeneity assumption is based on the information contained in Table 5–1. In order to make the data comparable among the three periods we restricted the countries included in the sample to thirty-six (Mauritius and Surinam were dropped from the sample for lack of labor data).

The results of our estimations are summarized in Table 5–6. Comparing the estimates of the per capita production function with those of the unrestricted form in Table 5–1, we see that the land coefficients become smaller and the livestock coefficients become larger. This appears to be caused by high intercorrelation between land area per worker and livestock per worker. Differences in the two sets of estimates do not seem to imply different conclusions. The production parameters seem relatively stable over time. The null hypothesis of the equality of the production coefficients in the years 1955, 1960, and 1965 is accepted according to the results of analysis of variance (Table 5–7).

Table 5–7. Analysis of variance for testing stability of agricultural production function over 1955–60–65

	Degree of freedom	Sum of squares	Mean square
1955 (Q13)	29	0.3562	
1960 (Q12)	29	0.4117	
1965 (Q14)	29	0.5321	
Sum	87	1.3000	0.0149
1955–60–65 pooled (Q18)	99	1.4822	
Difference	12	0.1482	0.0124
F_e = difference/sum			0.953

[30] Griliches, "Research Expenditures"; Hiromitsu Kaneda, "Substitution of Labor and Non-labor Inputs and Technical Change in Japanese Agriculture," *Review of Economics and Statistics* 47 (May 1965): 163–71.

Part III Agricultural Growth in the United States and Japan

CHAPTER SIX

Resource Constraints and
Technical Change [1]

In the previous chapter we investigated the sources of agricultural productivity differences among countries. The results of the analysis implied that even in situations characterized by severe constraints on the supply of land or labor a potential for dramatic growth of agricultural output still exists. Realization of this potential depends on growth of technical inputs and human capital. The intercountry cross-section data did not enable us, however, to analyze the dynamic process by which specific economies have overcome resource constraints by generating a sequence of innovations leading to the substitution of technical inputs such as fertilizer and machinery for land and labor.

In this chapter and the two chapters which follow we explore this process by analyzing the historical experiences of agricultural development in the United States and Japan for the period 1880–1960. As we have seen in Chapter 4 (Figures 4–5 and 4–6), the experiences of the United States and Japan seem to have important implications for two groups of countries: (a) countries of the new continents which have a favorable man-land ratio and (b) countries in Asia which have an unfavorable man-land ratio. In terms of the hypothesis postulated in Chapter 4, agricultural growth in these two countries has been achieved through movement along a common metaproduction function under conditions of extreme difference in resource constraints. The influence of resource endowments on technical changes in agriculture can be usefully illustrated by analyzing these two extreme cases.

The data on which it has been necessary to draw in conducting this study are subject to substantial limitations (see Appendix C).[2] Since much of the data

---

[1] This chapter draws heavily on Yujiro Hayami and V. W. Ruttan, "Factor Prices and Technical Change in Agricultural Development: The United States and Japan, 1880–1960," *Journal of Political Economy*, 78 (September/October 1970): 1115–41.

[2] See the comparison of various time series of agricultural production and productivities in the United States by Charles O. Meiburg and Karl Brandt, "Agricultural Productivity in the United States: 1870–1960," *Food Research Institute Studies* 3 (May 1962): 63–85. We

are admittedly crude and comparability of the data for the two countries is less adequate than we would prefer, analysis must of necessity deal with only the broadest trends in the comparative growth experiences of the two countries.

First let us describe the trends in factor prices and in several significant factor-product and factor-factor ratios in the course of agricultural development in the United States and Japan. After presenting this background material, we will specify more precisely our hypothesis concerning the relationship between factor prices and technical change. We will then subject the hypothesis to a statistical test using time-series data from the United States and Japan.

RESOURCE ENDOWMENTS, PRODUCTION, AND PRODUCTIVITY

In this section we attempt to characterize the differences and similarities in agricultural growth patterns in the United States and Japan for the period of 1880–1960. We first point to the extreme differences in factor endowments and factor prices in the two countries. We then compare changes in agricultural output and productivity in the two countries.

Resource Endowments and Prices

Japan and the United States are characterized by extreme differences in relative endowments of land and labor (Table 6–1). In 1880 total agricultural land area per male worker was thirty-six times as large in the United States as in Japan, and arable land area per worker was ten times as large in the United States as in Japan. The differences have widened over time. By 1960 total agricultural land area per male worker was ninety-seven times and arable land area per male worker was forty-seven times as large in the United States as in Japan.

---

adopted the USDA agricultural output series because it is consistent with the definition of agricultural output in our intercountry data. Reliability of agricultural production statistics in Meiji, Japan, has been strongly questioned by Nakamura. See James I. Nakamura, *Agriculture Production and the Economic Development of Japan: 1873–1922* (Princeton: Princeton University Press, 1966). The questions regarding the official statistics of Japan raised by Nakamura have been widely discussed by Japanese and other scholars: Yujiro Hayami, "On the Japanese Experience of Agricultural Growth," *Rural Economic Problems* 4 (May 1968): 79–88; Yujiro Hayami and Saburo Yamada, "Agricultural Productivity at the Beginning of Industrialization," *Agriculture and Economic Development: Japan's Experience,* ed. Kazushi Ohkawa, Bruce F. Johnston and Hiromitsu Kaneda (Tokyo: University of Tokyo Press, 1969), pp. 105–35; J. I. Nakamura, "The Nakamura *Versus* the LTES Estimates of Growth Rate of Agricultural Production," *Keizai Kenkyu* 19 (October 1968): 358–62. Appraisals by other scholars include: Henry Rosovsky, "Rumbles in the Ricefields: Professor Nakamura vs. the Official Statistics," *Journal of Asian Studies* 27 (February 1968): 347–60, and Colin Clark's review of Nakamura's book in the September 1967 issue of *Journal of Agricultural Economics.*

Table 6-1. Land-labor endowments and relative prices in agriculture: United States and Japan, selected years

	1880	1900	1920	1940	1960
U.S.A.					
(1) Agricultural land area (million ha.)	202	319	363	411	435[a]
(2) Arable land area (million ha.)	76	129	189	187	181[a]
(3) Number of male farm workers (thousand)	7,959	9,880	10,221	8,487	3,973
(4) (1)/(3) (ha./worker)	25	32	36	48	109
(5) (2)/(3) (ha./worker)	10	13	18	22	46
(6) Value of agricultural land ($/ha.)	47	49	171	78	285[a]
(7) Value of arable land ($/ha.)	163	129	352	180	711[a]
(8) Farm wage rate ($/day)	0.90[b]	1.00[c]	3.30	1.60	6.60
(9) (6)/(8) (days/ha.)	52	49	52	49	43
(10) (7)/(8) (days/ha.)	181	129	107	113	108
JAPAN					
(11) Agricultural land area (thousand ha.)	5,507	6,031	6,957	7,100	7,043
(12) Arable land area (thousand ha.)	4,748	5,200	5,997	6,121	6,071
(13) Number of male farm workers (thousand)	7,842	7,680	7,593	6,365	6,230
(14) (11)/(13) (ha./worker)	0.70	0.79	0.92	1.12	1.13
(15) (12)/(13) (ha./worker)	0.61	0.68	0.79	0.96	0.97
(16) Value of arable land (yen/ha.)	343	917	3,882	4,709	1,415,000
(17) Farm wage rate (yen/day)	0.22	0.31	1.39	1.90	440
(18) (16)/(17) (days/ha.)	1,559	2,958	2,793	2,478	3,216

[a] 1959.   [b] 1879 or 1880.   [c] 1899.

Note: See the sources of data in Appendix C. Agricultural land areas in Japan are estimated by multiplying arable land areas by 1.16 which is the ratio of agricultural land area to arable land area in the 1960 Census of Agriculture.

The relative prices of land and labor also differed sharply in the two countries. In 1880 in order to buy a hectare of arable land (compare column 10 and column 18 in Table 6-1) it would have been necessary for a Japanese hired farm worker to work nine times as many days as a U.S. farm worker. In the United States the price of labor rose relative to the price of land, particularly between 1880 and 1920. In Japan the price of land rose sharply relative to the price of labor, particularly between 1880 and 1900. By 1960 a Japanese farm worker would have to work thirty times as many days as a U.S. farm worker in order to buy one hectare of arable land.

Production and Productivity Growth

In spite of these substantial differences in land area per worker and in the relative prices of land and labor, both the United States and Japan experienced relatively rapid rates of growth in production and productivity in agriculture (Table 6-2). During the entire eighty-year period agricultural output increased at the annual compound rate of 1.5 percent in the U.S. and 1.6 percent in Japan; total inputs (aggregates of conventional inputs) increased at 0.8 per-

Table 6–2. Changes in output, input, productivity, and factor proportions in U.S. and Japanese agriculture, 1880–1960, selected years

	Index, 1880 = 100					Annual compound rate of change				
	1880	1900	1920	1940	1960	1880 to 1900	1900 to 1920	1920 to 1940	1940 to 1960	1880 to 1960
United States										
Output (net of seeds and feed)	100	155	180	232	340	2.2	0.8	1.3	1.9	1.5
Total inputs	100	138	172	181	190	1.6	1.1	0.3	0.2	0.8
Total productivity (output/total inputs)	100	112	105	128	179	0.6	−0.3	1.0	1.7	0.7
Number of male workers	100	124	128	107	50	1.1	0.2	−0.9	−3.9	−0.9
Output per male worker	100	125	141	217	680	1.1	0.6	2.2	5.8	2.4
Agricultural land area	100	157	180	203	215	2.3	0.7	0.6	0.3	1.0
Arable land area	100	170	249	246	238	2.7	1.9	−0.1	−0.2	1.1
Output per ha. of agricultural land	100	99	100	114	158	−0.1	0.1	0.7	1.6	0.5
Output per ha. of arable land	100	91	72	94	143	−0.5	−1.1	1.4	2.1	0.4
Agricultural land area per male worker	100	127	141	190	430	1.2	0.5	1.5	4.2	1.9
Arable land area per male worker	100	137	195	230	476	1.6	1.7	0.8	3.7	2.0
Japan										
Output (net of seeds and feed)	100	149	232	264	358	2.1	2.2	0.7	1.5	1.9
Total input	100	105	119	127	156	0.2	0.6	0.3	1.0	0.6
Total productivity	100	142	195	208	229	1.9	1.6	0.4	0.5	1.0
Number of male workers	100	98	97	81	79	−0.1	0	−0.9	−0.1	−0.3
Output per male worker	100	152	239	326	453	2.2	2.2	1.6	1.6	1.9
Arable land area (= Agric. land area)	100	110	126	129	128	0.5	0.7	0.1	0	0.3
Output per ha. of arable land	100	135	184	205	280	1.6	1.5	0.6	1.5	1.3
Arable land area per male worker	100	112	130	159	162	0.6	0.7	1.0	0.1	0.9

Note: Flow variables, such as output and total inputs, are five-year averages centering the year shown. Stock variables, such as land and labor, are measured in the year shown.

Source: Data from Appendix Table C–2 and Table C–3.

cent in the U.S. and 0.6 percent in Japan; and total factor productivity increased at 0.7 percent in the U.S. and 1.0 percent in Japan. It is remarkable that essentially similar over-all growth rates were attained under the extremely different factor proportions which characterize Japan and the United States.

Although there is resemblance in the over-all rates of growth in production and productivity, the time sequences of the relatively fast growing phases and the relatively stagnant phases differ between the two countries. Figure 6–1 indicates that in the United States agricultural output grew rapidly up to 1900; then the growth rate decelerated. From the 1900's to the 1930's there was little gain in total productivity. This stagnation phase was succeeded by a dramatic rise in production and productivity in the 1940's and 1950's. Japan experienced rapid increases in agricultural production and productivity from 1880 up to the 1910's, then entered into a stagnation phase which lasted until the mid-1930's. Another rapid expansion phase commenced during the period of recovery from the devastation of World War II. Roughly speaking, the United States experienced a stagnation phase two decades earlier than Japan and also shifted to the second development phase two decades earlier.

Components of Labor Productivity Growth

There have been, in the course of U.S. and Japanese agricultural development, substantial differences in the growth of labor productivity. For expository purposes the growth in output per worker is partitioned between two components—land area per worker and land productivity, as follows:

$$\frac{Y}{L} = \frac{A}{L} \frac{Y}{A}$$

where

Y = output	Y/L = labor productivity
L = labor	A/L = land area per worker
A = land area	Y/A = land productivity

Given the differences in the prices of land and labor in the United States and Japan we would expect that growth in output per worker (Y/L) in the United States would be closely associated with changes in land area per worker (A/L), and in Japan with changes in land productivity (Y/A).

These expectations are confirmed by the data on land area per male worker and output per hectare plotted in Figure 6–2. In the United States land area per worker (A/L) rose much more rapidly than in Japan. In Japan land productivity (Y/A) rose much more rapidly than in the United States. As shown below (pages 128–32), for the period 1880–1960 increase in land area per worker explains more than 80 percent of the labor productivity growth in the United States, whereas it explains less than 40 percent in Japan.

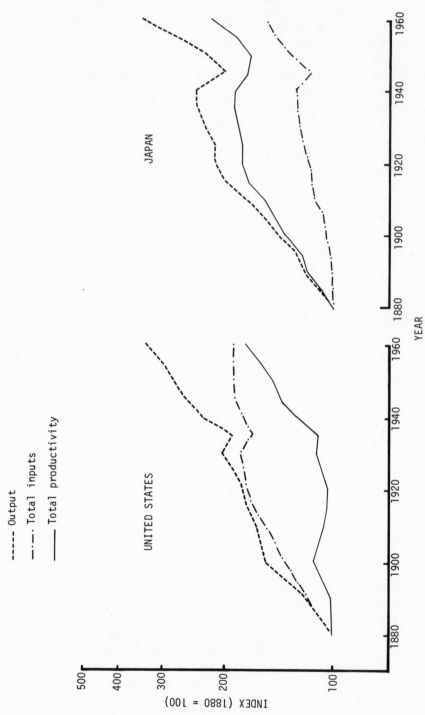

FIGURE 6–1. Changes in agricultural output, total input, and total productivity (1880 = 100), the United States and Japan, 1880–1960.

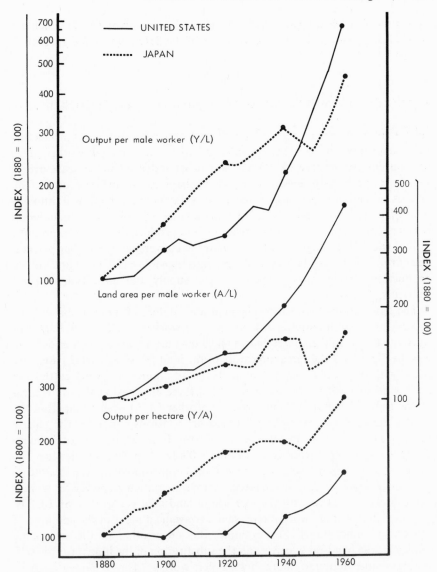

FIGURE 6-2. Changes in labor productivity, land-labor ratio, and land productivity (1880 = 100) (in logs.), the United States and Japan, 1880–1960. (Data from Appendix Table C–2 and Table C–3.)

Both the United States and Japan experienced successive stages of rapid growth and relative stagnation followed again by rapid growth in labor productivity. In the United States the stagnation phase was associated with a reduction in the rate of growth in land area per worker (A/L). In Japanese agriculture it is clearly the movements in land productivity (Y/A) which are most closely associated with the sequence of the development and stagnation phases.

PROGRESS IN MECHANICAL AND BIOLOGICAL TECHNOLOGY

In agriculture it appears consistent with the technical conditions of production (as discussed in Chapter 3) to consider growth in land area per worker (A/L) and output per hectare (Y/A) as "somewhat independent, at least over a certain range."[3] As discussed in previous chapters, the major source of increases in land area per worker has been progress in mechanical technology which facilitated the substitution of other sources of power for human labor. Similarly, the major source of increase in land productivity has been progress in biological technology which facilitated the conversion of a higher percentage of the solar energy falling on an area into higher levels of plant and animal production through improvements in the supply and utilization of plant nutrients.

The associations between mechanical and biological innovations and the contrasting growth patterns in land area per worker (A/L) and in land productivity (Y/A) in the United States and Japan are shown in Figures 6–3 and 6–4. In Figure 6–3 the three indicators of the land-labor ratio (A/L) are compared with the number of work animals (horses, mules, and work cattle) and tractor horsepower per worker.[4] Although there are considerable differences in the three indicators of land area per worker (A/L) when comparing the United States and Japan, their differences are relatively minor and the general pattern is not altered by the choice of indicator. In the United States the number of work animals increased up to the 1920's and then began to decline. The increase in tractor horsepower more than compensated for the decline in workstock. Over-all, it seems that the increase in nonhuman power per worker was closely associated with the increase in land area per worker (A/L). The increases in power per worker represent a convenient index of the adoption of mechanical innovations. For example, the substitution of the self-raking reaper for the hand-rake reaper and the substitution of the binder for the self-raking reaper required more horses per worker. Those innovations involved the substitution of power for labor, thereby causing an increase in the land area used per worker in agriculture.

In Japan, corresponding to the slow rate of growth in land area per worker

---

[3] Zvi Griliches, "Agriculture: Productivity and Technology," *International Encyclopedia of the Social Sciences*, vol. 1 (New York: Macmillan and Free Press, 1968), pp. 241–45.

[4] When it is difficult to choose a single data series to adequately represent a single variable, it is reasonable to try several alternatives and to accept the results as conclusive only if the several results are consistent with each other.

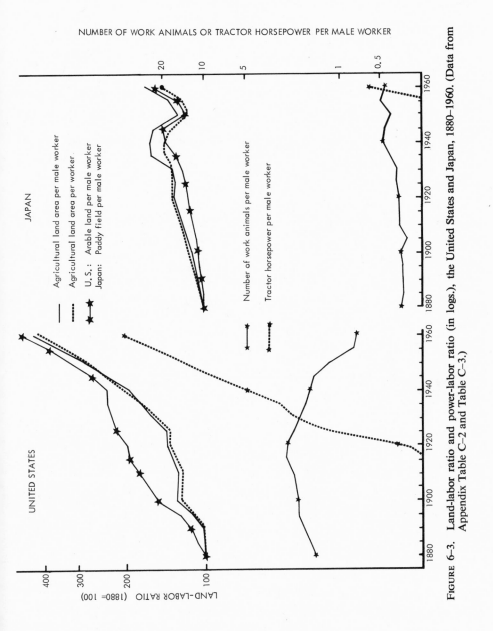

FIGURE 6–3. Land-labor ratio and power-labor ratio (in logs.), the United States and Japan, 1880–1960. (Data from Appendix Table C–2 and Table C–3.)

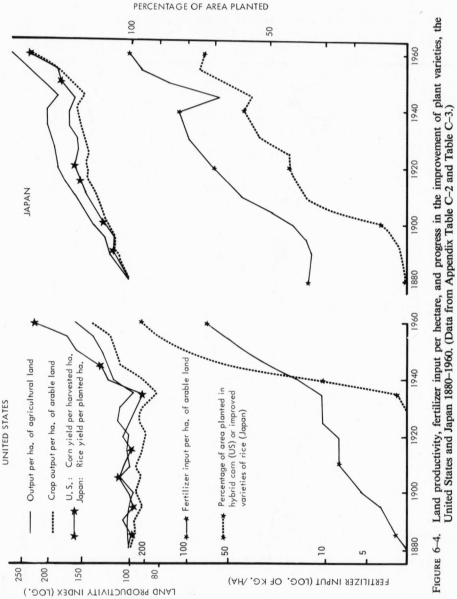

FIGURE 6–4. Land productivity, fertilizer input per hectare, and progress in the improvement of plant varieties, the United States and Japan 1880–1960. (Data from Appendix Table C–2 and Table C–3.)

(*A/L*), the number of work animals increased slowly and the introduction of the tractor started only after World War II.

Figure 6–4 illustrates the contrasting relationship between land productivity (*Y/A*) and the progress of biological technology in the United States and Japan. Here, again, three indicators of land productivity (*Y/A*) are shown in order to check whether different conclusions are implied by the different choices of data. The percentages of total corn area planted to hybrid corn and of total rice area planted to improved varieties are treated as proxy variables representing an index of advances in biological technology in the United States and Japan respectively.

The evidences from these two crops is certainly not conclusive (the percentages are poor proxies even for corn and rice improvements). However, it seems fairly safe to say, based on a comparison of the corn and rice adoption ratios with the trends in fertilizer inputs, that in Japan the significant yield-increasing innovations date from the 1880's, while in the United States they began only in the 1930's. The yield-increasing varieties are almost invariably associated with high levels of plant nutrient utilization. Biological innovations of the yield-increasing type involve the development of crop varieties which can respond to higher levels of fertilization. The parallel increases in fertilizer input per hectare and in percentage of the area planted in improved rice varieties in Japan indicate that the significant biological innovations were already under way in Japan as early as the 1880's. In the United States the introduction of hybrid corn (and other high-yielding crop varieties) is closely associated with the growth of fertilizer consumption. A major factor in the development, introduction, and adoption of hybrid corn, and other new crop varieties, was greater responsiveness to the higher-analysis commercial fertilizers which were becoming available at continuously lower real prices.

In connection with the complementarity between fertilizer input and the development of yield-increasing varieties, it is suggestive that Japan's level of fertilizer input per hectare in the 1880's was almost the same as the level in the United States in the 1930's. Furthermore, these dates represent the beginning of periods in which advances in biological technology, accompanied by rapid growth in fertilizer consumption, began to exert a significant impact on crop production in both countries.

This parallelism does not appear to hold for the period before the 1930's. Initially, increases in fertilizer input were not accompanied by increases in yield per hectare in the United States. This contradiction was apparently due to the use of commercial fertilizers primarily for the purpose of offsetting declining yields resulting from depletion of soil fertility. Prior to 1930, use of commercial fertilizer was concentrated in the South for the production of cotton and tobacco, crops which were classified as soil depleting.[5] Depletion

[5] Rosser H. Taylor, "The Sale and Application of Commercial Fertilizer in the South Atlantic States to 1900," *Agricultural History* 21 (January 1947): 46–52.

of the soil fertility from virgin land would have been significant, especially in the newly opened Great Plains (see pages 138–53, Chapter 7). The increase in commercial fertilizer input per hectare and the stagnant or even declining land productivity (Y/A) between 1880 and 1935 is consistent with the inference that the supply of plant nutrients from all sources (including both natural and commercial sources) was stagnant or even declining during this period.

Increases in power per worker and in fertilizer input per hectare were accompanied by dramatic declines in the price of machinery (a proxy for the price of power and machinery) relative to the wage rate and the price of fertilizer relative to the price of land (Figure 6–5). These trends in factor price ratios, along with the trends in the price of land relative to labor (Table 6–1), are consistent with the hypothesis that the differential progress in mechanical and biological technologies in the United States and Japan represented a process of dynamic factor substitution in response to the changes in relative factor prices.

INDUCED PROGRESS IN TECHNOLOGY: A HYPOTHESIS

In the previous sections we have observed sharp contrasts in the patterns of agricultural growth in the United States and Japan. In the United States it was primarily the progress of mechanization which facilitated the expansion of agricultural production and productivity by increasing the area operated per worker. In Japan it was primarily the progress of biological technology, represented by seed improvements which increased the yield response to higher levels of fertilizer application, which permitted the rapid growth in agricultural output in spite of severe constraints on the supply of land. U.S. agriculture has experienced significant biological innovations since the 1930's, and farm mechanization has been progressing at an accelerating pace since the 1950's. In Japan, the impact of biological technology has exerted a dramatic impact on the growth of production and productivity throughout much of the period since 1870.

In this section we investigate in greater detail the manner in which differences in factor price movements in Japan and the United States have influenced the process of technical change and the choice of inputs in the two countries. The argument is developed that the contrasting patterns of productivity growth and factor use in U.S. and Japanese agriculture can best be understood in terms of a process of dynamic adjustment to changing relative factor prices along a metaproduction function—dynamic in the sense that production isoquants change in response to the changes in relative factor prices.

In the United States the long-term decline in the prices of land and machinery relative to wages (Table 6–1 and Figure 6–5) could be expected to

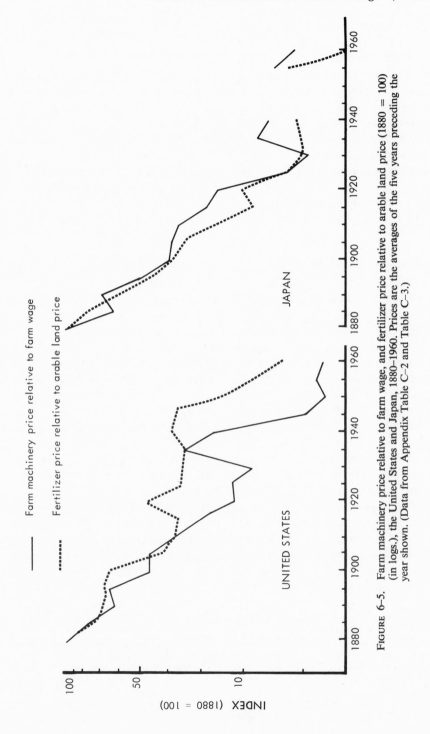

FIGURE 6-5. Farm machinery price relative to farm wage, and fertilizer price relative to arable land price (1880 = 100) (in logs.), the United States and Japan, 1880–1960. Prices are the averages of the five years preceding the year shown. (Data from Appendix Table C–2 and Table C–3.)

encourage the substitution of land and power for labor. This substitution generally involved progress in the application of mechanical technology to agricultural production. With fixed technology represented by a certain type of machinery, there is little possibility of factor substitution. For example, an optimum factor combination with the reaper (such as the McCormick or Hussey), assuming two weeks for harvesting and two shifts of horses, was approximately five workers, four horses (two horses for original models), and 140 acres of wheat. Only when a new technology, in the form of the binder, was introduced was it possible for the farmer to change this proportion to two workers, one reaper (binder), four horses and 140 acres.[6] Although we do not deny the possibility of substitution within a limited range (e.g., through change from two shifts to three shifts of horses), such enormous changes in factor proportions as observed in Figure 6–3 and Figure 6–4 could hardly occur as a result of substitution among available alternatives in the absence of new technical possibilities.

Dramatic increases in land area and power per worker of the magnitude that occurred in the United States indicate a response to mechanical innovations which raised the marginal rate of substitution in favor of both land and power for labor.[7] This has been a continual process. The introduction of the tractor, which can be considered as the single most important mechanical innovation in agriculture, greatly raised the marginal rate of substitution of power for labor by making it much easier to command more power per worker. Substitution of higher powered tractors for low powered tractors has a similar effect.

In Japan the supply of land was inelastic and the price of land rose relative to wages. It was not, therefore, profitable to substitute land and power for labor. Instead, the new opportunities arising from continuous declines in the price of fertilizer relative to the price of land were exploited through advances in biological technology. Seed improvements were directed to the selection of more fertilizer responsive varieties. The traditional varieties had equal or higher yields than the improved varieties at the lower level of fertilization, but they did not respond to higher application of fertilizer (as illustrated in Table 3–2, Chapter 3). With fixed biological technology represented by a certain variety of seed, the elasticity of substitution of fertilizer for land was low. The enormous changes in fertilizer input per hectare, as observed in

---

[6] Leo Rogin, *The Introduction of Farm Machinery in Its Relation to the Productivity of Labor in the Agriculture of the United States during the Nineteenth Century* (Berkeley: University of California Press, 1931).

[7] This is consistent with the emphasis on the importance of the effect of mechanical innovations on the substitution between new and old machinery in terms of the relative price changes as analyzed by David: Paul A. David, "The Mechanization of Reaping in the Ante-Bellum Midwest," *Industrialization in Two Systems*, ed. Henry Rosovsky (New York: Wiley, 1966), pp. 3–39. In fact the decline in the price of new machines (relative to old machines) in efficiency terms represents a measure of the contribution of the farm machinery industry to technical changes in agriculture.

Japan since 1880 and in the United States since the 1930's, reflect not only the effect of a decline in the price of fertilizer but the development of fertilizer-responsive crop varieties in order to take advantage of the decline in the real price of fertilizer.

In Japan, based on a result of the secular trends of rising wages and drastically falling fertilizer prices relative to land prices, there was a strong inducement for farmers and experiment station workers to develop the biological innovations such as the high-yielding, fertilizer-responsive crop varieties. It is significant that in the United States the biological innovations represented by hybrid corn began about ten years after the rate of increase in arable land area per worker decelerated (around 1920), and that biological innovations and fertilizer application were accelerated after acreage restrictions were imposed by the government. It seems that the changes in the land supply conditions coupled with a dramatic decline in fertilizer price induced a more rapid rate of biological innovations in the United States after the 1930's. It may be that when the increase in fertilizer input per hectare resulting from this relative price decline exceeded the amount of natural fertility depleted from the soil demand for biological innovations became a pressing need, which, coupled with the change in the supply condition of arable land, induced the dramatic advances in biological technology in the United States since the 1930's.

In terms of our hypothesis postulated in Chapter 4 such adjustments in factor proportions in response to changes in relative factor prices represent movements along the iso-product surface of a metaproduction function. This is illustrated in Figure 6–6. U in Figure 6–6 (left) represents the land-labor isoquant of the metaproduction function, which is the envelope of less elastic isoquants such as u_0 and u_1 corresponding to different types of machinery or technology. A certain technology represented by u_0 (e.g., the reaper) is created when a price ratio, p_0, prevails for a certain length of time. When the price ratio changes from p_0 to p_1, another technology represented by u_1 (e.g., combine) is induced.

The new technology represented by u_1, which enables enlargement of the area operated per worker, generally corresponds to a higher intensity of power per worker. This implies the complementary relationship between land and power, which may be drawn as a line representing a certain combination of land and power $[A, M]$. In this simplified presentation, mechanical innovation is conceived as the substitution of a combination of land and power $[A, M]$ for labor (L) in response to a change in wage relative to an index of land and machinery prices, though, of course, in actual practice land and power are substitutable to some extent.

In the same context, the relation between the fertilizer-land price ratio and biological and chemical innovations, such as the development of crop varieties which are more responsive to application of fertilizers, is illustrated in Figure 6–6 (right). V represents the land-fertilizer isoquant of the metaproduction

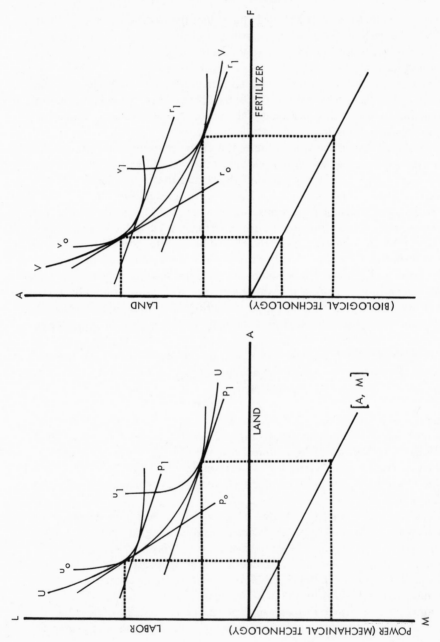

FIGURE 6-6. Factor prices and induced technical change.

function, which is the envelope of less elastic isoquants, such as v_0 and v_1, corresponding to varieties of different fertilizer responsiveness. A decline in the price of fertilizer relative to the price of land from r_0 to r_1 makes it more profitable for farmers to search for crop varieties described by isoquants to the right of v_0. The farmers also press public research institutions to develop new varieties. Through a kind of dialectic process of interaction among farmers and experiment station workers, a new variety, such as that represented by v_1, is developed.

Such movements along the metaproduction function may be inferred from Figure 6–7, in which the U.S. and Japanese data on the relationship between

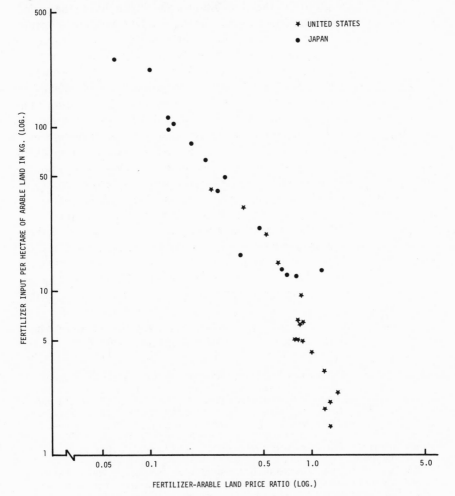

FIGURE 6–7. Relation between fertilizer input per hectare of arable land and fertilizer-arable land price ratio (= hectares of arable land which can be purchased by one ton of $N + P_2O_5 + K_2O$ contained in commercial fertilizers), the United States and Japan: quinquennial observations for 1880–1960. (Data from Appendix Table C–2 and Table C–3.)

fertilizer input per hectare of arable land and the fertilizer-land price ratio is plotted. Despite the enormous differences in climate and other environmental conditions, the relation between these variables is almost identical in both countries. This suggests that U.S. and Japanese agricultural growth has involved a movement along a common metaproduction function.[8]

A STATISTICAL TEST*

The hypothesis developed in the previous section can be summarized as follows: Agricultural growth in the United States and Japan during the period 1880–1960 can best be understood when viewed as a dynamic factor substitution process. Factors have been substituted for each other along a metaproduction function in response to long-run trends in relative factor prices. Each point on the metaproduction surface is characterized by a technology which can be described in terms of specific sources of power, types of machinery, crop varieties, and animal breeds. Movements along this metaproduction surface involve technical changes. These technical changes have been induced to a significant extent by the long-term trends in relative factor prices.

As a test of this hypothesis, we have tried to determine the extent to which the variations in factor proportions, as measured by the land-labor, power-labor, and fertilizer-land ratios, can be explained by changes in factor price ratios. In a situation characterized by a fixed technology it seems reasonable to presume that the elasticities of substitution among factors are small; and this permits us to infer that innovations were induced, if the variations in these factor proportions are consistently explained by the changes in price ratios.[9] The historically observed changes in those factor proportions in the United States and Japan are so large that it is hardly conceivable that these changes represent substitution along a given production surface describing a constant technology.

In order to have an adequate specification of the regression form, we have to be able to infer the shape of the underlying metaproduction function and

---

[8] Griliches has shown, using a distributed lag model, that increases in fertilizer input by United States farmers can be explained solely in terms of the decline in fertilizer prices. See Zvi Griliches, "The Demand for Fertilizer: An Economic Interpretation of a Technical Change," *Journal of Farm Economics* 40 (August 1958): 591–606. The relation he estimated can be identified as the movement along the metaproduction function. The decline in the prices of fertilizer to farmers is a reflection of technical changes in the fertilizer industry. See Gian S. Sahota, *Fertilizer in Economic Development: An Econometric Analysis* (New York: Praeger, Inc., 1968).

* Readers who are not interested in the technical detail may wish to skip this section.

[9] A direct test of the induced innovation hypothesis would involve a test for non-neutral change in the production surface. A possible approach is suggested in Paul A. David and Th. van de Klundert, "Biased Efficiency Growth and Capital-Labor Substitution in the U.S., 1899–1960," *American Economic Review* 55 (June 1965): 357–94.

the functional form of the relationship between changes in the production function and in factor price ratios. Because of a lack of adequate a priori information, we have simply specified the regression in log-linear form with little claim for theoretical justification.[10] If we can assume that the production function is linear and homogeneous, the factor proportions can be expressed in terms of factor price ratios alone and are independent of product prices.

Considering the crudeness of data and the purpose of this analysis, we used quinquennial observations (stock variables measured at five-year intervals and flow variables averaged for five years) instead of annual observations for the regression analysis. A crude form of adjustment is built into our model, since our data are quinquennial observations and prices are generally measured as the averages of the past five years preceding the year when the quantities are measured (for example, the number of workers in 1910 is associated with the 1906–10 average wage).

The results of regression analyses are summarized in Tables 6–3 and 6–4. Table 6–3a presents the regressions for land-labor and power-land proportions for the United States. In those regressions we originally included the fertilizer-labor price ratio as well. But, probably due to high intercorrelation between machinery and fertilizer prices, either the coefficients for the fertilizer-labor price ratio were insignificant or they resulted in implausible results for the other coefficients.[11] This variable was dropped in the subsequent analysis.

As shown in Table 6–3a for the United States more than 80 percent of the variation in the land-labor ratio and in the power-labor ratio is explained by the changes in their price ratios. The coefficients are all negative and are significantly different from zero at the standard levels of significance (1 percent and 5 percent), except the land-price coefficients in regressions (W2) and (W4). Such results indicate that the marked increases in land and power per worker in U.S. agriculture over the past eighty years have been closely associated with declines in the prices of land and of power and machinery relative to the farm wage rate. The hypothesis that land and power should be treated as complementary factors is confirmed by the negative coefficients. This seems

[10] The derivation of factor demand functions from a multifactor production function with different elasticities of substitution seems to suggest a possibility for improving the present specification. See such attempts in Zvi Griliches, "Notes on the Role of Education in Production Function and Growth Accounting" (University of Chicago: Center for Mathematical Studies in Business and Economics, Report No. 6839, 1969), mimeo.; "A Note on Capital-Skill Complementarity" (University of Chicago: Center for Mathematical Studies in Business and Economics, Report No. 6905, 1969), mimeo. Our regressions are similar to Griliches' but our factor prices do not measure the costs of factor services other than fertilizer. See Appendix C.

[11] Some of the coefficients of our prices turned positive, e.g., the coefficients of land price relative to wage in Regressions (1) and (2). An exponential time trend was also included. The results were totally implausible due to multicolinearity (the simple correlation between time and the machinery price relative to wage was as high as 0.95).

Table 6–3a. Regressions of land-labor ratios and power-labor ratios on relative factor prices: United States, 1880–1960 quinquennial observations

| Regression number | Dependent variables | Coefficients of price of | | Coeff. of det. (adj.) | S. E. | Durbin–Watson statistics |
		Land relative to farm wage	Machinery relative to farm wage			
	Land-labor ratios:					
(W1)	Agricultural land per male worker	−0.451 (0.215)	−0.486 (0.120)	0.828	0.0844	1.29
(W2)	Arable land per male worker	−0.035 (0.180)	−0.708 (0.101)	0.882	0.0706	1.37
(W3)	Agricultural land per worker	−0.492 (0.215)	−0.463 (0.120)	0.828	0.0789	1.34
(W4)	Arable land per worker	−0.077 (0.182)	−0.686 (0.102)	0.879	0.0713	1.41
	Power-labor ratios:					
(W5)	Horsepower per male worker	−1.279 (0.475)	−0.920 (0.266)	0.827	0.1865	1.33
(W6)	Horsepower per worker	−1.321 (0.474)	−0.898 (0.265)	0.828	0.1863	1.36

Note: Equations are linear in logarithm. Inside of the parentheses are the standard errors of the estimated coefficients.

Source: Data from Appendix C: Number of workers = U3, Number of male workers = U4, Agricultural land area = U5, Arable land area = U6, Power in horsepower equivalents = U7 + U8, Farm wage = U18, Land price = U20, Machinery price = U21

to indicate, that, in addition to the complementarity along a fixed production surface, mechanical innovations which raise the marginal rate of substitution of power for labor tend to also raise the marginal rate of substitution of land for labor.

The results from using the same regressions for Japan (Table 6–3b) are greatly inferior in terms of statistical criteria. This is probably because the ranges of observed variation in the land-labor and in the power-labor ratios are too small in Japan to detect any significant relationships between the factor proportions and price ratios. It may also reflect the fact that the mechanical innovations in Japan were developed and adopted primarily to increase yield, rather than as a substitute for labor.

The results for the United States of the regression analyses of the determinants of fertilizer input per hectare of arable land are presented in Table 6–4a. The results indicate that variations in the fertilizer-land price ratio alone explain almost 90 percent of the variation in fertilizers. It also shows that the wage-land price ratio is a significant variable, indicating a substitution relationship between fertilizer and labor. Over a certain range, fertilizer input can be substituted for human care for plants (for example, weeding). A more important factor in Japanese history would be the effects of substitution of

Table 6–3b. Regressions of land-labor ratios and power-labor ratios on relative factor prices: Japan, 1880–1960 quinquennial observations

Regression number	Dependent variables	Coefficients of price of		Coeff. of det. (adj.)	S. E.	Durbin–Watson statistics
		Land relative to farm wage	Machinery relative to farm wage			
	Land-labor ratios:					
(W7)	Arable land per male worker	0.159 (0.110)	−0.219 (0.041)	0.751	0.0347	1.17
(W8)	Arable land per worker	0.230 (0.049)	−0.155 (0.019)	0.914	0.0156	1.71
	Power-labor ratios:					
(W9)	Horsepower per male worker	−0.665 (0.261)	−0.299 (0.685)	0.262	0.2191	0.60
(W10)	Horsepower per worker	−0.601 (0.236)	−0.228 (0.620)	0.266	0.1982	0.61

Note: Equations are linear in logarithms. Inside of the parentheses are the standard errors of the estimated coefficients.

Source: Data from Appendix C: Number of workers = J3, Number of male workers = J4, Arable land area = J6, Power in horsepower equivalents = J7 + J8, Farm wage = J18, Land price = J20, Machinery price = J21.

commercial fertilizer for the labor allocated to the production of self-supplied fertilizers such as animal and green manure.[12]

A comparison of Table 6–4a with Table 6–4b indicates a striking similarity in the structure of demand for fertilizer in the United States and Japan. The results in these two tables seem to suggest that, despite enormous differences in climate, initial factor endowments, and social and economic institutions and organization, in the United States and Japan the agricultural production function, the inducement mechanism of innovations, and the response of farmers to economic opportunities have been essentially the same.

The possibility of structural changes in the metaproduction function over time, as suggested by some of the low Durbin–Watson statistics in Tables 6–3 and 6–4, was tested by separate regression analyses for 1880–1915 and 1920–

[12] Biological innovations represented by improvements in crop varieties, characterized by greater response to fertilizer, tend to be land-saving and labor-using. The yield potential of the improved varieties is typically achieved only when high levels of fertilization are combined with high levels of crop husbandry and water management. On this score, the introduction of high-yielding varieties enhances the substitution of fertilizer and labor for land. On the other hand, commercial fertilizers have significant labor saving effects as they substitute for self-supplied fertilizers. In Japan, the production of such self-supplied fertilizers as manure, green manure, compost, and night soil has traditionally occupied a significant portion of a farmer's work hours. With the increased supply of commercial fertilizers, farmers can divert their labor to the improvements in cultural practices in such forms as better seed bed preparation and weed control.

Table 6–4a. Regressions of fertilizer input per hectare of arable land on relative factor prices: United States, 1880–1960 quinquennial observations

| | Coefficients of prices of | | | | | |
Regression number	Fertilizer relative to land	Labor relative to land	Machinery relative to land	Coeff. of det. (adj.)	S. E.	Durbin–Watson statistics
(W11)	−1.622 (0.200)	1.142 (0.275)	0.014 (0.286)	0.950	0.1042	2.08
(W12)	−1.615 (0.134)	1.138 (0.255)	—	0.954	0.0968	2.09
(W13)	−1.951 (0.166)	—	—	0.895	0.1406	0.77
·(W14)	−1.101 (0.184)	1.134 (0.173)	−0.350 (0.214)	0.969	0.0816	1.38
(W15)	−1.357 (0.102)	1.019 (0.168)	—	0.970	0.0832	1.15
(W16)	−1.707 (0.154)	—	—	0.884	0.1481	0.84

Note: Equations are linear in logarithms. Inside of the parentheses are the standard errors of the estimated coefficients.

Source: Data from Appendix C: Fertilizer input = U9, Arable land area = U5. In case of (W11), (W12), and (W13), Farm wage = U11, Land price = U9, Machinery price = U21, Fertilizer price = U23. In case of (W14), (W15), and (W16), Farm wage = U18, Land price = U20, Machinery price = U21, Fertilizer = U24.

60. The results summarized in Table 6–5 do not suggest that any significant structural changes occurred between those two periods.[13]

Over-all, the results of the statistical analysis are consistent with the hypothesis stated at the beginning of this section; in both Japan and the United States factors have been substituted for each other along a meta-production function, primarily in response to long-run trends in factor prices.

IMPLICATIONS

The results of the regression analysis indicate that the enormous changes in factor proportions which have occurred in the process of agricultural growth in the United States and Japan are explainable in terms of changes in factor price ratios. In spite of strong reservations regarding the data and the methodology, when we relate the results of the statistical analysis to the historical knowledge of the progress in agricultural technology, we conclude that such

[13] Because of the small number of observations involved, the inferences from this test are relatively weak.

Table 6–4b. Regressions of fertilizer input per hectare of arable land on relative factor prices: Japan, 1880–1960 quinquennial observations

| Regression number | Coefficients of prices of | | | Coeff. of det. (adj.) | S. E. | Durbin–Watson statistics |
	Fertilizer relative to land	Labor relative to land	Machinery relative to land			
(W17)	−1.437 (0.238)	0.662 (0.244)	0.236 (0.334)	0.973	0.0865	2.45
(W18)	−1.274 (0.057)	0.729 (0.220)	—	0.974	0.0810	2.45
(W19)	−1.211 (0.071)	—	—	0.953	0.1036	1.52
(W20)	−1.248 (0.468)	1.217 (0.762)	−0.103 (0.708)	0.878	0.1820	1.76
(W21)	−1.313 (0.131)	1.145 (0.556)	—	0.888	0.1670	1.79
(W22)	−1.173 (0.126)	—	—	0.860	0.1794	1.52

Note: Equations are linear in logarithms. Inside of parentheses are the standard errors of the estimated coefficients.

Source: Data from Appendix C: Fertilizer input = J9, Arable land area = J5. In case of (W17), (W18), and (W19), Farm wage = J17, Land price = J19, Machinery price = J21, Fertilizer price = J22. In case of (W20), (W21), and (W22), Farm wage = J18, Land price = J20, Machinery price = J21, Fertilizer price = J23.

changes in input mixes represent a process of dynamic factor substitution along a metaproduction function accompanying changes in the production surface induced primarily by changes in relative factor prices.

This conclusion, if warranted, represents a key to understanding the success of agricultural growth in the two countries. The basis for the contrasting patterns of factor price changes is the difference in factor supply conditions. In the United States, the land supply for agriculture has been more elastic than the labor supply. In Japan, the labor supply has been more elastic than the land supply. With the increased demand for farm products in the course of economic development, the price of the less elastic factor tends to rise relative to the prices of the more elastic factors. Given the differences in supply elasticities, agricultural growth in both countries accompanied contrasting changes in land-labor price ratios. Prices of agricultural inputs, such as fertilizer and machinery supplied by the nonfarm sector, tended to decline relative to the prices of land and labor. Such trends induced farmers, public research institutions, and private agricultural supply firms to search for new production possibilities that would offset the effects of the relative price changes. Thus, mechanical innovations of a labor-saving type were induced in the United States and biological innovations of a yield-increasing type

Table 6–5. Analysis of variance for testing structural change of regression relations between 1880–1915 and 1920–60

Regression number	Residual sum of squares			Number of parameters p	Sample size		F—statistics	
	1880–1915 s_1	1920–1960 s_2	1880–1960 s		1880–1915 n_1	1920–1960 n_2	Computed F_c	Theoretical F
(W1)	0.00314	0.07898	0.08719	3	8	9	0.23	3.59
(W2)	0.00123	0.05539	0.06099	3	8	9	0.28	3.59
(W3)	0.00282	0.07788	0.08709	3	8	9	0.29	3.59
(W4)	0.00103	0.05443	0.06233	3	8	9	0.45	3.59
(W5)	0.00284	0.39095	0.42588	3	8	9	0.30	3.59
(W6)	0.00277	0.38936	0.42512	3	8	9	0.31	3.59
(W7)	0.00052	0.00865	0.01241	3	8	7	1.06	3.86
(W8)	0.00146	0.00046	0.00250	3	8	7	0.93	3.86
(W9)	0.00344	0.46381	0.49381	3	8	7	0.17	3.86
(W10)	0.00346	0.38035	0.40415	3	8	7	0.16	3.86
(W11)	0.01295	0.03399	0.11470	4	8	9	3.25	3.63
(W12)	0.01856	0.06597	0.11472	3	8	9	1.31	3.59
(W13)	0.07902	0.09521	0.27809	2	8	9	2.43	3.80
(W14)	0.00582	0.03278	0.07027	4	8	9	1.85	3.63
(W15)	0.01578	0.03771	0.08473	3	8	9	2.14	3.59
(W16)	0.02107	0.23481	0.30829	2	8	9	1.33	3.80
(W17)	0.01602	0.03085	0.06462	4	8	7	0.66	4.12
(W18)	0.01872	0.03859	0.06754	3	8	7	0.54	3.86
(W19)	0.05996	0.04582	0.12952	2	8	7	1.01	3.98
(W20)	0.11286	0.01408	0.28639	4	8	7	2.20	4.12
(W21)	0.11312	0.06828	0.28694	3	8	7	1.75	3.86
(W22)	0.12274	0.15434	0.38845	2	8	7	2.21	3.98

Note: $F_c = \dfrac{s - s_1 - s_2}{s_1 + s_2} \cdot \dfrac{n_1 + n_2 - 2p}{p}$; F: theoretical value at 5 percent level.

were induced in Japan.[14] Since the 1930's, the decline in the price of fertilizer has been so dramatic that innovations in U.S. agriculture shifted from a predominant emphasis on mechanical technology to the development of new biological innovations in the form of crop varieties and production practices developed in response to lower cost fertilizers.[15]

Rapid growth in agriculture in both countries could not have occurred without such dynamic factor substitution. If factor substitution had been limited to substitution along a fixed production surface, agricultural growth would have been severely limited by the inelastic supply of the more limiting factors. Development of a continuous stream of new technology, which altered the production surface to conform to long-term trends in factor prices, was the key to success in agricultural growth in the United States and Japan.

For both the United States and Japan, vigorous growth in the industries which supplied machinery and fertilizers at continuously declining relative prices has been an indispensable requirement for agricultural growth. Equally important were the efforts in research and extension to fully exploit the opportunities created by industrial development. Without the creation of fertilizer-responsive crop varieties, the benefits from the lower fertilizer prices would be limited. The success in agricultural growth in both the United States and Japan seems to lie in the capacity of their farmers, research institutions, and farm supply industries to exploit new opportunities in response to the information transmitted through relative price changes.

Agriculture in the United States and Japan, starting from entirely different initial factor endowments and factor supply conditions, experienced comparable rates of growth in production and productivity over the 1880–1960 period. There is little reason to believe that presently developing countries cannot attain the same success if they exploit the opportunities available to them. Their patterns of growth would be expected to be different than either the United States or Japan, since factor supply conditions reflect the unique endowments of each country, and product demand in most developing countries is rising at a rate that exceeds the historical rates experienced in either Japan or the United States. Efforts must be directed to create a unique pattern of growth for each developing country. An important element in this effort appears to be a system which accurately reflects the economic implications of factor endowments to producers, public institutions, and private industry.

[14] Adjustments of production techniques to factor price ratios are not confined to agriculture. In the early phase of Japan's modern economic growth, we see a continuous sequence of modifications of "borrowed techniques" to conform to the factor price ratios which were different from those in western countries. See Gustav Ranis, "Factor Proportions in Japanese Economic Development," *American Economic Review* 47 (September 1957): 594–607.

[15] Between the late 1920's and the early 1960's corn yields in the U.S. corn belt increased from approximately 30 to 70 bushels per acre. This increase was accounted for by three interrelated factors: hybrid seed, higher planting rates, and increased use of nitrogen fertilizer. See Lawrence H. Shaw and Donald D. Durost, *The Effect of Weather and Technology on Corn Yields in the Corn Belt, 1929–62* (Washington: U.S. Department of Agriculture, Economic Research Service, Agricultural Economic Report No. 80, July 1965).

CHAPTER SEVEN

Science and Progress in Agriculture

A dvances in agricultural science and technology clearly represent a necessary condition for releasing the constraints on agricultural production imposed by inelastic factor supplies. Yet, for a country in the early stages of economic development, technical innovations are among the more difficult products to produce. Institutionalization of the process by which a continuous stream of new agricultural technology is made available to a nation's farmers is particularly difficult to achieve.

In both Japan and the United States the "socialization" of agricultural research has been deliberately employed as an instrument of modernization in agriculture. In both countries the modernization process involved the development of experiment station and industrial capacity capable of producing the biological and mechanical innovations adapted to factor supply conditions. In this chapter, we review the process by which the scientific and technological capacity to produce technical change in agriculture was effectively institutionalized in the two countries.

THE SOCIAL CLIMATE FOR SCIENTIFIC RESEARCH

Public support for education and research as an instrument of economic progress represents a major institutional innovation in modern society. In Germany this innovation was initiated with the deliberate intention of utilizing education and research as an engine of economic growth.[1] At the middle of the nineteenth century Germany was a generation behind Britain in industrial and agricultural development. Public support for advances in science,

---

[1] David S. Landes, "Technological Change and Development in Western Europe, 1750–1914," *The Cambridge Economic History of Europe VI. The Industrial Revolution and After, Part I*, ed. H. J. Habakkuk and M. Postan (Cambridge: Cambridge University Press, 1966), pp. 274–601.

technology, and education was undertaken for the deliberate purpose of overcoming the gap in industrial technology and economic power between Germany and Great Britain.

Britain, which led the world in the industrial revolution, left technical training and scientific research to private enterprise, due to its strong laissez-faire tradition, while "the German states generously financed a whole gamut of institutions, erecting buildings, installing laboratories, and above all maintaining competent and, at the highest level, distinguished faculties."[2] In the latter half of the nineteenth century Britain fell behind Germany in human capital formation, including (a) the ability to read, write, and calculate; (b) the engineer's combination of scientific principle and applied training; and (c) a high level of scientific knowledge, theoretical and applied, with the possible exception of the working skills of the craftsman and mechanic.[3] As a result, there was a rapid closing of the gap in industrial productivity between Britain and Germany in the 1860's and 1870's; and Germany emerged as an industrial leader in fields such as chemicals and electrical machinery.

Although Britain, at the beginning of the nineteenth century, was regarded by continental reformers as the "school for agriculture," it was not a coincidence that the first publicly supported agricultural research institution was set up in Germany rather than Britain. It had been a British tradition since Tull and Townsend (admired by such great pioneers in German agricultural science as Albrecht Thair) that agricultural improvements were carried out by country gentlemen. The famous Rothamsted Experimental Station was established (1843) and financed personally by Sir J. B. Lawes throughout the nineteenth century. The Edinburgh Laboratory (founded in 1842), from which early advocates of the state agricultural experiment stations in the U.S. (such as J. P. Norton and Samuel Johnson) received great inspiration, was supported by the Agricultural Chemistry Association of Scotland, a voluntary agricultural society. The laboratory was dissolved in 1848 due to the association members' hastiness in their demand for practical results.

In contrast, a publicly supported agricultural experiment station was successfully established in Germany (at Möckern, Saxony) in 1852 as an answer to the "search, stirring in the German provinces since the publication of Liebig's treatise in 1840, for methods of applying science to agriculture."[4] The Saxon farmers drafted a charter for the station, which the Saxon government legalized by statute, and secured an annual appropriation from the government to finance the experiment station operations. Although the German system of agricultural research evolved later than the British, it provided a

---

[2] Landes, "Technological Change," p. 571.
[3] Ibid., pp. 566–67.
[4] H. C. Knoblauch et al., *State Agricultural Experiment Stations: A History of Research Policy and Procedure* (Washington: U.S. Department of Agriculture, Miscellaneous Publication No. 904, May 1962), p. 16.

more effective environment for the "enlargement" of new scientific and technical knowledge. As a specialized institution, operating under its own charter and supported by the state, it was not as subject to the pressures for immediate practical results as the privately supported research of the English landowners or even the co-operatively organized Edinburgh Laboratory. The development of publicly supported agricultural research institutions was based on the establishment, in Germany, of a social and political climate which regarded science and technology as instruments of economic growth and which viewed their advance as a major responsibility of the state.[5]

The German concept of socialized agricultural research was transplanted to the United States and Japan and has evolved beyond the German model in response to the enormous differences in resource endowments and social and economic traditions of the two countries. Japan and the United States, as relative late-comers in industrial development, were responsive to the role of education and research as a means for economic growth. This was fertile soil into which the concept of socialized agricultural research could be transplanted and grown. Agriculture in these two countries was characterized by predominantly peasant or family operated farms, in contrast to the large-scale system of farming in England and Prussia. Individual farmers in the United States and Japan had but limited capacity to conduct research and little possibility of realizing a significant share of any gains from the results of research. The gains from technical progress tended to be rapidly externalized with consumers rather than farm producers realizing the major share of the returns. Under such conditions, there were strong social incentives to socialize scientific research in agriculture.

SCIENCE AND TECHNOLOGY IN UNITED STATES AGRICULTURE

A belief that the application of science to the solution of practical problems represented a sure foundation for human progress has been a persistent theme in the intellectual and economic history of the United States. The nation "was born of the first effort in history to marry scientific and political ideas."[6] However, the institutionalization of public responsibility for advances in science

---

[5] W. O. Atwater, *Agricultural-Experiment Stations in Europe* (Washington: U.S. Department of Agriculture, Report of the Commissioner of Agriculture for the year 1875, 1876), pp. 517–24.

[6] Don K. Price, *The Scientific Estate* (Cambridge: Harvard University Press, 1965), p. 5. According to Price, "The United States was founded at a time when philosophers were beginning to believe in the perfectibility of mankind. Ever since Benjamin Franklin and Thomas Jefferson, Americans have been inclined to put their faith in a combination of democracy and science as a sure formula for human progress" (p. 1).

and technology, as an instrument of national economic growth, developed slowly.[7]

Progress in Mechanical Technology in the Nineteenth Century

In the nineteenth century progress in agricultural science and technology was, as in England, primarily the product of innovative farmers, inventors, and the emerging industrial sector. Progress in mechanical technology was impressive throughout the last half of the nineteenth century,[8] and advances in tillage and harvesting machinery, induced by the westward march of the land frontier and the associated shortage of labor relative to land, resulted in rapid growth of labor productivity. Mechanization was the most important single source of labor productivity growth.[9] In the case of the small grains (wheat and oats) most of the increase in labor productivity was accounted for by mechanization of seeding and of harvest and postharvest operations. In the case of corn, nearly all of the decline in labor inputs per acre occurred from improvements in preharvest operations.

The advances in mechanical technology were not accompanied by parallel advances in biological technology.[10] Nor were the advances in labor produc-

[7] Even as late as 1860 "the United States still hesitated to embrace the theory that the government should have a permanent scientific establishment.... Sciences that only the government could easily coördinate, such as meteorology and aid to agriculture, failed to find adequate organizational expression. The attempts of the government to use science in regulation and aid of technology had been timid and intermittent." A. Hunter Dupree, *Science in the Federal Government: A History of Policies and Activities to 1940* (Cambridge: Harvard University Press, 1957), p. 114. See also I. Bernard Cohen, *Science and American Society in the First Century of the Republic* (Columbus: Ohio State University, 1961).

[8] Leo Rogin, *The Introduction of Farm Machinery in Its Relation to the Productivity of Labor in the Agriculture of the United States During the Nineteenth Century* (Berkeley: University of California Press, 1931); Clarence H. Danhof, *Change in Agriculture: The Northern United States, 1820–1870* (Cambridge: Harvard University Press, 1969); Irwin Feller, "Inventive Activity in Agriculture, 1837–1890," *Journal of Economic History* 22 (December 1962): 560–77. Feller indicates that "while considerable inventive activity was devoted towards agriculture in the early nineteenth century, these efforts did not have an appreciable effect on output until the middle of the century" (p. 561). The same point has been made in a letter from Wayne D. Rasmussen, August 12, 1970.

[9] William N. Parker and Judith L. V. Klein, "Productivity Growth in Grain Production in the United States, 1840–60 and 1900–10," *Output, Employment and Productivity in the United States after 1800*, NBER Studies in Income and Wealth, vol. 30 (New York: Columbia University Press, 1966), pp. 523–82. In the case of wheat, approximately 60 percent of the growth in labor productivity was due to mechanization, 20 percent was due to the westward shift in the location of production, and 20 percent due to changes in land yields and interaction effects. There is some evidence that Parker and Klein underestimate the contribution of the westward movement to expansion of agricultural production. See Franklin M. Fisher and Peter Temin, "Regional Specialization and the Supply of Wheat in the United States 1867–1914," *Review of Economics and Statistics* 52 (May 1970): 134–49.

[10] This is not to imply that significant advances in biological technology were not achieved; for example, "all of the farmers of the Lower South accepted as their standard strain a new upland cotton developed by Southwestern plant breeders during the early decades of the 1800's. This new variety, the famous Mexican hybrid, improved the yield and

tivity accompanied by comparable advances in land productivity. In most areas fertility and the yields of staple crops declined within a decade or two after settlement. By 1800 declines in fertility and yields were characteristic of even the more fertile areas of the East. By the 1840's declines in productivity were beginning to be serious in Ohio and by the 1860's as far west as Iowa. In the meantime efforts were being made in the Eastern states to introduce the English "new husbandry." Improved breeds of livestock were introduced from England. Use of natural organic (animal manure, green manure, and guano) and mineral (gypsum, lime, and lime phosphate) fertilizers was being initiated on a modest scale. "The English succeeded in inducing American farmers to adopt their livestock, but they were less successful in persuading Americans to use English field culture and agricultural machinery."[11] The aggregate impact of the new crop production technology was barely sufficient to offset the effects of soil depletion on yields.[12]

Explanations for the differential advances in mechanical and biological technology in U.S. agriculture in the nineteenth century can be sought in both the state of scientific development on which advances in mechanical and biological technology draw and in the economic environment in which American farmers operated prior to 1860.[13] It has been pointed out, for example, that "invention in biology and chemistry was, by modern standards, far less advanced in the nineteenth century than invention of mechanical equipment."[14]

A more fundamental response must be sought in the economic environment in which American farmers operated during the nineteenth century. During the first half of the century, labor was too expensive relative to land, even in the older areas of the country, to economically employ labor-intensive systems of conservation farming.[15] Instead, mechanical technology was sought in order to increase the land area that each worker could cultivate. The Civil

---

quality of American cotton to such an extent that it deserves to rank alongside Eli Whitney's gin in the Old South's hall of fame" (p. 95). John Hebron Moore, "Cotton Breeding in the Old South," *Agricultural History* 30 (July 1956): 95–104. See also, Rosser H. Taylor, "The Sale and Application of Commercial Fertilizer in the South Atlantic States to 1900," ibid. 21 (January 1947): 46–52.

[11] Rodney C. Loehr, "The Influence of English Agriculture on American Agriculture, 1775–1825," ibid. 11 (January 1937): 12.

[12] Danhof, *Change in Agriculture*, pp. 251–77.

[13] For a general discussion of historical evidence on whether technical change is knowledge induced or demand induced see Jacob Schmookler, *Invention and Economic Growth* (Cambridge: Harvard University Press, 1966). Based on an extensive review of 235 important inventions in agriculture, 284 in petroleum refining, 185 in paper making, and 230 in railroading between 1800–1955, Schmookler concludes that technical change has been primarily demand-induced, pp. 66, 67, 176.

[14] Parker and Klein, "Productivity Growth," p. 525.

[15] Danhof, *Change in Agriculture*. According to Danhof, "the approach to soil utilization pursued by the majority of farmers was a product of the circumstances in which early settlers had found themselves. The known fertility-maintaining practices . . . were impractical because . . . the available labor was fully occupied to more immediate advantage . . . including the clearing of new land" (p. 251). "The maximum returns desired were obtained by cultivating with a minimum of labor the largest possible acreage planted in the most imme-

War added further impetus, in the form of labor shortages and inflation of product prices, for farmers to adopt mechanical technology.

In an economic environment characterized by a strong demand for labor-saving mechanical technology, the industrial sector responded by introducing a continuous stream of new mechanical equipment. Advances in the design and diffusion of tillage, seeding, and harvesting equipment resulted in a system of agriculture based on "horse mechanization," even though mechanization of motive power was not developed until introduction of the tractor (see Figure 3-1). The introduction of wire fencing sharply reduced the cost of enclosing the western lands and the conversion from a grazing to a crop agriculture.[16]

During the nineteenth century the process by which new mechanical and other industrial inputs were generated by the private industrial sector appeared to be relatively consistent with the demand for progress in mechanical technology by the agricultural sector. The typical process by which new mechanical technology was introduced involved initial invention and production by innovating farmers, inventors, mechanics, or small machinery firms. After demonstration of the technical feasibility and market potential, the production rights were typically acquired by larger firms, which proceeded to make further engineering improvements and adapt the design to the requirements of mass production and distribution.[17]

The patent system provided sufficient protection to induce inventors and manufacturers to undertake the research and development costs necessary to introduce a continuous stream of new industrial inputs designed to bring more land into cultivation and to reduce labor requirements per unit area.[18]

---

diately valuable crops. ... Most farms were established with acreages that required many years to bring into cultivation, and as long as virgin land remained available, the breaking of new land was the reaction to declining fertility" (p. 252). "Among those who did attempt to apply fertility conservation and renovating techniques, many found returns inadequate, so that they too joined the search for new lands" (p. 253).

[16] Earl W. Hayter, "Barbed Wire Fencing—A Prairie Invention; Its Rise and Influence in the Western States," *Agricultural History* 13 (October 1939): 189–207.

[17] See Walter Prescott Webb, *The Great Plains* (Boston: Ginn and Company, 1931), pp. 295–318, for a history of the farmer invention of the barbed wire fence, the litigation over patent rights, and the final monopolization of barbed wire production by a subsidiary of U.S. Steel. For a more recent example see James H. Street, "Mechanizing the Cotton Harvest," *Agricultural History* 31 (January 1957): 12–22.

[18] "The patent system raises the returns to invention and innovation by increasing the costs and difficulties of imitation. It makes private property out of what otherwise would, in the absence of secrecy, be in the public domain." Richard R. Nelson, Merton J. Peck, and Edward D. Kalachek, *Technology, Economic Growth, and Public Policy* (Washington: The Brookings Institution, 1967), p. 160. Nelson et al., also point out that "broadening of the incentive to invent is one of the most important social benefits of the patent system. These benefits do not come without cost. ... the patent system involves a transfer of income from the general public or a subgroup of the public to successful innovators. ... Rather than tapping public tax revenues, the patent system effects the income transfer by granting the inventor a monopoly right. ... It is in the social interest that existing knowledge be free for use wherever it may be of positive social value. In contrast, it is in the interest of a particular producer to limit the use of knowledge so as to give it a scarcity value" (pp. 161, 162).

By the beginning of the twentieth century the earlier consistency between the pattern of technical change generated in the industrial sector and the growth requirements of American agriculture was breaking down. The rate of growth in labor productivity was beginning to decline, growth of total productivity was turning negative, and the rate of growth of agricultural output fell below the rate of growth in demand. Prices of agricultural products were beginning to rise relative to the general price level. In spite of a continued flow of new mechanical technology, U.S. agriculture appeared to be entering a period of diminishing returns consistent with the classical model of economic development. These changes set the stage for a dramatic increase in investment in public sector agricultural research and for advances in biological technology.

Setting the Stage for Advances in Biological Technology, 1860-1920

The institutionalization of public sector responsibility for research in the agricultural sciences and technology in the United States can be dated from the 1860's. The Act of May 15, 1862, "establishing the United States Department of Agriculture" and the Act of July 2, 1862, "donating public lands to the several states and territories which may provide colleges for the benefit of American agriculture and the mechanic arts" became the first federal legal authority under which a nationwide agricultural research system was to develop.

The institutional pattern that emerged for the organization of agricultural research drew heavily on the German experience.[19] As noted earlier, a tradition of public support for research laboratories and agricultural experiment stations had been established in Germany in the 1850's. A number of the leaders in the movement to establish state experiment stations had studied in Germany, and there was a substantial traffic of young Americans to European, particularly German, centers of study for graduate education in the fields of agricultural science. The results of foreign training were, however, not unlike those observed in many underdeveloped countries today. "European professors were puzzled by American students who, after beginning well abroad, lapsed into mediocrity upon returning home. And one recalls cases in which Americans, inspired by European science, actually began to make basic contributions; but never went on to a fulfillment of the potentialities so revealed."[20]

In institutionalizing agricultural research the United States created a dual

---

[19] Knoblauch, *State Agricultural Experiment Stations*. The role of Samuel W. Johnson of the Yale Analytical Laboratory was particularly significant. "Samuel W. Johnson spent a lifetime searching for the most effective ways to institutionalize research in agriculture. . . . . he studied science in German laboratories and personally observed the German experiment station movement in its infancy. He became America's first advocate calling for a similar movement in the United States" (p. 14).

[20] Richard Harrison Shryock, "American Indifference to Basic Science During the Nineteenth Century," *The Sociology of Science*, ed. Bernard Barber and Walter Hirsch (New

federal-state system. The federal system developed more rapidly than the state system. Yet it was not until the later years of the nineteenth century that the U.S. Department of Agriculture achieved any significant capacity to provide the scientific knowledge needed to deal with urgent problems of agricultural development. The emergence of a viable pattern of organization, toward the end of the century, involved breaking away from a discipline-oriented pattern of organization and the organization of scientific bureaus focusing on a particular set of problems or commodities.[21] Dupree cites the Bureau of Animal Industry, established in 1884, as an example: "The Bureau of Animal Industry thus had most of the attributes of the new scientific agency at its birth—an organic act, a set of problems, outside groups pressing for its interests, and extensive regulatory powers."[22]

The capacity of the land-grant colleges to produce new scientific and technical knowledge for agricultural development was even more limited than the Department of Agriculture. The first state experiment station, the Connecticut State Agricultural Experiment Station, was not established until 1877. Prior to passage of the Hatch Act in 1887, which provided federal funding for the support of land-grant college experiment stations, only a few states were providing any significant financial support for agricultural research at the state level.[23]

It was well after the turn of the century before the new state experiment stations could be regarded as productive sources of new knowledge or significant contributors to productivity growth in U.S. agriculture.[24] And it was not until 1914, with the passage of the Smith-Lever Act, that a firm institutional basis, in the form of a co-operative federal-state extension service, was established for the educational functions of the Department of Agriculture and the land-grant colleges.[25] By the early 1920's a national agricultural

York: The Free Press of Glencoe, 1962), pp. 104–5. Shryock attributes this lack of accomplishment in basic science to orientation toward applied science which "seems to promise most for utility in the near future" (p. 110).

[21] ". . . the department gradually evolved an adequate social and political mechanism, the government bureau. . . . The ideal new scientific bureau had clearly defined characteristics. In the first place, the center of interest was a problem, not a scientific discipline. . . . Thus the ideal bureau chief sought continuity by means of a grant of power in the organic act of Congress. . . . In the second place, the ideal bureau aimed at a stable corps of scientific personnel which was not only competent but also loyal to the bureau and confident that its work was important to the country. . . . In the third place, the ideal bureau established as harmonious relations as possible with many groups outside itself," Dupree, *Science in the Federal Government*, pp. 158–59.

[22] Ibid., p. 165.

[23] Knoblauch, *State Agricultural Experiment Stations*, pp. 29–52. Prior to the passage of the Hatch Act in 1887 only four of the land-grant colleges had established experiment stations—California in 1880, Tennessee in 1882, Wisconsin in 1883, and Kentucky in 1885.

[24] Ibid., pp. 191–206.

[25] Prior to 1914, "the state experiment stations and colleges, along with the agricultural journals, had borne the brunt of extension work for many years in a disorganized way. . . . In 1914 the Smith-Lever Act put the Extension Service on a separate and permanent basis. One feature of the law was the '50–50' plan by which each federal dollar was matched by one from the states." Dupree, *Science in the Federal Government*, pp. 181, 182.

Table 7-1. Expenditures on agricultural research and extension in the United States (in millions of current dollars) 1880–1965

Year	Public extension	State experiment station research		U.S.D.A. research	Research by private industrial firms[a]	Agriculturally-related research[b]
		Fed. funds	Non-fed. funds			
1880	—	—	0.1	0.5		
1890	—	0.7	0.2	0.8		
1900	—	0.7	0.3	0.8		
1910	—	1.3	1.3	4		
1920	1.5	1.4	6	7		
1930	2.4	4	12	15		
1935	20	4	10	12		
1940	33	7	13	22		
1945	38	7	18	23		
1950	75	13	47	47		
1955	101	19	71	54		
1960	142	31	111	92	325	
1965	175	47	180	167	460	365

[a] The estimated expenditures for research by private firms for 1960 and 1965 are the only estimates available for this effort. The 1960 estimate includes some agriculturally related research.

[b] Research indirectly related to agriculture. This includes research by private foundations and non-land-grant universities.

Source: Robert E. Evenson, *The Contribution of Agricultural Research and Extension to Agricultural Production* (Ph.D. dissertation, University of Chicago, 1968), p. 3.

research and extension system had been effectively institutionalized at both the federal and state levels.

In reviewing the history of the previous sixty years, the appropriate question is not what had the system contributed to the growth of agricultural production and productivity but why had it contributed so little? There are several answers. In total, federal and state expenditures on agricultural research were less than $2.0 million in 1900 and less than $15 million in 1920 (Table 7-1). But why, in spite of more than half a century of effort, had the evolution of public sector investment in agricultural research proceeded so slowly? The answer must be sought in the same conditions that induced the rapid development of mechanical technology in American agriculture before 1900. Neither movements in relative factor prices nor factor-product price ratios were such as to induce yield-increasing innovations or the adoption of available yield-increasing technology until the closing years of the nineteenth century.

Progress in Biological Science and Technology—The Case of Corn Improvement

The institutional innovations in the organization of public sector agricultural research, development, and extension between 1860 and 1920 proved capable, during the 1920–65 period, of absorbing new resources at a relatively rapid rate and of generating rapid growth in new scientific and technical knowledge. By and large, the private sector had contributed little to advances in biological technology. Similarly, public sector agricultural research institutions were much more effective in generating advances in biological (or biological and chemical) technology than in generating advances in mechanical technology. In this section we devote special attention to the institutional aspects of technical advance in corn production.

Corn (maize) has occupied a unique role in U.S. agricultural development from colonial times to the present. It was indigenous to the Americas at the time of their discovery. Maize culture represented the agricultural basis for the pre-Columbian civilization. In the United States it has, in the past, occupied an important role as both a food grain for human consumption and as a feed grain for work animals. It is valued today, however, primarily as a feed grain for meat animals.

In 1960 corn accounted for more than three-fifths of the total energy production from the basic food and feed crops produced in the U.S.[26] It occupied an even more dominant role in 1870. After 1870 corn production increased rapidly to the mid-1920's, declined from 1925 to 1937, and rose rapidly again after 1937 (see Figure 7-1). Between 1870 and the mid-1920's corn yields per acre remained essentially unchanged at approximately twenty-seven bushels per acre. From the early 1920's until the end of the drought years of the 1930's national average corn yields actually declined.

The first third of the twentieth century was clearly a period of relative stagnation in corn production. Increases in acreage, which had sustained growth in output in the nineteenth century, were no longer an important source of growth after 1900. The growth of demand pressed against supply. Corn prices, which had started to rise relative to the general price level in the 1880's, rose dramatically between 1900 and 1920. James O. Bray and Patricia Watkins have argued that the declining yield trend, despite the movement toward better land, "suggests that increases in the total production of corn between 1870 and 1937 were, to a large degree, brought about by fertility-depleting operations. Capital in soil fertility was transformed into animals and machines which, in turn, enabled the process to be accelerated. . . . After the beginning of the 20th century, the effectiveness of further improvements in extractive techniques began to be restricted by the fertility barrier."[27] The evidence from corn yields during the first third of the twentieth century clearly supported the view of the English classical economists concerning diminishing returns to additional "doses" of land and labor.

By the mid-1920's, however, three developments were beginning to call into question the implications of projections based on the classical model. These

[26] James O. Bray and Patricia Watkins, "Technical Change in Corn Production in the United States, 1870–1960," *Journal of Farm Economics* 46 (November 1964): 751–65.

[27] Ibid., pp. 760–61.

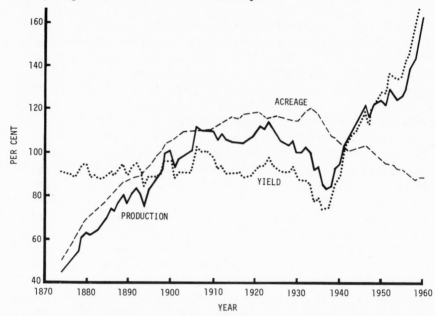

FIGURE 7-1. U.S. acreage, yield, and production of corn, 1870–1960. Index numbers of five-year moving average; 100 = period mean for each series. (*Source:* James O. Bray and Patricia Watkins, "Corn Production in the United States, 1870–1960," *Journal of Farm Economics* 46 [November 1964]: 753).

included: (a) mechanization of motive power; (b) the invention of hybrid corn; and (c) sharply declining real costs in the production of commercial fertilizer.

The critical significance of the mechanization of motive power—the substitution of tractors for horses—was that it sharply reduced the demand for corn and other feed grains as an energy source for draft power.[28] Feed accounted for approximately three-fourths of the cost of maintaining horses.[29] As "tractorization" continued it also released the constraints on labor productivity imposed by farm production of power and fuel in the form of horses and feed grains, and on the size of equipment imposed by the capacity of horse-powered machines.

Increasingly intensive efforts to improve corn yields through the selection and the diffusion of the best varieties produced by farmers and commercial

[28] The effects of this change on productivity have been described by Sherman E. Johnson, *Changes in American Farming* (Washington: U.S. Department of Agriculture Misc. Pub. No. 707, December 1949).

[29] Naum Jasny, "Tractor versus Horse as a Source of Farm Power: Their Competition in Various Countries of the World," *Agricultural Economic Review* 25 (December 1935): 708–23. According to Jasny, substitution of tractors for horses was affected by the relative prices of feed and fuel, the relative prices of horses and tractors, the price of labor, and the number of horses or tractor days of work per horse or per tractor per year.

"seedmen" and the efforts to develop more effective cultivation practices were made by the land-grant college experiment stations and extension services and the U.S. Bureau of Plant Industry after 1900.[30] These efforts had little impact on yield at the farm level until the introduction of hybrid varieties in the 1920's and 1930's.

The development of hybrid corn has been characterized as the most significant contribution in applied biology in the first half of the twentieth century.[31] It involved not one, but several, inventions. These included the crossing techniques for producing hybrid corn plants developed by William Beal at the Michigan Agricultural Experiment Station; the studies of inheritance by George H. Schull at the Carnegie Institution, which led to the understanding of the theoretical basis for hybrid vigor; and the invention by Donald Jones at the Connecticut Agricultural Experiment Station of the double-cross method of mass seed production. Jones also made a second important contribution by presenting a genetic interpretation of hybrid vigor.

The work by Beal was completed before the turn of the century; Schull presented his results in papers published in 1908 and 1909; Jones's work was conducted between 1915–17. According to Paul C. Mangelsdorf, "hybrid corn was transformed from Schull's magnificent design to the practical reality it now is when Jones' method of seed production made it feasible and his theory of hybrid vigor made it plausible."[32] By the early 1920's hybrid corn breeding programs were initiated in many states; by the 1930's hybrid corn was in commercial production on a substantial scale; and by 1950 more than three-fourths of the total corn acreage in the United States was planted to hybrid corn.

The production of commercial varieties of hybrid corn involves three complex steps:[33] (a) isolation of inbred lines; (b) testing of inbred lines in various crossing combinations to determine their hybrid performance; and (c) combining the selected inbred lines to produce commercial hybrid seed. Because second-generation progeny of a hybrid decline markedly in yield, the farmer cannot save his own seed but must buy new hybrid seed each season. Furthermore, hybrid corn varieties must be individually "tailored" to a particular environment. The primary factors limiting geographic adaptability are varietal

---

[30] The efforts made in Illinois and Iowa have been carefully documented in Martin L. Mosher, *Early Iowa Corn Yield Tests and Related Later Programs* (Ames: Iowa State University Press, 1962).

[31] Paul C. Mangelsdorf, "Hybrid Corn," *Scientific American* 185 (August 1951): 39–47. The basic reference on the biological aspects of corn improvement is George F. Sprague, ed., *Corn and Corn Improvement* (New York: Academic Press, 1955). For more personal accounts see Herbert Kendall Hayes, *A Professor's Study of Hybrid Corn* (Minneapolis: Burgess Publishing Co., 1963) and A. Richard Crabb, *The Hybrid Corn Makers: Prophets of Plenty* (New Brunswick: Rutgers University Press, 1947).

[32] Mangelsdorf, "Hybrid Corn," p. 42.

[33] Ibid., p. 43; H. D. Hughes, "Introduction," to Crabb, *Hybrid Corn Makers*, pp. xv–xxv.

sensitivity to temperature and to "photo-period" (flowering is triggered by day length). These factors limit adaptability in a north-south direction but not necessarily in an east-west direction. Other ecological factors, such as rainfall and pathogens, combine to make most hybrid corn varieties relatively "location specific."

The development of hybrid corn, therefore, represents an "invention of a method of inventing" varieties adapted to each growing region, rather than the invention of varieties that can then be diffused from the original location through normal marketing and extension education processes.[34] As a result, the successful development and diffusion of commercial hybrid corn varieties was characterized by the evolution of an increasingly complex research, development, distribution, and educational system involving close co-operation among public sector research and extension agencies, a series of public, semi-public, and co-operative foundation seed-producing organizations, and private sector research and marketing agencies.[35,36]

Entry of the private sector into the development and marketing of new hybrid corn varieties was encouraged by the complex technology of seed production. The existence of proprietary lines of superior inbred lines provided a protection to the innovating firm, similar to the protection afforded to mechanical inventions by the patent system.[37] As a result, the private sector has come to play a more significant role in the development of new hybrid corn varieties than in most other areas of crop improvement. By the mid-1950's the private sector had become the dominant source of new hybrid corn research, although inbred lines released by the experiment stations continued to be of great importance to the hybrid seed industry. Griliches estimated that as of 1955 the U.S. Department of Agriculture had spent approximately $300,000, the state agricultural experiment station $650,000, and the private seed companies $1,900,000 on hybrid corn research.[38] The expanded role of the private sector in varietal improvement and in the production and distribution of seed resulted in the allocation of much larger resources to the effort to achieve corn yield increases, than if the effort had been confined primarily to the public sector.

[34] Zvi Griliches, " 'Hybrid Corn': An Exploration in the Economics of Technological Change," *Econometrica* 25 (October 1957): 501–22.

[35] Albert H. Moseman, *Building Agricultural Research Systems in the Developing Nations* (New York: Agricultural Development Council Inc., 1970).

[36] Crabb, *Hybrid Corn Makers*. See also Griliches, " 'Hybrid Corn': An Exploration"; and Hayes, *A Professor's Study of Hybrid Corn*.

[37] There has been considerable discussion among plant breeders of the need for more formal incentives comparable to patent protection. See S. O. Fejer, "The Problem of Plant Breeders' Rights," *Agricultural Science Review* (Third Quarter 1966): 1–7. See also the testimony presented at the Hearing before the Subcommittee on Agricultural Research and General Legislation of the Committee on Agriculture and Forestry, United States Senate, 91st Congress, Second Session, on S.3070, June 11, 1970 (Washington: USGPO, 1970).

[38] Zvi Griliches, "Research Costs and Social Returns: Hybrid Corn and Related Innovations," *Journal of Political Economy* 66 (October 1958): 419–31.

By introducing a significant shift up and to the right along the metaproduction function in the yield-response curve, the use of both higher levels of fertilizer and higher levels of management became profitable (see pp. 83–85). There has, almost since the introduction of hybrid corn, been a continuing argument regarding the relative contribution of the new varieties themselves, as compared to the contribution of higher levels of fertilization and advances in the level of crop management. According to D. Gale Johnson and Robert L. Gustafson, the corn yield increase between 1920–29 and 1946–54 was due, in approximately equal proportions, to seed improvement, higher levels of fertilization, and increase in mechanization.[39] Lawrence H. Shaw and Donald D. Durost indicate that the main variables involved in increases in corn yields since 1950 are higher levels of nitrogen fertilization and increased plant population per acre.[40] Prior to the introduction of hybrid corn, intensive efforts to induce farmers to utilize fertilizer and advanced management practices were relatively unsuccessful. Recent corn improvement work has been directed to the development of varieties that are increasingly efficient in energy and nutrient conversion. The higher levels of fertilization and the higher plant populations would not have been profitable in the absence of varietal improvement, and the higher yield ceilings associated with the improved hybrids have made it profitable to develop and adopt more effective plant protection materials and practices.

It is clear that the technical changes in fertilizer production and marketing did lead to a substantial decline in the real price of fertilizer relative to the price of corn and relative to the price of land.[41] This decline in the price of fertilizer, together with the shift in the fertilizer-response curve resulting from the new hybrids, resulted in the corn yield explosion of 1940–70 (see Figure 7–1). Furthermore, we would hypothesize that the advances in fertilizer technology were themselves induced, at least in part, by the same technical and economic forces that led to the introduction of hybrid corn. Both were part of the effort to overcome the technical stagnation in corn production and the

[39] D. Gale Johnson and Robert L. Gustafson, *Grain Yields and the American Food Supply: An Analysis of Yield Changes and Possibilities* (Chicago: University of Chicago Press, 1962), p. 92. See also Bray and Watkins, "Technical Change in Corn Production," p. 761.

[40] Lawrence H. Shaw and Donald D. Durost, *The Effect of Weather and Technology on Corn Yields in the Corn Belt, 1929–62* (Washington: U.S. Department of Agriculture, Economic Research Service, Agricultural Economic Report No. 80, July 1965).

[41] The contribution of technical change in fertilizer production and distribution to the decline in the price of fertilizer relative to other input and product prices has been documented by S. G. Sahota, "The Sources of Measured Productivity Growth: United States Fertilizer Mineral Industries, 1936–1960," *Review of Economics and Statistics* 48 (May 1966): 193–203; Gian S. Sahota, *Fertilizer in Economic Development: An Econometric Analysis* (New York: Praeger, 1968). Between 1936 and 1960 the price of fertilizer declined by 52 percent relative to the GNP implicit price deflator. Of this total decline (a) 26 percent was accounted for by productivity increases in the fertilizer sector; (b) 12 percent by increased competition; and (c) 10 percent by decline in the price of inputs used by the fertilizer industry.

rising relative prices of corn, and of agricultural commodities generally, in the latter part of the nineteenth and early part of the twentieth centuries.

Public sector research played an important role in the evolution of fertilizer technology and in the diffusion of fertilizer use. The National Fertilizer Development Center operated by the Tennessee Valley Authority has been an important source of new knowledge of the physical and chemical properties of fertilizer materials, of soil-fertilizer-plant relationships, and of new technology in the field of process engineering.[42] There is also evidence that public sector fertilizer research has contributed to the decline in the real price of fertilizers to farmers through efforts to maintain and strengthen competition in the fertilizer industry.[43]

Agricultural Research Productivity and Priorities

It is only during the last two decades that quantitative measures of the supply, demand, and productivity of public sector agricultural research have become available. In the early 1950's total productivity data, such as that presented in Chapter 6 (Table 6–2), became available, indicating that less than half of the recent increases in agricultural output in the United States was accounted for by growth in inputs.[44] These were followed by a series of studies designed to measure the returns to public sector investment in agricultural research in hybrid corn, sorghum, poultry, and other individual commodities. These studies, typically, indicated exceptionally high rates of returns or cost benefit ratios (Table 3–1).

Robert E. Evenson's comprehensive study also provides considerable insight into the time and spatial dimensions of research productivity.[45] His data indicate a median time lag between research investment and impact on production of approximately five to eight years. The total lag between investment and the production impact represents a combination of three separate lags. These include (a) the lag between expenditure of research funds and economically relevant discoveries of new knowledge; (b) the lag between the

[42] Tennessee Valley Authority, *The TVA Fertilizer Program* (Knoxville: Tennessee Valley Authority, September 1965).

[43] Jesse W. Markham, *The Fertilizer Industry* (Nashville: The Vanderbilt University Press, 1958). Vernon W. Ruttan, "Positive Policy in the Fertilizer Industry," *Journal of Political Economy* 68 (February 1960): 634.

[44] Glen T. Barton and Martin R. Cooper, "Relation of Agricultural Production to Inputs," *Review of Economics and Statistics* 30 (May 1948): 117–26; Theodore W. Schultz, *Economic Organization of Agriculture* (New York: McGraw-Hill, 1953), pp. 99–124; Vernon W. Ruttan, "The Contribution of Technological Progress to Farm Output: 1950–75," *Review of Economics and Statistics* 38 (February 1956): 61–69.

[45] Robert Eugene Evenson, *The Contribution of Agricultural Research and Extension to Agricultural Production* (University of Chicago, Department of Economics, Ph.D. thesis, 1968). Robert E. Evenson, "Economic Aspects of the Organization of Agricultural Research," *Resource Allocation in Agricultural Research*, ed. Walter L. Fishel (Minneapolis: University of Minnesota Press, forthcoming, 1971).

discovery of new knowledge and the adoption of the new inputs or techniques embodying this new knowledge by the producer; and (c) a depreciation or obsolescence effect. This obsolescence effect will be positively related to the rate at which new knowledge is provided which renders obsolete old practices and inputs.

Evenson's results are also consistent with the proposition that differences in the rate of growth in agricultural output among states are influenced by differences in research expenditure.[46] Thus, while much agricultural research is clearly "pervasive,"—with an impact on agricultural output in other states —it is, on balance, sufficiently "location specific" to influence state economic growth. These results suggest that the demand for the results of agricultural research is rationally shared by the entire agribusiness complex of a state. The agricultural supply, production, and marketing sectors share in the effects of differential growth in agricultural output resulting from public sector investment in research and extension. In addition the multiplier effects of income generated in the agricultural and agribusiness sectors result in a substantial spillover into growth in demand for the consumer goods and service industries.

The results of the studies focusing on the returns to public sector investment are consistent with the induced development model. Public sector investment in agricultural research in the U.S. has grown rapidly since the 1920's, in response to the high rates of return flowing from such investment. Furthermore, the resources allocated to agricultural research, at least at the state level, have borne a close relationship to the perceived distribution of returns from such investment.

There are two major unresolved issues that will face the United States agricultural research system as it continues to evolve. One issue centers around the bias in the direction of research activity induced by the price and resource use distortions of the agricultural commodity programs of the 1950's and 1960's. It is clear that these programs have not only distorted resource use at the farm level they have also induced distortions in the allocation of research resources.

[46] Latimer and Paarlberg had earlier presented data indicating that the knowledge generated by the state experiment stations was highly pervasive and did not exert a differential impact on state output. Robert Latimer and Don Paarlberg, "Geographic Distribution of Research Costs and Benefits," *Journal of Farm Economics* 47 (May 1965): 234–41. Dalrymple has indicated, however, that the results presented in the *Journal of Farm Economics* article are inconsistent with one of the models employed by Latimer in his thesis. See Dana G. Dalrymple, "Public Investment in Agricultural Research and Education: Some Comments," ibid. 47 (November 1965): 1020–22. In addition to Evenson's work, evidence is presented in two other studies which indicate a differential impact of research and education on agricultural output at the state level; Zvi Griliches, "Research Expenditures, Education, and the Aggregate Agricultural Production Function," *American Economic Review* 54 (December 1964): 961–74; and T. D. Wallace and D. M. Hoover, "Income Effects of Innovation: The Case of Labor in Agriculture," *Journal of Farm Economics* 48 (May 1966): 325–36.

The point is illustrated by an example from research on tobacco.[47] Throughout most of the history of the tobacco program, the price of flue-cured tobacco was maintained by land-use controls which sharply limited the acreage an individual farmer could plant to tobacco and raised the price of land with tobacco allotments.[48] During the period of acreage controls plant breeders, agronomists, and research workers directed their activity to improving yields in response to the institutionally determined "scarcity" of land on which tobacco could be grown. The result was a dramatic increase in yield per acre. The new high-yielding tobacco varieties were, however, typically inferior in quality to the older varieties. The result was excessive accumulation by the government of low quality tobacco. In 1965 quantitative marketing controls were substituted for acreage controls. This led to a shift in emphasis by farmers away from practices designed to increase yields and toward practices designed to improve quality. It also led to a shift in emphasis by tobacco breeders to the development of varieties characterized by higher quality rather than higher yields. In North Carolina, where most flue-cured tobacco is produced, the aggregate effect of the change in policy has been a decline in the average yield and an increase in average quality.

Other illustrations could also be presented of the distortions in the allocation of research resources by the agricultural programs which have made land a relatively "scarce" factor of production. In the United States the effect has been to induce agricultural scientists, in both public and private sector research institutions, to place greater stress on land-saving innovations than would appear consistent with resource endowments. As a result, both market price relationships and an induced bias in technical innovations have contributed to the substitution of industrial inputs for land. The convergence toward the Japanese pattern of resource use has, therefore, been somewhat more rapid than if price ratios accurately reflected relative resource endowments and product demand.

A second major issue centers around the future role of the public and the private sector as sources of new knowledge and new inputs in American agriculture. New scientific and technical knowledge is increasingly available to the farmer in the form of inputs purchased from the industrial sector. This is now characteristic of the significant number of biological inputs—new varieties of hybrid corn, higher analysis fertilizer, and more efficient animal

---

[47] This information is based on material provided to the authors by Professor James Seagraves, Department of Agricultural Economics, North Carolina State University, Raleigh, North Carolina, March 1970.

[48] For evidence on the impact of the tobacco program on land values see W. L. Gibson, Jr., C. J. Arnold, and F. D. Aigner, *The Marginal Value of Flue-Cured Tobacco Allotments* (Blacksburg: Virginia Agricultural Exeriment Station Technical Bulletin No. 156, January 1962); Frank H. Maier, James L. Hendrick, and W. L. Gibson, Jr., *The Sale Value of Flue-Cured Tobacco Allotments* (Blacksburg: Virginia Agricultural Experiment Station Technical Bulletin No. 148, April 1960).

feeds—as well as the inputs associated with mechanical technology. As a result, a smaller share of the new knowledge is channeled to the farmer directly from the agricultural experiment station or extension service. The ability to embody the new knowledge in the form of inputs which can be sold directly to the farmer by the industrial sector has acted to induce increases in research investment in the production of new biological technology by the private sector. By the mid-1960's approximately half of the agricultural research expenditures in the United States were being made by the private sector (Table 7-1).

A major implication of this development is that if investment in public sector agriculture research is to continue to produce a relatively high rate of return, resources must be shifted away from the applied end of the spectrum and toward the more basic end. There are two concerns in a system in which applied research and development is concentrated in the private sector and basic research in the public sector institutions. One is the bias in private sector research toward innovations which can be embodied in the form of proprietary products. A second concern centers on the possible reduction in the effectiveness of information flows and resource allocation as compared to a system in which extension, development, applied research, and basic research are combined within a single administrative system. As the relative role of the private sector as a source of biological technology continues to expand, institutional innovations to provide more effective linkages between public and private sector research will become increasingly important.

SCIENCE AND TECHNOLOGY IN JAPANESE AGRICULTURE[49]

Until shortly before the beginning of the Meiji Period (1868–1911), Japan had been isolated from the influence of western technology for more than two centuries.[50] Because of the real danger of colonization by the western powers, quick acquisition of western technology and industrial productivity was regarded as of utmost urgency. Progress in education, science, and technology was viewed, as in Germany, as an effective instrument of national progress.

---

[49] This section heavily depends on Nogyo Hattat Sushi Chosakai (Research Committee for the History of Agricultural Development), *Nihon Nogyo Hattat Sushi* (History of Japanese Agricultural Development), 10 volumes (Tokyo: Chuokoronsha, 1953–1958): henceforth abbreviated as NNHS. Its abbreviated edition is Seizo Yasuda, ed., *Meiji Iko ni Okeru Nogyo Gijutsu no Hattatsu* (Progress of Agricultural Technology since Meiji) (Tokyo: Nogyo Gijutsu Kyokai, 1952). English readers may refer to Takekazu Ogura, ed., *Agricultural Development in Modern Japan* (Tokyo: Fuji Publishing Co., Ltd., 1963).

[50] Interest in western science by Japanese intellectuals had, however, developed rapidly during the last century of the Tokagawa period. See Donald Keene, *The Japanese Discovery of Europe, 1720–1830* (rev., Stanford: Stanford University Press, 1969). In spite of their isolation Keene argues that, "by the end of the eighteenth century the Japanese were better acquainted with European civilization than the people of any other non-western country" (p. 123).

Productivity growth in agriculture, the dominant sector of the economy, was required not only to contribute to social welfare by increasing the consumers' surplus but also was essential to finance industrialization and various modernization measures.

Leaders of the new Meiji government felt this need keenly. Partly because the need was so urgent and partly because they were impressed by the superiority of western industrial technology, their first attempt to develop agriculture was the direct importation of the large-scale farm machinery and implements employed in England and the United States. It was natural for the Meiji leaders, reasoning from the analogy with industrial technology, to identify western agricultural technology as modern large-scale farm machines. This identification was not unique to Japanese leaders.

In 1870 Hirotumi Ito (later to be a prime minister) brought back from the U.S. 700 dollars worth of farm machinery. In order to exhibit the new machines, and the ones to be imported later, the Western Farm Machinery Exhibition Yard was opened in 1871 in Tsukiji, Tokyo. The operations of the machines were demonstrated at the Naito Shinjuku Agricultural Station (set up in 1873). In 1879 the Mita Farm Machinery Manufacturing Plant was established to produce farm machinery modeled after the imported models.

The government also invited instructors from Britain to the newly opened Komaba Agricultural School (founded in 1877 and redesignated the University of Tokyo, College of Agriculture, in 1890), and from the U.S. to the Sapporo Agricultural School (in 1875) which was designed to develop the last frontier, Hokkaido.[51] The curriculum at the new agricultural colleges was based on the same view of the requirements for agricultural development that led to the importation of Anglo-American mechanical technology.

This trial represented one example of the broad effort to borrow agricultural and industrial technology from the western world. But, unlike the case in industry, this trial was entirely unsuccessful, except in Hokkaido. The factor endowments in Japanese agriculture (average arable land area per worker of less than 0.5 hectare) were simply incompatible with the large-scale machinery of the Anglo-American type. A farmer, observing the imported machinery, remarked, "these machines may be applicable in the vast area as in Hokkaido, but it would be as if a camel were to dress in the hide of an elephant to use them in the small patches of land as in our region."[52] While the importation of modern industrial machinery, as in the Tomioka Model Silk Reeling Plant, led to the modern industrial development, the importation of farm machinery completely failed to provide a momentum for agricultural development.[53]

---

[51] John A. Harrison, "The Capron Mission and the Colonization of Hokkaido, 1868–1875," *Agricultural History* 25 (April 1951): 135–42.

[52] *NNHS*, vol. 2, p. 114.

[53] The government also tried to transplant foreign plants and livestock. The Mita Botanical Experiment Yard (1874), the Shimofusa Sheep Farm (1875), the Kobe Olive Farm

The teaching of the British instructors at the Komaba School was equally ineffective. Kizo Tamari, a first graduate of the Komaba School and later a professor at the University of Tokyo, recollected in his memorial lecture, ". . . instructions concerning agronomy were based on the extensive livestock farming in England and hardly applicable to the real problems of Japan. . . . How could one translate such words as 'plow,' 'harrow,' 'furrow,' and 'rotation'? First of all, did such things even exist in Japan?"[54]

Rationalization of Indigenous Techniques

The Meiji government quickly perceived the failure of the attempt to develop a mechanized agriculture of the Anglo-American type and redirected its agricultural development policy toward the search for a modern technology compatible with the factor endowments of Japanese economy.

In 1881, as soon as the contracts of the British agricultural instructors at the Komaba School were completed they were replaced by a German agricultural chemist (Oskar Kellner) and a German soil scientist (Max Fesca). The curriculum of agricultural education in Japan was reorganized to place primary emphasis on German agricultural chemistry and soil science of the von Liebig tradition.

The facilities for the demonstration of the Western machinery, plants, and livestock were largely discontinued during the 1880's. The newly founded Ministry of Agriculture and Commerce (1881) established an Itinerant Instructor System in 1885, in which the instructors traveled throughout the country holding agricultural extension meetings. The government employed as instructors not only the graduates of the Komaba School but also veteran farmers (*rōnō*), in order to combine the best practical farming experience with the new scientific knowledge of the inexperienced college graduates. In contrast with the earlier emphasis on the direct transplanting of western technology, the itinerant instruction system was designed to diffuse the best seed varieties already in use by Japanese farmers and the most productive cultural practices used in the production of Japan's traditional staple crops, rice and barley. In order to provide better information for the itinerant lecturers, the Experiment Farm for Staple Cereals and Vegetables was set up in 1886. In 1893 the experimental farm at Nishigarhara was further strengthened and designated the National Agricultural Experiment Station, with six branches over the nation. The itinerant instruction system was subsequently absorbed into the program of the National Agricultural Experiment Station.

The initial research conducted at the Experiment Farm for Staple Crops and Vegetables and at the National Agricultural Experiment Station was primarily at the applied end of the research spectrum. The major projects

---

(1877), and the Harima Grape Farm (1880) represent such trials. This effort also failed because the importation was not selective and there was no adequate basis of adaptive research.

[54] *NNHS*, vol. 9, p. 761.

were simple field experiments comparing the various varieties of seeds or various husbandry techniques (for example, checkrow planting of rice seedlings versus irregular planting). Facilities, personnel, and, above all, the state of knowledge did not permit conducting research beyond simple comparative experiments.

Nevertheless, such experiments provided a basis for the rapid growth of agricultural productivity during the latter years of the Meiji period. This was because of the existence of substantial indigenous technological potential which could be further tested, developed, and refined at the new experiment stations, combined with a strong propensity to innovate among farmers with whom the research workers interacted effectively.

During the 300 years of the Tokugawa period preceding the Meiji Restoration farmers were subject to the strong constraints of feudalism. Personal behavior and economic activity were highly structured within a hierarchical system of social organization. Farmers were bound to their land and were, in general, not allowed to leave their village except for such pilgrimages as the Ise-Mairi (the Pilgrimage to the Ise Grand Shine). Neither were they free to choose what crops to plant nor to choose what varieties of seeds to sow. Barriers which divided the nation into feudal estates actively discouraged communication. In many cases, feudal lords prohibited the export of improved seeds or cultural methods from their territories. Under such conditions diffusion of superior seeds and husbandry techniques from one region to another was severely limited. Although the Tokugawa period was characterized by significant growth in agricultural productivity, Japanese agriculture entered the Meiji period with a substantial backlog of unexploited indigenous technology.[55]

With the reforms of the Meiji Restoration such feudal restraints were removed. Farmers were free to choose what crops to plant, what seeds to sow, and what techniques to practice. Nationwide communication was facilitated with the introduction of modern postal service and railroads. The cost of information diffusion concerning new technology was greatly reduced. The land tax reform, which granted a fee simple title to the farmers and transformed a feudal share crop tax to a fixed rate cash tax, increased the farmers' incentive to innovate.

The farmers, especially of the *gōnō* class (landlords who personally farm part of their holdings), vigorously responded to such new opportunities. They

---

[55] Japanese agriculture "underwent notable technological (though not mechanical) changes long before the modern period. Between 1600 and 1850 a complex of such changes greatly increased the productivity of land, altered that of labor both in specific operations and over-all, and contributed to lasting changes in agrarian institutions. ... Few changes were the result of inventions; most resulted from the spread of known techniques from the localities in which they had been developed to areas where they were previously unknown or unused." Thomas C. Smith, *The Agrarian Origins of Modern Japan* (Stanford: Stanford University Press, 1959), p. 87.

voluntarily formed agricultural societies called *nodankai* (agricultural discussion society) and *hinshukokankai* (seed exchange society) and searched for higher pay-off techniques. Such rice production practices as use of salt water in seed selection, improved preparation and management of nursery beds, and checkrow planting were discovered by farmers and propagated by the itinerant instructors, and sometimes enforced by the sabers of the police. The major improved varieties of seeds, up to the end of the 1920's, were also the result of selections by veteran farmers. For example, the *Shinriki* variety, which was more widely diffused in the western half of Japan than any other single variety that has since been propagated, was selected in 1877 by Jujiro Maruo, a farmer in the Hyogo prefecture (the variety was called *Shinriki* meaning the "Power of God" by the farmers who were surprised by its high yield). Also, the *Kameno-o* variety, which was propagated widely and contributed greatly to stabilizing the rice yield in northern Japan, was selected in 1893 by Kameji Abe, a farmer in the Yamagata prefecture. The development and diffusion of these *rōnō* varieties were initiated within the western part of Japan, which includes the most advanced regions (Kinki and Northern Kyushu). Then this process was transmitted to the relatively backward eastern part of Japan (Figure 7–2).[56]

Experiment station research was successful in testing and refining the results of farmer innovations. The *rōnō* techniques (veteran farmers' techniques) were based on experiences in the specific localities where they originated. They tended to be location-specific and to require modification when transferred to other localities. Simple comparative tests effectively screened the *rōnō* techniques and varieties, thereby reducing greatly the cost of technical information for farmers. Slight modification or adaptations of indigenous techniques on the basis of experimental tests often gave them universal applicability. A good example is the technique of rice seed sorting in salt water. Jikei Yokoi, who later became a foremost leader of agriculture and agricultural science in Japan, found this technique practiced by farmers when he was a young instructor at a vocational agricultural school in the Fukuoka prefecture. After he perfected the technique and it was subjected to repeated tests at the national experiment station, it was propagated throughout Japan. It is interesting that a person like Yokoi, who advocated very strongly the superiority of modern agricultural science over the *rōnō* knowledge throughout his life, contributed to the propagation of the *rōnō* technique.

The techniques developed by veteran farmers were strongly constrained by the resources available to Japanese farmers. In Japan the major motivation was, of necessity, to increase land productivity. The success of agricultural productivity growth in the Meiji period was achieved by a reorientation of

[56] See Yujiro Hayami and Saburo Yamada, "Technological Progress in Agriculture," *Economic Growth: The Japanese Experience Since the Meiji Era*, ed. Lawrence Klein and Kazushi Ohkawa (Homewood, Illinois: Richard D. Irwin, Inc., 1968), pp. 135–61.

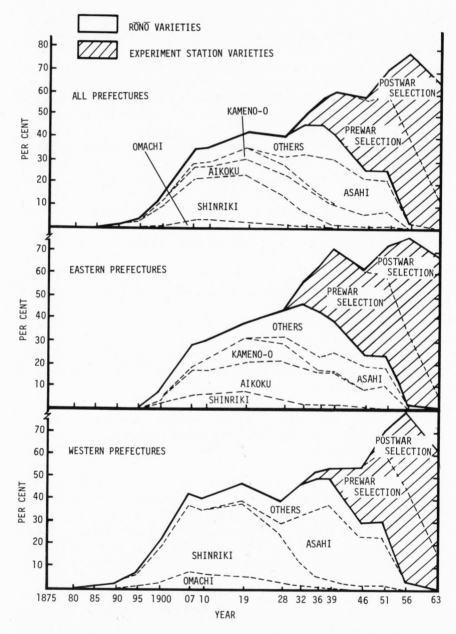

FIGURE 7–2. Changes in the percentage of area planted in improved varieties to total area planted in rice, Japan, 1875–1963. (*Source:* Yujiro Hayami and Saburo Yamada, "Technological Progress in Agriculture," *Economic Growth: The Japanese Experience Since the Meiji Era*, ed. L. R. Klein and Kazushi Ohkawa [Homewood, Illinois: Irwin, 1968], pp. 135–61.)

agricultural development policy toward the development of a technology suited to the resource endowment situation in Japan. Effective interaction between farmers and scientists was deliberately encouraged as part of the process of screening, adapting, and diffusing the best indigenous technology.

Another important element in the effective response of technical change to Japanese resource endowments was improvement in the supply of inputs which substitute for land, i.e., fertilizer. This depended on the progress in the intersectoral division of labor accompanying industrialization and economic growth. Agricultural suppliers, particularly fertilizer supply firms, perceived the pressing demand by farmers for land substitutes and exploited the opportunity. Improved efficiency in transportation, especially the introduction of the steamship, greatly reduced the cost of herring meals from Hokkaido. Search for a cheaper source of nitrogen brought about the enormous inflow of Manchurian soybean cake in the 1900's and 1910's.

The story of Kumejiro Tagi, founder of the Tagi Fertilizer Company, illustrates the interaction between farmers and agricultural supply firms. Tagi belonged to the *gōnō* class in the Hyogo prefecture where he owned eleven hectares of arable land, of which he cultivated a little less than a hectare himself. He also manufactured soya sauces as a family enterprise. Perceiving the strong demand for fertilizer and the rising price of sardine meals Tagi started the manufacture of bonemeal. Overcoming several difficulties, including the repulsion against animal bones among farmers and his employees due to the Buddhist tradition, he further expanded his enterprise during the fertilizer shortage of the Sino-Japanese War (1894–95) and developed it to become one of the largest producers of superphosphate of lime and mixed fertilizer. His vigorous extension and sales promotion activities, more than his engineering dexterity, have been identified as the secret of his success.[57]

The increasing demand for fertilizer induced innovations in the fertilizer industry. These innovations reduced the cost of fertilizer and induced further innovations of the fertilizer-using type in crop varieties and production. The history of seed improvement in Japan is a history of developing varieties that were increasingly more fertilizer-responsive. Varieties selected by *rōnō* in response to the inflow of cheap Manchurian soybean cakes (such as *Shinriki* and *Kameno-o*) were characterized by high fertilizer-responsiveness—varieties which did not easily lodge and were less susceptible to disease at higher levels of nitrogen application. Both economic logic and pressure from farmers pressed agricultural scientists to develop a technology geared to the high levels of fertilizer application and yield, the so-called "fertilizer consuming rice culture."[58] In this respect the discipline of agricultural chemistry and soil science of the German tradition was extremely effective.

---

[57] Nippon Kagakushi Gakkai, ed., *Nippon Kagaku Gijutsushi Taikei* (History of Japanese Science) vol. 22 (Tokyo: Daiichi Hoki Shuppan, 1967), pp. 383–85.
[58] Ogura, *Agricultural Development in Modern Japan*, pp. 365–77.

Through the dialectic interaction among farmers, scientists, and agricultural supply firms in response to relative factor prices which reflected Japan's resource endowments, Japan was able to evolve a unique and highly productive system of agricultural technology called *Meiji Noho* (Meiji Agricultural Technology).

Toward Scientific Maturity in Experiment Station Research

The high pay-off of simple applied agricultural research in the Meiji period was based on the backlog of indigenous technological potential previously dammed by the feudal constraints.[59] This potential was exhausted as it was exploited. In due course it became necessary for the research institutions to recharge the declining potential by conducting more sophisticated and basic research. By the beginning of this century the accumulation of human capital and scientific knowledge had approached the stage where such research could be initiated. In addition to the national system, the prefectures had gradually established their own experiment stations. This trend was encouraged by the Law of State Subsidy for Prefectural Agricultural Experiment Stations (1899), and in 1900, twelve new stations were set up, bringing the total number of prefectural stations to thirty-three. Those prefectural stations gradually accepted responsibility for conducting the more applied research tests and demonstrations. Agricultural associations organized under the Agricultural Association Law (1899) into a pyramidal structure, with the Imperial Agricultural Association on the top and village associations on the bottom, began to take on extension activities by employing agricultural technicians (the number of these extension workers grew to 5,200 in 1914, 10,000 in 1924, and 14,000 in 1933). Relieved of those activities, the National Experiment Station could now direct its resources towards more basic research.

Thus, for the first time, in 1904, the National Agricultural Experiment Station launched an original crop breeding project at the Kinai Branch with Koremochi Kato in charge of rice breeding. The objective of this project was to develop new seed varieties by cross breeding. It took almost two decades before new varieties of major practical significance were developed, though the project contributed greatly to the accumulation of experience and knowledge.[60] Another project was started in 1905 at the Rikuu Branch to improve rice varieties by pure line selection. This approach brought about quicker practical results. Thereafter the main efforts of crop breeding in the *Taisho* Era (1912–25) were directed to pure line selection.

Although scientific research gradually evolved into a major source of new

[59] See evidence in Hayami and Yamada, "Technical Progress"; also, Smith, *Agrarian Origins of Modern Japan.*

[60] The first variety of major practical significance developed by hybridization was the *Rikuu No. 132* (1922). This variety was characterized by the stronger cold weather resistance and replaced *Kameno-o* in Northern Japan.

biological technology, Japanese agriculture continued to rely heavily on *rōnō* techniques during the *Taisho* era and even into the early period of the *Showa* era (1926–present). Major rice varieties were still predominantly of *rōnō* selection. The *Asahi* variety, which substituted for *Shinriki* because of its high responsiveness to ammonium sulphate, was selected (1911) by Shinjiro Yamamoto, a farmer in Kyoto. The *Ginbozu* variety, which was propagated in the north central region because of its strong pest and insect resistance under the high application of nitrogen, was selected (1907) by Iwajiro Ishiguro in the Toyama prefecture. The pure line selection at the experiment stations was essentially a sophistication of *rōnō* varieties. It contributed to productivity growth through the exploitation of indigenous potential rather than creating new potential.

The exploitation and consequent exhaustion of indigenous potential became evident in the 1910's. The rate of increase in rice yield started to decelerate. When this productivity lag coincided with the increase in demand due to World War I, Japan had to face a population-food problem. The rising price of food, which exceeded increases in wage rates, caused serious disruption in urban areas and culminated in the *Kome Sodo* (Rice Riot) of 1918. The riot, triggered by fishermen's wives in the Toyama prefecture, swept over all the major cities in Japan.

The first reaction of the government was to increase rice imports from the overseas colonies, Taiwan and Korea. Through the squeeze on income in Taiwan and Korea by taxes and monopoly sales, on the one hand, and the investment in irrigation and agricultural research, on the other, Japan was successful in organizing large-scale rice imports from the colonial territories. The importation of colonial rice, which coincided with the contraction of demand after World War I, was successful in bringing down the price of rice to consumers. It also had the effect of reducing income and dampening production incentives for Japanese agriculture (see Chapters 9 and 10).

The government reacted by partially blocking rice imports from the colonies. At the same time the government tried to rescue domestic agriculture by investing in research and physical infrastructure. Under such circumstances, the nationwide co-ordinated crop breeding program called the "Assigned Experiment System" (the System of Experiment Assigned by the Ministry of Agriculture and Forestry) was established, first for wheat (1926) and second for rice (1927).[61]

Under the Assigned Experiment System the national experiment stations were given the responsibility for conducting hybridization up to the selection of the first several filial generations. The regional stations, in each of eight regions, conducted further selections so as to achieve adaption to the regional ecological conditions. The varieties selected at the regional stations were then

---

[61] This system was expanded to cover other crops and livestock. See Ogura, *Agricultural Development in Modern Japan*, p. 326.

sent to prefectural stations to be tested for the acceptability in specific localities. The varieties developed by this system were called *Norin* (abbreviation of the Ministry of Agriculture and Forestry) varieties.[62]

This system was outstandingly successful. *Norin No. 1* was selected in 1931 at the headquarters of Hokuriku (north central region) located at the Niigata prefectural station. This variety proved to be superior in yield, fertilizer responsiveness, early maturity (a required character in northern regions), and palatability. *Norin No. 1* spread rapidly, especially after 1935, and was planted in approximately 160 thousand hectares in 1939. It saved rice farming in this region, which was on the verge of collapse due to the competition of colonial rice.

It appears that with the establishment of the Assigned Experiment System, scientific research finally had become a major supplier of new technological potential and a dominant source of productivity gain in agriculture. The *Norin* numbered varieties successively replaced older varieties in the latter half of the 1930's (see Figure 7–3). If the supply of fertilizer and agricultural inputs had not been restricted due to the diversion of resources for the production of munitions during World War II, Japanese agriculture would have probably experienced a second epoch of agricultural productivity growth beginning in the late 1930's. The history of the Assigned Experiment System seems to suggest that the institutional response to changes in the supply of factors and products, reflected by changes in relative prices, occurs with a significant time lag. The production of new knowledge embodied in new varieties and materials occurs only after a further lag. The first crossing of parents of *Norin No. 1* was made in the Rikuu Branch of the National Experiment Station in 1922. The fifth filial generation was sent to the Niigata regional headquarters of the Assigned System in 1927, and three years later *Norin No. 1* was selected as the eighth filial generation. Further tests at prefectural stations were involved before it was finally recommended by extension workers.

The agricultural stagnation in Japan during the interwar period seems to be explained by this time lag in the adjustment of the public research complex to changes in the demand and supply of production factors and products. The Japanese experience was, in this respect, similar to the U.S. experience discussed earlier in this chapter.

Science and Technology in Modern Japanese Agriculture

The rapid agricultural growth in the post World War II period was not only a recovery phenomenon but it was based on the technological potential accu-

[62] It is of interest that the Mexican dwarf wheat which is revolutionizing Mexican and Indo-Pakistan agriculture was based on the *Norin* wheat varieties brought back to the U.S. by C. S. Salmon, a USDA scientist on loan to the occupation Army as an agricultural adviser. See Ralph D. Wennblom and Glenn Lorang, "Shorter Wheats for Everybody," *Farm Journal* 93 (July 1969): 16–17, 27–28.

mulated under the Assigned Experiment System. The potential was quickly realized when industry supplied enough fertilizers. In fact, the government placed the first priority on the fertilizer and coal mining industries in the postwar recovery program called *Keisha Seisan* (Differential Production Development).

The postwar agricultural growth was further enhanced by the supply of new industrial inputs, such as chemical pesticides, insecticides, and garden-type tractors and tillers. Such inputs were based on the progress of industrial technology and scientific knowledge accumulated during the war. Agricultural scientists developed techniques that pushed forward the "fertilizer consuming rice culture" to its extreme. This involved a dynamic interaction among various scientific and engineering disciplines. Increased fertilizer application made rice plants susceptible to pests and insects, which induced research on agricultural chemicals, in plant physiology and in entomology. Success in these areas reinforced the development of varieties that were even more responsive to high levels of fertilizer application.

The effective interaction among farmers, scientists, and agricultural supply firms, which led to the success in *Meiji* agricultural growth, continued to operate in the postwar years. Development of *Hoonsechu Nawashiro* (semi-irrigated cover-protected nursery bed), which contributed so greatly to the postwar expansion of rice culture in northern Japan, represents a remarkable example. This technique was originally devised by Toyojiro Ogino, a farmer in the Nagano prefecture. In the process of developing this practice he asked advice of the prefectural experiment station. The Nagano Agricultural Experiment Station, and later the Tokyo College of Agriculture and Forestry, co-operated with him to perfect this seed bed technique.[63] Industry also contributed to its development. Originally oil paper was used for cover protection. A new industrial product, the vinyl sheet, greatly increased the maneuverability and the degree of protection. The high pay-off of the technique, when completed, was demonstrated by its rapid propagation. Within ten years nearly 100 percent of the farmers adopted it in the regions where seed bed protection was needed.

The success of Japanese agricultural development over the long run has been due to the effective response of farmers, scientists, and agricultural supply industries to factor and product price relationships which have reflected the resource endowments of the Japanese economy. It appears, however, that since the mid-1960's government policies have contributed to a significant malallocation of resources in both agricultural production and agricultural research. The restrictions on growth of farm size, under land reform legislation, have discouraged the introduction of labor saving mechanical technology at a time when labor shortages are emerging as a secular feature of the

[63] *Nogyo Hyakka Jiten* (Encyclopedia of Agriculture), vol. 2 (Tokyo: Nosei Chosa Iinkai, 1966), p. 715.

Japanese economy. The pressure by farmers for high price supports for rice has pushed the price paid to Japanese farmers to more than double the world price. This has resulted in surplus rice production and is blocking the development of a feed-livestock system of agriculture at a time when the demand for livestock products is rising rapidly.

In the 1880's, under the depression due to the monetary reform by the Finance Minister Masayoshi Matsukata, there was strong agitation for the reduction of the newly established land tax, an essential revenue source for Japanese industrial development. At that time the *Nogakukai* (Agricultural Science Association) issued the *Konoronsaku* (A Treatise on the Strategy of Agricultural Development) in which they rejected the argument for a land tax reduction and advocated "more positive measures to develop agriculture such as agricultural schools, experiment stations, itinerate lectures, and agricultural societies" to reduce the burden of farmers.[64] The establishment of the National Agricultural Experiment Station represented the response to this plea. In retrospect the policies advocated by the Agricultural Science Association were remarkably successful. In the 1930's farmers benefited more from the development of *Norin No. 1*, produced by the Assigned Experiment System, than from the measures to block the import of colonial rice.

Today the widening income differential between agricultural and non-agricultural occupations represents a serious social and economic problem. Still it must be questioned whether high price supports are the most effective or desirable method to solve this problem when evaluated either in terms of the welfare of farmers or of the nation. Rather it would seem appropriate for Japan to review the process by which agricultural science was induced to respond to price relationships among production factors and between factors and products which reflected the factor endowments of the economy. Japan now needs to follow these same guides in designing an agricultural technology suitable to an environment in which labor is becoming an increasingly expensive factor of production and in which cereals occupy a declining role in per capita consumption and are declining in value in world markets.

CONCLUSIONS AND IMPLICATIONS

Two major conclusions may be drawn from the historical review of the role of science and technology in the agricultural development of the United States and Japan.

First, the history of agricultural innovation in Japan and the United States is consistent with the proposition that innovative efforts in both the private and public sectors have been directed toward saving the relatively scarce fac-

[64] *NNHS*, vol. 3, p. 255.

tors of production. In both countries advances in mechanical and biological technology responded to changing relative factor prices and the prices of factors relative to products to ease the constraints imposed by inelastic supplies of land and labor. In both countries the development of a dual federal-state (United States) or national-provincial (Japan) system of research administration contributed to the effectiveness with which public sector research resources were mobilized around problems of broad national significance, while at the same time developing the capacity to respond to the specific problems of regions and localities.

Second, the experience of both the United States and Japan suggests that public sector investment in education in the biological sciences related to agriculture and in experiment station research capacity is essential if a nation is to successfully test and diffuse the indigenous technology employed by its own farmers, transfer and adapt the agricultural technology developed in other countries, and conduct the basic and applied research necessary to provide its farmers with a continuous stream of new biological and chemical technology. This implication, which will be examined in greater detail in subsequent chapters, is particularly significant for most developing countries since their factor endowments clearly suggest that their optimum path of technical progress would place a relatively heavy emphasis on biological technology.

The history of both Japan and the United States also suggests that the public sector must play an important role in the advance of biological technology if the pattern of technical progress is to approach an optimal rate or avoid bias in the direction of mechanical technology and those areas of biological technology which can be embodied in proprietary products.

The homogeneity of agricultural products and the small size of the farm firm, even in western economies, make it difficult for the individual agricultural producer to either bear the research costs or capture the gains from innovations leading to advances in biological technology. Innovations in biological technology, typified by the breeding of new plant varieties or new cultural practices, can be copied or reproduced by other firms. Furthermore, the benefits of rapid diffusion of agricultural technology tend to be rapidly transmitted from farm producers to consumers through lower product prices. It seems clear, from both economic logic and economic history, that as land begins to act as a serious constraint on the growth of agricultural output, public sector investment in agricultural research designed to increase the rate of advance in biological technology can have a relatively high social return.

It also seems apparent that failure to effectively institutionalize public sector agricultural research can result in serious distortion of the pattern of technological change and resource use. Mechanical technology has been much more responsive than biological technology to the inducement mechanism as it operates in the private sector. Failure to balance the effectiveness of the private sector in responding to inducements for advances in mechanical technology, and in those areas of biological technology in which advances in knowledge can be embodied in proprietary products, with institutional innovations capable of providing an equally effective response to inducements for advances in biological technology leads to a bias in the productivity growth path that may not be consistent with relative factor endowments. It seems reasonable to hypothesize that failure to invest in public sector experiment station capacity is one of the factors responsible in some developing countries for the unbalanced adoption of mechanical, relative to biological, technology. Failure to develop adequate public sector research institutions has also been partially responsible in some countries for the almost exclusive concentration on research expenditures on the plantation crops and for concentration on the production of export crops, such as bananas and sugar, in the plantation sector.

It also seems clear that the effective institutionalization of public sector agricultural research will involve new institutional innovations rather than the direct transfer of the Japanese or the U.S. models. Neither the English nor the German models, on which the Japanese and U.S. agricultural research system drew for initial inspiration, were adequate to the needs of Japan or the United States. Both the Japanese and United States experience is consistent with the proposition that the transfer of institutions appears to be even more difficult and requires more time than the transfer of agricultural technology. A major challenge for the developing countries is to develop the scientific and institutional capacity to design location-specific agricultural technology adapted to the technological and economic environment in which the new agricultural technology is to be employed.

Part IV   Can Growth Be Transferred?

CHAPTER EIGHT

Theory and History of
International Technology Transfer

In our attempt to explain productivity differentials among countries (Chapter 5) a substantial share of the differences are accounted for by differences in the proxy variables for knowledge (general and technical education). The more detailed comparisons between the United States and Japan (Chapters 6–7) indicate that dialectic interaction among farmers, public institutions, and private farm supply firms resulted in a highly developed mechanical technology in U.S. agriculture and a highly developed biological technology in Japanese agriculture consistent with the resource endowments of the two countries.

It was also argued that the conventional treatment of technical change in agriculture in most development models, as a factor which shifts the production function without imposing any substantial demands on resource inputs, is inadequate. The production of technical change in agriculture imposes a substantial pressure on resource utilization, particularly the relatively limited pool of scientific and technical manpower available to the agricultural sector in most developing economies. The short-run supply of such manpower, and of the new scientific and technical knowledge required for agricultural development, appears to be relatively inelastic with respect to increases in expenditures on research personnel in both developed and less developed countries. It is our hypothesis that technical change is one of the more difficult products for a country in the early stages of economic development to produce.

Enormous agricultural productivity differences among countries seem to imply that less developed countries can acquire substantial gains in agricultural productivity by borrowing advanced technology existing in developed countries. In fact this was the premise on which the "diffusion model" was adopted as a major foundation for technical assistance after World War II, leading to an "extension bias" in aid programs in the 1950's (Chapter 3).

Efforts to achieve agricultural development by the direct transfer of foreign technology have been largely unsuccessful. Modern agricultural technology has evolved largely in the developed countries of the temperate zone and is primarily adapted to their ecology and factor endowments. Inadequate recognition of the location-specific character of agricultural technology was a major reason for the lack of effectiveness of much of the technical assistance effort of national and international agencies during the 1950's and 1960's. Major emphasis was placed on extension projects designed primarily to transfer materials and practices from the developed to the less developed countries and on the implementation of multipurpose, and frequently superficial, "community development" efforts. In reviewing the agricultural efforts of the 1950's and early 1960's, Moseman points out that "this 'extension bias' met with only limited success because of the paucity of applicable indigenous technology and the general unsuitability of U.S. temperate zone materials and practices to tropical agricultural conditions."[1]

Yet the effective transfer of technology is critically important to the agricultural development process. Although there exist a few ready-made technologies (for example, particular machinery or seeds) for international diffusion, transfer of knowledge and the development of indigenous capacity to generate an ecologically adapted and economically viable agriculture technology is vital to the progress of less developed countries.

In this chapter we attempt to draw from earlier research on the diffusion of culture and technology insights that may contribute to a more adequate understanding of the processes involved in the international diffusion of agricultural technology. This analysis leads us to place particular emphasis on adaptive research and development as the critical elements in the international transfer of agricultural technology. Finally, we specify the implications of our analysis for the continued diffusion of the technical potential opened up by the "green revolution" of the late 1960's. The hypotheses developed in this chapter are examined in greater detail in Chapters 9 and 10, where we attempt to place the changes that are now under way in grain production in the tropics in historical perspective. In Chapters 9 and 10 we draw particularly on the impact of the diffusion of Japanese rice technology in Taiwan and Korea.

DIFFUSION MODELS AND INTERNATIONAL TECHNOLOGY TRANSFER

There are multiple traditions of research on diffusion processes: in anthropology, economics, geography, sociology, and other disciplines. Each tradition has evolved a somewhat different model of the diffusion process.[2] Aside from

[1] Albert H. Moseman, *Building Agricultural Research Systems in the Developing Nations* (New York: Agricultural Development Council, Inc., 1970), p. 71.

[2] For a review of these several traditions see Elihu Katz, Herbert Hamilton, and Martin L. Levin, "Traditions of Research on the Diffusion of Innovation," *American Sociological*

differences in terminology, real differences among these models exist because they are concerned with different aspects of diffusion phenomena.

The main focus of sociologists and geographers has been on the impact of communication (or interaction) and sociocultural resistance to innovation on the pattern of diffusion over time and across space. There has been particular concern with understanding how the different sociocultural characteristics of adopters create a spectrum ranging from innovators to laggards, and how these characteristics determine the means of communication that are most effective in accelerating the diffusion process.[3] The models of economists have focused on how economic variables such as the profitability of innovation and the asset position of firms influence the rate of diffusion.[4]

These models have, with a few exceptions, only limited relevance for the international transfer of technology in agriculture. They have typically been designed to describe or analyze diffusion within a particular area over time. The attributes of the technology and the attributes of potential adopters are taken as given.[5] The assumption of ready availability and of direct transferability of the technology within the area represents a critical limitation in utilizing these diffusion models to understand the process of international diffusion of technology in situations where variations in ecological conditions and factor endowments among countries severely restrict the direct transfer of agricultural technology.

Review 28 (April 1963): 237–52; Everett M. Rogers, *Diffusion of Innovations* (New York: The Free Press of Glencoe, 1962); Allan Pred, "Postscript," in Torsten Hägerstrand, *Innovation Diffusion as a Spatial Process* (Chicago: University of Chicago Press, 1967), pp. 299–324; Delbert T. Myren, *Bibliography: Communications in Agricultural Development* (Mexico: Rockefeller Foundation, 1965); Lawrence A. Brown, *Diffusion Processes and Location: A Conceptual Framework and Bibliography* (Philadelphia: Regional Science Research Institute, 1968).

[3] See George M. Beal and Joe M. Bohlen, *The Diffusion Process* (Ames: Iowa State Agricultural Experiment Station, Special Report No. 18, March 1957); also Joseph E. Kivlin, Prodipto Roy, Frederick E. Fleigel, and Lalit K. Sen, *Communication in India: Experiments in Introducing Change* (Hyderabad: National Institute of Community Development, May 1968).

[4] Zvi Griliches, " 'Hybrid Corn:' An Exploration in the Economics of Technological Change," *Econometrica* 25 (October 1957): 501–22; "Hybrid Corn and the Economics of Innovation," *Science* 132 (July 29, 1960): 275–80; Edwin Mansfield, "Technical Change and the Rate of Imitation," *Econometrica* 29 (October 1961): 741–66; "The Speed of Response of Firms to New Techniques," *Quarterly Journal of Economics* 77 (May 1963): 291–311; "Size of Firm, Market Structure, and Innovation," *Journal of Political Economy* 71 (December 1963): 556–76; "Intrafirm Rates of Diffusion of an Innovation," *Review of Economics and Statistics* 45 (November 1963): 348–59.

[5] This has been of concern to some of the leaders in the field of diffusion research. Hägerstrand, in summarizing his work, points out: "In the models attention was directed to the processes of change, to how the distribution of g_n generates the distribution of g_{n+1}. The location of the starting point of the diffusion process was stated among the assumptions. However, we observe that when agricultural indicators and agricultural elements are involved, the same small areas within the region seem repeatedly to be the starting points for new innovation. ... The origin of such centers is a problem in itself." Hägerstrand, *Innovation Diffusion*, p. 293.

The study by Griliches of the diffusion of hybrid corn represents a rare attempt to incorporate the mechanism of local adaptation into a diffusion model.[6] The study is of relevance because the diffusion of hybrid corn among geographic areas, through the development of locally adapted varieties, is similar to our view of the process of the international technology transfer in agriculture. "Hybrid corn was the invention of a method of inventing, a method of breeding superior corn for specific locations. It was not a single invention immediately available everywhere. The actual breeding of adaptable hybrids had to be done separately for each area. Hence, besides the differences in the rate of adoption of hybrids by farmers . . . we have also to explain the lag in the development of adaptable hybrids for specific areas."[7,8]

The procedure employed by Griliches was to summarize the diffusion path for each hybrid corn maturity area by fitting an S-shaped logistic trend function to data on the percentage of corn area planted with hybrid seed. The logistic trend function is described by three parameters—an origin, a slope, and a ceiling. Griliches used differences in the *slope*, which measures the rate of acceptance, and the *ceiling*, which measures the percentage of acceptance at which use of hybrid seed tended to stabilize, of the S-shaped logistic curve to measure changes in the demand for hybrid seed. He interpreted his results

[6] Griliches, " 'Hybrid Corn': An Exploration"; and "Hybrid Corn and Economics." The Griliches study is also of interest because subsequent discussions helped to clarify the role of economic and sociocultural factors in the diffusion process. See Lowell Brandner and Murray A. Straus, "Congruence Versus Profitability in the Diffusion of Hybrid Sorghum," *Rural Sociology* 24 (December 1959): 381–83; Zvi Griliches, "Congruence versus Profitability: A False Dichotomy," ibid. 25 (September 1960): 354–56; Everett M. Rogers and A. Eugene Havens, "Adoption of Hybrid Corn: A Comment," ibid. 27 (September 1962): 328–30; Zvi Griliches, "Profitability versus Interaction: Another False Dichotomy," ibid. 27 (September 1962): 327–30; Jarvis M. Babcock, "Adoption of Hybrid Corn: A Comment," ibid. 27 (September 1962): 332–38; Gerald E. Klonglan and E. Walter Coward, Jr., "The Concept of Symbolic Adoption: A Suggested Interpretation," ibid. 35 (March 1970): 77–83; Kenneth J. Arrow, "Classification Notes on the Production and Transmission of Technological Knowledge," *American Economic Review* 59 (May 1969): 29–35. Arrow points out that "the economists are studying the demand for information by potential innovators and sociologists the problems in the supply of communication channels" (p. 33).

[7] Griliches, " 'Hybrid Corn': An Exploration," p. 502.

[8] The technology of hybrid corn breeding is considerably more sophisticated than the production of new varieties by "crossing." "Hybrid corn is the product of a controlled, systematic crossing of specially selected parential strains called 'inbred lines.' These inbred lines are developed by inbreeding, or self-pollinating, for a period of four or more years. Accompanying inbreeding is a rigid selection for the elimination of those inbreds carrying poor heredity, and which, for one reason or another, fail to meet the established standards." N. P. Neal and A. M. Strommen, *Wisconsin Corn Hybrids* (Madison: Wisconsin Agricultural Experiment Station, Bulletin 476, February 1948), p. 4. "[The inbred lines] are of little value in themselves for they are inferior to open-pollinated varieties in vigor and yield. When two unrelated inbred lines are crossed, however, the vigor is restored. *Some* of these hybrids prove to be markedly superior to the original varieties. The development of hybrid corn, therefore, is a complicated process of continued self-pollination accompanied by selection of the most vigorous and otherwise desirable plants. These superior lines are then used in making hybrids." R. W. Jugenheimer, *Hybrid Corn in Kansas* (Manhattan: Kansas Agricultural Experiment Station, Circular 196, February 1939), pp. 3–4.

as indicating that differences among regions in the rate (slope) and level (ceiling) of acceptance are both functions of the profitability of a shift from open-pollinated to hybrid corn. Variations in these two parameters among regions are thus explained in terms of farmers' profit-seeking behavior. In this respect Griliches' model is similar to other diffusion models employed by economists.

What makes Griliches' study unique and relevant to the problem of international technology transfer is that he incorporated into his model the behavior of public research institutions and private agricultural supply firms in making locally adapted hybrid seeds available to farmers. He identified the date of *origin* as the date at which an area began to plant 10 percent of its ceiling acreage to hybrid corn as an indicator of commercial availability. The 10 percent level was chosen as the origin to indicate that the development had passed through the experimental stage and that superior hybrids were available to farmers in commercial quantities. The average lag between technical availability and commercial availability was approximately two years. He attempted to explain variations in the date of origin, or of commercial availability, by the size and density of the hybrid seed market, estimated from the size and density of corn production.

From this analysis Griliches derived the conclusion that both the efforts of the agricultural experiment stations and the commercial seed companies were guided by the expected return to research, development, and marketing costs. In spite of the lack of a direct market test of the returns to research and development, in the case of the publicly (U.S.D.A. and state) supported experiment stations, the "contribution of the various experiment stations is strongly related to the importance of corn in the area. In the 'good' corn areas the stations did a lot of work on hybrids and in the marginal areas, less."[9] This implies, as hypothesized in our discussion of the induced development model (pages 53–63) that public research institutions are motivated and in fact attempt to maximize social returns (social returns of the region) to their research expenditure.

Similar inter-regional variations in development and marketing activities are consistent with the private profit maximization behavior of the commercial seed companies. Larger size and higher density of market imply larger potential sales and lower marketing costs of the firms. In addition, the cost of commercial development of local hybrids would be lower in those regions characterized by the most intensive hybrid corn research.[10]

One of the great merits in the Griliches model is that it incorporates the mechanism of local adaptation in the inter-regional transfer of agricultural technology. This mechanism is based on the behavior of public research institutions and private agricultural supply firms. Modification of the model is

[9] Griliches, " 'Hybrid Corn': An Exploration," p. 511.
[10] A. Richard Crabb, *The Hybrid-Corn Makers: The Prophets of Plenty* (New Brunswick: Rutgers University Press, 1947).

needed, however, when we apply it to the study of international technology transfer.

In the United States there exists a large stock of scientific and technical manpower, a well-structured federal-state experiment station network, and vigorous entrepreneurship in private farm supply firms. The mechanism for inducing the research and development necessary for local adaptation of technology functions efficiently. When these conditions are not met, even if the expected pay-off from the transfer of a particular technology is potentially very high, the supply of adaptive research may be very inelastic. The problem of facilitating international technology transfer as an instrument of agricultural development is, therefore, how to institutionalize an elastic supply of adaptive research and development. We hypothesize that the most serious constraints on the international transfer of agricultural technology are: limited experiment station capacity in the case of biological technology and limited industrial capacity in the case of mechanical technology. The inelastic supply of scientific and technical manpower represents a critical limiting factor in both cases.

PHASES OF INTERNATIONAL TECHNOLOGY TRANSFER

The international diffusion of agricultural technology is not new. The classical studies by Sauer and Vavilov indicate that intercountry and intercontinental diffusion of better husbandry practices and of crop varieties and livestock breeds was a major source of productivity growth even in prehistory.[11] It is well known that transfer of new crops (potatoes, maize, tobacco, etc.) from the new continents to Europe, after the discovery of America, had a dramatic impact on European agriculture.[12] Before agricultural research and extension were institutionalized, this diffusion took place as a by-product of travel and communication undertaken for other purposes. Over a long gestation period (several decades or centuries) exotic plants and techniques were gradually adapted to local conditions.

This natural diffusion can be a significant source of agricultural productivity growth in preindustrial economies in which the required rate of growth in agricultural output is in the range of 1.0 percent per year. This does not seem

---

[11] See Carl O. Sauer, *Agricultural Origins and Dispersals: The Domestication of Animals and Foodstuffs* (2nd ed.; Cambridge: Massachusetts Institute of Technology Press, 1969), pp. 113–34; N. I. Vavilov, *The Origin, Variation, Immunity and Breeding of Cultivated Plants*, trans. from the Russian by K. Starr Chester, *Chronica Botanica*, vol. 13, nos. 1–6 (1949–50). See also David R. Harris, "New Light on Plant Domestication and the Origins of Agriculture: A Review," *Geographical Review* 57 (January 1967): 90–107.

[12] See Folke Dovring, "The Transformation of European Agriculture," *The Cambridge Economic History of Europe, VI, The Industrial Revolution and After, Part II*, ed. H. J. Habakkuk and M. Postan (Cambridge: Cambridge University Press, 1966), pp. 604–72.

consistent with the requirements of economies characterized by modern rates of growth in demand for agricultural output in the range of 3 to 6 percent per year.

It appears useful to distinguish the three phases of international technology transfer as: (a) material transfer; (b) design transfer; and (c) capacity transfer. The first phase is characterized by the simple transfer or import of new materials such as seeds, plants, animals, machines, and techniques associated with these materials. Local adaptation is not conducted in an orderly and systematic fashion. The naturalization of plants and animals tends to occur primarily as a result of "trial and error" by farmers.[13]

In the second phase, the transfer of technology is primarily through the transfer of certain designs (blue prints, formula, books, etc.). During this period the imports of exotic plant materials and foreign equipment are made in order to obtain new plant breeding materials or to copy equipment designs, rather than for their use in direct production. New plants and animals are subject to orderly tests and are propagated through systematic multiplication. Domestic production of the machines imported in the previous phase is initiated. This phase usually corresponds to an early stage of evolution of publicly supported agricultural research in that experiment stations conduct, primarily, simple tests and demonstrations.

In the third phase, the transfer of technology is made through the transfer of scientific knowledge and capacity which enable the production of locally adaptable technology, following the "proto-type" technology which exists abroad. Increasingly, plant and animal varieties are bred locally to adapt them to local ecological conditions. The imported machinery designs are modified in order to meet climatic and soil requirements and factor endowments of the economy. An important element in the process of capacity transfer is the migration of agricultural scientists. In spite of advances in communications, diffusion of the ideas and craft of agricultural science depends heavily on extended personal contact and association.[14] The transfer of scientists is often of critical importance to ease the constraint of the short supply of scientific and technical manpower in the less developed countries. It is necessary in order to speed up the entrance of these countries into the capacity transfer phase. These phases of international technology transfer can be illustrated for

---

[13] See, for example, R. H. Green and S. H. Hymer, "Cocoa in the Gold Coast: A Study in the Relations between African Farmers and Agricultural Experts," *Journal of Economic History* 26 (September 1966): 299–319. The crucial innovations leading to the rapid growth of Gold Coast cocoa production "were made in the 1880's by Ghanaians, and they succeeded in spite of, not because of, the colonial Department's efforts" (p. 302).

[14] For interesting insight into the relationships between the transfer of ideas and the migration of individuals and groups see Warren C. Scoville, "Minority Migrations and the Diffusion of Technology," ibid. 11 (Fall 1951): 347–60: Fritz E. Redlich, "Ideas—Their Migration in Space and Transmittal Over Time," *Kyklos* 6 (1953): 301–22; Robert Solo, "The Capacity to Assimilate an Advanced Technology," *American Economic Review* 56, Papers and Proceedings (May 1966): 91–97.

biological technology by the international transfer of sugar cane technology; and for mechanical technology by the transfer of tractors from the United States to the USSR and Japan.

Transfer of Biological Technology: The Case of Sugar Cane[15]

Evenson's study of the development of sugar cane varieties is of interest because it represents a major example of the international transfer of biological technology in agriculture, and because the process has evolved from a simple transfer of plants to the phase of capacity transfer.

Evenson identified four stages of development in sugar cane varieties: Stage 1—Natural Selection (Wild Canes). The cane plant reproduces asexually. Until the late 1800's relatively few wild or native varieties were commercially produced. These varieties apparently were the result of natural asexual reproduction. They were transmitted between countries, but the transmission was extremely slow. For example, the "Bourbon" cane, the major Stage I cane in the nineteenth century, was not introduced to the British West Indies until 1785, almost a hundred years after it was a commercial cane in Madagascar.

Stage II—Sexual Reproduction (Noble Canes). The discovery of the fertility of the sugar cane plant in 1887, independently in Barbados and in Java, established the basis for the breeding of new varieties. Under proper conditions the cane plant can be induced to flower and produce seedlings. Each new seedling is then a potential new variety since it can be reproduced asexually. The early man-made varieties were produced using the existing commercial 80-chromosome cane species *Saccharum Officinarum* as parent varieties. Between 1900 and 1920 numerous varieties resulted from this effort. These varieties were transferred widely over the world from experiment stations in Java, India, Barbados, British Guiana, and Hawaii; and when introduced they appeared to be definitely superior to the native varieties. Only simple tests and demonstrations are required, if any, for recipient countries to propagate these varieties. In many cases, however, they were susceptible to diseases and their yield advantages were lost.

Stage III—Interspecific Hybridization (Nobilization).[16] The experiment

---

[15] This section is based on R. E. Evenson, J. P. Houck, Jr., and V. W. Ruttan, "Technical Change and Agricultural Trade: Three Examples—Sugarcane, Bananas, and Rice, "*The Technology Factor in International Trade*, ed. Raymond Vernon (New York: Columbia University Press, 1970), pp. 415–80; Robert Evenson, "International Transmission of Technology in the Production of Sugar Cane," (University of Minnesota Agricultural Experiment Station Scientific Journal Paper No. 6805, 1969); Robert E. Evenson and Manuel L. Cordomi, "Responsiveness to Economic Incentives by Sugarcane Producers in Tucuman, Argentina" (New Haven: Department of Economics, Yale University, 1969), mimeo. draft.

[16] Interspecific hybrids should be distinguished from single- or double-cross hybrids. Interspecific hybrids are produced by the crossing of two species. The backcross method may be used as in the above case to transfer a single, readily identifiable characteristic

station in Java (Proefstation Oost Java, P.O.J.) achieved a major advance in cane breeding by introducing the species *Saccharum Spontaneum* into their breeding programs after 1915. Through a series of crosses and back crosses new interspecific hybrids were developed that incorporated the hardiness and disease-resistance of this noncommercial species. Later, the station at Coimbatore, India, developed a series of tri-hybrid canes by introducing a third species, *Saccharum Barberi*. The local *S. Barberi* species resulted in new varieties adaptable to local climate, soil, and disease conditions. The Stage III varieties were disease-resistant and high-yielding, notably those from Java and India. They were transferred to every producing country in the world. While this international transmission was widespread, it did not occur easily without the aid of research and extension efforts in the recipient countries.

Stage IV—Location Specific Breeding. The Coimbatore, India, station set the stage for modern breeding activity. More than 100 experiment stations are now in existence. In most cases they are pursuing programs which involve systematic selfing and crossing of parent varieties suitable to the specific soil, climate, disease, and economic conditions of relatively small regions. Very little international transfer of varieties is now taking place, as most regions are producing cane from varieties produced by the region's experiment station.

It appears possible to interpret sugar cane variety transfers during Evenson's Stages I and IV as clearly belonging to the material transfer and the capacity transfer stages, respectively. Stage II appears to be a transition from the material transfer to the design transfer; and Stage III a transition from the design transfer to the capacity transfer.

Significant implications of this sequence are the increasingly important role which public research has played in developing and "naturalizing" of sugar cane varieties and the sequence running from initial international diffusion of superior varieties to the international diffusion of the capacity to "invent" location-specific varieties superior to the "naturalized" varieties.

Transfer of Mechanical Technology: The Tractor in Russia and Japan

There has been increasing interest in the process of international diffusion and transfer of industrial technology. The enhanced role of technological change in economic growth and international competition has resulted in growing dissatisfaction with the treatment of technical change in the theory of international trade.[17] Most of the studies have emphasized the process and

---

such as disease resistance, from one variety to another. The backcross method can not be expected to improve the variety more than the increment achieved by the addition of the single selected character. This is in contrast to "hybrid vigor" obtained by combining inbred lines (as in corn).

[17] G. S. Maddala and Peter T. Knight, "International Diffusion of Technical Change—A Case Study of the Oxygen Steel Making Process," *Economic Journal* 77 (September 1967): 531–58. William Gruber, Dileep Mehta, and Raymond Vernon, "The R & D Factor in

impact of diffusion of known technology rather than the transfer of capacity to invent new technology.[18] A few studies have focused on the implications of alternative national strategies of technological development for economic growth and power.[19]

In the field of agriculture one of the dramatic examples was the Soviet adoption of American mechanical technology, particularly the tractor, during the 1924–33 decade. Also of interest is the transfer of small-scale mechanical equipment to Japan since the mid-1950's. In both cases the experiment station occupied a relatively minor role in comparison to the transfer of biological technology. An important element in the transfer of machine technology in agriculture in both the USSR and Japan was the domestic manufacturing and design capacity.

The tractor occupied an important role, for both ideological and practical reasons, in the development of agriculture in the USSR.[20] The transfer of American machinery technology to the USSR has been documented by Dana G. Dalrymple,[21] and the three phases in the evolution of technology transfer can be observed.

Material transfer—Importation: In 1924 there were only about 1,000 tractors in operation in the USSR. By 1934 the number had increased to over 200,000. Approximately half of this total was imported, mostly from the United States. After 1931 imports dropped sharply.

Design transfer—Domestic Production: Tractor production in the USSR rose from 17 in 1924 to close to 5,000 in 1929. By 1933, production exceeded 50,000 and in 1934 approximated 100,000 units. This development was heavily dependent upon the contributions of U.S. technology. The early Russian tractors were direct copies of U.S. models, primarily Fordson and International Harvester machines. The Russian tractor manufacturing plants were designed by American firms and constructed under the direction of U.S. construction engineers who had been associated with similar developments in Detroit and Chicago. Russian technical teams visited Detroit and Chicago,

---

International Trade and International Investment of United States Industries," *Journal of Political Economy* 75 (February 1967): 20–37; Daniel L. Spencer and Alexander Woroniak, eds., *The Transfer of Technology to Developing Countries* (New York: Praeger, 1967); Raymond Vernon, ed., *The Technology Factor*.

[18] Woodruff presents a historical description of evolution in the process of international transfer of rubber manufacturing technology. See W. Woodruff, "An Inquiry into the Origins of Invention and the Intercontinental Diffusion of Techniques of Production in the Rubber Industry," *Economic Record* 38 (December 1962): 479–97.

[19] See the review by Robert Gilpin, "Technological Strategies and National Purpose," *Science* 169 (July 1970): 441–48.

[20] Robert F. Miller, *One Hundred Thousand Tractors* (Cambridge: Harvard University Press, 1970), pp. 63–98.

[21] Dana G. Dalrymple, "American Technology and Soviet Agricultural Development, 1924–1933," *Agricultural History* 40 (July 1966): 187–206; "The American Tractor Comes to Soviet Agriculture: The Transfer of a Technology," *Technology and Culture* 5 (Spring 1964): 191–214.

and American foremen were imported to train the workmen and help run the new plants. "Thus by the early to middle 1930's the Russians were producing reproductions of three American tractors, in plants designed by Americans, built under American supervision, and initially operated under American supervision. In this way . . . the Russians were able to acquire quickly and with very little effort the technical knowledge of tractor production which had taken years to develop in this country."[22]

Capacity transfer: Beginning in 1922, the Russians also began to import to the USSR American farmers and American farm management specialists to advise in the organization of large-scale mechanized farming units and to instruct in the use of tractors. American influence in the adaptation of mechanized production to the economic and technical conditions of Russian agriculture was, however, less pervasive than it was in the importation and production of tractors. From the beginning, the productive use of the new equipment was hampered by improper use and inadequate maintenance. Nevertheless, the Russians have developed a pattern of machine operation consistent with scarcity of capital relative to labor in the economy:

> rates of scrapping are about twice as high as those in the United States. . . .
> utilization to full capacity on huge farm units leads to a more rapid wearing out
> of machines. In recent years the supply of new tractors to agriculture in the Soviet
> Union has been larger than in the United States; yet the total tractor fleet in the
> USSR increases only slowly. The Soviet tractor figures confirm that the use of
> men and machines in the USSR is *machine-centered*, as would be expected in a
> low-income economy. In the United States and western Europe, with high and
> rapidly rising per-capita incomes, the use of machines centers around the use of
> manpower, aiming at maximizing the efficiency of labor committed to agricultural
> production by means, among other things, of some excess capacity in tractors
> and other heavy machines.[23]

A remarkable aspect in the Soviet adoption of U.S. machine technology is that it has continued to center on large-scale tractors. There is still no indication that machine size has been reduced to be more consistent with factor endowments of the economy. This seems to be explainable in terms of the Russian motivation to mechanize agriculture. The Soviet efforts at farm mechanization were inseparably related to Stalin's policy of heavy industrialization:

> The overriding economic goal of the Soviet Union has long been to catch up with
> and exceed the highest productive indices of capitalist industry. . . . Much of the
> capitalization for this process was to come from the export of agriculture products.

---

[22] Dalrymple, "The American Tractor Comes to Soviet Agriculture," p. 201.
[23] Folke Dovring, "Soviet Farm Mechanization in Perspective," *Slavic Review* 25 (June 1966): 289–90.

To obtain agricultural goods for export, as well as to gain economic and political independence from the peasantry, Stalin chose to collectivize agriculture. Collectivization was at first to be done slowly, but Stalin soon changed his mind and elected to push the program through with all haste. One of the subsequent costs he may not have expected was the widespread slaughter of livestock. This led to a severe loss of draft power. To make up for the loss and to help weld the collective farms into collective units, it was felt necessary to push large-scale mechanization faster than had been anticipated. This meant that mechanization had to be pressed simultaneously with the development of basic industry, instead of letting agricultural industry follow. . . . Stalin's decision to develop basic industry at the expense of agriculture entailed collectivization of agriculture. But the process of collectivizing led to a need for a certain minimal development of agricultural industry.[24]

In short, farm mechanization was designed to procure an agricultural surplus for industrialization (by means of compulsory delivery) while breaking the economic power of the peasantry—the fortress of conservatism. In terms of this goal, the development of efficient small-scale machinery, consistent with the peasant or family farm mode of production, was considered undesirable. Big tractors were a means of forcing peasants to adapt to the socialist mode of production.

Given the factor endowments in Russia, however, it was inevitable that this large-scale mechanization has led to a significant malallocation of resources in the Soviet agriculture:

By tailoring agriculture to big tractors, it has forced agriculture into an absurd, bimodal structure of farm sizes, i.e., exceedingly large state and collective farms and tiny plot farms, a bimodal structure based on big tractors and many hoes. Both types are highly inefficient. Suppose that on the large state and collective farms only the costs of tractors and the machinery to match them mattered; even then it would be more economical to have a complementary assortment of tractors consisting of large, intermediate, and small types instead of only very large tractors. . . . Meanwhile, the millions of plot farms are restricted to many hoes and to an extremely intensive use of labor. . . . Suppose these plot farms were increased to no more than 10 acres and suppose small hand (garden-type) tractors and complementary machines and equipment were made available; total agricultural production in the Soviet Union would rise sharply.[25]

Bias toward large-scale in the Soviet farm mechanization had its own rationale in terms of motivation and policy for the promotion of socialist development. It is beyond the scope of this study to evaluate this whole policy complex. It does seem apparent, however, that the Russians had to pay the

[24] Dalrymple, "American Technology and Soviet Agricultural Development," p. 204.
[25] Theodore W. Schultz, *Transforming Traditional Agriculture* (New Haven: Yale University Press, 1964), p. 123.

cost of tailoring agriculture to imported technology (big tractors) rather than tailoring the machine technology to their agriculture.

"Mini-tractorization," an introduction of the small-scale tractors of less than ten horsepower in postwar Japan represents a clear contrast to this Russian experience. Before World War II, mechanization in Japan was restricted to irrigation, drainage, and postharvesting operations; tractors were introduced only on an experimental scale.[26] The number of hand tractors on farms rose sharply from virtual nonexistence in the 1940's to 89,000 in 1955, to 517,000 in 1960, and to 2,500,000 in 1965. Before 1960 large-scale riding tractors were employed almost exclusively in the construction industry.[27]

This postwar spurt of Japanese tractorization may partly be explained by increased income of farm households, due to the land reform and relatively high food prices in the early postwar period; the high income induced farmers to lessen hard manual labor by means of automotive power. A more critical factor appears to be the supply pressure of the machinery industry. From the beginning of modern economic growth until the end of World War II, the Japanese machinery industry depended heavily on military procurement. When this favored market was eliminated, after World War II, the industry was left with significant idle capacity, especially of engineering and technical manpower, and was forced to divert part of its capacity to agriculture.[28] Domestic production of hand tractors increased from only 60 in 1945, to 34,000 in 1955, to 305,000 in 1960, and to 437,000 in 1965.

Under the strong supply pressure of the machinery industry, Japan bypassed the phase of material transfer-importation and soon entered into the capacity-transfer phase. These small-scale tractors were imported from abroad only to the extent of borrowing designs.[29] The first tractors manufactured in Japan (called "power cultivators") were subject to several defects: heavy body weights relative to the power they could generate and engines without waterproof devices, which made operations in wet paddy fields difficult.[30] These defects were soon corrected. Two major developments which brought about the rapid growth of tractorization in the mid-1950's were an increase in the power of the "power cultivators" from less than five h.p. to the range of five

[26] See the process of farm mechanization in the prewar period in Takekazu Ogura, ed., *Agricultural Development in Modern Japan* (Tokyo: Fuji Publishing Co., 1963), pp. 410–22.

[27] Introduction of riding tractors for farm field operations began in Hokkaido in the late 1950's, and has been progressing rapidly with labor outmigration from agriculture. The number of riding tractors on farms reached 38,000 in 1966. See *Norinsho Tokeihyo 1966/67* (Statistical Year Book of the Ministry of Agriculture and Forestry 1966/67), (Tokyo, 1967), p. 67.

[28] Seiichi Tobata and Shigeto Kawano, ed., *Nihon no Keizai to Nogyo* (The Economy and Agriculture of Japan) vol. 2 (Tokyo: Iwanami, 1956), pp. 231–61.

[29] The major source of supply of large-scale riding tractors has been imports from abroad. With respect to large-scale tractors and machinery, Japan is now in the process of transition from material transfer to design transfer.

[30] Nobufumi Kayo, *Nihon Nogyo no Kikaika Kadai* (Problems of Agricultural Mechanization in Japan) (Tokyo: Nosei Chosa Iinkai, 1962), pp. 41–66.

to ten h.p., which permitted a depth of cultivation comparable to the depth of horse plowing; and the development of the small hand tractors of three to five h.p., with interchangeable attachments. These modifications made it possible to replace draft animals completely by small-scale tractors.[31]

Extremely rapid progress in the "mini-tractorization" has puzzled many Japanese agricultural economists. Some have suspected its efficiency and have developed a hypothesis of "over-mechanization" based on demonstration effects and other psychological elements.[32] Keizo Tsuchiya's recent study, however, indicates that increased utilization of tractors can be explained by the efforts of farmers to reduce production costs in response to rising wage rates relative to the price of agricultural machines and equipment without invoking such psychological factors.[33]

In contrast to the Russian experience, of modifying agricultural production units to conform to the requirements of mechanization, the Japanese experience involved the tailoring of tractors, and other farm machinery, to the size of the individual production unit. Due to the spectacular industrial growth in the 1960's, Japan has now entered into a phase of chronic labor shortage. To sustain national economic growth, transfer of labor from agriculture to more productive sectors should be accelerated. In order to transfer a significant amount of labor without causing a decline in agricultural production, measures have to be taken to consolidate small farms into the larger units that can realize the benefit of large-scale mechanization. Japan is now facing the problem of tailoring its agricultural structure to changing national resource endowments. There is a real danger that the very existence of an efficient system of small-scale mechanical technology may work as a barrier to structural adjustments during the next several decades. In order to avoid this possibility, it will be necessary to produce a continuous sequence of efficient systems of mechanical technology consistent with the changing factor endowments of the economy.

TECHNOLOGY TRANSFER AND THE EMERGENCE OF NEW GRAIN PRODUCTION POTENTIAL IN THE TROPICS[34]

Technological transfer is intimately linked with institutional development. The most dramatic example of agricultural technology transfer during the last

---

[31] Ibid.

[32] These views were surveyed in ibid., pp. 35–40.

[33] Keizo Tsuchiya, "Economics of Mechanization in Small-Scale Agriculture," *Agriculture and Economic Growth: Japan's Experience*, ed. Kazushi Ohkawa, Bruce F. Johnston, and Hiromitsu Kaneda (Tokyo: University of Tokyo Press, 1969), pp. 155–72; Keizo Tsuchiya, "The Role and Significance of Mechanization in Japanese Agriculture," *Journal of the Faculty of Agriculture, Kyushu University* 16 (July 31, 1970): 169–77.

[34] This section draws heavily on Vernon W. Ruttan, "The International Institute Approach," *Agents of Change: Professionals in Developing Countries*, ed. Guy Benveniste and Warren F. Iichman (New York: Praeger, 1969), pp. 220–28.

Table 8–1. Estimated area planted in high-yielding varieties (HYV) of rice and wheat in West, South, and Southeast Asia

	Rice				Wheat			
	1966/ 67	1967/ 68	1968/ 69	1969/ 70	1966/ 67	1967/ 68	1968/ 69	1969/ 70
	Thousand acres							
Turkey					1	420	1,430	1,540
Iran							25	222
Afghanistan					5	54	302	361
Nepal			105	123	16	61	133	186
West Pakistan		10	761	1,239	250	2,365	5,900	7,000
East Pakistan	1	166	382	652			20	NA
India	2,195	4,408	6,625	10,800	1,270	7,270	11,844	15,100
Ceylon			17	65				
Burma		8	412	356				
Malaysia	104	157	225	316				
Laos	1	3	5	5				
Vietnam		1	100	498				
Indonesia			488	1,850				
Philippines	204	1,733	2,500	3,346				
Total	2,505	6,486	11,620	19,250	1,542	10,170	19,654	24,409

Source: Dana G. Dalrymple, *Imports and Plantings of High-Yielding Varieties of Wheat and Rice in the Less Developed Nations*, Foreign Economic Development Service, U.S. Department of Agriculture, in co-operation with Agency for International Development (Washington, D.C., Jan. 1971), pp. 35, 36.

several decades has involved the development and rapid diffusion of new high-yielding varieties (HYV's) of rice, wheat, and maize in the tropics (Table 8–1).[35,36] The development and rapid diffusion of the new cereals technology was made possible by a series of institutional innovations in the organization, management, and financing of agricultural research in the less developed countries of the tropics.

Of particular significance in the present context is the fact that the development of the HYV's represents a process of agricultural technology transfer

[35] "The word 'revolution' has been greatly abused, but no other term adequately describes the effects of the new seeds on the poor countries where they are being used. Rapid increases in cereal production are but one aspect of the agricultural breakthrough. . . . The new seeds are bringing far-reaching changes in every segment of society. They may be to the agricultural revolution in the poor countries what the steam engine was to the Industrial Revolution in Europe." Lester R. Brown, Statement at the U.S. House of Representatives Committee on Foreign Affairs, December 5, 1969, *Symposium on Science and Foreign Policy— The Green Revolution* (Washington: U.S. Government Printing Office, 1970), p. 80.

[36] For a concise documentation see Dana G. Dalrymple, *Imports and Plantings of High-Yielding Varieties of Wheat and Rice in the Less Developed Nations*, Foreign Economic Development Service, U.S. Department of Agriculture, in co-operation with Agency for International Development (Washington, D.C., January 1971). For a dramatic story of these developments see E. C. Stakman, Richard Bradfield, and Paul C. Mangelsdorf, *Campaigns Against Hunger* (Cambridge: Harvard University Press, 1967). For a cautionary note see Clifton R. Wharton, Jr., "The Green Revolution: Cornucopia or Pandora's Box?," *Foreign Affairs* 47 (April 1969): 464–76.

from the temperate zone to tropical and subtropical zones through the transfer of scientific knowledge and capacity. Furthermore, this development was directed to the improvement in yield of the staple food crops consumed domestically rather than to the "enclave" tropical export commodities which had received attention under colonial administration. These new HYV's adaptable to tropical ecologies were initially developed by international teams of scientists drawing on the principles that emerged in the process of developing HYV's that had been introduced earlier in Japan, the United States, and other temperate zone developed countries.[37]

Within the tropics the diffusion of the new cereals technology from Mexico (wheat) and the Philippines (rice) was characterized by an initial materials-transfer stage. The initial impact of the diffusion of the new varieties on grain production in Pakistan, India, Malaysia, Turkey, Mexico, and other countries, involved the direct transfer of seed of the new varieties from Mexico and the Philippines; and of fertilizer, insecticides, and fungicides from Japan, the United States, and Western Europe. In other countries, such as Thailand, the impact was delayed until the design and capacity transfer stage could be achieved, in order to maintain the quality characteristics of the Thai varieties which are important in the export market for Thai rice. In the countries that benefited initially from capacity transfer, there has been a rapid movement to develop the local experiment station capacity that will permit them to move to the design-transfer and capacity-transfer stages in the development of ecologically adapted varieties. There is also, in many countries, a move toward the development of a domestic fertilizer and agricultural chemical industry based primarily on developed country designs.[38]

The adaptive research that led to the development of HYV's was primarily conducted at a new set of international agricultural research centers. These centers are typically supported by major U.S. Foundations. They are staffed by international teams of scientists of various agricultural science disciplines

---

[37] Peter R. Jennings, "Plant Type as a Rice Breeding Objective," *Crop Science* 4 (January–February 1964): 13–15; E. A. Jackson, "Tropical Rice: The Quest for High Yield," *Agricultural Science Review* 4 (Fourth Quarter 1966): 21–26. The Jennings article represents the classic statement of the new crop breeding strategy focusing on models of biologically efficient plant types.

[38] The role of material transfers on the initial impact of the new grain varieties on production has been documented in a series of country papers prepared for the 1969 spring review at the US AID. The material presented in the country papers has been summarized in two papers: Wayne A. Schutjer and E. Walter Coward, Jr., "Planning Agricultural Development—The Matter of Priorities," *Journal of Developing Areas*, forthcoming 1971, and E. Walter Coward, Jr., and Wayne A. Schutjer, "The Green Revolution: Initiating and Sustaining Change," paper presented at Annual Meeting of the Rural Sociological Society, 1970. The contribution of material inputs is also emphasized in Wayne Schutjer and Dale Weigle, "The Contribution of Foreign Assistance to Agricultural Development," *American Journal of Agricultural Economics* 51 (November 1969): 788–97. The results obtained by Schutjer and Coward in the AJAE article do not reflect the significance of capacity transfer. It was only after the new production functions characterized by a higher response to material inputs were developed that the material transfers became profitable.

and by in-service trainees and co-ordinated by a common orientation to produce major breakthroughs in the yield potentials of certain staple cereals. Establishment of these research-training centers can be considered as an institutional innovation facilitating the transfer of an "ecology-bound" location-specific agricultural technology from temperate zone developed countries to tropical zone developing countries. It is useful, therefore, to review the evolution of these institutions, particularly the International Center for Corn and Wheat Improvement (CIMMYT) in Mexico and the International Rice Research Institute (IRRI) in the Philippines. Similar international centers have recently been established in Colombia and Nigeria. The new international centers are also exerting a major impact on the organization of national research systems.

CIMMYT and IRRI do not, of course, represent completely new concepts of research organization. Commodity-centered research institutes established in the tropics under British and Dutch colonial auspices have been responsible for substantial productivity gains in the production of tropical export crops such as rubber and sugar. The new international institutes represent an extension and further evolution of an already established institutional pattern.[39]

The Rockefeller Foundation Agricultural Sciences program, which eventually led to the establishment of CIMMYT and IRRI, was initiated in 1943 with the establishment of the Office of Special Studies (Oficina de Estudios Especiales) in the Mexican Ministry of Agriculture.[40] Field research programs

---

[39] "... commodity research stations were established by the British in tropical Africa and later turned into regional institutes. A Cocoa Research Institute was launched in Ghana in 1938 followed by the Oil Palm Research Station in Nigeria in 1939. Beginning in 1957, these national commodity research stations were regionalized and the West African Cocoa Research Institute (Sierra Leone), West African Oil Palm Research Institute (Nigeria), West African Maize Research Institute (Nigeria), the West African Institute for Social and Economic Research (Nigeria), plus five other West African Research Institutes were established. As West African nations gained independence, starting with Ghana in 1957, problems emerged which led to the breakup of all the West African institutes. ... the British acted with impressive foresight in developing biological research stations in Africa ...," in Carl K. Eicher, "Regional Programming for Rural Development in Tropical Africa: Implications for AID," paper presented at a conference on African Development from a Regional Perspective, Warrenton, Virginia, November 14–16, 1969, mimeo. For a more detailed treatment of colonial research in the areas under British administration see Charles Jeffries, *A Review of Colonial Research, 1940–1960* (London: H. M. S. O., 1964). For a comment on the inadequacy of the colonial research effort see Green and Hymer, "Cocoa in the Gold Coast."

[40] The decision to initiate the program was made following the report in 1941 of a survey team consisting of Richard Bradfield (professor of agronomy and head of the Department of Agronomy, Cornell University), Paul C. Mangelsdorf (professor of plant genetics and economic botany, Harvard University) and E. C. Stakman (professor of plant pathology and head of the Department of Plant Pathology, University of Minnesota). The team was sent to Mexico as a result of a request to the Rockefeller Foundation from the Mexican Ministry of Agriculture following a visit to Mexico by Vice President Henry Wallace. For further background see Arthur T. Mosher, *Technical Cooperation in Latin-America Agriculture* (Chicago: University of Chicago Press, 1957), pp. 100–26; L. M. Roberts, "The Rockefeller Foundation Program in the Agricultural Sciences," *Economic Botany* 15 (October–December 1961):

were first initiated with wheat and corn. The program later expanded to include field beans, potatoes, sorghum, vegetable crops, and animal sciences. A common pattern of staffing was followed for each commodity program.[41] A U.S. specialist was brought in as each commodity program was initiated. Each specialist assembled a staff of young Mexican college graduates who were trained in research methods and practices, as part of the research program, rather than through a formal program of graduate studies.

In retrospect, the staffing program adopted by the Foundation and centered around a project leader for each commodity did have one major limitation. In situations where progress depended on the solution to a complex set of interrelated problems in varietal improvement and crop-production practices, the commodity specialist was rarely able to bring to bear the range of disciplinary knowledge and technical skill needed to achieve progress in crop production. This can be illustrated by comparing the relative progress of the wheat and corn programs. The wheat program achieved technical success earlier and its impact on yield per hectare and on total wheat production has been greater than for the other commodity programs. New wheat varieties were being distributed to farmers by the fall of 1948. By 1956 the production impact was sufficient to make Mexico independent of imported wheat.

The rapid progress of the wheat program was clearly related to the special competence of the early leaders of the wheat program in the fields of plant pathology and genetics and the fact that stem rust was a dominant factor limiting wheat yields. It was also facilitated by effective institutional linkages with related programs in the U.S. and elsewhere.[42]

Improvement in corn yields occurred much more slowly. In addition to a more complex set of biological factors, the institutional considerations involved in seed multiplication, distribution, and diffusion were more difficult.

296–301; Ralph W. Richardson, Jr., "A Pattern of Practical Technical Assistance: The Rockefeller Foundation's Mexican Agricultural Program," *Agricultural Science Review* 2 (Winter 1964): 12–20; Stakman, Bradfield, and Mangelsdorf, *Campaigns Against Hunger*; Delbert T. Myren, "The Rockefeller Foundation Program in Corn and Wheat in Mexico," *Subsistence Agriculture and Economic Development*, ed. Clifton R. Wharton, Jr. (Chicago: Aldine, 1969), pp. 438–52.

[41] Sterling Wortman, "Approaches to the World Food Problems," paper presented at Southwest Agricultural Forum, Tulsa, Oklahoma, January 19, 1967.

[42] "The initial varieties raised were selected from hybrid materials furnished by McFadden of the USDA staff working at the Texas Agricultural Experiment Station. Borlaug also continued to draw heavily on the materials available to him from Kenya, Australia, and the United States, with particularly close ties to Dr. B. B. Bayles who was in charge of the USDA program on wheat improvement. Subsequently, Dr. O. A. Vogel of the USDA staff at Pullman, Washington, contributed significantly by furnishing hybrids involving the short-strawed, high-yielding Norin selection which had been introduced from Japan in 1947 by Dr. S. C. Salmon of the USDA. This strong tie to the experience and materials in the U.S. and elsewhere was an important factor in the steady growth of the wheat project, together with the fact that the short-strawed, high-yielding, disease-resistant, fertilizer-responsive varieties were particularly well-suited for the irrigated areas in Northwest Mexico," in letter from A. H. Moseman, January 3, 1969.

In retrospect, it appears that success would have been more rapid if initial efforts had been directed to the development of high-yielding synthetic varieties rather than double-cross hybrids.

In situations where the technical, production, and organizational problems were relatively complex, requiring contributions from a broad spectrum of biological and social scientists, the staffing pattern worked out during the early years of the Mexican program was not entirely consistent with rapid progress in the solution of research and production problems. In these more complex situations a multidisciplinary team approach emerged as a more appropriate strategy than the simple commodity specialist approach of the early years.

A major source of strength in the success of the Rockefeller Foundation program in Mexico was its economical use of the scarce professional manpower available in Mexico, both at the beginning and throughout the program. The shortage of professional manpower and of indigenous educational resources was conducive to the development of an internship system which intimately linked professional education with investigation.[43]

By 1963 agricultural science had been successfully institutionalized in Mexico. On December 30, 1960, the Office of Special Studies was dissolved and merged into a new National Institute of Agricultural Research (INIA) under Mexican direction. The Rockefeller Foundation program staff in Mexico was reorganized into a new International Center for Corn and Wheat Improvement (CIMMYT).[44] The shift of the national program to Mexican management involved serious emotional strain. One of the more difficult problems faced by the Rockefeller Foundation staff in making the transition was the recognition that they would occupy a marginal role in a program which

[43] "In 1943 there was not a single Mexican in the field of agricultural sciences with a doctoral degree and only a few with a Master's degree. By the end of 1945 the Office of Special Studies employed seven Rockefeller Foundation scientists and 25 Mexican 'interns.' Even at its peak in the late 1950's the Rockefeller Foundation staff in Mexico consisted of less than twenty scientists. By 1963 over 700 young Mexicans had served for one or more years as interns in the Officina de Estudios Especiales. About 250 of the best interns had received fellowships for study in universities in the United States or elsewhere. There were 156 Mexicans with M.S. degrees and eighty-five with Ph.D. degrees in the agricultural sciences. Of the twenty-seven interns who entered the program in the first two years, all but four were still engaged professionally in the field of agriculture in Mexico in 1963." Charles M. Hardin, "The Responsibility of American Colleges and Universities: Definition and Implementation," paper read in Section O of the American Association for the Advancement of Science, New York, December 28, 1967.

[44] "In 1960 it was anticipated that the Rockefeller Foundation staff would be accommodated in the facilities of INIA at Chapingo and would continue to work in the respective departments in very much the same manner as USDA personnel associated with specific departments in the state agricultural experiment station cooperative programs, but would be devoting major time and effort to the development of international dimensions. . . . The decision to establish the International Center for Corn and Wheat Improvement (CIMMYT) came several years later and provided for a more specific and prominent identity for the Foundation supported personnel in Mexico," Moseman (see footnote 42).

they had developed. In technical assistance programs, the disengagement phase is often more difficult than the institution-building phase.

The significance of the disengagement is that it symbolized Mexican success of agricultural science as a career service which men could enter with confidence that their contributions would be rewarded both in money and in professional recognition. It is also significant that on May 14, 1963, advanced degrees in the agricultural sciences were conferred for the first time in Mexico. Mexico's new capacity to produce trained manpower in the agricultural sciences is developing in response to the demand for scientific manpower generated by the success of the initial thrust of the technical revolution in Mexican agriculture.

The establishment of the International Rice Research Institute (IRRI) in the Philippines in 1962 represents a second major landmark in the evolution of the agricultural science program of the Rockefeller Foundation. The IRRI was jointly financed by the Ford and Rockefeller Foundations and established as an international research and training institute, rather than as a component of a national ministry of agriculture. It was staffed by an international team of scientists representing eight different nationalities. Recognition of the complexity of the problem of achieving higher yield potentials and of the multidisciplinary competence that would be required to solve the biological problems posed thereby and to achieve rapid increases in total national and regional output were recognized and carefully structured into the staffing plan.[45] An intensive program of seminars and research program reviews was initiated to focus the efforts of the diverse multinational and multidisciplinary team on a common set of objectives and to achieve the complementarity among the several disciplines necessary to invent, introduce, and diffuse a new high-productivity rice technology.

The location of the IRRI in Los Baños, adjacent to the University of the Philippines College of Agriculture (UPCA), made professional resources available to the IRRI that had not been available in Mexico. The UPCA had already developed relatively strong departments in several fields of agricultural science. Joint appointments of IRRI staff to the UP graduate school strengthened the graduate research capacity of the UPCA. This arrangement

[45] "The scientific staff has been cosmopolitan from the beginning. . . . as shown by the following list: agronomy, Moomaw, Hawaii; plant breeding and genetics, Beachell and Jennings, United States, and Chang, Taiwan; soils, Ponnamperuma, Ceylon; plant physiology, Tanaka, Japan, and Vergara, Philippines; plant pathology, Ou, Taiwan; entomology, Pathak, India; chemistry and biochemistry, Akazawa, Japan, and Juliano, Philippines; microbiology, MacRae, Australia; statistics, Oñate, Philippines; agricultural economics, Ruttan, United States; agricultural engineering, Johnson, United States; communications [and sociology], Byrnes, United States." Stakman, Bradfield, and Mangelsdorf, *Campaigns Against Hunger*, p. 298. See also Randolph Barker, "The Contribution of the International Rice Research Institute to Asian Agricultural Development," *Change in Agriculture*, ed. A. H. Bunting (London: Gerald Duckworth and Co., Ltd., 1970), pp. 207–18.

permitted many of the IRRI trainees to work toward M.S. degrees under the direction of an IRRI staff member while simultaneously engaging in a highly complementary research "internship" at the Institute.

Within six years after the initiation of the research program at the IRRI, a series of new rice varieties with yield potentials roughly double that of the varieties that were previously available to farmers in most areas of Southeast Asia had been developed. By the late 1960's progress had proceeded far enough to have a measurable impact on aggregate production.[46]

The significance of the international institute experience, both in Latin America and in Asia, goes well beyond the impact of the new wheat, corn, and rice technology in at least two respects. The most important contribution was the evolution of an institutional pattern for the organization of scientific resources which can be replicated for a wide variety of crops and localities with a reasonable probability of success. It is now possible to organize a multidisciplinary team of biological, physical, and social scientists capable of adapting any new biological and chemical technology for crop production to local growing conditions and to make this technology available to farmers in a form that they are capable of accepting within the relatively short period of five to ten years.

According to Wayne D. Rasmussen, the "systems approach," in which the multidisciplinary teams of scientists co-operate to solve a problem, characterizes modern development in agricultural technology in the United States and other developed countries, in contrast to the traditional "component approach," in which individual inventors and scientists work sporadically according to their inspirations and insights.[47] The international institute experience clearly demonstrates the possibility of transmitting the "systems approach" to the less developed countries.

A second contribution of the new international centers was the evolution of a technique for establishing a set of linkages with national and local education and research centers. This technique includes activities such as exchanges of staff, professional conferences, support of graduate and postgraduate training, personal consultations, and exchanges of genetic materials. An institutional infrastructure that is capable, at least in part, of offsetting the inability to fully exploit the economies of scale, which characterize the larger national research systems, is evolving. This communications function of the interna-

---

[46] These developments have been widely reported in the popular press typically in a highly exaggerated form. For a more careful assessment see International Rice Research Institute, *Annual Report: 1967* (Los Baños, 1967); E. A. Jackson, "Tropical Rice," pp. 21–26; Randolph Barker, "Economic Aspects of New High-Yielding Varieties of Rice: IRRI Report," *Agricultural Revolution in Southeast Asia: Impact on Grain Production and Trade*, vol. I (New York: Asia Society, 1970), pp. 29–53.

[47] Wayne D. Rasmussen, "Advances in American Agriculture: The Mechanical Tomato Harvester as a Case Study," *Technology and Culture* 9 (October 1968): 531–43.

tional institutes is particularly important for the experiment stations located in the smaller countries where the development of a broad-based national research system is limited.

The international research-training institute approach clearly represents an effective institutional innovation in the process of technology transfer. It has been particularly effective in situations characterized by a supply of indigenous scientific manpower and experiment station capacity that is inadequate to achieve effective realization of the scale economies inherent in research and development activities, and in fostering the development of regional research and training infrastructure which can contribute to the support of self-sustaining progress of agricultural technology. The next stage in this development must be the strengthening of national research and production education systems.[48] In a few countries this may mean the building of new national research systems. In most countries the task is much more complex. It involves the transformation of existing national research systems into productive sources of new technical knowledge.[49]

In the next chapter, we will attempt to analyze the economic forces that induced the development of the new cereals technology, including the institutional innovations for the international transfer of technology.

[48] Delane E. Welsch and Ernest W. Sprague, "Technical and Economic Constraints on Grain Production in Southeast Asia," Asia Society, *Agricultural Revolution*, pp. 13–28.

[49] See, for example, the discussion of the agricultural research system in Brazil in G. Edward Schuh, *The Agricultural Development of Brazil* (New York: Praeger, 1970), pp. 227–40. In spite of substantial investment in agricultural research the impact on productivity has been small. According to Schuh much of the productivity increase that has been observed in Brazilian agriculture "comes from a change in product mix, and not from an increase in yields or productivity for the same crop" (p. 184).

CHAPTER NINE

A Perspective on Induced
Transfer of Technology[1]

In the previous chapter the new tropical grain production technology was viewed as occurring as a result of agricultural technology transfer between different ecological zones through the transfer of scientific knowledge, the development of local experiment station capacity, and the transfer of material inputs. This process involved institutional innovations designed to promote the capacity transfer. In this chapter, we analyze the economic forces that have induced international and national agencies to change development policies and to design institutional innovations leading to the creation of a new potential for grain production in the tropics.

We hypothesize that the efforts of the international and national agencies to transmit the new technology represented by high-yielding varieties (HYV) were undertaken because the expected gains from transferring this new technology into the tropics had risen high enough to pay for the cost of technology transfer, including the cost of building new institutions. The rise in the pay-off was primarily due to rapid growth in the demand for food output in most developing countries—reflected in the rise in food grain prices—and improvements in the supply of agricultural inputs, and a decline in the real prices, particularly fertilizer, which are required to realize the output potentials of HYV's. A critical element in this process is a rational response by public agencies to economic incentives rather than the response by profit maximizing firms, on which traditional arguments of induced innovations have been based.

In order to explore this process, the experience of transmitting rice production technology from Japan to Taiwan and Korea during the interwar period seems particularly instructive. Although this technology transfer was based on Japanese colonialist ambitions, it represented a significant success in the transmission of agricultural technology through the transfer of scientific

---

[1] This chapter draws heavily on Yujiro Hayami, "Elements of Induced Innovation: A Historical Perspective for the Green Revolution," *Explorations in Economic History*, forthcoming 1971.

knowledge, with the deliberate intention of transforming traditional peasant agriculture. The long-term historical statistics of product and factor prices in Japan, Taiwan, and Korea enable us to infer the price mechanisms which induced the transfer of technology through scientific research; this appears to parallel what is happening in Asia today.

First we will further elaborate the model developed in Chapter 4, in order to discuss with greater precision the nature of HYV's in their relation to a critical complementary input—fertilizer. Then we will review the fertilizer-rice price ratios which prevailed in selected Asian countries on the eve of the green revolution, in contrast with the time-series data for Japan. From these observations we will postulate a hypothesis concerning the innovation-inducement mechanism. This hypothesis will be tested against the experience of Japan, Taiwan, and Korea. Because of the dominance of rice in the agriculture of Japan, Taiwan, and Korea, our discussion will be concentrated on rice.[2] As is the case in any historical inference, the analyses of the historical experiences of Japan, Taiwan, and Korea in this chapter and the next chapter are of limited relevance to the economic policy problems of contemporary developing countries. The differences in factor mobility and trade relationships, as between today's independent developing countries and colonial Taiwan and Korea in the interwar period, should be kept in mind in drawing inferences for contemporary development problems from the history of Japan, Taiwan, and Korea. The experience of Japan, Taiwan, and Korea does, however, represent a useful historical experiment for testing our induced-development hypothesis.

AN INDUCED DEVELOPMENT HYPOTHESIS FOR THE NEW CEREALS TECHNOLOGY

The high-yielding rice varieties recently developed in tropical Asia, as the "proto-type HYV's" in Japan (demonstrated in Table 3–2, Chapter 3), are distinguished by high fertilizer responsiveness. Their fertilizer-responsive capacity is fully realized only when they are accompanied by better husbandry practices (for example, weed and insect control) and by adequate water control. Traditional varieties have long survived with little fertilization under

[2] Data used for Japan, Taiwan, and Korea cover periods after the cadastral surveys were completed (the cadastral survey was completed in 1890 in Japan; 1906 in Taiwan; 1918 in Korea). Reliability of data after the cadastral surveys is also subject to criticism. See James I. Nakamura, *Agriculture Production and the Economic Development of Japan: 1873–1922* (Princeton: Princeton University Press, 1966); *Incentives, Productivity Gap, and Agricultural Development in Japan, Taiwan, and Korea* (New York: Columbia University, Economics Department, 1969) mimeo. The questions regarding the official statistics of Japan raised by Nakamura have been widely discussed by Japanese and other scholars (see footnote 1 in Chapter 6). Although the data for Taiwan and Korea need to be examined in more detail, we will resort in this study to official statistics.

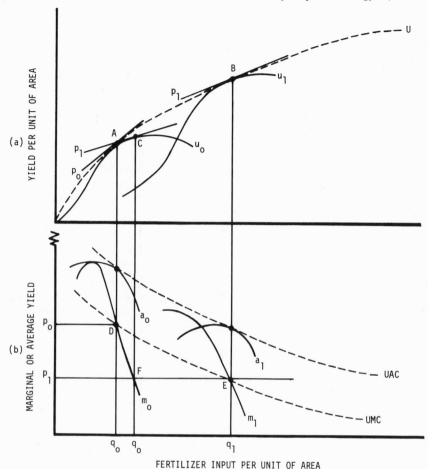

FIGURE 9-1. Hypothetical process of the induced development of a high-yielding variety (HYV) of rice.

unfavorable environmental conditions, including a precarious water supply and rampant weeds. In such conditions the traditional varieties represented an optimum technology.[3]

The fertilizer response curves for the traditional varieties and the HYV's are typically drawn as u_0 and u_1, respectively, in Figure 9-1a (same as Figure 4-8). We assume the metaproduction function (U) which is the envelope of many such response curves, each representing a variety characterized by a different degree of fertilizer responsiveness; a_0 and m_0, a_1, and m_1, and UAC and UMC in Figure 9-1b are the average and marginal product curves corre-

---

[3] Tadayo Wataabe and Keizaburo Kawaguchi, "Increasing the Rice Yield in South and Southeast Asia," *Asian Survey* 8 (October 1968): 820–28.

sponding, respectively, to u_0, u_1, and U; u_0 represents an optimum (profit-maximizing) variety for the fertilizer-rice price ratio, p_0; and u_1 represents an optimum for p_1. However, even if the fertilizer-rice price ratio declines from p_0 to p_1, individual farmers cannot move from A (or D) to B (or E), and will be trapped at C (or F) unless u_1 becomes available. C represents an equilibrium for a response curve (u_0) that is actually available for farmers, but a disequilibrium in terms of potential alternatives described by the metaproduction function (u_1). It is hypothesized that the development of a new variety (u_1) is undertaken when the benefit of adjustment from C (or F) to B (or E) exceeds the cost of development of u_1. This is an oversimplified picture. The location and shape of the fertilizer response curve depends on the conditions of water control and husbandry practices. If water supply and control are inadequate, the HYV's would fail to show the fertilizer-responsive character. On the other hand, it is quite possible that in the paddy fields having good irrigation and drainage facilities the HYV's produce higher yields than the traditional varieties, even at the zero level of artificial fertilization. In such fields, significant amounts of plant nutrients are supplied from the efficient decomposition of organic materials and from nutrients carried in by irrigation water. Yield response to fertilizer is also dependent on effective weed control, because short-stalked HYV's are more subject to competition for sunlight from vigorous growth of weeds encouraged by the high level of fertilization. Application of herbicides and weed-preventing practices, such as checkrow planting, become of crucial importance in accurate measurement of the fertilizer response relationships. (We again emphasize that in this formulation the fertilizer input per hectare should be regarded as an index representing the level of the package of inputs complementary with fertilizer in realizing the yield potential of the HYV's).[4]

Adjustments along the metaproduction function involve time and costs. The development of fertilizer-responsive HYV's requires investment in research. Better husbandry practices must be developed and learned. Complementary investment in irrigation and drainage may be required to secure adequate control of water. It takes time to reorient the efforts of public agencies in such directions in response to price changes. It is particularly costly and time-consuming to build adequate institutions and competent research staff.

These processes may be inferred with respect to Table 9–1, which compares for Japan and other selected countries in Asia the price of fertilizers relative

---

[4] The choice of varieties (u_0 or u_1) depends not only on fertilizer and rice prices but also on the costs of water control and cultural practices. It is a reasonable assumption, however, that the rise in marginal productivity of fertilizer due to the development of the HYV's (u_1) raises the marginal productivities of these complementary inputs. A decline in the price of fertilizer can thus play a leading role in changing the economic return on investment in developing the HYV's. And the development of higher yielding varieties can sharply increase the return on investment in irrigation and in plant protection.

Table 9-1. Fertilizer-rice price ratios and rice yields per hectare in selected Asian countries and in Japan, 1883–1962

Country	Currency unit	Price of fertilizer: per m. ton of nitrogen (1)	Price of rice: per m. ton of milled rice (2)	Fertilizer-rice price ratio (1)/(2)	Rice yield per hectare: m. ton of paddy (3)
Intercountry comparison 1963–65					
India	rupee	1,750	595[a]	2.9	1.5
			723[b]	2.4	
Pakistan (East)	rupee	1,632	780	2.1	1.7
Philippines	peso	1,048	530	2.0	1.3
Thailand	U.S. dollar	229	70	3.3	1.6
Japan	1,000 yen	97	99	1.0	5.0
1955–57					
India	rupee	1,675	417[a]	4.0	1.3
			505[b]	3.3	
Pakistan (East)	rupee	1,322	511	2.6	1.4
Philippines	peso	962	352	2.7	1.1
Thailand	U.S. dollar	393	79	5.0	1.4
Japan	1,000 yen	119	77	1.5	4.8
Japan's time series					
1958–62	1,000 yen	100	85	1.2	4.9
1953–57	1,000 yen	113	75	1.5	4.2
1933–37	yen	566	208	2.7	3.8
1923–27	yen	1,021	277	3.7	3.6
1913–17	yen	803	125	6.4	3.5
1903–07	yen	815	106	7.7	3.1
1893–97	yen	670	69	9.7	2.6
1883–87	yen	450	42	10.7	n.a.

[a] Price at Sambalpur (Orissa).

[b] Price at Bombay. (1) Price paid by farmers. Intercountry data: average unit price of nitrogen contained in ammonium sulphate; 1963–65 data are the averages for 1962/63–1964/65; 1955–57 data are the data of 1956/57; government subsidies of 50 percent for 1963–65 and of 40 percent for 1955–57 are added to Pakistan's original data. Japan data: average unit price of nitrogen contained in commercial fertilizers. (2) This is the wholesale price at milled rice basis. Japan data are converted from brown rice basis to a milled rice basis assuming 10 percent for processing cost. (3) Japan data are converted from a brown rice basis to a milled rice basis assuming 0.8 for a conversion factor.

Source: Intercountry data: FAO, *Production Yearbook*, various issues. Japan data: Kazushi Ohkawa et al. (ed.), *Long-term Economic Statistics of Japan*, Vol. 9 (Tokyo: Toyokeizaishimposha, 1966), pp. 202–3; Nobufumi Kayo (ed.) *Nihon Nogyo Kisotokei*, (Tokyo: Norin Suisangyo Seisankojokaigi, 1958), p. 514; Toyokeizaishimposha, *Bukku Yoran* (Tokyo, 1967), p. 80; Institute of Developing Economies, *One Hundred Years of Agricultural Statistics in Japan* (Tokyo, 1969), p. 136.

to the price of rice and rice yield per hectare of paddy area planted. It shows (a) that the higher rice yield per hectare in Japan than in Southeast Asian countries is associated with a considerably lower price of fertilizer relative to the price of rice; (b) a high inverse association between the rice yield per hectare and the fertilizer-rice price ratio in the Japanese time-series data; (c) a substantial decline in the fertilizer-rice price ratios in the Asian countries from 1955–57 to 1963–65 in other Asian countries, associated with only small gains in rice yield per hectare; and (d) that fertilizer-rice price ratios in the Southeast Asian countries today are much more favorable than those which prevailed in Japan at the beginning of this century and earlier.

If we consider the yield comparisons in Table 3–2, it seems reasonable to infer that the considerable differences in the rice yield and the price ratios between Japan and Southeast Asian countries can best be interpreted in terms of the different fertilizer response curves as shown by u_0 and u_1 in Figure 9–1. The consistent rise in the rice yield per hectare, accompanied by the consistent decline in the fertilizer-rice price ratio in the historical experience of Japan, indicates a process of movement along the metaproduction function. The history of the development of Japanese agricultural technology, including the deliberate efforts of veteran farmers to select and propagate superior varieties, the vigorous activities in experiment stations and other research institutions, and the remarkable shifts of rice varieties over time, is clearly inconsistent with an assumption of movement along a fixed production response curve (u_0).

When we examine the data for Southeast Asia, some intriguing questions remain unanswered. Why did rice yields per hectare in the Southeast Asian countries increase so slowly from 1955–57 to 1963–65, in spite of the substantial decline in the fertilizer-rice price ratio? And, why did rice yields in these countries remain at low levels despite fertilizer-rice price ratios which were more favorable than in Japan at the beginning of this century? The answer must be sought in the time lag required to move along the metaproduction function. This time lag tends to be extremely long in situations characterized by lack of adequate institutions and human capital to generate the flow of new techniques. Apparently before 1960 the countries in Southeast Asia, even though the fertilizer-rice price ratio declined from p_0 to p_1, could not move from A (or D) to B (or E) in Figure 9–1 because of a lag in the investment by public agencies in the experiment station capacity necessary to create a new technology (u_1). They seem to have been trapped at C (or F).

The dramatic appearance of the HYV's after 1965 can be interpreted in this light. The efforts of the International Rice Research Institute, the University of the Philippines College of Agriculture, and the Bureau of Plant Industry in the Philippines, of the Japanese plant breeders in Malaysia under the Colombo Plan, of the Indian Council of Agricultural Research, and of various other national research organizations were designed to develop fertilizer-responsive HYV's. By the mid-1960's a number of varieties satisfying these requirements, including IR-8, C4-63 Malinja, and ADT-27, were being released to farmers. It is hypothesized that these innovations were induced by a potential high pay-off of investment in crop breeding research, thus permitting the adjustment from C (or F) to B (or E). Because the "proto-type HYV's" were already

in existence in Japan, the United States, and other temperate zone rice producing countries, it was possible to realize major advances in potential productivity from a relatively modest research investment. A critical element is that
realization of the high pay-off to investment in research was dependent on a
social decision to invest in research rather than on decisions made by individual firms. The farms operated by Asian producers are, except in the cases
of a few export commodities, too small to capture the gains necessary to pay
for research investments. It is only when public agencies (or semi-public
agencies such as foundations) perceive this opportunity and allocate funds for
such research that technological transfer or development becomes feasible.

Declines in the price of fertilizer relative to the price of rice during the
1950's and 1960's were the result of increased productivity in the chemical
fertilizer industry in the developed countries, which was transmitted to less
developed countries through international trade, and rapid shifts in rice
demand due to population growth which outpaced production increases. In
most parts of Asia characterized by high population density the increase in
population and food demand has resulted in increasing pressure against land.
It seems reasonable to hypothesize that the pay-off of the crop breeding research was enhanced by the capacity of the HYV's to facilitate the substitution
of an increasingly abundant factor (fertilizer) for an increasingly scarce factor
(land). It seems valid to regard the agricultural research which produced the
new fertilizer-responsive varieties as a response to a decline in the price of
fertilizer relative to the price of land and to the price of rice. In the absence
of a decline in the real price of fertilizer, such research might not have been
attempted[5] and, even if attempted, the results would have been incompatible

---

[5] "Organized agricultural research was established in India before independence but until
very recently few resources were devoted to the development of high yielding varieties of
rice and wheat. The puzzle is, why this long neglect of the advances in biological information
in developing new and better varieties? It is not because there have been no competent agricultural scientists in India specializing on rice and wheat varieties. It is my contention that
they saw the demand of farmers for varieties that would perform best given the depleted
soils, the weather uncertainties, the limited control of water and the poor farm equipment
that characterize so much of India. Their assessment was undoubtedly correct, and given
these circumstances, the gains in agricultural productivity from research were meager. It is
also clear that the new high yielding varieties of wheat and rice are strongly dependent upon
fertilizer, whereas the research entrepreneurs of India were serving a country with virtually
no commercial fertilizer. To contend that Indian agricultural scientists should have anticipated the recent marked increases in the supply of fertilizer available to farmers in India
seems far-fetched to me. . . . Now that there is awareness of these new possibilities, government and farmers are using their influence in bringing about change." T. W. Schultz, "The
Allocation of Resources to Research," *Resource Allocation in Agricultural Research*, ed.
Walter L. Fishel (Minneapolis: University of Minnesota Press, forthcoming, 1971). This
view by Schultz emphasizes only one aspect of the phenomenon. Another important aspect
in the reorientation of research efforts by Indian scientists is the development of new varieties
by IRRI and CIMMYT; these varieties provided the prototype for Indian plant breeders by
establishing new possibilities and new concepts ("plant-type" concepts, etc.). It seems
likely that if such a prototype had not been provided, the response of Indian scientists (and
of scientists in other countries of Southeast Asia) to the increased availability and lower
prices of fertilizer would have been further delayed.

with price relationships among factors and products and would have been similar to earlier attempts to introduce mechanization in tropical rice production. Success of research depends on whether it is directed to the generation of a technology compatible with the market prices that reflect product demand and factor endowments of the economy.

TRANSFER OF RICE PRODUCTION TECHNOLOGY FROM JAPAN TO TAIWAN AND KOREA

In this section we attempt to test the hypothesis proposed in the previous section against the experience of transmitting Japanese rice technology to Taiwan and Korea during the 1920's and the 1930's. To be more specific, a hypothesis to be tested is that (a) fertilizer-rice price ratios in Taiwan and Korea before the 1920's had already been favorable enough to make it rewarding to develop the fertilizer-responsive HYV's, but due to the lack of local research and development capacity in Taiwan and Korea this opportunity had not been exploited; (b) only when the colonial governments, pressed by the demand from the mother country, responded to this opportunity by investing in rice breeding research, were the HYV's adaptable to the local ecologies of Taiwan and Korea actually developed; and (c) these HYV's represent a technical change biased toward the fertilizer-using and land-saving direction that was compatible with changes in the factor endowments of the economy. As is the case with the recent development of HYV's in tropical Asia, this represents a transfer of "prototype" agricultural technology existing in developed countries (Japan) to less developed countries (Taiwan and Korea), through the transfer of scientists. It is hypothesized that institutional innovations and the increased public investment in research leading to this technology transfer were induced by the high social pay-off expected from adjustment from a secular disequilibrium (*C* in Figure 9–1) to a secular equilibrium (*B* in Figure 9–1), although the social pay-off in this case was primarily in terms of the benefits to Japan rather than to Taiwan and Korea.[6]

---

[6] This technology transfer involved relatively minor costs because it did not cause major changes in agrarian structure; peasant or small-scale farms based on family labor continued to be basic units of production. Whether this will be the case with the green revolution remains a major unsolved question. See Bruce F. Johnston and John Cownie, "The Seed-Fertilizer Revolution and Labor Force Absorption," *American Economic Review* 59 (September 1969): 569–82 and John Cownie, Bruce F. Johnston and Bart Duff, "The Quantitative Impact of the Seed-Fertilizer Revolution in West Pakistan: an Exploratory Study," *Food Research Institute Studies in Agricultural Economics, Trade, and Development*, vol. 9, No. 1 (1970): 57–95. For an extreme example of the impact of technical change on the demand for labor see Richard H. Day, "The Economics of Technological Change and the Demise of the Sharecropper," *American Economic Review* 57 (June 1967): 427–49; also Andrew Schmitz and David Seckler, "Mechanized Agriculture and Social Welfare: The Case of the Tomato Harvester," *American Journal of Agricultural Economics* 52 (November 1970): 569–77.

Background

The recent development of new HYV's in the tropics involved the application of science to the production problems of peasant agriculture, with the ultimate goal of promoting over-all economic growth. This was the process of agricultural development in Japan, Taiwan, and Korea until the collapse of the Japanese Empire during World War II. The primary purpose was to finance and support industrial development in metropolitan Japan by generating agricultural surpluses through increased productivity. The technological potentials available in the late nineteenth and early twentieth centuries were first exploited in domestic agriculture in Japan, and when they were exhausted, the colonial agricultural development policy was launched.

This process is reflected in the movements in rice production and yield per hectare in Japan, Taiwan, and Korea (Figures 9–2 and 9–3).[7] The major source of rice output increase necessary to meet the increase in consumer demand, associated with rapid industrialization and urbanization in Japan through the first two decades of the twentieth century, was primarily yield increases in domestic agriculture in the western part of Japan until around 1905 and in the eastern part from 1905 to 1920. These differential rates of growth in the East and West reflect the lag in diffusion of improved varieties and techniques to the East.

As we indicated in Chapter 7, the agricultural productivity growth of Japan in the Meiji Period (1868–1911) was supported by the propagation of techniques, practiced by the better farmers, which were screened and tailored by experiment station workers following the modern agricultural science traditions observed in Germany. The initial phase of rice yield increase was caused by the diffusion of superior varieties selected by veteran farmers (*rōnō*) in the western part of Japan, which included the most advanced regions (Kinki and Northern Kyushu). The superior varieties in the West provided the prototype for farmers and experiment station workers in the East in developing improved varieties for their ecologies. Regional patterns in the spread of the *rōnō* varieties (Figure 7–3 (Chapter 7)) are consistent with movements in rice yields (Figure 9–3).

It appears that this process of rice productivity growth in Meiji Japan—a significant decline in the fertilizer-rice price ratio, the spread of improved varieties, increases in fertilizer input and rice yield per hectare from 1895 to 1915 (rows 1–4, Table 9–2)—indicates movement along the metaproduction function in response to a decline in the fertilizer-rice price ratio, as represented by a movement from *A* to *B* in Figure 9–1.

The development and diffusion of these high-yielding varieties were also

---

[7] It should be remembered that double cropping of rice is commonly practiced in Taiwan while it is virtually nonexistent in Japan and Korea. Productivity of land in Taiwan is, therefore, higher, relative to Japan and Korea, than the rice yield per hectare planted indicates.

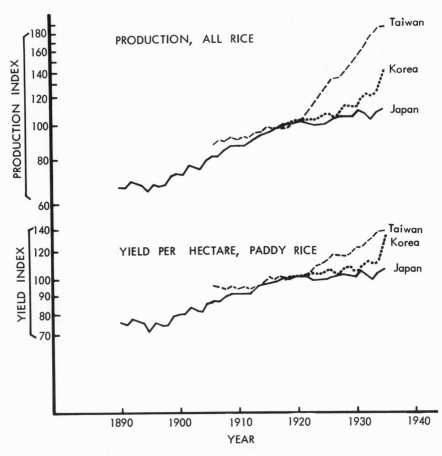

FIGURE 9-2. Indices (in logs.) of total production and yield per hectare of rice, Japan, Korea, and Taiwan, five-year moving average, 1890–1935. 1917–22 = 100. (*Sources:* Japan—*LTES*, Vol. 9, pp. 166–67; *Norimsho Ruinen Tokeihyo* [Historical Statistics of Ministry of Agriculture and Forestry], [Tokyo, 1945], p. 24. Korea—*Chosen Sotokutu Tokeihyo* [*Statistical Yearbook of Government General Korea*], 1925 issue [p. 94], 1930 issue [p. 92]. Taiwan—Chinese-American Joint Commission on Rural Construction Taiwan Agricultural Statistics, [Taipei, 1966], pp. 23–27.)

based on the relatively well-established water control facilities in Japanese paddy fields, which raised the potential pay-off of the HYV's. Even at the beginning of the Meiji Restoration almost 100 percent of the paddy fields in Japan were irrigated, although the water supply was not necessarily sufficient and appropriate drainage was lacking in many cases.[8] These irrigation systems

---

[8] The fact that no statistics have ever been collected on the irrigated area is consistent with the fact that in Japan "paddy field" and "irrigated field" have been regarded as identical. Construction of drainage facilities has been the primary objective in land improvement projects in Japan.

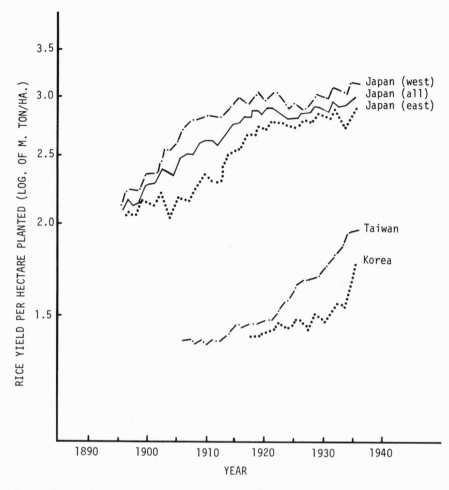

FIGURE 9-3. Rice yields per hectare planted for Japan, Taiwan, and Korea, five-year moving average, 1895–1935. (*Sources:* Nobufumi Kayo, *Nihon Nogyo Kiso Tokei* [Basic Statistics of Japanese Agriculture] [Tokyo: Norin-Suisangyo Seisansei Kojo Kaigi, 1958]: 607–52; Taiwan Government-General, *Taiwan Nogyo Nenpo* [Yearbook of Taiwan Agriculture], [Taipei], various issues; Korea Government-General, *Nogyo Tokeihyo* [Agricultural Statistics] [Seoul], various issues.)

had been built during the long peaceful feudal Tokugawa period, primarily by communal labor under the encouragement of feudal lords.

As described in Chapter 7, the exploitation of indigenous potential and the lag in scientific research in supplying new potential, when confronted with the expansion of demand due to World War I, resulted in a serious rice shortage and forced the rice price upward to an unprecedented level. This caused serious disruption in the urban areas, culminating in the *Kome Sodo* (Rice Riot) in 1918.

Table 9–2. Fertilizer-rice price ratio, seed improvement, fertilizer input and rice yield per hectare: Japan, Taiwan, and Korea, selected years

	1895	1905	1915	1920	1925	1930	1935
Japan							
1) Fertilizer-rice price ratio (m. tons of brown rice purchasable with a ton of $N + P_2O_5 + K_2O$)	7.0	5.2	4.4	3.5	3.0	3.0	2.2
2) Ratio of area planted in improved varieties to total paddy area planted in rice	0.04	0.30	0.40	0.42	0.42	0.56	0.56
3) Fertilizer input per ha. (kg. of $N + P_2O_5 + K_2O$)	13	24	49	63	79	96	104
4) Rice yield per ha. (m. tons of brown rice)	2.06	2.46	2.79	2.91	2.84	2.89	3.04
Taiwan							
5) Fertilizer-rice price ratio (m. tons of brown rice purchasable with a ton of $N + P_2O_5 + K_2O$)					4.5	4.5	4.2
6) Ratio of area planted in Ponlai varieties to total paddy area planted in rice					0.13	0.23	0.46
7) Fertilizer input per ha. (kg. of $N + P_2O_5 + K_2O$)				12	20	33	55
8) Rice yield per ha. (m. tons of brown rice)			1.47	1.47	1.63	1.75	1.97
Korea							
9) Fertilizer-rice price ratio (m. tons of brown rice purchasable with a ton of $N + P_2O_5 + K_2O$)				3.3	3.0	3.5	2.5
10) Ratio of area planted in Japanese varieties to total paddy area planted in rice				0.22	0.57	0.72	0.84
11) Fertilizer input per ha. (kg. of $N + P_2O_5 + K_2O$)				1.3	3.4	12	28
12) Rice yield per ha. (m. tons of brown rice)				1.43	1.50	1.48	1.82

Notes: Data are five-year averages, centering at the years shown except for arable land area which is measured at the years shown.

1) Unit price of plant nutrients in commercial fertilizer divided by unit price of rice. (Source: Kazushi Ohkawa et al. [ed.], Long-term Economic Statistics of Japan since 1868 [abbreviated as LTES] 9 [Tokyo: Toyokeizaishimposha, 1966]: 146–47, 166–68 and 194–201.)

2) Series J10 in Appendix Table C–3.

3) Plant nutrients contained in commercial fertilizers per hectare of arable land. (Source: Series J6 and J9 in Appendix Table C–3.)

4) Yield per hectare planted in paddy rice. (Source: Series J10 in Appendix Table C–3.)

5) Unit price of plant nutrients in commercial fertilizer divided by unit price of rice. Commodity flow estimates of fertilizer consumption (production + import − export) after 1932 were spliced to the estimates for preceding years based on rural survey by multiplying by the 1929–32 average ratio. (Source: Michio Kanai, "Taiwan," Koshinkoku Nogyo Hatten no Shojoken (Conditions of Agricultural Development in Less Developed Countries) in Chujiro Ozaki (ed.) [Tokyo: Institute of Development Economies, 1968], pp. 82–112 and 101; Taiwan Government-General, Taiwan Nogyo Nenpo [Yearbook of Taiwan Agriculture], various issues.)

6) Taiwan Nogyo Nenpo, various issues.

7) Plant nutrients contained in commercial fertilizers applied to crops other than sugar cane per hectare of arable land area minus sugar cane area. Kanai's estimates of total plant nutrient consumption were apportioned to sugar cane and other crops in proportion to the values of commercial fertilizers applied to sugar cane. The data of fertilizer applications by crops are available only until 1932. The data after 1932 were estimated by fixing the compositions to 1929–32 values. (Source: Kanai, "Taiwan"; Taiwan Nogyo Nenpo, various issues. The 1920 figure is estimated by linear extrapolation using the rate of growth from 1925 to 1930.)

8) Yield per hectare planted in paddy rice. (Source: Taiwan Nogyo Nenpo, various issues.)

9) Unit price of plant nutrients in commercial fertilizers divided by unit price of rice. (Source: Korea Government-General, Nogyo Tokeihyo [Agricultural Statistics], various issues.)

10) Nogyo Tokeihyo, various issues.

11) Plant nutrients contained in commercial fertilizers per hectare of arable land. (Source: Nogyo Tokeihyo, various issues.) Total quantities of plant nutrients were calculated from the quantities of individual fertilizer consumed using the following conversion factors:

	Fish meal	Bone meal	Other animal matters	Soy-bean cake	Other oil seed cakes	Brans	Other vegetable matters	Ammonium sulphate	Sodium nitrate	Superphosphate of lime	Potassium sulphate	Other chemical fert.	Mixed fert.
N	0.08	0.04	0.08	0.07	0.06	0.02	0.06	0.21	0.15	0	0	0.08	0.08
P_2O_5	0.07	0.23	0.07	0.01	0.03	0.04	0.02	0	0	0.17	0	0.08	0.08
K_2O	0.03	0	0.03	0.02	0.01	0.02	0.02	0	0	0	0.50	0.05	0.05

12) Yield per hectare planted in paddy rice. (Source: Nogyo Tokeihyo, various issues.)

Japan was then faced with a choice between high rice prices, high cost of living, and high wages, on the one hand, and a drain on foreign exchange by large-scale rice imports on the other. Both were unfavorable to industrial development. The reaction of the government was to organize programs to import rice from the overseas territories of Korea and Taiwan. In order to release rice for export to Japan, short-run exploitation policies which involved importing millet to Korea from Manchuria forced Korean farmers to substitute lower quality grain for rice in domestic consumption. A similar squeeze was also practiced in Taiwan, forcing Taiwanese farmers to substitute sweet potatoes for rice in their diet. This was enforced by a squeeze on real income through taxation and government monopoly sales of such commodities as liquor, tobacco, and salt. The longer-run program was to introduce development programs designed to increase the yield and output of rice in those colonial territories.[9] Before the rice riot, "development efforts in Taiwan were concentrated on sugar production and little was done in Korea. It was claimed that the development of rice production in those overseas territories should be suppressed since it would foster competition against Japanese agriculture."[10]

Under the program titled *Sanmai Zoshoku Keikaku* (Rice Production Development Program), the government invested in irrigation and water control and in research and extension, in order to develop and diffuse high-yielding Japanese rice varieties adapted to the local ecologies of Korea and Taiwan. The expenditure for agricultural development by the Government-General of Korea before and after the start of the Rice Production Development Program (1920) clearly indicates this drastic policy reorientation. The total agricultural development expenditure jumped from a 1915–19 total of 3.5 million yen to a 1920–24 total of 18.6 million yen; expenditure for experiment stations increased from 1.1 million yen to 2.8 million yen; and the expenditure for land improvement projects, including irrigation and drainage facilities, went from

[9] This reorientation of the colonial agricultural development policy, in response to the shortage of rice in Japan, is clearly described by Tobata and Ohkawa in reference to Korea: "Since the Rice Riot Japan has faced a so-called 'population-food problem.' Rapid increase in population and even more rapid increase in nonagricultural population, as the result of industrial development, have been pressing the need for an increase in rice production. In Japan, however, rice farming had already approached a technical limit of intensification, and economically there was little possibility of increasing rice production. Therefore, the solution of the population-food problem was sought in the direction of enlarging the rice production area. In this connection Korea represented the biggest hope, where extensive and underdeveloped farming have been practiced without progress for hundreds of years. It was anticipated that if Korean agriculture were to be developed by the weapons of modern science it would be possible to increase its intensity as well as to expand the paddy field area." Seiichi Tobata and Kazushi Ohkawa, *Chosen Beikoku Keizairon* (A Treatise on Rice Economy in Korea) (Tokyo: Nihon Gakujutsu Shinkokai, 1935), p. 7.

[10] Nihon Nogyo Hattatsushi (History of Japanese Agricultural Development), 10 volumes (Tokyo: Chuokoronsha, 1953–1958), henceforth abbreviated as *NNHS*, vol. 9, p. 597.

only 334 thousand yen to 12 million yen.[11] Rapid increases in rice yields in Taiwan and Korea, accompanied by stagnation in Japanese rice yields, were the result of this policy reorientation.

Taiwan Case

The most spectacular success was attained in Taiwan with the development of the Ponlai varieties. The Ponlai varieties are rice varieties "developed by cross-breeding of Japanese varieties or between Japanese and traditional Taiwan (Chailai) varieties to have photo-sensitivities different from the original Japanese varieties."[12] They are more fertilizer-responsive, high-yielding, with adequate water control and cultural practices, and are better suited to the Japanese taste than are the Chailai varieties (Indica).

It was not easy to adapt Japanese varieties to the tropical climate of Taiwan. Even before the policy reorientation after the Rice Riot, when the effort of the Government-General was directed to improving the Chailai varieties to satisfy Taiwan's domestic demand, research to adapt Japanese varieties to tropical ecology had been conducted, although on a small scale. A breakthrough occurred when Eikichi Iso of the Agricultural Division, Central Research Institute of the Government-General, found that the Japanese varieties could be grown successfully by reducing by one-half the time the rice seedlings remained in the nursery bed.[13]

With this breakthrough, and under the pressing demand of Japan, the Government-General shifted the emphasis from improvement of the Chailai varieties to the development and propagation of the Ponlai varieties. Areas planted with the Ponlai varieties grew from 400 hectares in 1922, the first year this statistic was recorded, to 131 thousand hectares in 1930, and 296 thousand hectares (almost one-half of the paddy field area planted) in 1935. This rapid diffusion was based on the high pay-off of the Ponlai varieties. According to the rice production costs survey conducted by the Government-General in 1926–27, both profit (total revenue minus total cost) and farm family income (profit plus family labor wages) per *chia* (0.97 hectare) were very much higher with the Ponlai varieties than with the Chailai varieties (Table 9–3).

In the cost comparison in Table 9–3 differences in (a) fertilizer expense; (b) wages; and (c) rent are particularly significant. Larger expenditures for fertilizer for the production of Ponlai varieties clearly reflect their higher

[11] Kuro Kobayakawa, (ed.), *Chosen Nogyo Hattatsushi: Seisakuhen* (History of Korean Agriculture: Policy Volume) (Tokyo: Yuhokyokai, 1959), pp. 117–18.

[12] Eikichi Iso, *Horaimai Danwa* (Discourse on the Ponlai Rice) (Yamaguchi: Udokukai, 1964), p. 18.

[13] From fifty to sixty days to twenty to forty days in the first crop: from thirty to forty days to fifteen to twenty days in the second crop. Ibid., pp. 76–77.

Table 9–3. Comparison of the costs of Ponlai and Chailai rice production per *chia**

	1926 second crop			1927 first crop		
	Ponlai (1)	Chailai (2)	(1)–(2)	Ponlai (3)	Chailai (4)	(3)–(4)
			yen			
Seed	8.12	3.97	4.15	8.31	4.17	4.14
Fertilizer[a]	51.26	25.50	25.76	63.58	26.90	36.68
Wage:	112.38	93.86	18.52	126.20	103.83	22.37
Family labor	73.30	54.57	18.73	81.51	62.75	18.76
Hired labor	39.08	39.29	−0.21	44.69	41.08	3.61
Implements and building	3.76	4.24	−0.48	4.55	4.83	−0.28
Miscellaneous	2.46	1.01	1.45	9.25	11.73	−2.48
Tax and rate	1.41	1.66	−0.25	1.81	1.57	0.24
Rent	147.20	121.70	25.50	176.40	133.42	42.98
Total cost	326.59	251.94	75.15	390.10	286.45	103.65
Total revenue[b]	382.04	285.31	96.73	466.76	285.26	181.50
Profit[c]	55.45	33.37	22.18	76.66	−1.19	77.85
Farm family income[d]	128.75	87.94	40.81	158.17	61.56	96.61

* 1 chia = 0.97 hectares.
a Include self-supplied fertilizers.
b Include the value of straw.
c Profit = total revenue − total cost.
d Farm family income = profit + wage for family labor.

Sources: Taiwan Government-General, Bureau of Colonial Development, *Shuyonosan-butsu Keizai Chosa* (Economic Survey of Major Agricultural Products) No. 6, pp. 11, 48–49, 62–63, 82–83, 112–13, 241, 249; and No. 9, pp. 11, 13, 15, 17, 50–51, 64–65, 118–19, 152–53 (Taipei, 1928). Data are for tenant farmers.

fertilizer-responsiveness.[14] Higher wage costs show that the Ponlai varieties require more labor and better husbandry, including checkrow planting, deep plowing, more intensive weeding, and insect control. Higher rent for the Ponlai varieties indicates that these varieties were grown in areas with better water control. It appears that the economic implications of the Ponlai varieties

[14] The fertilizer-responsive character of the Japanese varieties from which the Ponlai varieties were developed relative to the Chailai varieties is demonstrated by the following results of experiments, which compare the average fertilizer responses of four Japanese varieties and four Chailai varieties:

	No fertilization	Level of ordinary fertilization	Double of ordinary level of fertilization
		metric tons per hectare[a]	
Taiwan Chailai	2.024	2.701	2.815
Japanese Ponlai	1.587	2.713	3.081

a Brown rice basis.

Source: NNHS, vol. 9, p. 221.

for Taiwan in the 1920's were essentially equivalent to those of "miracle rice" in the tropics today.[15]

A remarkable aspect of the rapid diffusion of the Ponlai varieties during the 1920's and 1930's is that it was not accompanied by an appreciable decline in fertilizer prices relative to rice prices, as was the case with the improved varieties in Japan prior to 1920 (compare row 1 and row 5 in Table 9–2). As discussed previously, the spread of improved varieties in Japan, accompanied by a decline in the fertilizer-rice price ratio, suggests movement from A to B in Figure 9–1. In contrast, the rapid propagation of the Ponlai varieties in Taiwan, without any significant decline in the fertilizer-rice price ratio, seems to indicate a movement from C to B. Since Taiwan had been included in the Japanese empire common market, it seems reasonable to assume that the fertilizer price in Taiwan declined relative to rice price, parallel with its decline in Japan prior to 1920 (from p_0 to p_1). In the absence of comparable levels of development of scientific knowledge in Taiwan, this opportunity could not be exploited, and rice production in Taiwan was trapped at C on the response curve of the Chailai varieties (u_0). When foreign (Japanese) agricultural scientists turned their attention to this situation, in response to the demand of the mother country, the potential was exploited through the dramatic development and propagation of the Ponlai varieties (u_1).

Korean Case

The Korean experience as summarized in Table 9–2 (rows 9–12) indicates: (a) the ratio of the price of fertilizer relative to the price of rice was almost as low as in Japan; (b) propagation of Japanese varieties in the 1920's was not accompanied by a significant reduction in the relative price of fertilizer; and (c) in spite of an earlier start in propagation of Japanese varieties, fertilizer input per hectare in the 1920's was at a much lower level than in Taiwan; and the rice yield did not start to increase until the late 1920's.

Korea was situated closer to Manchuria, Japan's major supplier of nitrogen in the form of the soybean cake until the 1920's. In the 1930's Japanese industrialists, attracted by abundant hydroelectric power, built large-scale modern nitrogen plants in North Korea. Korean agriculture thus had access to cheaper sources of plant nutrients than did Taiwan. Rapid diffusion of Japanese rice varieties and rapid yield increases, in spite of rather stagnant relative prices of fertilizer, can be explained in terms of the movement from C to B in Figure 9–1. This is the same as in the case of Taiwan.

There is, however, an apparent contradiction in the Korean experience. In

---

[15] Randolph Barker and E. V. Quintana, "Returns and Costs for Local and High Yielding Rice Varieties," *Philippine Economic Journal* 7 (Second Semester, 1968): 145–61. The entire issue contains the papers presented at a seminar-workshop on the economics of rice production held at the International Rice Research Institute, December 8–9, 1967.

Table 9-4. Irrigation and double-cropping ratios in paddy field: Korea and Taiwan, selected years

		Year				
		1915	1920	1925	1930	1935
Taiwan						
1) Paddy area	1,000 ha.	343	367	374	396	479
2) Sugar cane area	1,000 ha.	83	105	127	106	118
3) Irrigated area	1,000 ha.	239	268	350	442	466
4) Double-cropping paddy area	1,000 ha.		246	266	292	313
5) Ratio of irrigated area	(3) ÷ [(1) + (2)]	0.56	0.57	0.70	0.88	0.78
6) Ratio of double-cropping area	(4) ÷ (1)		0.67	0.71	0.74	0.65
Korea						
7) Paddy area	1,000 ha.	1,168	1,531	1,551	1,605	1,668
8) Irrigated paddy area	1,000 ha.			758	953	1,152
9) Double-cropping paddy area	1,000 ha.	160	240	266	353	429
10) Ratio of irrigated area	(8) ÷ (7)			0.49	0.59	0.69
11) Ratio of double-cropping area	(9) ÷ (7)	0.14	0.16	0.17	0.22	0.26

Note: (1) Area of paddy field; (2) area of sugar cane harvested; (3) irrigated arable land area; (7) area of paddy field; (8) irrigated paddy field area.

Sources: Taiwan—Taiwan Government-General, *Taiwan Nogyo Nenpo* (Yearbook of Taiwan Agriculture), various issues. Korea—Korea Government-General, *Nogyo Tokeihyo* (Agricultural Statistics) and *Chosen Tochikairyo Jigyo Yoran* (Summary Report of Korean Land Improvement Projects), various issues.

spite of an earlier start in the diffusion of Japanese varieties, the level of fertilizer input per hectare was low and the yield take-off lagged in Korea relative to Taiwan. The key to this contradiction seems to be the difference in the level of irrigation and water control. Table 9-4 compares progress in paddy field irrigation between Taiwan and Korea. Since data on the area of irrigated paddy fields are not available for Taiwan, we calculated the ratio of irrigated paddy field area to total paddy field area on the assumption that irrigation was developed only for rice and sugar production (which seems a rather reasonable approximation). The ratios thus calculated check well with the ratios of double-cropped paddy areas. In Taiwan, irrigation is required for double-cropping of rice.

From Table 9-4 it is apparent that irrigation construction lagged in Korea compared with Taiwan. In terms of the ratio of irrigated paddy area to total paddy area, Korea in 1925 did not reach the level of Taiwan in 1915. Judging from the movements in double-cropping ratios (which are not comparable with Taiwan in absolute level because of the different climate) it seems reasonable to assume that progress in water control in Korea was greatly accelerated during the 1925–35 period. This is compatible with the expenditure patterns for land improvement projects of the Government-General as seen earlier. In the literature on Korean agriculture it is common to identify the lack of irrigation as the critical cause for low productivity. Tobata and Ohkawa wrote in 1935:[16] "The first technical condition of rice production is nothing but water control. But paddy field in Korea is so called 'rain-fed paddy field,' . . . accordingly marshy paddy field with drainage difficulty, which is considered of low quality in Japan is considered good paddy field. . . . Who would dare to apply fertilizers under such conditions?" It was natural to place a high investment priority on irrigation when the Rice Production Development Program was initiated in 1920.

The climate of Korea is much more like that of Japan than is Taiwan's. Rice varieties from northern Japan were directly transferable to Korea. But due to the precarious water supply, even in most of the so-called "irrigated paddy field" areas, the Japanese varieties introduced into Korea were not the high fertilizer-responsive varieties. Koremochi Kato, Director of the Agricultural Experiment Station in Korea remarked in 1926:[17] "It is natural that our experiment station since its establishment has worked to select those from many Japanese varieties, which have better results under low level of fertilization. . . . But, as water control has been developing recently farmers have been increasing fertilizer application and have become dissatisfied with the results." In response to the demand for fertilizer-responsive varieties the South Korea Branch of the Agricultural Experiment Station was set up in 1930, with the primary purpose of developing fertilizer-responsive HYV's. During the 1930's, varieties with higher fertilizer responsiveness, such as *Ginbozu* and *Rijuu No. 132*, rapidly replaced less fertilizer-responsive Japanese varieties, such as *Tamanishiki* and *Kokurato*.[18]

In short, for almost a decade the development of HYV's in Korea, comparable to the Ponlai varieties, lagged relative to development of HYV's in Taiwan due to the constraint of water control, which worked to depress the pay-off of investment in developing the HYV's. We may then ask, why was irrigation developed earlier in Taiwan? Many factors were involved: (a) annexation of Korea to Japan occurred a decade later than for Taiwan, so that investment in infrastructure in general was later in starting;[19] (b) irrigation had been developed in Taiwan during the early days of colonization to promote the production of sugar cane, and the facilities could be utilized for rice production; (c) production of Korean rice (Japonica) had been a direct menace

[16] Tobata and Ohkawa, *Chosen Beikoku Keizairon*, pp. 2–3.

[17] *NNHS*. vol. 9, pp. 176–77.

[18] The area planted to *Tamanishiki* and *Kokurato* was more than 30 percent of the area planted to rice and close to 50 percent of the area planted to Japanese varieties in Korea during the late 1920's. According to the experiments conducted by the Agricultural Experiment Station of the Government-General of Korea for 1927–29, both those two varieties recorded lower yields in high fertilization plots, while such varieties as *Ginbozu* recorded higher yields in the high fertilization plots. *NNHS*, vol. 9, pp. 177–78.

[19] Taiwan was conceded to Japan by China in 1895 as a result of the Sino-Japanese War. Korea became a protectorate of Japan in 1905, and it became a territory of Japan in 1910.

Table 9–5. Factor shares in the cost of rice production, Japan and Taiwan

	Japan 1925–27 average	Taiwan			
		Ponlai		Chailai	
Factor		1926 Second crop	1927 First crop	1926 Second crop	1927 First crop
Fertilizer[a]	15.9	15.7	16.3	10.0	9.4
Wage	35.8[b]	34.4	32.2	37.3	36.2
Rent	41.5	45.1	45.2	48.3	46.6
Others	6.8	4.8	6.3	4.3	7.2
Total cost	100.0	100.0	100.0	100.0	100.0

[a] Include self-supplied fertilizer.
[b] Includes livestock labor.
Note: Japan: Calculated from Yukio Ishibashi, *Teikoku Nokai Kome Seisanhi Chosa Shynsei* (Compilation of Rice Production Cost Survey by the Imperial Agricultural Society) (Tokyo: The National Research Institute of Agriculture, 1961), pp. 82–95. Data are for tenant farmers. Taiwan: Calculated from Table 9–3.

to Japanese rice producers and was suppressed, while Taiwan Chailai rice (Indica) was not a direct competitor; (d) the Taiwan Government-General enjoyed revenue surpluses during the half decade preceding 1910 (called the "Golden Age" of the Taiwan Government-General's treasury) and could afford to invest in large-scale construction of physical infrastructure, including railways, ports, and irrigation.[20]

Transfer of Production Function: A Process of Biased Technical Change

It appears that the emergence and propagation of HYV's in Taiwan and Korea during the 1920's and 1930's can be represented by the movement from *C* to *B* in Figure 9–1. This movement was made possible by the organized research of Japanese agricultural scientists and investment in irrigation by the colonial governments. This process of technology transfer involved the transfer of "prototype" Japanese rice production technology to Taiwan and Korea through co-ordinated adaptive research.

This process is illustrated in Table 9–5, which compares factor shares in the cost of rice production in Japan with those of the Ponlai and Chailai varieties in Taiwan. The factor shares in the case of the Ponlai varieties are very similar to those in Japan. If we assume a production function of the Cobb–Douglas type and equilibrium under competitive factor markets, the factor shares represent production elasticities of the respective inputs. In the propagation of the Ponlai varieties, Japan's rice production technology was assimilated by Taiwan.

Both in the cases of Japan and of the Ponlai varieties in Taiwan, the share

[20] Shigeto Kawano, *Taiwan Beikoku Keizairon* (A Treatise of Rice Economy in Taiwan) (Tokyo: Yuhikaku, 1941), p. 11; Tadao Yanaihara, *Teikokushugika no Taiwan* (Taiwan under Imperialism) (Tokyo: Iwanami, 1929), pp. 91–117.

accounted for by fertilizer is larger and the share accounted for by rent is smaller than in the case of the Chailai varieties. This clearly reflects the fertilizer-using and land-saving character of the new technology embodied in fertilizer-responsive HYV's. This bias in technical change was consistent with a land-saving demand of the Taiwan economy in which the population pressure against land was raising the price of land relative to the prices of other factors.[21]

Figure 9-4 shows the changes in fertilizer's share in the total output in Japan, Taiwan, and Korea. Due to data limitations, self-supplied fertilizers, such as manure and compost, are not included in the fertilizer totals. In Taiwan, because of its special nature, the sugar cane sector is excluded from the calculations (fertilizer input in sugar cane is deducted from total fertilizer inputs and sugar cane output is deducted from total agricultural output).[22] There is a remarkable association between the movement of fertilizer's share and of rice yield per hectare (Figure 9-3) in Japan, Taiwan, and Korea. This suggests strongly that growth in rice yields in these three regions was a process of replacement of traditional varieties by fertilizer-responsive HYV's (for example, Chailai by Ponlai). It indicates the process of assimilation of Japanese technology by Taiwan and Korea. In other words, it represents the transfer of Japan's agricultural production function to Taiwan and Korea.

Fertilizer's share of output in Japan rose rapidly until the end of the 1910's and decelerated thereafter. This corresponds to the emergence and propagation of HYV's based on the exploitation of technological potential through a dialectic process of farmers' trials and scientific research, followed by the exhaustion of the yield potential of the *rōnō* varieties, as discussed previously. This movement in fertilizer's share may appear to be similar to what Bent Hansen has called the learning process in reference to Egyptian and U.S. agriculture: the process by which farmers learn how to use new inputs, i.e., chemical fertilizers.[23] Our interpretation of the experience of Japan, Taiwan, and Korea is somewhat different. Even though farmers are well-informed about the properties of new fertilizers, the shift to a new production function is difficult for individual farmers unless more fertilizer-responsive HYV's are made available. The growth in fertilizer's share in Japan, Taiwan, and Korea in Figure 9-4 involved not only farmers' learning but also the creation of new

[21] During the period 1920–35 arable land area increased by 11 percent and agricultural population by 21 percent, resulting in a decline in the land-man ratio of 10 percent in Taiwan. In Korea, during the same period, arable land area increased by 3 percent and agricultural population by 11 percent, resulting in a decline in a land-man ratio of 8 percent. Although comparable data are unavailable for Taiwan and Korea, Japan recorded a rise in the price of arable land relative to the prices of other inputs from 1880 to 1960 (Table 6–1, Chapter 6).

[22] Sugar cane was produced either by plantations owned by sugar companies or by peasant farmers by contract under the supervision and guidance of the sugar companies. Fertilizer inputs in sugar cane were high even before the 1910's.

[23] Bent Hansen, "The Distributive Shares in Egyptian Agriculture, 1897–1961," *International Economic Review* 9 (June 1968): 175–94.

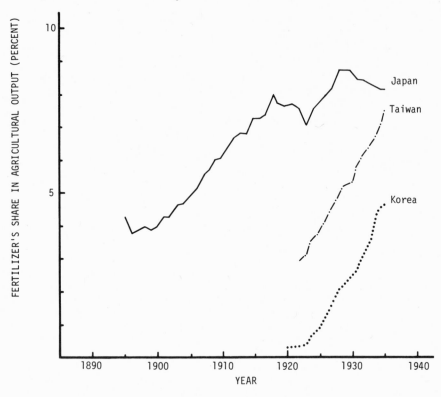

FIGURE 9-4. Fertilizer's share in agricultural output for Japan, Taiwan, and Korea, five-year moving average, 1895–1935. (*Sources:* Kazushi Ohkawa et al. [ed.], *Long-term Economic Statistics since 1968*, 9 [Tokyo: Toyokeizaishimposha, 1966]: 146–47 and 194–95; Taiwan Government-General, *Taiwan Nogyo Nenpo* [Yearbook of Taiwan Agriculture], various issues; Korea Government-General, *Nogyo Tokeihyo* [Agricultural Statistics], various issues.)

Note: Fertilizer's share is the total value of commercial fertilizer consumption divided by the gross value of agricultural production (both in current prices). In the case of Taiwan, fertilizers applied to sugar cane and sugar cane production are deducted, respectively, from fertilizer consumption and agricultural production (see estimation procedures in the note to Table 9–4).

technology through a dialectic interaction between farmers' experience and scientific research, and its transfer through adaptive research.

IMPLICATIONS FOR THE RECENT DEVELOPMENT OF HYV'S IN THE TROPICS

We have hypothesized that the technical basis of the "green revolution" has involved a movement from a production function which had been optimum for the factor and product prices which once prevailed in premodern society to another production function optimum at currently prevailing prices. This adjustment process lagged until the mid-1960's in most parts of Asia, because of the lack of investment in the local research and development capacity needed to make this adjustment possible. Disequilibria in terms of the meta-production function had accumulated and induced the transfer of scientific research capacity to tropical and subtropical Asia. When co-ordinated research by international teams of scientists was applied to this wide technological gap, the adjustment took a revolutionary form.

Japan's experience in the Meiji period indicates that in the creation and diffusion of more fertilizer-responsive HYV's the effective interaction among innovative veteran farmers and emerging agricultural science brought about continuous adjustments in response to declining fertilizer-rice price ratios. This Japanese experience suggests that movements along the metaproduction function can be accomplished relatively smoothly, given the existence of indigenous human capital and an adequate institutional and physical infrastructure.

Without these two factors, disequilibrium had mounted in Taiwan until about 1920 when Japan, in order to alleviate her own food problem, transferred to Taiwan the technical knowledge embodied in Japanese agricultural scientists. This resulted in a dramatic success in the creation of the Ponlai varieties. The experience of Taiwan has special relevance in that it involved the transfer of technology to a different climatic condition, where the direct transfer of seeds and techniques was not feasible. Korea's adjustment lagged behind that of Taiwan, mainly because of a lag in the construction of physical infrastructure, especially irrigation. Korean experience is particularly relevant for many areas in Southeast Asia where the adjustment to a new optimum through the diffusion of HYV's may be severely constrained both by limitations in human capital and by inadequate physical infrastructure, especially water control facilities. It appears possible to interpret the experience of Taiwan and Korea as representing the response of public agencies (colonial governments) to a potential high pay-off (for Japan) of investment in research leading to adjustments from a secular disequilibrium toward an equilibrium for the fertilizer-rice price ratios prevailing at that time.

Viewed from the historical perspective of agricultural development in Japan, Taiwan, and Korea, the recent development of HYV's in Asia represents a response by national and international agencies to changes in product and factor prices, particularly rice and fertilizer prices, resulting from changes in rice demand and in the technology of fertilizer production during the 1950's and the early 1960's. Also it appears that the technical changes embodied in the new high-yielding cereal varieties is biased toward saving the increasingly scarce factor (land) and using the increasingly abundant factor (fertilizer) in the economy. It clearly indicates a rational response of public agencies to economic forces. Although an initial success has been achieved, the adjustment has not yet been completed. It can be sustained for some time if investment in research and irrigation is sufficiently high. It is anticipated that sustained progress will become increasingly difficult and costly as the adjustment process continues. The supply of land with better water control and farmers with better knowledge and skill will progressively be exhausted. Larger areas of HYV's will require more research for protection from insects and pests and for protection of their high-yielding properties from genetic degeneration. Above all, when technology in less developed countries approaches the prototype technology of developed countries, the breakthroughs necessary for further advancement will become more costly.[24]

The issue that continues to face the countries that are now experiencing the "green revolution" is whether the potential commodity surpluses resulting from the new biological technology will be used to generate viable economic growth in the total economy or will be absorbed by even higher levels of population growth. Most developing economies face the choice between the historical examples provided by Java and Japan—between involution and development.[25] Their successes will, to a large extent, depend on the flexibility and efficiency of public institutions in responding to the economic opportunities available to them. In considering these alternatives it is useful to review, in the next chapter, the impact on Japanese agricultural development of the earlier transfer of a high productivity cereal technology to Taiwan and Korea.

[24] Albert H. Moseman, *Building Agricultural Research Systems in the Developing Nations* (New York: Agricultural Development Council, Inc., 1970), pp. 95–115.

[25] Clifford Geertz, *Agricultural Involution; The Process of Ecological Change in Indonesia* (Berkeley: University of California Press, 1966); Johnston and Cownie, "The Seed-Fertilizer Revolution."

CHAPTER TEN

Technology Transfer, Trade, and Agricultural Transformation

Successful transfer and diffusion of agricultural technology represents a necessary condition for agricultural and economic development. The introduction of an advanced technology, leading to rapid productivity and output growth, into less developed countries typically results in imbalance and disequilibria which require major economic and social adjustments. The effects of these changes may not be confined to the impact transmitted through domestic product and factor markets. It frequently spills over into the international economic system through its impact on price and trade relationships in the markets for the commodities that are experiencing rapid growth in productivity.

In this chapter, we focus on changes in agricultural transformation and trade, which are required in moving from the successful transfer of technology in one sector of the economy to success in over-all development. The problem is first discussed in reference to the emerging problems associated with the "green revolution" of the late 1960's and early 1970's. Second, the economic consequences of the transfer of rice production technology from Japan to Taiwan and Korea are analyzed. This experience can be viewed as a small-scale "historical experiment" that is particularly relevant to the current development in Asia, as analyzed in the previous chapter. From the experience of Japan, Taiwan, and Korea we draw inferences regarding the possible consequences of technology transfer and the economic policies necessary to transfer the potential gains of productivity growth into a basis for sustained agricultural and economic development.

THE TRANSFER OF TECHNOLOGY: THE SECOND GENERATION PROBLEMS

It is almost inevitable that the dramatic transfer of technology which generated the "green revolution" would result in a heavy imbalance in the relatively underdeveloped economies of the tropics where these changes are occurring.[1] The imbalance takes the form of a number of bottlenecks in production, distribution, and trade. As discussed in Chapter 9, inadequate investments in the creation of local experiment station capacity and in the maintenance and development of irrigation facilities represent a serious bottleneck for the full realization of the production potential of the new seed-fertilizer technology.

More immediate bottlenecks are emerging due to the inadequate capacity of the marketing system in many areas to handle the sharp increase in the marketable surplus. In the spring of 1968 Northern India found the existing marketing facilities inadequate for handling the increased output of wheat. Substantial amounts of grain were stored in schools or even left uncovered on the ground. In the Philippines, lack of artificial drying facilities for rice harvested during the monsoon season has represented a bottleneck for the expansion of double-cropping of rice.

Lack of effective input and credit markets also represents constraints on progress in agricultural production. In order to exploit the production potential of HYV's, fertilizer and other technical inputs must be supplied at the right time and at the right places. Farmers require credit in order to meet the increased cash outlay for the procurement of larger amounts of technical inputs.

These bottlenecks impede the realization of the production potential of new technology. At the same time, however, they can be powerful sources of forward and backward linkages in Hirschman's sense in transmitting the impact of the new technology in agricultural production to other sectors of the economy.[2] A marketing bottleneck resulting from rapid growth in production, for example, implies that the pay-off to investment in agricultural marketing is increased by the development of HYV's. If investment is induced by the increase in the pay-off, the marketing bottleneck will not only be eased but additional nonfarm employment and income will be created.

If this mechanism functions properly, the new seed-fertilizer technology can realize its production potential and at the same time contribute to sustained growth in the nonagricultural sector of the economy. A secular consequence of rapid growth in agricultural output, relative to demand, is a downward

---

[1] See for discussions of the second generation problems of the green revolution, Clifton R. Wharton, Jr., "The Green Revolution: Cornucopia or Pandora's Box?," *Foreign Affairs* 47 (April 1969): 464–76; House of Representatives Committee on Foreign Affairs, *Symposium on Science and Foreign Policy—The Green Revolution* (Washington, D.C.: U.S. Government Printing Office, 1970); Lester R. Brown, *Seeds of Change: The Green Revolution and Development in the 1970's* (New York: Praeger, 1970); Walter P. Falcon, "The Green Revolution: Generations of Problems," *American Journal of Agricultural Economics* 52 (December 1970): 698–710; Hiromitsu Kaneda, "Economic Implications of the 'Green Revolution' and the Strategy of Agricultural Development in West Pakistan," *Pakistan Development Review* 9 (Summer 1969): 112–43.

[2] Albert O. Hirschman, *The Strategy of Economic Development* (New Haven: Yale University Press, 1958).

shift in the aggregate cost and supply schedules for food staples. The effect is to transfer at least part of the gain in agricultural productivity from farmers to other sectors of the economy. When the aggregate supply of commodities which are characterized by inelastic demand, such as staple cereals, shifts downward, the decline in the prices may exceed the increase in the output, resulting in a decline in the income of farmers.[3]

More serious is the possibility of widening income disparity among farmers. The income position of farmers who have no access to new technology, due, for example, to the lack of irrigation facilities, will become relatively worse as the aggregate supply schedule shifts to the right. Declining prices and widening income disparity among farm producers may cause significant social tension and disruption in rural areas and major political instability at the national level.[4]

These problems can be magnified in the international dimension. As traditional food deficit countries, such as the Philippines and Pakistan, shift from a grain-importing to a grain-exporting status and other countries, such as India and Indonesia, reduce the gap between production and utilization, substantial price disruption is likely in international markets. This would have severe repercussions on the foreign exchange earnings of food-exporting countries, such as Thailand and Burma, and may result in significant reduction in the trade among countries in Asia.[5]

These are the possible but not, of course, necessary consequences of the "green revolution." Technical progress or decline in the cost schedule of any one commodity in any region can result in higher returns to all resources in the economy, if resources are reallocated efficiently. If, as the HYV's spread, land, labor, and other resources are diverted from the production of food cereals to the production of commodities characterized by a more elastic demand in domestic and export markets, such as livestock products, both the income of farmers and the welfare of consumers will be increased. The reallocation of resources, leading to a transformation of the agricultural sector made possible by technical progress in cereal production, represents a critical process in over-all agricultural and economic development.

This is, however, an extremely difficult task. In many cases human skill,

<hr />

[3] This process has been documented for U.S. agriculture by Willard W. Cochrane, *Farm Prices, Myth and Reality* (Minneapolis: University of Minnesota Press, 1958).

[4] Francine R. Frankel, "India's New Strategy of Agricultural Development: Political Costs of Agrarian Modernization," *Journal of Asian Studies* 28 (August 1969): 693–710; Guy J. Pauker, "Political Consequences of Rural Development Programs in Indonesia," *Pacific Affairs* 41 (Fall 1968): 386–402.

[5] The trade implications of the green revolution are discussed in a series of papers presented at a meeting of the SEADAG Rural Development Seminar in Honolulu in June of 1969. See particularly Martin E. Abel, "Prospects for Rice and Corn Production and Trade in the 1970's," *Agricultural Revolution in Southwest Asia*, vol. 1 (New York: The Asia Society, 1970), pp. 105–22; Quentin W. West, "World Grain Production Prospects and Trade Stabilization Measures in Southeast Asia," ibid., pp. 148–65.

capital, and cultural patterns in rural sectors are inseparably linked with the production of traditional crops, which impedes resource reallocation. For example, it is often difficult to plant crops other than rice in wet paddy fields or to find remunerative markets for alternative crops. Farmers who have been accustomed to a rice or wheat monoculture system cannot easily be converted to become efficient livestock operators or vegetable producers. The technological and economic foundations for the development of modern feed-livestock farming in the tropics will involve far more difficult and complex research than was involved in developing the high-yielding cereal varieties. The inter-regional and interindustrial reallocation of agricultural labor associated with the reallocation of agricultural resources among commodities and geographic areas is a problem that many developed countries have failed to solve.

Yet agricultural transformation corresponding to changes in product and factor prices and to changes in comparative advantages among regions and countries is, in the long run, the key to success in leading to over-all economic growth from the successful transfer of new technology into the food cereal sector. Failure to achieve such a transformation can dampen the whole process of economic development. This is illustrated by the experience of Japan following the successful diffusion of rice production technology to Taiwan and Korea after World War I.

TAIWAN RICE, KOREAN RICE, AND JAPANESE AGRICULTURAL STAGNATION[6]

In Chapter 9 we traced the similarities in the transfer of rice production technology to the tropical rice-producing areas of Asia during the late 1960's and early 1970's and the colonial development of Taiwan and Korea by Japan. In this section, we analyze the impact on economic growth in Japan of the successful transfer of rice technology to the two colonial areas. The results of our analysis suggest that the imports of rice from Taiwan and Korea to Japan as the result of colonial agricultural development were, to a substantial degree, responsible for the stagnation of Japanese agriculture during the interwar years. At the same time they also contributed to industrial growth by keeping the industrial wage low and the return to capital high, without causing a serious drain on foreign exchange. The increased supply of colonial rice did not

---

[6] The material in the following sections of this chapter draws heavily on two earlier papers: Yujiro Hayami and V. W. Ruttan, "Korean Rice, Taiwan Rice, and Japanese Agricultural Stagnation: An Economic Consequence of Colonialism," *Quarterly Journal of Economics* 84 (November 1970): 562–89; R. E. Evenson, J. P. Houck, Jr., and V. W. Ruttan, "Technical Change and International Trade: Three Examples—Sugarcane, Bananas, and Rice, "*The Technology Factor in International Trade*, ed. Raymond Vernon (New York: Columbia University Press, 1970), pp. 415–80.

produce an agricultural transformation comparable to that of nineteenth-century England. Rather it produced agricultural stagnation and low farm income, which may have been largely responsible for the general economic and political instability of the interwar period.

Japanese Agricultural Stagnation: A Hypothesis

The rapid increase in rice production in Taiwan and Korea after World War I resulted from the successful transfer of Japanese rice production technology to the two colonial areas. This increase, when coupled with policies to extract the potential income growth from Taiwanese and Korean farmers by taxation and government monopoly sales, created the tremendous rice surplus which flooded into the Japanese market. As shown in Table 10–1, during the twenty years from 1915 to 1935 net imports of rice from Korea to Japan rose from 170 to 1,212 thousand metric tons per year, and net imports from Taiwan rose from 113 to 705 thousand metric tons. As a result of the inflow of colonial rice, the net import of rice rose from 5 to 20 percent of the domestic production.[7]

Such large-scale imports of rice, a commodity characterized by a relatively inelastic demand schedule, could be expected to lower the price and discourage the production of rice in Japan. In fact, as shown in Table 10–2, the price of rice and the internal terms of trade, as measured by the price of rice deflated by the general price index, continued to decline from 1920 to the catastrophe of the *Nogyo Kyoko* (Agricultural Depression) in 1929–32.[8]

This contrasts with the price movements for 1890–1920. The price of rice rose continuously and the terms of trade were favorable for rice immediately after 1890 and were relatively stable between 1895 and 1915. The fact that the

---

[7] A somewhat similar phenomenon occurred during the 1890–1905 period. Increase in the supply (and presumably consumption) of rice outpaced domestic production, although the 1905 (1903–07 average) observation includes the abnormal years of the Russo–Japanese War (1904–05). The fact that Japan shifted from a net exporter to a net importer of rice during the last decade of the nineteenth century pressed the government to take measures to encourage agricultural production, including the establishment of the National Agricultural Experiment Station (1896), the Law of State Subsidy for Prefectural Agricultural Experiment Stations (1899), and the Arable Land Replotment Law (1899). Due to the existence of indigenous technological potential that was not being fully exploited, these government efforts were effective and contributed to the advances in rice production and in yield per hectare during the first two decades of this century. As a result, Japanese agriculture continued to supply about 95 percent of the rapidly growing domestic rice consumption during this period.

[8] The decline in the price of rice is partly ascribed to an unfavorable shift in the demand for rice. Demand for food, as well as for other consumer goods, declined as a result of the decline in consumer income resulting from the deflation policy Japan adopted in order to return to the gold standard at the prewar parity. The income elasticity of demand for rice and staple foods declined as a result of urbanization and of changes in the occupational distribution of the labor force. Also, labor's share of income tended to decline: See Table 4, p. 79, and Table 7, p. 85, in Mataji Umemura, *Chingin Koyo Nogyo* (Wage, Employment and Agriculture) (Tokyo: Taimindo, 1961).

Table 10-1. Production, import, and available supply of rice in Japan, 1890–1935*

Year	Supply $Q = Z + K$	Production Z	Net import Total K	Net import Korea K_k	Net import Taiwan K_f	Production	Net import Total $k = K/Z$	Net import Korea $k_k = K_k/Z$	Net import Taiwan $k_f = K_f/Z$
			(1,000 m. tons)				(percent)		
1890	5,813	5,861	−48			100	−0.8		
1895	5,700	5,651	49			100	0.9		
1900	6,578	6,372	206			100	3.2		
1905	7,539	6,943	596			100	8.6		
1910	7,923	7,588	335			100	4.4		
1915	8,692	8,286	406	170	113	100	4.9	2.1	1.4
1920	9,720	8,838	882	360	132	100	10.0	4.1	1.5
1925	10,043	8,700	1,343	640	278	100	15.4	7.3	3.2
1930	10,483	9,070	1,413	974	389	100	15.6	10.7	4.3
1935	11,290	9,414	1,876	1,212	705	100	19.9	12.9	7.5

* Five-year averages centering the years shown. Rice in brown (husked but not polished) rice basis.

Sources: Z: Kazushi Ohkawa et al. (ed.), Long-term Economic Statistics of Japan (LTES), vol. 9, (Tokyo: Toyokeizaishimposha, 1966), pp. 166–68. K: LTES 6 (1967): 150–52. K_k and K_f: Bureau of Statistics, Office of the Prime Minister, Japan Statistical Yearbook (Tokyo, 1949), pp. 630–31.

internal terms of trade remained stable without an appreciable increase in rice imports during 1900–15 may indicate a relative balance in the growth of agriculture and industry during the "big spurt" period of industrialization in Japan from the Russo–Japanese War (1904–05) to World War I.[9] Farmers' real income from rice, measured as the total value of rice production at the farm, deflated by the general price index, went up rapidly, mainly as a result of growth in physical production. A sharp rise in the price of rice resulted from the boom of World War I, which culminated in the Rice Riot in 1918.

Sharp changes in the rates of growth in rice production and productivity are associated with changes in the rice price trend. From 1890 to 1920, the area planted in rice and the yield per hectare planted grew, respectively, by 0.44 and 0.94 percent per year, while total production increased by 1.38 percent per year. In contrast, the growth rates declined to 0.16 for area, 0.24 for yield, and 0.40 for production between 1920 and 1935.

In Chapter 7 we have identified the exploitation and consequent exhaustion of the technological backlog existing at the beginning of the Meiji period as the major cause for the emergence of the growth and stagnation phases in Japanese agriculture before and after the late 1900's. The seed improvement index in Table 10–2 was calculated in an attempt to quantify the influence of diffusion of improved seeds on the national average yield. This index is based on the weighted averages of the areas planted in the respective varieties, using as weights the standard yields of various varieties (see Appendix D). The standard yields, which are fixed by regions, were based on the reports of comparative-yield tests at various experiment stations. The annual growth rate of this index declined drastically from 1890–1920 to 1920–35, reflecting the saturation in the spread of improved varieties.

It seems reasonable, however, to hypothesize that, in the absence of such large-scale rice imports from Taiwan and Korea, the agricultural stagnation in the 1920's and 1930's might not have been so pronounced and the agricultural depression not so disastrous.

Counterfactual Analysis of Japanese Agricultural Stagnation

In order to assess the influence on Japanese agriculture of the transfer of rice technology to Taiwan and Korea and the consequent increase in imports of rice from the two colonies, we present two hypothetical or "counterfactual" calculations to illustrate how production and price could have changed after 1920.[10]

[9] Kazushi Ohkawa and Henry Rosovsky, "The Role of Agriculture in Modern Japanese Economic Development," *Economic Development and Cultural Change*, vol. 9, part 2 (October 1960): 43–67.

[10] For a discussion of the role of counterfactual models in the study of economic history, see Robert William Fogel, "The Specification Problem in Economic History," *Journal of Economic History* 27 (September 1967): 283–308.

Table 10–2. Area, yield, production, price, and seed improvement indexes for rice in Japan, 1890–1935*

Year	Area planted A (1,000 ha.)	Yield per unit area $Y = Z/A$ (m. ton/ha.)	Production Z (1,000 m. ton)	Price $P = V/Z$ (yen/m. ton)	Farm value of production V (mil. yen)	General price index I (1934–36 = 100)	Deflated price P/I (yen/m. ton)	Deflated value production V/I (mil. yen)	Seed improvement index S (1890 = 100)
1890	2,717	2.16	5,861	42	243	31.7	131	767	100.0
1895	2,752	2.05	5,651	57	323	35.8	160	902	100.8
1900	2,813	2.27	6,372	79	501	47.4	166	1,057	101.6
1905	2,862	2.43	6,943	91	633	55.7	164	1,136	104.3
1910	2,933	2.59	7,588	104	790	60.3	173	1,310	105.1
1915	3,029	2.74	8,286	106	882	66.4	160	1,328	105.8
1920	3,094	2.86	8,838	242	2,140	131.3	184	1,630	106.2
1925	3,129	2.78	8,700	224	1,944	128.3	174	1,515	105.8
1930	3,203	2.83	9,070	143	1,297	104.5	137	1,241	105.8
1935	3,169	2.97	9,414	179	1,673	101.9	174	1,642	107.4
				Annual compound rate of growth (%)					
1890–1920	0.44	0.94	1.38	6.09	7.47	4.95	1.14	2.52	0.20
1920–1935	0.16	0.24	0.40	−2.05	−1.65	−1.70	−0.35	0.05	0.07

* Five-year averages centering the years shown. Rice in brown (husked, but not polished) rice basis.

Sources: A: Ministry of Agriculture and Forestry, Norinsho Ruimento-keihyo (Historical Statistics of Ministry of Agriculture and Forestry) (Tokyo, 1955), p. 24. Z: Kazushi Ohkawa et al. (ed.), Long-term Economic Statistics of Japan (abbreviated as LTES), vol. 9 (Tokyo: Toyo-keizaishimposha, 1966), pp. 166–68. V: LTES, vol. 9, pp. 146–47. I: LTES, vol. 8 (1967), Series 1, Table 1, p. 134. S: See Appendix D.

In Case 1 we assume that the ratio of net imports of rice to domestic production remained the same as in 1913–17. In Case 2 we assume, in addition to the assumption of a constant import ratio, that the seed improvement index continued to grow at the 1890–1920 rate. The method employed in the counterfactual calculations is explained in a supplement to this chapter (pages 215–18). The results are summarized in Table 10–3. In order to make comparisons between actual and hypothetical growth paths of the Japanese rice economy, the results in Table 10–3 are plotted in Figures 10–1 and 10–2.

Figure 10–1 shows that the decline in the rate of growth in the seed improvement index and the increase in the imports of colonial rice explain most of the decline in the rate of growth in rice yield and production during the interwar period. The rates of growth in hypothetical yield and production

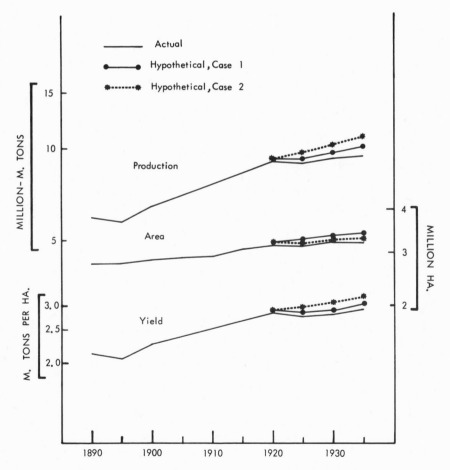

FIGURE 10–1. Area, yield, and production of rice (in logs.) in Japan, 1890–1935.

Table 10–3. Actual and hypothetical paths of growth of area, yield, production, and price of rice in Japan, 1920–35*

Year	Area planted A	Yield per unit area Y	Production Z	Price P	Farm value of production V	Price deflated by general price index P/I	Value production deflated by general price index V/I
	(1,000 ha.)	(m. ton/ha.)	(1,000 m. ton)	(yen/m. ton)	(mil. yen)	(yen/m. ton)	(mil. yen)
			Actual				
1920	3,094	2.86	8,838	242	2,140	184	1,630
1925	3,129	2.78	8,700	224	1,944	174	1,515
1930	3,203	2.83	9,070	143	1,297	137	1,241
1935	3,169	2.97	9,414	179	1,673	174	1,624
			Hypothetical Case 1				
1920	3,116	2.87	8,954	257	2,307	196	1,757
1925	3,204	2.85	9,126	284	2,587	221	2,016
1930	3,280	2.90	9,514	181	1,726	173	1,652
1935	3,277	3.07	10,064	250	2,496	244	2,450
			Hypothetical Case 2				
1920	3,116	2.87	8,954	257	2,307	196	1,757
1925	3,170	3.02	9,335	254	2,366	197	1,844
1930	3,219	3.10	9,886	150	1,480	143	1,416
1935	3,223	3.23	10,402	212	2,195	207	2,164
			Annual compound rate of growth from 1920 to 1935 (%)				
Actual	0.16	0.24	0.40	−2.05	−1.65	−0.35	0.05
Case 1	0.34	0.44	0.78	−0.18	0.51	1.88	2.21
Case 2	0.21	0.79	1.00	−1.30	−0.30	0.40	1.40

* Five-year averages centering the years shown. Rice in brown (husked, but not polished) rice basis.

Case 1: Assumes the net import of rice stayed at the 1913–17 level relative to domestic production.

Case 2: Assumes, in addition to the assumption of Case 1, the seed improvement index continued to grow at the 1880–1920 rate.

See pp. 230–35 for computational procedures.

224

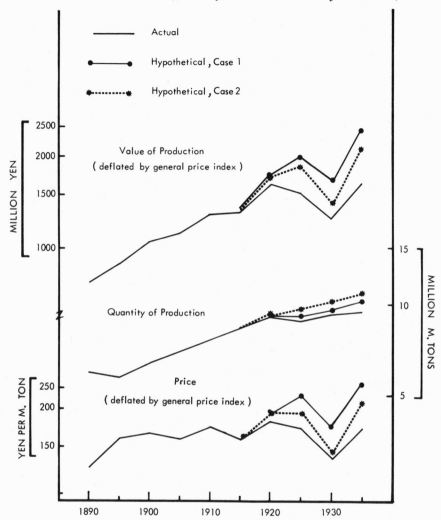

FIGURE 10–2. Production of rice (in logs.) in Japan, 1890–1935.

declined slightly from 1890–1920 to 1920–35, but it is unlikely that anything resembling the "epochal" change in the rate of growth of actual rice production would have occurred if imports had been held at the 1913–17 level relative to production and the seed improvement index had continued to rise at the 1890–1920 rate (Case 2). It is also clear that imports of rice from the colonial areas (Case 1) is not, by itself, an adequate explanation for the decline in the rate of growth of rice production in the interwar period. The "technology gap" between the exploitation of the yield gains from the diffusion of the superior varieties of farmers' selections and the introduction of the new experiment station varieties exerted a major impact on dampening the rate of growth of rice production in Japan during the interwar period.[11]

The influence of rice imports did exert a sizable impact on rice prices and the incomes of rice producers in Japan. Under the assumption of Case 1, production went up less rapidly than during 1890–1920, while the internal terms of trade for rice improved and the real income of farmers from rice rose after 1920 as rapidly as before 1920. Even in Case 2, where imports are held at the 1913–17 ratio and yield technology represented by seed improvement is assumed to continue at the earlier rate, the terms of trade improved gradually, except during the depression, and the real incomes of rice producers rose significantly over the period 1920–35, in contrast to almost no change under the conditions that actually prevailed.

In an economy which is closed, in the sense that there is no international trade, and in which there is no technological progress and no capital accumulation in agriculture, industrialization and economic growth will eventually lead to a point that the terms of trade deteriorate for industry and the supply price of labor from agriculture to industry will rise in terms of industrial products, the "shortage point" of Fei and Ranis.[12] Until World War I Japan was able to prolong the arrival of this point by exploiting the technological potential in the traditional peasant agriculture. Industrial development was supported by the very elastic supply of labor from agriculture.[13] Colonial policy seems to have been designed to postpone the arrival of the "shortage point" further and to make the progress of industrialization easier by expanding the supply of rice in the domestic market through imports from the colonies. Success of this policy kept the industrial wage low and the competitive position of industrial products strong in the international market. If the same amount of rice were supplied from foreign countries, there would have

---

[11] The data presented in Table 10–1 indicate that the rate of growth in the supply (presumably consumption) of rice declined after 1920 (from the annual compound rate of 1.7 percent during the 1890–1920 period to 1.0 percent during the 1920–35 period). Population continued to grow at an annual rate of about 1.0 percent for both periods. The stagnation of per capita rice consumption, if due to a decline in demand, might be expected to have a significant influence on production and productivity trends, although in an open economy domestic consumption does not represent a direct constraint on domestic production. The present analysis indicates the stagnation of domestic rice production and productivity in Japan can be consistently explained by two major factors: the exhaustion of indigenous technological potential and the importation of colonial rice. This does not, however, refute the hypothesis that demand contraction may have also contributed to the decline. A quantitative analysis of the influence of demand contraction on domestic rice production during this period awaits future analysis.

[12] Gustav Ranis and J. C. H. Fei, "A Theory of Economic Development," *American Economic Review* 51 (September 1961): 533–65.

[13] It is questionable if there existed the unlimited supply of labor in the sense of Ranis and Fei, but a recent study by Minami indicates that there was a situation which could well be identified as the unlimited supply of labor from agriculture to industry. See Ryoshin Minami, "The Turning Point in the Japanese Economy," *Quarterly Journal of Economics* 82 (August 1968): 380–402.

been a significant foreign exchange drain and the import of capital goods would have been curtailed.

This success was a mixed blessing for Japan. It depressed the price and the income of farmers and contributed to serious social disorders in the agricultural sector. The so-called military reformists made this social unrest and disorder among farmers the springboard for the invasion of Manchuria in 1931 and for the other military adventures which followed. The policy decision concerning the rice supply after the Rice Riot in 1918 had thus not only economic but significant social and political implications.[14]

Why did the economic effects of a colonial development policy fail, in Japan, to produce the "classical" results associated with the importation of cheap grain into nineteenth-century England from colonial and other newly settled areas? The answer seems, at least in part, to be associated with the different structure of agriculture and the different pattern of industrial development in the two countries at the time the policies of dependence on overseas sources of food supply were initiated.

The inflow of grain to England, following the repeal of the Corn Laws in 1846, was accompanied by the continuing absorption of labor into the industrial sector and a transformation of the agricultural sector away from grain production and toward a more extensive system of livestock agriculture.[15]

---

[14] It is interesting to consider what would have happened if the colonial development policies had been accompanied by land reform and other economic democratization measures in Japan similar to those implemented during the U.S. occupation after World War II. Land reform might have (a) raised the rate of growth in agricultural production by increasing the incentives of farmers; (b) improved the level of income and living of farmers and contributed to social and political stability of the rural sector; and (c) expanded the domestic market for industrial products through the increased consumption by farmers depressing the incentives to the imperialistic expansion of the overseas market. On the other hand, the improved level of income and consumption of farmers might have depressed industrial growth by (a) decreasing the net outflow of savings from agriculture to industry and (b) shifting upward the schedule of labor supply to industry, which was determined by the level of living in the rural sector, with a possible rise in the industrial wage rate. A more extensive analysis is required to evaluate the over-all effects of alternative land tenure policies on economic growth and social and political development.

[15] The shift away from grain production toward mixed farming characterized by "high feeding" of livestock was pronounced during the two decades following the repeal of the Corn Laws. Prior to 1850 livestock feeding was justified primarily on the basis of the value to the grain enterprise of the manure produced by the livestock. After 1850 livestock production became profitable in its own right. For an excellent assessment of the changes in farming during this period, see E. L. Jones, "The Changing Basis of English Agricultural Prosperity, 1853–73," *Essays in Agrarian History*, vol. II, ed. W. E. Minchinton (Newton Abbot: David and Charles Ltd., 1968) pp. 219–36 (reprinted from *Agricultural History Review* vol. 10, part 2 (1962): 102–19. Jones summarized the factors responsible for the shift as follows: "after the Repeal the altered relative value of wheat and livestock products, due to imports which prevented a rise in the price of wheat, the growth of population, and rising real incomes of which an increasing proportion was spent on livestock products" (p. 229). He also quotes an observation by James Caird made in 1878, "Thirty years ago probably not more than one-third of the people of this country consumed animal food more than once a week. Now, nearly all of them eat it, in meat or cheese or butter, once a day. ... The leap which the consumption of meat took in consequence of the general rise of wages in all branches of trade and employment, could not have been met without foreign supplies" (p. 227).

The transformation was facilitated by rising incomes in the industrial sector which stimulated the demand for the products of an animal agriculture.[16]

A number of obstacles prevented Japan from achieving a similar agricultural transformation in response to rising imports and declining prices of grain during the interwar period. Japanese agriculture was rigidly locked into a sophisticated labor-intensive system of crop production, highly dependent on irrigation and fertilizer as the leading inputs.[17] There was not a fully adequate basis, in either agricultural research or industrial infrastructure, to make a rapid transformation from grain production to a more diversified agricultural system. Furthermore, the rise in imports of grain was not accompanied, in Japan, by a rapid growth in the demand for labor by the industrial sector. The demand for labor in the industrial sector slackened after 1920 as a result of (a) the contraction of world demand for the products of Japanese industry after World War I; (b) the contraction of domestic demand due to the deflation policy adopted to permit a return to the gold standard at a prewar parity; and (c) the adoption of an industrial rationalization policy in an attempt to stay competitive in world markets. This rationalization policy placed major emphasis on attempts to increase productivity and to save labor through more capital-intensive methods of production.[18] Finally, income levels in the urban industrial sector of the Japanese economy remained too low to create a large increase in the demand for the products of a more diversified agriculture.

CURRENT DEVELOPMENT AND THE EXPERIENCE OF JAPAN

The foregoing analysis of Japanese agricultural stagnation during the interwar period is suggestive of the problem that countries experiencing rapid growth in grain production, as a result of the new cereals technology, may experience during the 1970's. The problem of converting current or potential food surpluses into a basis for sustained economic growth poses an extremely difficult problem for most countries of South and Southeast Asia during the next decade. The continuing decline of export opportunities and prices is expected to limit the opportunity to use surplus grain production to earn the foreign exchange needed to finance domestic development. Furthermore, the relatively large share of the population engaged in agricultural production and the slow (absolute) growth in nonfarm employment opportunities limits the economic gains that can be realized by using the surpluses primarily to support employ-

---

[16] Phyllis Deane and W. A. Cole, *British Economic Growth, 1688–1959, Trends and Structure* (Cambridge: The Cambridge University Press, 1962), pp. 154–81.

[17] Shigeru Ishikawa, *Economic Development in Asian Perspective* (Tokyo: Kinokuniya Bookstore, 1967) pp. 84–122.

[18] Ohkawa and Rosovsky, "The Role of Agriculture," pp. 68–83.

ment in the urban industrial sectors unless the transfer of surpluses is also accompanied by lower food prices.

Thus, if developed countries do not adopt less protectionist policies with respect to their domestic agriculture, the economies of Southeast Asia are likely to face difficulties during the 1970's similar to those faced by the Japanese economy during the interwar period. The main difference is that the downward pressure on rice prices in these countries will come from increased supplies generated from internal rather than colonial sources.

The Japanese experience indicates that the economic and social conditions of Asian agriculture make it extremely difficult to achieve a structural transformation comparable with the agricultural transformation in nineteenth-century England. Unique patterns and processes of agricultural transformation will have to be discovered which are feasible for Asian conditions.

In contrast to the interwar period, aggregate world trade is expanding even though trade in food grains may decline. The demand for feed grains and luxury food items is increasing rapidly. Maize in Thailand and asparagus and mushrooms in Taiwan represent examples of success in diverting resources from food grains to production of commodities characterized by expanding world demand. It is suggestive that these successes were achieved in the traditional food surplus countries in Asia.

Another possibility is that, as the reduced real cost and prices of food staples become reflected in wage rates, downward shifts will result in the cost schedule for rubber, copra, plywood, and other tropical export commodities. If this counteracts effectively the competition from synthetics and temperate zone agricultural products, the traditional export crop sector might again emerge as a leading sector in tropical economies.

Whether these possibilities materialize depends, to a large extent, on the efficient allocation of agricultural research. Research is essential to discover and develop new profitable crops. The competitive position of traditional export crops must be maintained and reinforced by continuous improvements in technology. It is unlikely that countries in South and Southeast Asia can attain a successful agricultural transformation if technical progress brought about by the transfer of scientific knowledge and capacity is limited to the food cereal sector.

Critical to the efficient reallocation of resources, including research resources, is an efficient system of prices which accurately reflects changes in the demand and supply of outputs and inputs in the economy. If the governments of South and Southeast Asian countries divert substantial resources to maintain the level of food cereal prices that prevailed in the late 1960's, the result will be malallocation of resources not only by farmers but also by agricultural scientists and agricultural supply firms. In consequence, the cost schedules of these surplus commodities will continue to shift downward relatively more rapidly, enlarging the disequilibria.

The developing countries do not have the resources to duplicate the costly programs that have characterized agricultural commodity policy in the developed countries during the past two decades. The developed countries can bear the heavy direct costs and the waste of resources resulting from high agricultural price supports. In most developed countries, agriculture generates less than 10 percent of national income. The price supports have been effective in easing the social tensions associated with agricultural transformation among the rural population. Developing countries in the tropics, with a relatively large share of their income generated in the agricultural sector, do not have either the administrative capacity or the resources to pursue high price-support policies. Though painful, they are forced to follow a route toward agricultural transformation under efficient price signals. Price-support programs can be used for stabilization purposes and as a guide to efficient resource-use decisions, if they are not distorted by overly ambitious income transfer objectives.[19]

The problem of attaining an efficient reallocation of agricultural resources, while maintaining sufficient equity in welfare among the rural population and between rural and urban sectors, will require extreme skill. It may generate more social tension than the political structures of many developing countries seem able to absorb.

SUPPLEMENT: THE METHOD OF COUNTERFACTUAL CALCULATIONS*

In this supplement we explain the details of the method applied to the counterfactual calculations of agricultural production and price after 1920 (pages 218–28).

Model

The basic model for these counterfactual calculations is the equilibrium of demand and supply. We will use the notation for the actual values of variables

---

[19] "In their drive for greater social equity, or perhaps a more egalitarian society, many developing nations have forgotten that prices and wages have the role of allocating resources as well as producing income. ... This means that developing countries with weak administrative structures should not generally attempt to achieve equity, or social goals, through price and wage manipulations. ... A classic example of this occurred in India in the early 1960's. In an effort to hold food prices to 'fair' levels for urban consumers as food production lagged, farm prices were depressed by government-requisitioning procedures. ... The effort to achieve an equity goal—namely, low food prices for urban consumers—acted to dampen down food production at the very time that an expansion was desperately needed." Willard W. Cochrane, *The World Food Problem; A Guardedly Optimistic View* (New York: Crowell, 1969), pp. 287–88. More recently a number of developing nations, the Philippines and Pakistan in particular, have been unable to maintain announced price support levels. In general, price support actions may have made a greater contribution to price instability than to stability in most developing economies.

* Readers who are not interested in technical detail may wish to skip this section.

as specified in Tables 10–1 and 10–2, and identify the hypothetical values with a prime (′).

Since the actual total supply of rice, Q, can be considered identical to total demand, the equilibrium of demand and supply can be written as:

1) $$Q = (1 + k) Z,$$

where Q is total consumption, Z is domestic production, and k is the ratio of net import (and inventory change) to production. We assume that the above equilibrium relation holds at some actual price, P, and that an equilibrium level of consumption, imports, and production could be specified at some hypothetical price P' as:

2) $$Q' = (1 + k') Z'.$$

If we assume a typical constant elasticity demand function as:

3) $$Q = Q_0 P^\eta,$$

where income and other demand shifters are included in Q_0, the relation between Q and Q' is:

4) $$Q' = Q \left(\frac{P'}{P}\right)^\eta,$$

where η is the price elasticity of demand for rice.

If we assume a constant elasticity supply function as:

5) $$Z = Z_0 P^\gamma S^\delta,$$

where supply shifters other than S are included in Z_0, the relation between Z and Z' is:

6) $$Z' = Z \left(\frac{P'}{P}\right)^\gamma \left(\frac{S'}{S}\right)^\delta,$$

where γ is the price elasticity of supply, S is the seed improvement index, and δ the elasticity of supply with respect to the seed improvement index. Since the following identity holds,

7) $$Z = A\,Y,$$

where A is the area planted (in hectares) and Y is the yield per hectare (in metric tons). If we assume an area response function as:

8) $$A = A_0 P^\alpha$$

and a yield response function as:

9) $$Y = Y_0 P^\beta S^\delta,$$

where α and β are respectively the elasticities of area response and yield response ($\gamma = \alpha + \beta$ and $Z_0 = A_0 Y_0$), the relations between A, A', and Y and Y' are:

10) $$A' = A \left(\frac{P'}{P}\right)^\alpha$$

11)
$$Y' = Y \left(\frac{P'}{P}\right)^{\beta} \left(\frac{S'}{S}\right)^{\delta}.$$

Replacing equations (4) and (6) for Q and Z in equation (2) we have:

12)
$$Q \left(\frac{P'}{P}\right)^{\eta} = (1 + k') Z \left(\frac{P'}{P}\right)^{\gamma} \left(\frac{S'}{S}\right)^{\delta}.$$

From equations (1) and (12) we obtain the formula used to calculate the equilibrium price of rice in Japan under the hypothesized conditions:

13)
$$P' = P \left(\frac{1 + k'}{1 + k}\right)^{\frac{1}{\eta - \gamma}} \left(\frac{S'}{S}\right)^{\frac{\delta}{\eta - \gamma}}.$$

The hypothetical area, yield, and production can be calculated for P' by equations (10), (11), and (7), respectively.

Estimation of Parameters

The problem is now to obtain empirical estimates of five parameters: elasticity of area response to price (α); elasticity of yield response to price (β); elasticity of supply with respect to price (γ); the elasticity of supply with respect to the seed improvement index (δ); and the price elasticity of demand for rice (η).

The estimate of the price elasticity of demand (η) is available from Ohkawa's classical study of the food economy of prewar Japan.[20] His estimates of the price elasticity of demand for rice were based on household survey data of 1931/32–1938/39 for the urban population, and on 1920–38 market data for the rural population. These estimates differ for different occupational, regional, and income groups, but cluster around the mode, minus 0.2. We will adopt minus 0.2 as the elasticity of demand with respect to price (η), since this figure is also consistent with the various estimates of income elasticity of demand for rice.

The supply parameters represent our own estimates. Apparently no study of the supply response of rice has been conducted in Japan. We chose to estimate area response and yield response separately and to obtain an estimate of the aggregate supply elasticity by adding the area and yield elasticities. An important consideration in using this approach is the difference in the time lag required to make adjustments in response to price changes between the area and yield responses. The yield response is essentially a short-run phenomenon, depending primarily on the time it takes to adjust various inputs, such as fertilizer, to a change in price. Area response involves a long-run adjustment period. In Japan, the area planted in upland rice is negligible (less

[20] Kazushi Ohkawa, *Shokuryo Keizai no Riron to Keisoku* (Theory and Measurement of Food Economy) (Tokyo: Nihonhyoronsha, 1945), pp. 9–34, 77–96.

than 5 percent of the total area planted in rice) and no competitive crop exists for rice on the paddy land during the summer crop season. Therefore, the area planted in rice is almost completely determined by the available paddy field area. It requires substantial investment to expand the paddy field area (for example, by shifting upland crop fields to paddy fields), because such a change in land use must be accompanied by an extension of the irrigation system. Because of the large capital investment involved in paddy field development, the short-run response in the area planted to rice to a change in price is limited. The longer-run response may, however, be substantial. Because of the significance of lags in the response of area to price, we employ a distributed lag model of the Koyck–Nerlove type for the analysis of area response. The basic model used is:

14) $$a_t^* = \alpha_0 + \alpha p_{t-1} + \alpha_c p_{c(t-1)}$$

and

15) $$a_t \times a_{t-1} = \lambda (a_t^* - a_{t-1}),$$

where a_t, p_t, and p_{ct} are the logarithmic transformations of area planted in rice, rice price, and the price of competitive crops, respectively. a_t^* is the long-run equilibrium area (in logarithm) for certain levels of p_t and p_{ct}. Equations (10) and (11) reduce to:

16) $$a_t = \lambda \alpha_0 + \lambda \alpha p_{t-1} + \lambda \alpha_c p_{c(t-1)} + (1 - \lambda) a_{t-1}$$

which we will use for the regression analysis.[21] The prices of rice employed in the models estimated were deflated by the general price index, which, to some extent, reflects the changes in the cost of opening new paddy fields. An important variable lacking from our model is public investment in riparian and irrigation works. It is assumed that such government investment is induced in the long-run by price trends and, in that sense, is incorporated into our distributed lag models.[22]

The yield-response model is specified as:

17) $$y_t = \beta_0 + \beta p_t + \delta s_t,$$

[21] Several variations of the area response model were tried, for example, using net income or profit instead of price. The estimates of such models were inferior to the present model.

[22] This assumption is based on the following reasoning: The government, whether democratic or not, would try to perceive and respond to economic and political opportunities. If the price of agricultural products goes up, the benefit-cost ratio of irrigation and water control investment would improve. In that situation, farmers, landlords, and consumers would press for greater investment in such facilities. The government, sensitive to this demand, would allocate a larger amount of funds for irrigation and water control. This would increase national wealth and might also result in an increase in government revenue under an appropriate tax system. Whether the present distributed lag specification of geometric convergence is adequate for describing this process is, of course, open to challenge.

where y_t, p_t, and s_t are the logarithmic transformations of rice yield per hectare, rice price, and the seed improvement index, respectively. For purposes of estimation, we deflated the rice price by the fertilizer price index, in order to reflect the changes in the price of the major current input item.

The results obtained from estimating equations (16) and (17) by least squares are summarized in Table 10–4. In area response the coefficients of the price of competitive products were nonsignificant, and the estimation was repeated after dropping that variable. The estimates of the response of rice area with respect to the price of rice are significant at or near the 5 percent level. The magnitudes of the price coefficients are small and the coefficients of the lagged independent variable are close to one, indicating that the short-run response to price in area planted in rice is very small; but the long-run response is relatively large. This was the expected result, considering the long time required to adjust the paddy field area. The long-run elasticity, allowing infinite time adjustment, is in the order of 0.4–0.6. Such estimates are not incompatible with the results of estimation of area response elasticity in other Asian countries.[23]

The price coefficients in the yield-response regressions are positive and significant at or near the 5 percent level. The seed improvement index variable is also highly significant. The price coefficients, especially in case of $(Y - 1)$, are consistent with the results obtained in a study of fertilizer demand obtained in an earlier study by Yujiro Hayami.[24] In that study, the estimates of the elasticity of demand for fertilizer, with respect to the price of fertilizer, relative to the price of farm products center around 1.5 and the estimates of the elasticity of rice production to fertilizer center around 0.15. Considering the ratio of rice production to total agricultural production in value terms is about 0.55, those estimates imply that the price elasticity of rice-yield response to rice price is around 0.12 ($= 1.5 \times 0.15 \times 0.55$), which is compatible with the results of direct estimation in Table 10–4.

From the results of the estimation of the yield-response relation, we decided to adopt a yield-response elasticity (β) of 0.1 and a seed improvement elasticity (δ) of 3.0. The problem of deciding on an appropriate area response parameter (α) from the results of estimation of the distributed lag area response model is more difficult. The model provides us with a short-run elasticity (allowing a one-year adjustment period) and a long-run elasticity (allowing an infinite ad-

[23] Raj Krishna, "Agricultural Price Policy for Economic Development," *Agricultural Development and Economic Growth*, ed. Herman M. Southworth and Bruce F. Johnston (Ithaca: Cornell University Press, 1967), pp. 497–540; and Mahar Mangahas, Aida E. Recto, and V. W. Ruttan, "Market Relationships for Rice and Corn in the Philippines," *Philippine Economic Journal* 5 (First Semester 1966): 1–27.

[24] Yujiro Hayami, "Nogyo Seisanryoku no Hinogyoteki Kiso" (Nonagricultural Sector as the Basis of Agricultural Productivity), *Keizaiseichoriron no Tenbo* (Perspective for the Theory of Economic Growth), ed. Jinkichi Tsukui and Yasusuke Murakami (Tokyo: Iwanami, 1968), pp. 218–33.

justment period), neither of which is adequate for our purpose. The span of time we are concerned with is the twenty years from 1915 to 1935. We chose ten years as the average adjustment period and selected an area response elasticity (α) of 0.1, based on the range of results shown in the last column of Table 10–4. It should be recognized that this is a convention adopted for computation ease. It has some intuitive appeal but little theoretical justification.

The results of applying the specified parameters to the previous model are shown in Table 10–3.

Table 10-4. Least squares estimates of area and yield response of rice production to price, based on 1890–1937 annual time-series data

Regression number	Equations estimated	Coeff. of determination (adjusted)	Standard error of estimate (adjusted)	Durbin–Watson statistics	Long-run price elasticity	
					Infinite time adjustment[a]	Ten-years adjustment[b]
	Area response					
A-1	$a_t = 0.0529 + 0.0083\,p_{1(t-1)} + 0.0034\,p_{c(t-1)} + 0.9833\,a_{t-1}$ (0.0069) (0.0107) (0.0223)	0.9872	0.00654	2.35	0.497	0.071
A-2	$a_t = 0.0691 + 0.0092\,p_{1(t-1)} + 0.9785\,a_{t-1}$ (0.0058) (0.0163)	0.9874	0.00641	2.34	0.428	0.077
A-3	$a_t = 0.0719 + 0.0138\,p_{2(t-1)} + 0.0026\,p_{c(t-1)} + 0.9787\,a_{t-1}$ (0.0076) (0.0101) (0.0219)	0.9876	0.00643	2.39	0.648	0.113
A-4	$a_t = 0.0848 + 0.0150\,p_{2(t-1)} + 0.9749\,a_{t-1}$ (0.0070) (0.0162)	0.9878	0.00273	2.39	0.598	0.122
	Yield response					
Y-1	$Y_t = -6.6713 + 0.1287\,p_{3t} + 2.8219\,s_t$ (0.0626) (1.1903)	0.6356	0.08731	2.28		
Y-2	$Y_t = -8.0034 + 0.0673\,p_{4t} + 4.2887\,s_t$ (0.0395) (0.8052)	0.7490	0.03112	2.18		
Y-3	$Y_t = -6.6695 + 0.0911\,p_{5t} + 3.5058\,s_t$ (0.0615) (1.1485)	0.6199	0.03872	2.32		
Y-4	$Y_t = -14.6023 + 0.0831\,p_{6t} + 3.6244\,s_t$ (0.0606) (1.1672)	0.6173	0.08346	2.34		

* Variables are a – log A: area planted in rice (1,000 ha.); Y – log Y: rice yield per hectare planted (m. tons); p_1 – log (P/I): unit farm price of rice deflated by general price index (yen per m. ton); p_2 – log of calendar year average of wholesale price of rice deflated by general price index (yen per m. ton); p_3 – log of unit farm price of rice of previous year deflated by fertilizer price index of current year (yen per m. ton); p_4 – log of calendar year average of wholesale price of rice of previous year deflated by fertilizer price index of current year (yen per m. ton); p_5 – log of rice year (November of previous year to October of current year) average of wholesale price of rice deflated by fertilizer price index of current year (yen per m. ton); p_6 – log of January–July average of wholesale price of rice deflated by fertilizer price index of current year (yen per m. ton); p_e – log of price index of farm products except rice deflated by general price index; s – log of S: seed improvement index.

a (Coefficient of p_{t-1}) ÷ (coefficient of a_{t-1}).
b (Coefficient of p_{t-1}) × [1 – (coefficient of a_{t-1})⁹] ÷ (coefficient of a_{t-1}).

Sources: Table 1, except: wholesale prices of rice (monthly prices at Fukagawa Rice Market in Tokyo): Nobufumi Kayo (ed.), Nihon Nogyo Kiso Tokei (Basic Statistics of Japanese Agriculture) (Tokyo: Norin-Suisangyo Seisansei Kojo Kaigi, 1958), p. 514.

Fertilizer price index: Kazushi Ohkawa et al. (ed.), Long-term Economic Statistics of Japan, (LTES), vol. 9 (Tokyo: Toyokeizaishimposha, 1966), pp. 192–93.

Price index of farm products except rice: Price indexes by major commodity groups in LTES, vol. 8 (1967), pp. 168–70, aggregated with 1934–36 value weights in LTES, vol. 8, p. 78.

Part V   Retrospect and Prospect

CHAPTER ELEVEN

Disequilibrium in World Agriculture

In the international economic system that emerged by the end of the nineteenth century, agricultural commodities and raw materials were exported from the most recently settled countries of the temperate region and from the tropical-colonial areas to the developed countries. Industrial products were exported by the developed countries to the less developed world. It was believed to be to the economic advantage of both the developed (DC) and the less developed (LDC) countries for each nation to pursue its comparative "natural advantage." This system gradually broke down after World War I.[1]

By the end of World War II, a massive disequilibrium had emerged in world agriculture. During the first two decades after World War II, the policies pursued by the developed and developing countries intensified the disequilibrium in agricultural production and productivity and in the welfare of rural people between the developed and less developed countries of the world.[2] Agricultural productivity differences between the developed and less developed countries widened (Chapter 4). A fundamental restructuring of agricultural trade relations occurred, and the developing countries became, on balance, net importers rather than net exporters of food.

It is clear, from the policies adopted by both the developed and the less developed countries that these changes have reflected a widening disequilibrium in world agriculture rather than adjustments along a dynamic equi-

[1] Harry G. Johnson, *Economic Policies Toward Less Developed Countries* (Washington: The Brookings Institution, 1967), pp. 48–52; W. Arthur Lewis, *Aspects of Tropical Trade, 1883–1965* (Wicksell Lectures, 1969) (Stockholm: Almquist and Wiksell, 1969); Alex F. McCalla, "Protectionism in International Agriculture Trade, 1850–1968," *Agricultural History* 43 (July 1969): 329–43.

[2] Both the less developed and the developed countries are extremely heterogeneous. They have followed widely different agricultural development and trade policies. The policies discussed in this section should be taken as fairly typical rather than as descriptive of all countries in either group.

librium path. The policies that were adopted resulted in an extreme distortion of prices in factor and product markets in both international and internal trade. Movements of factors and products among countries were dampened by the nationalistic trade and development policies adopted by both the developed and less developed countries. Both market and nonmarket incentives for the allocation of resources in current production and in capital investment and technological development were distorted. In this chapter we attempt to explore how this disequilibrium emerged in the postwar world within the perspective generated from the analysis in the previous chapters. First, we identify the basic forces that resulted in the disequilibrium and the nature and origin of these forces. We also explore some of the efforts that have been made to reverse the trend toward disequilibrium and the reasons why so little success has been achieved.

The approach employed in this section represents a departure from that employed in earlier chapters. It is less firmly based on the results of our own research. Rather it represents an attempt to employ the induced development model, developed and tested in earlier chapters, to illuminate a number of major considerations in the development of effective agricultural development strategies.

THE SOURCES OF DISEQUILIBRIUM

The basic cause of the widening disequilibrium in world agriculture is the lag of the less developed countries in shifting from a natural resource-based agriculture to a science-based agriculture. Agriculture in the developed countries evolved throughout the era of modern economic growth from a resource-based industry to a science-based industry.

In the developed countries human capital and technical inputs, as demonstrated by the intercountry production function analysis (Chapter 5), became a dominant source of growth in agricultural output. The basis for comparative advantage shifted from the natural resource endowments to the endowments of scientific and industrial capacity. The shift in comparative advantage in agricultural production from the less developed to the developed countries was accelerated after World War II.

Differences in output per hectare and in output per worker between the DC's and LDC's widened cumulatively during the first two decades after World War II (Chapter 4). For example, between 1960–64 (average) and 1968 the developed countries increased cereal output by 123 million tons. The developing countries, with twice as many inhabitants and much higher population growth rates, increased cereal production by only fifty-two million tons.[3]

[3] Lyle P. Schertz, "The Green Revolution: Production and World Trade," *Columbia Journal of World Business* 5 (March–April 1970): 53–59.

A significant unanswered question is why the technological lag between the developing and developed countries continued to widen throughout most of the post-World-War-II period in spite of extensive technical assistance programs by the international aid agencies and the agricultural programs adopted by the developing countries.

In retrospect, it seems clear that the breakdown in the international economic system after World War I and during the Great Depression, and the domestic economic policies adopted by both developed and less developed countries after World War II, contributed to a widening rather than a narrowing of the disequilibrium in world agriculture. Typically, the developed countries adopted a policy of protecting domestic agriculture by supporting agricultural prices and imposing barriers, including tariffs, quotas, and levies, on agricultural imports. On the other hand, the less developed countries adopted policies which forced the agricultural sector to bear the costs of protecting domestic industry. These included policies to help finance industrialization, such as the use of state marketing monopolies to stabilize agricultural prices at relatively low levels and the taxation of agricultural exports to keep food prices low for industrial workers. In order to protect less efficient domestic producers, the prices of agricultural inputs, such as fertilizer, were often concurrently maintained well above world price levels.[4] As a result agricultural commodities were significantly overvalued in the developed countries and undervalued in the less developed countries. Surplus agricultural commodities from the developed countries were dumped into international markets through both commercial and concessional trade channels, further aggravating the disequilibrium.

The resulting distortion of prices in factor and product markets resulted in significant malallocation in the resources available for agricultural development. Our analyses of the historical experiences of the United States and Japan (Chapters 6–7), and of the international technology transfer (Chapters 8–10) indicate that market prices represent a powerful co-ordinating force on the resource allocation decisions, not only of private producers but also of scientists and public administrators.

The analysis in Chapter 9 suggests that the anticipation of rising food grain prices and of falling fertilizer prices represented critical factors in inducing institutional innovations in research organization and investment in research, leading to the revolution in food grain production in the tropics since the mid-1960's. Our analysis suggests that the movement toward the restoration of equilibrium in world agriculture, through developments such as new grain varieties, would have begun much earlier and on a much larger scale if agricultural, industrial, and trade policies had not so effectively distorted price relationships throughout much of the postwar period.

[4] See the literature summarized by Theodore W. Schultz, *Economic Growth and Agriculture* (New York: McGraw-Hill, 1968), pp. 17–41.

In addition, the allocation of funds by national and international agencies for agricultural development of the less developed countries has been far from efficient, even when we take into account the misallocation due to price distortions. Priorities in agricultural development were focused primarily on: (a) institutional reforms in the fields of land tenure, marketing, and credit organizations; (b) development of extension and production education systems; and (c) investment in physical infrastructure, especially large-scale land and water resource developments. There was substantial underinvestment in agricultural research. This imbalance led to (a) a widening of productivity differences; (b) failure to build viable agricultural institutions; and (c) low returns to capital applied to the land.

In the following sections we will review in greater detail the economic policies that contributed to a widening of the disequilibrium in world agriculture.

Agricultural Protectionism in the Developed Countries

Agricultural protectionism in the developed countries has been a major factor contributing to disequilibrium in world agriculture. One of the principal obstacles that the developing countries face as they attempt to increase factor productivity, achieve a more rapid rate of growth in production, and expand agricultural exports is the excess production capacity in the developed countries at prevailing prices.

In the United States, productive capacity is so enormous that in 1970 approximately fifty million acres of cropland had been withheld from production for more than a decade. Dumping of agricultural exports in international markets has been encouraged through sales on concessional terms, such as the sale of agricultural commodities for foreign currencies under Public Law 480 and through two-price systems, under which the farmer receives a relatively high price for the share of his product which is sold in the domestic market and a price which reflects the international market conditions for the share of his product that is exported.

In Western Europe grain prices in the European Economic Community (EEC) countries are in many cases double world prices. Export subsidies are so large that they undercut the prices of other exporters as far away as Southeast Asia. In 1969 the handling, storage, and disposal of dairy surpluses cost the EEC countries nearly one billion dollars.[5] Even the United Kingdom has followed a persistent policy of increased self-sufficiency in agriculture. Japan is also highly protectionist. In the late 1960's Japan shifted from its long-term role as a major rice importer to a rice exporter. Prices paid to Japanese producers for rice have been more than double world prices. Production has also

[5] Schertz, "The Green Revolution," p. 56.

been encouraged by subsidies for paddy development. Imports of such products as beef and tropical fruits have been severely restricted.

The increasing agricultural protectionism of the developed countries since World War II has been fundamentally different in its rationale, though perhaps not in its impact on trade, from the earlier protectionism which followed the industrial revolution. Historically, the demand for agricultural protectionism has rested (a) on the wide differential in productivity and income between workers in the agricultural and industrial sectors and (b) on a loss of comparative advantage relative to foreign agricultural producers, as nations have shifted an increasing share of their resources from agriculture to industry during the process of modernization. The demand for protection by the agricultural producers in the developed countries since World War II has rested on a different basis. As agriculture in the developed countries has shifted from a resource-based to a science-based industry, productivity growth in agriculture has often exceeded productivity growth in the industrial sector.[6] Confronted with a relatively inelastic demand for agricultural products in domestic markets, agricultural producers in the industrial countries have demanded protection against declining domestic prices.

The governments of the developed countries have responded to the demands of agricultural producers by erecting an increasingly complex system of national policies for the protection of domestic agriculture. These systems have typically involved some combination of: (a) devices which directly discourage imports (import duties, quantitative restrictions, state trading, and multiple exchange rates); (b) devices which directly encourage exports (export subsidies and multiple exchange rates); and (c) devices which directly encourage domestic production (price supports and deficiency payments). The net effect has been an increase in the degree of protectionism. Although the complexity of the "new protectionist" devices makes comparisons difficult, estimates based on data up through the early 1960's show an increase in agricultural protectionism in most of the developed countries since World War II.[7]

The response of national economic policy to either the "old" or the "new" protectionism has varied widely among nations. In nineteenth-century Great Britain, where the comparative advantage clearly rested in the industrial sector and foreign markets for industrial products were highly elastic, agricultural protectionism was forced to give way to free trade. The Corn Laws were re-

[6] For example, Chandler estimated that from 1946 to 1958 output per man hour of labor and the rate of technological progress (based on the Solow formula) increased by 90.4 percent and 79.1 percent, respectively, in the farm sector, while they increased only 25.1 percent and 12.1 percent, respectively, in the nonfarm sector. See Cleveland A. Chandler, "The Relative Contribution of Capital Intensity and Productivity to Changes in Output and Income in the U.S. Economy, Farm and Nonfarm Sectors," *Journal of Farm Economics* 44 (May 1962): 335–48.

[7] Rachel Dardis and Elmer W. Learn, *Measures of the Degree and Cost of Economic Protection of Agriculture in Selected Countries* (Washington: U.S. Department of Agriculture, Economic Research Service, Technical Bulletin No. 1384, 1967).

pealed in 1846, well over half a century after the Industrial Revolution had resulted in a clear shift of comparative advantage from agriculture (particularly in grain production) to manufacturing. It seems likely that the conditions that led to the repeal of the Corn Laws were unique, even in Great Britain. In his classic history of the English Corn Laws, Donald Grove Barnes points out that "only for a brief period in Great Britain were the interests of the manufacturers and consumers identical. Both wanted cheap food, although for different reasons, and hence they united against their common enemy, the agriculturists, and brought in free trade. But in no other country has this union of the trading and manufacturing interests with the consumers taken place, because their interests have never been identical."[8]

It seems apparent that the failure of the other developed countries to follow the example of Great Britain in the latter half of the nineteenth century reflected a situation where the comparative advantage of the industrial sector was less clear and foreign markets for industrial products were viewed as less elastic. The response of France and Germany to the large-scale inflow of grains from the new continents, which coincided with the world depression during the 1870's and 1880's, was protectionist. The tariff on grain imports introduced in Germany by Bismarck in 1879 was the result of a united campaign by Junkers and iron-steel industrialists to protect both agricultural and industrial products. Later, in the 1890's, the tariff rate was reduced as policy was reoriented toward trade expansion (Caprivi's Der Neue Kurs), but the protection was never completely abandoned. In France tariffs on agricultural produce were revived by Méline in 1892, strengthened in 1895, raised again after World War I, and supplemented again during the Great Depression of the 1930's. Support for protectionist policies was based both on the weak competitive position of French industry and on the threat of lower priced grain imports from Russia, Australia, and America.[9]

In those countries where tariff protection for agriculture has prevailed the longest, it has contributed to a cumulative weakening of the competitive position of agriculture. It has preserved an inefficient agricultural structure and has contributed to a widening productivity gap and a demand for further increases in protection for agriculture. In France the "protectionist policies tended, as always, to preserve the agricultural *status quo*, the existing allocation of resources, peasant farming, *parcellement*, and all the rest of it."[10] A

---

[8] Donald Grove Barnes, *A History of the English Corn Laws From 1660–1846* (New York: Augustus M. Kelley, 1961, reprinted from the original 1930 edition), p. 239.

[9] For a comparison of the responses of Great Britain, Germany, France, Italy, and Denmark to the world decline in the price of wheat after 1870, see C. P. Kindleberger, "Group Behavior and International Trade," *Journal of Political Economy* 50 (February 1951): 30–46. See also, Gordon Wright, *Rural Revolution in France: The Peasantry in the Twentieth Century* (Stanford: Stanford University Press, 1964), pp. 6–18; *Nogyo Hyakka Jiten* (Encyclopedia of Agriculture), vol. 6 (Tokyo: Nosei Chosa Iinkai, 1967), pp. 126–28, 140–41.

[10] A. Whitney Griswold, *Farming and Democracy* (New York: Harcourt, Brace, and Co., 1948), p. 120.

succession of aristocratic, republican, and socialist governments discovered that the economic demands of the peasantry were stronger than economic theory.[11]

The Great Depression in the 1930's was the final blow to trade liberalism. Countries throughout the world raised tariff walls. This was the period when agricultural price supports emerged as a permanent feature of the United States agricultural policy. The tariffs, price supports, and production quotas were originally designed as emergency measures to relieve agricultural prices and income from collapse due to rapidly contracting demand against the inelastic supply of agricultural products during the depression of the 1930's.[12] The persistence and further strengthening of protectionist policies in the industrial countries during the postwar period has been due, to a substantial degree, to rapid growth in agricultural output in the developed countries due to the rapid shift from a resource-based agriculture to a science-based agriculture and a secular decline in the income elasticity of demand for food by consumers. The result was a shift in the internal terms of trade against agriculture.

The impact of rapid growth in labor productivity pressing against an inelastic demand for farm products created particularly difficult resource adjustment problems. In the United States, for example, labor productivity rose by more than 3.0 percent per year between 1925 and 1950 and at more than 6.0 percent per year during the 1950's and 1960's. The growth of demand was less than 2.0 percent per year. The slow expansion in demand for farm products and the rapid growth in labor productivity in agriculture placed the major burden of adjustments to the shift in the domestic terms of trade against agriculture on the intersector labor markets. Labor market adjustments of this magnitude, involving a transfer of farm labor to the nonfarm sector at a rate of more than 4 percent per year, have been extremely difficult to achieve even in a rapidly growing urban industrial economy. The burden of adjustment was particularly difficult in those regions where local nonfarm employment has expanded slowly and for the older farm workers, the less well-educated, and the ethnic and racial minorities.[13] In this environment, in order to ease the burden of adjustment, agricultural producers have pressed for increased agricultural protectionism as well as for more effective domestic price supports and and land-use controls.[14]

The economic rationale for protectionist policies has been strengthened by a

[11] Ibid., p. 117.

[12] D. Gale Johnson, "The Nature of the Supply Function for Agricultural Products," *American Economic Review* 40 (September 1950): 539–64.

[13] Vernon W. Ruttan, "Agricultural Policy in an Affluent Society," *Journal of Farm Economics* 46 (December 1968): 1100–20.

[14] ". . . nationalism in developed countries justifies protection as a means of preserving old industries at the expense of both the consumer and the foreigner, particularly the poor foreigner, who could supply the product cheaper," Harry G. Johnson, *Economic Policies*, p. 79.

number of social and political factors. In France, Japan, and the United States there has been a broad base of public support by farmers for protection from the full impact of market forces. Agricultural "fundamentalism"—the view that an agrarian system in which the basic unit of production was the family farm, owned and operated by the cultivator, represented the only sound foundation of social equality and political stability—has persisted. In Western Europe the economic position of the peasantry has been reinforced by political alliances between the peasant parties and the moderate and conservative parties against the "left."

Perhaps of equal importance in explaining the continued use of protectionist devices, price supports, and land-use controls to manage agricultural prices and output has been a dramatic rise in the capacity of the government administration and control that started in World War I and has greatly accelerated since World War II—by what Hicks has termed the "Administrative Revolution in Government."[15] Before this revolution the tariff was the only practical technique available to governments to manipulate prices, manage production, and redirect income flows in favor of or against agriculture. Today the governments of the developed countries have the capacity to administer a much more complex and precise set of policy measures and direct controls. Furthermore, the economic growth of the total economy and the relative decline of the agricultural sector have made both the government and the general public in the developed countries much less sensitive to the distortions in resource use and the social costs incurred as a result of the policies adopted to protect agriculture from market forces.

The effect of failure of developed countries to manage price and trade policies in the mutual interests of both the developed and the developing countries is illustrated in an extreme form in the case of sugar.[16]

World sugar trade is characterized by special marketing arrangements between exporting and importing countries. Less than 50 percent of total exports enter international trade channels without any preferential arrangements. The

---

[15] "It is impossible to have a strong administration ... unless it can be paid for. ... But the 'amount' of control that can be 'purchased' for a given expenditure may be large or may be small; there can be no doubt that in the Modern Phase it has been very sharply increased. The change that has ensued is so important, and so potent, that we cannot get on without naming it; ... the *Administrative Revolution*. It is partly a matter of organization ... but it is partly ... a matter of application of capital equipment. Modern governments, one would guess, over-use the aeroplane; but where would they be without the telephone—and the typewriter? The contribution of the computer ... is only beginning to be seen. It is already the case that it would be easier (technically) to govern New Zealand from London than it was to govern Scotland from London in the eighteenth century," John Hicks, *A Theory of Economic History* (London: Oxford University Press, 1969), pp. 99, 162.

[16] For a history of sugar policy see Vladimir P. Timoshenko and Boris C. Swerling, *The World's Sugar: Progress and Policy* (Stanford: Stanford University Press, 1957). Also Donald C. Horton, "Policy Directions for the United States Sugar Program," *American Journal of Agricultural Economics* 52 (May 1970): 185–96. For current data and policy reviews see U.S. Department of Agriculture, *Sugar Reports*.

governments of nearly every sugar-producing country exercise some degree of control over the production, refining, and marketing of sugar. Most importing countries have preferential arrangements with dependent overseas territories or independent countries with whom they have close political ties. In addition, most importing countries impose tariffs or quotas to protect their domestic producers.

In the case of the United States the sugar industry was protected and regulated solely by tariff duties prior to 1934. During 1934 the United States established more restrictive import policies under the Jones–Costigen Act in order to protect domestic producers and traditional foreign suppliers from the economic disorganization in world trade that accompanied the Great Depression. Since 1934 the basic structure of the United States sugar policy has involved (a) the establishment of an annual domestic marketing quota for sugar based on an estimate of consumption requirements; (b) a division of this quota between domestic and foreign producers; and (c) an allocation of the domestic quota among mainland and offshore (Hawaii and Puerto Rico) sugar beet and cane producers and of the foreign quota among supply nations.

The Jones–Costigen Act has been modified eight times since 1934, but the basic structure has remained unchanged. The effect of the revisions during the 1950's was to increase the share of the total quota going to domestic producers and to reduce the share available to foreign producers.

The quotas that are made available to foreign suppliers are particularly valuable to them since they receive the U.S. quota price, less transportation costs, and an import duty of 0.62 cents (formerly 0.50 cents) per pound. This is between two and three times the price at which sugar has been available on the international market in recent years (Figure 11–1). The result is that domestic producers, foreign suppliers, and sugar processing and refining organizations engage in extensive public relations and lobbying activities designed to influence the size of quota allocations. Quota allocations have been made to some countries in which production is so inefficient that they have gone on the open market to supply part of their own requirements after exporting their quota to the U.S.

The sugar policy of the United States has clearly been successful in achieving high and relatively stable prices for domestic sugar producers. Prices to foreign quota holders have also been well above the level that would have prevailed in the absence of a quota system. Prices in the "free market" have been lower. It is also clear that this has been an expensive program for U.S. consumers and taxpayers and that it has worked to the long-term disadvantage of tropical exporting countries. Participation of foreign suppliers in the premium system has enabled U.S. producers to escalate the domestic share of the total quota without substantially increasing program costs.

Estimates of the resources that would be made available to the LDC's if the sugar-protecting countries were to replace the present restrictionist policies by

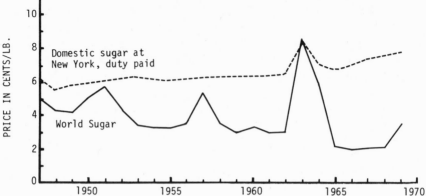

FIGURE 11-1. Spot prices of raw cane sugar. (*Sources:* World sugar: FAO Production Yearbook for 1947–66 data; USDA, Sugar Reports, for 1967–69 data. Domestic sugar: USDA, Sugar Situation and Sugar Reports.)
Note: "World sugar" refers to Cuba, Raw, 96°, export price; destinations other than the United States (No. 4 contract). f.o.b. From 1961, prices are No. 8 contract, bagged, f.o.b., and stowed at Greater Caribbean ports, including Brazil.

completely free trade in sugar indicate that free trade could be expected to lead to an annual increase of more than $1.0 billion in the net value of sugar exports by the developing countries.[17]

These estimates do not exhaust the benefits from free trade in sugar to either the developing or the developed countries. The distortion of sugar prices has clearly induced nonproductive resource shifts in the infrastructure serving agriculture. Investment in research on sugar beet production is one clear example. It is not likely in a free market situation that the United States and the other free world importing countries would regard investment in sugar beet research as having a much higher priority than investment in research on a minor crop, such as oats, since it is unlikely that under any conditions would it be profitable to produce sugar beets if sugar could be imported at less than four cents per pound.

The protectionist policies of the developed countries have also influenced the location and payoff to sugar cane research.[18] Prior to the increase in pro-

[17] Clayton Ogg, "Johnson and Johnson on Sugar Policy," (St. Paul: University of Minnesota, Department of Agricultural Economics, January 1971), mimeo. The estimates by Ogg represent a revision of earlier estimates by Harry G. Johnson, *Economic Policies*, pp. 87, 88, 257–66; and D. Gale Johnson, "Sugar Program: Costs and Benefits," *Foreign Trade and Agricultural Policy Technical Papers of the National Advisors Commission on Food and Fiber*, vol. 6 (Washington: U.S. Government Printing Office, August 1967), pp. 37–47. See also R. H. Snape, "Some Aspects of Protection in the World Sugar Industry," *Economica* 30 (February 1963): 63–73.

[18] Robert Evenson, "International Transmission of Technology in the Production of Sugar Cane" (University of Minnesota, Agricultural Experiment Station Scientific Journal Paper No. 6805, 1969).

tectionism associated with the Great Depression, it was possible for a less developed country to achieve a high return to investment in sugar cane research. The rapid growth of sugar production and exports in Java between the late 1800's and the early 1930's was based on the clear technical advantage resulting from development of the world's major sugar research station in Java (Proefstation Oost Java). By the late 1920's cane yields were the highest in the world in Java, and Java ranked second only to Cuba as a sugar exporter. The first international sugar agreement, negotiated in 1933, and other trade restraint policies adopted as a result of the Great Depression were disastrous to the Java sugar industry. Since World War II, sugar cane research investment has shifted primarily to importing countries and countries with protected markets in importing countries.

There have been a number of attempts to estimate the losses due to distortions of resource use as a result of protectionist trade policies. The estimates, as in the case of sugar, are substantial but not spectacular. In our judgment, the distortion of development incentive through the failure to employ efficiency prices in international transactions is much more serious than the short-run losses that have been calculated.

Resource Malallocation in the Less Developed Countries

A second factor contributing to the widening disequilibrium in world agriculture during the first two post-World-War-II decades has been the malallocation of resources resulting from domestic development policies adopted by the developing countries. Agricultural and industrial development policies have been adopted with almost complete disregard to factor endowments. The policies have reflected a combination of ideological bias on the part of the political elite and of analytical failure on the part of development planners.

These policies were adopted in an effort to remove the constraints imposed by the political and economic dominance of the metropolitan economies. The mercantile policies of the metropolitan countries, supported by the productivity of the industrial sector of the developed countries, had resulted in the decline of local handcraft and manufacturing production and increased specialization in raw material and commodity production.[19] The commodity and raw material producing sectors were frequently dominated by foreign capital and managed by foreign personnel.

A major objective of political leadership in most developing countries, whether impelled by a nationalist or a socialist ideology, has been an attempt

[19] For the theoretical formulation see Stephen Hymer and Stephen Resnick, "A Model of an Agrarian Economy with Nonagricultural Activities," *American Economic Review* 59 (September 1969): 493–506. For a historical review of the impact of colonial development policies in the economic structure of countries in Southeast Asia see Stephen A. Resnick, "The Decline in Rural Industry Under Export Expansion: A Comparison among Burma, Philippines and Thailand, 1870–1938," *Journal of Economic History* 30 (March 1970): 51–73.

to substitute new forms of economic organization for the "capitalist" form inherited from a period of colonial dominance or economic dependence, and to replace the traditional "exploitive" raw material and commodity producing sectors with an industrial structure that would reduce "dependence" on the metropolitan economies.[20]

Even when the motivation has been primarily nationalistic, there has generally been a preference for public enterprise over private enterprise and a distrust of the market mechanism in the allocation of resources and the direction of income flows. The implementation of nationalistic development policies has typically involved public ownership of the industries controlled by foreign capital and managed by foreign personnel, particularly those industries, such as public utilities, which tended to occupy a monopolistic position in the domestic market. In other sectors the thrust of nationalistic economic policy has frequently emphasized the development of indigenous "entrepreneurship" and the direction of industrial development along lines selected for their symbolic value in terms of concepts of "national identity" and "modernization." This typically involves the use of tax, tariff, foreign exchange, price policies, and direct controls to direct the flow of resources. Where socialist ideology has reinforced the nationalistic drive, public ownership tends to be more pervasive and may even extend, as in Tunisia in the late 1960's, to small-scale industry, distribution, and agriculture.

There was also a general failure to adopt policies consistent with rapid growth of output in the agricultural sector. In some cases these policies were directed to shifting income streams away from the traditional political elite whose economic base rested in the agricultural and plantation sectors. In other cases it was based on a presumption of low growth potential in the agricultural sector because of institutional constraints on the response of peasant producers to economic incentives. Industrialization was viewed as an effective means of breaking down the constraints on economic growth in economies where "too many peasants" were viewed as a major obstacle to economic growth.[21]

The net effect of the ideological perspectives and the analysis of development alternatives was typically to redirect income flows away from both the

[20] Harry G. Johnson, "A Theoretical Model of Economic Nationalism in New and Developing States," *Political Science Quarterly* 80 (June 1965): 169–85; Albert Breton, "The Economics of Nationalism," *Journal of Political Economy* 72 (August 1964): 376–86; M. Bronfenbrenner, "The Appeal of Confiscation in Economic Development," *Economic Development and Cultural Change* 3 (April 1955): 201–18; Martin Bronfenbrenner, " 'Capitalism' East and West: Horatio Alger and Simon Legree," *Ethics* 71 (April 1961): 188–94.

[21] See Raúl Prebisch, "Commercial Policy in the Underdeveloped Countries," *American Economic Review* 49 (May 1959): 251–73. For a critical review of the Prebisch thesis see M. June Flanders, "Prebisch on Protectionism: An Evaluation," *Economic Journal* 74 (June 1964): 305–26. Also see Gottfried Haberler, "An Assessment of the Current Relevance of the Theory of Comparative Advantage to Agricultural Production and Trade," *International Journal of Agrarian Affairs* 4 (May 1964): 130–49.

traditional elite and the peasantry and toward the middle class, particularly the educated middle class and organized labor. These policies cannot, of course, be evaluated only, or perhaps principally, in economic terms. "Even though nationalization may involve a substantial redistribution of real income toward the middle class at the expense of the mass of population, this redistribution may perform a necessary function in the early stages of forming a nation, in the sense that the existence of a substantial middle class may be a prerequisite of a stable society and democratic government. . . . an investment in the creation of a middle class, financed by resources extracted from the mass of the population by nationalistic policies, may be the essential preliminary to the construction of a viable national state."[22] It is useful, however, to inquire into the costs of such policies on national economic growth.

Regardless of the motivation, these policies have contributed to the widening of disequilibrium in world agriculture. Discrimination against agriculture in both factor and product markets has depressed production incentives. The new industries developed to foster nationalistic economic objectives have often not achieved the capacity to produce the new biological, chemical, and mechanical inputs essential for agricultural development. Price policies have been directed toward extracting an economic surplus from both the peasant and plantation sectors rather than toward the effective co-ordination of production decisions at the farm level and of intersector resource allocation decisions. Finally, the drive for industrialization has been accompanied by failure to invest in the development of the research necessary for the growth of agricultural productivity and output.

The characterization of the economic policies followed by the less developed countries has been necessarily rather general. It is useful, therefore, to examine the working out of these policies in a particular economy. The Philippines represents a useful example because of the relative success of the national development policies it has followed, as well as the limitations on development resulting from these policies. During the period since independence, the objective of Philippine national economic development has been to achieve "relatively and absolutely increasing per capita real income accruing to Filipinos, with an increasing relative share of aggregate income generated by manufacturing and a diminishing relative share of aggregate income generated by specialization and external trade in primary products and, equally important, both an absolute and relative increase in the share of Filipinos in the ownership and management of the productive assets of the economy."[23]

The policies that were adapted to implement these objectives were based on

---

[22] Harry G. Johnson, "A Theoretical Model of Economic Nationalism," p. 185.
[23] Frank H. Golay, *The Philippines: Public Policy and National Economic Development* (Ithaca: Cornell University Press, 1961), p. 10. See also the review of the Golay book by Amado A. Castro, "Economic Policy Revisited," *Philippine Economic Journal* 1 (First Semester 1962): 66–91.

the assumption that the export prospects for the traditional primary products produced by the Philippines (sugar, copra, abaca) were poor. It was concluded that the prospects for growth depended on the effective development of import-substituting industries. The legal and administrative devices employed to achieve industrial growth included (a) licensing of foreign exchange transactions; (b) administration by the government of large credit resources; and (c) use of the regulatory powers of the government to direct investment. The protective use of controls, the availability of foreign exchange at bargain prices, and the regulatory powers of the government were employed to direct resources into the manufacturing sector and into the hands of a new class of Filipino entrepreneurs. Industrial output expanded rapidly. "Between 1949 and 1960 income originating in manufacturing grew at the rate of 29% a year. Relatively, it moved faster than other sectors . . . accounting for 8.1 percent of the national income in 1949, and rising to 17.7% by 1960."[24]

In spite of impressive industrial growth the Philippine economy was beginning to experience serious difficulties by the late 1950's. There was a sharp deterioration in the balance of payments position. The foreign exchange rate (₱2/$1) was under severe pressure. Between 1960 and 1962 a series of "decontrol" measures and exchange reforms was undertaken. According to Benito Legarda, the "grand design of the whole reform" was "simultaneously to lift quantitative restrictions on trade and payments under what amounted to an open general license, while at the same time . . . to prevent runaway movements of the exchange rate by credit restraints and by securing financial backing, and also to provide new forms of protection . . . by raising tariff rates on certain items."[25] The effect of the decontrol was a substantial devaluation of the peso (to approximately ₱4/$1), a shift in the internal terms of trade against the emerging industrial sector, and a redirection of income flows toward the traditional commodity- and raw-material-producing sectors.

Throughout the 1960's there was a substantial professional debate concerning the effect of the economic policies of the 1950's and the reversal of economic policy in the 1960's. One major conclusion that emerged out of this debate is that the control policies of the 1950's had resulted in a severe distortion of incentives and had led to a composition of industrial output inconsistent with the nations' factor endowments. The new entrepreneurs, "encouraged by low prices on imported capital goods attributable to a policy of peso overvaluation, by incredibly low interest rates to favored industries . . . , and by high wages fostered by . . . minimum wage policy, . . . substituted

---

[24] Benito Legarda y Fernandez, "Foreign Exchange Decontrol and the Redirection of Income Flows," ibid. 1 (First Semester 1962): 22. See also Benito Legarda, Jr., "Philippine Economic Paradoxes," *Philippine Statistician* 13 (June 1964): 89–112; Benito Legarda, Jr., "Back to the 'Sugar Republic,'" *Far Eastern Economic Review* 46 (October 1969): 171, 172, 217.

[25] Legarda, "Foreign Exchange Decontrol," p. 21.

capital for labor wherever their production functions allowed such possibili- ties."[26] The commitment to an import substitution pattern of industrializa- tion, dependent on the growth of domestic consumer goods demand, set a relatively low ceiling on industrial growth. Furthermore, the effect of capital deepening at the firm level imposed severe constraints on the ability of the industrial sector to achieve gains in total factor productivity. The Philippine experience with a nationalistic import-substitution policy is in these respects quite similar to the experience in Latin America.[27]

It is possible to provide a more positive view of the Philippine economic policies of the 1950's. An expanded industrial base was established and a new entrepreneurial class was developed. Nevertheless, the policies of the 1950's had severely underestimated the elasticity of substitution between capital and labor in the industrial sector[28] and the response of agricultural production to changes in the prices of factors and products.[29] While the redirection of in- come flows resulting from the decontrol of the early 1960's did depress returns to the industrial sector, this did not significantly retard the growth of indus- trial output.[30] The decontrol resulted in a rapid rise in the price of the com- mercial export crops relative to the domestically consumed food crops. The shift in the terms of trade between the domestic food and commercial export crop sectors was associated with a significant shift of resources into export production and a rapid rise in the volume of export crop production and in export earnings (Figure 11–2). This response clearly exceeded the expectations of the analysts and planners who had designed the policies of the 1950's and the reforms of the 1960's.[31] As a result they paid a high price for the limited

[26] Jeffrey G. Williamson, "Dimensions of Postwar Philippine Economic Progress," *Quarterly Journal of Economics* 83 (February 1969): 107. See also John H. Power, "Import Substitution as an Industrialization Strategy," *Philippine Economic Journal* 5 (Second Semester 1966): 167–204; Robert J. Lampman, "The Sources of Post-War Economic Growth in the Philippines," ibid. 6 (Second Semester 1967): 170–88.

[27] Henry J. Bruton, "Productivity Growth in Latin America," *American Economic Re- view* 57 (December 1967): 1099–1116; Nathaniel H. Leff, "Export Stagnation and Autarkic Development," *Quarterly Journal of Economics* 81 (May 1967): 286–301.

[28] Gerardo P. Sicat, "Production Functions in Philippine Manufacturing," *Philippine Economic Journal* 2 (Second Semester 1963): 107–31; Gerardo P. Sicat, "Analytical Aspects of Two Current Economic Policies," ibid. 4 (First Semester 1965): 107–19.

[29] Mahar Mangahas, Aida E. Recto, and Vernon W. Ruttan, "Price and Market Rela- tionships for Rice and Corn in the Philippines," *Journal of Farm Economics* 48 (August 1966): 685–703 (see also *Philippine Economic Journal* [First Semester 1966]: 1–27); Randolph Barker, "The Response of Production to a Change in Rice Price," ibid. 5 (Second Semester 1966): 260–76. The data and analysis on which these articles are based are reported in greater detail in Mahar Mangahas, Aida E. Recto, Vernon W. Ruttan, *Production and Market Rela- tionship for Rice and Corn in the Philippines* (Los Baños, Philippines: International Rice Research Institute, Technical Bulletin No. 9, 1970).

[30] Malcolm Treadgold and Richard W. Hooley, "Decontrol and the Redirection of In- come Flows: A Second Look," *Philippine Economic Journal* 6 (Second Semester 1967): 109–28.

[31] Benito Legarda, "Foreign Exchange Decontrol"; "Philippine Economic Paradoxes"; "Back to the 'Sugar Republic.'"

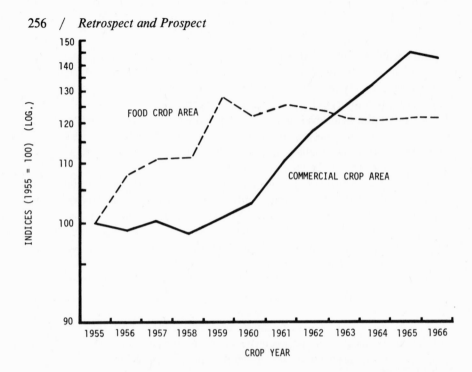

FIGURE 11-2. Land utilization indices: food crops and commercial crops, 1955–66. (*Source:* Malcolm Treadgold and Richard W. Hooley, "Decontrol and the Redirection of Income Flows: A Second Look," *Philippine Economic Journal* 7 [second semester 1967]: 118 and 119.)

Note: Crop area data refer to area harvested (except for tree crops). Data are on a crop year basis, ending June 1930. Data as reported by the Department of Agriculture and Natural Resources, Bureau of Agricultural Economics.

gains in industrial employment actually achieved and failed to create the growth of demand in rural areas necessary to sustain a viable import-substitution industrialization policy.

In spite of the continued growth of the export sector and the expansion of exports, the decontrol was not an unqualified success. One effect was an excess of domestic demand which "was concentrated particularly on food, the production of which failed to grow more rapidly in the post-decontrol era because of the greater price incentives to expand export crops."[32] The result was pressure on food prices, inflation in the cost of living index, and rising imports of food commodities, particularly rice, during the mid-1960's. The inflation tended to erode the gains from decontrol by pushing labor costs upward in the export industries and by pre-empting the gains in foreign exchange earnings for food imports.

The inability to expand food production in the face of rising demand during

[32] Treadgold and Hooley, "Decontrol and Redirection of Income Flows," p. 125.

the 1960's is itself a reflection of the failure, during both the colonial period and during the 1950's, to make the investments in land and water resource development, in experiment station capacity, and in the production of the industrial inputs needed to sustain growth in agricultural productivity. Throughout this period there was little change in agricultural productivity. Output expansion was largely accounted for by expansion of traditional inputs. Output per worker rose only slightly. Output per unit of land area declined. Total productivity remained approximately unchanged.[33]

In retrospect, as a result of the development policies adopted in the 1950's and 1960's, the Philippines has paid a relatively high price for economic growth. Capital investment in the industrial sector has purchased too few new jobs. Failure to make the investments in agricultural experiment station capacity and in the industrial inputs necessary to achieve productivity growth in agriculture imposed severe limitations on the ability of the agricultural sector to respond to growth in demand. In the 1950's growth of food crop production occurred at the expense of growth of export production. And in the 1960's growth of export crop production occurred at the expense of food crop production. Productivity growth was inadequate to release the constraints imposed by resource limitations to permit rapid growth in the production of both commercial export crops and domestic food crops.

By the late 1960's a new rice production technology, resulting primarily from the research at the International Rice Research Institute, the University of the Philippines College of Agriculture, and the Philippine Bureau of Plant Industry, was beginning to relax the constraints on productivity growth in food crop production. There are some indications that the experiences of the 1950's and the 1960's may now be leading to a new set of economic policies which redirect economic incentives in the agricultural and industrial sectors in such a way as to reduce the costs of economic growth.

Over the last several decades the developed countries have evolved an increasingly complex set of agricultural commodity and trade policies. The policies have been discriminatory, in that the most serious barriers have been against goods which the less developed countries typically have a comparative advantage in producing. The less developed countries have, in turn, adopted economic policies toward agriculture that had the net effect of reducing economic efficiency and impeding economic growth.

The net effect of these policies has been a failure to realize the potential contribution of agriculture to economic growth in the developing countries. The developed countries have been reaping growth dividends from the new production possibilities resulting from the advances in biological and mechanical technology, while paying high costs for the protection of agriculture. The less developed countries "have lagged seriously in taking advantage of modern

[33] Richard Hooley and Vernon W. Ruttan, "The Philippines," *Agricultural Development in Asia*, ed. R. T. Shand (Canberra: Australian National University Press, 1969), pp. 215–50.

agricultural inputs, and they have, in general, thwarted agriculture by imposing on it a set of inefficient prices, thereby concealing virtually all profitable investment opportunities in farming."[34]

There have been a number of attempts to reverse the trend toward disequilibrium in world agriculture. Much of this effect has centered around issues of institutional reform and investment in the organizational and physical infrastructure serving agriculture. In the next section we examine some of the attempts to remove some of the institutional constraints on the process of agricultural development.

INSTITUTIONAL REFORM

One of the basic premises of the agricultural development and technical assistance programs of the late 1940's and early 1950's was that institutional constraints represented the major barrier to technical change and to modernization in agriculture.[35] Major program priorities were placed on the reform of land tenure, marketing, and credit institutions. The perspective that emerges from our analysis is that changes which enhance the productivity potential of the human and material resources used in agricultural production represent the most effective incentive that a society can offer to agricultural producers for the transformation of traditional agriculture.

In our view, institutional reform is appropriately viewed more as a response to the new opportunities for the productive use of human and material resources opened up by advances in technology than as a precondition for agricultural development (see pages 53–63). The institutional reform that is appropriate for any economy depends both on its particular historical traditions and the economic opportunities available to it. If this view is correct, the returns to society from the resources devoted to the introduction of institutional reform, independent of the opportunities for growth available to the agricultural sector of a particular economy, are likely to be extremely low and, in some cases, negative.

---

[34] Theodore W. Schultz, *Economic Growth and Agriculture*, p. 15.

[35] See John M. Brewster, "Traditional Social Structure as Barriers to Change," *Agricultural Development and Economic Growth*, ed. Herman M. Southworth and Bruce F. Johnston (Ithaca: Cornell University Press, 1967), pp. 66–98. The institutional constraint perspective has recently been restated by Gunnar Myrdal, *Asian Drama: An Inquiry into the Poverty of Nations* (New York: Pantheon Books, 1968; paperback edition, New York: Twentieth Century Fund, 1968), 3 vols., "the success of technological reforms designed primarily to increase the cultivated acreage and raise agricultural yields through variations in techniques and the input of capital hinges largely on the extent of prior or at least simultaneous institutional changes" (p. 1260). For a comment on the Myrdal perspective see Kusum Nair, "Asian Drama—A Critique," *Economic Development and Cultural Change* 17 (July 1969): 449–59.

Land Tenure Reform [36]

Tenure reform has been viewed as essential to the mobilization of labor resources and the generation of productivity growth in both liberal and Marxist development perspectives. Among Western economists economic history and economic logic have combined to produce a remarkable unity in doctrine, to the effect that an agricultural sector organized on an owner-operator pattern achieves a more efficient allocation of resources and makes a greater contribution to national economic growth than under alternative systems. This perspective has led to a major emphasis on land reform in the technical and economic assistance efforts of a number of national and inter-national aid agencies.[37] The result has been a proliferation of land reform legislation in the developing world, particularly in Asia and Latin America, but very little land redistribution to peasant producers.[38]

The major conclusion which emerges from an analysis of the relationship between tenure and productivity within the framework of the neoclassical theory of the firm is "that there is no substitute, from the standpoint of sheer productivity, and irrespective of sociological considerations, for an owner-operated agricultural system."[39] The generalization is based on formal anal-ysis of the equilibrium levels of inputs and outputs under alternative "ideal type" tenure arrangements within the framework of the neoclassical theory of the firm. The deductions indicate that if farms were classified by size, tenure, and productivity, a productivity ranking would find the owner-operator at the

[36] The material discussed in this section is treated in greater detail in Vernon W. Ruttan, "Equity and Productivity Issues in Modern Agrarian Reform Legislation," *Economic Problems of Agriculture in Industrial Societies*, ed. Ugo Papi and Charles Nunn (New York: Macmillan [St. Martins Press], 1969), pp. 581–600.

[37] For a review of recent literature see Philip M. Raup, "Land Reform and Agricultural Development," ed. Southworth and Johnston, *Agricultural Development*, pp. 267–314; Doreen Warriner, *Land Reform in Principle and Practice* (London: Oxford University Press, 1969); E. B. Rice, *Design of the Review* (Washington: Agency for International Develop-ment, Spring Review of Land Reform, June 2–4, 1970). The AID review consists of a series of background studies, agricultural papers, and country papers.

[38] See, for example, Ernest Feder, "Land Reform Under the Alliance for Progress," *Journal of Farm Economics* 47 (August 1965): 652–88; Kusum Nair, *Blossoms in the Dust* (New York: Praeger, 1962). Feder points out that "the best visible result of the Alliance seems to be the enactment of a large number of land reform laws, which have become effec-tive instruments not for carrying out large scale reforms but for stalling them" (p. 652). Ac-cording to Nair, "though since 1947, India has enacted perhaps more land reform legislation than any other country in the world, it has not succeeded in changing in any essentials the power pattern, the deep economic disparities, nor the traditional hierarchical nature of inter-group relationships which govern the economic life of village society" (p. 196).

[39] Louis S. Drake, "Comparative Productivity of Share- and Cash-Rent Systems of Ten-ure," *Journal of Farm Economics* 34 (November 1952): 549. For the evolution of this analysis in U.S. literature, see Rainer Schickele, "Effect of Tenure Systems on Agricultural Effi-ciency," ibid. 23 (February 1941): 185–207; Earl O. Heady, "Economics of Farm Leasing Systems," ibid. 34 (August 1947): 659–78; D. Gale Johnson, "Resource Allocation Under Share Contracts," *Journal of Political Economy* 58 (April 1950): 111–23; Drake, "Compara-tive Productivity," pp. 535–50.

top, share tenants at the bottom, and part owners and lessees in an intermediate position in each size group.

The analytical deductions are generally regarded as consistent with historical experience.[40] The recent experience in Japan and Taiwan has been widely interpreted as supporting the proposition that an agrarian structure consisting of extremely small owner-cultivator family farms can be viable, reasonably efficient, and capable of sustaining rapid increases in agricultural productivity. Analysis of the earlier modifications in tenure arrangements in Japan, beginning with the abolition of feudal privileges and the conversion of the land tax to a cash rather than a commodity basis during the early years of the Meiji Restoration, also supports the proposition that the resulting improvements in incentives complemented efforts to introduce new varieties, higher levels of fertilization, and other changes in cultural practices.[41]

Analysis of land tenure data and land reform experiences in other developing countries, however, does not provide the same degree of support for either the logical deductions or the historical generalizations. The growing body of empirical evidence on the relationships among farm size, tenure, and productivity is frequently inconsistent with the ordering suggested by the logical deductions. In the smaller size ranges, share tenants frequently achieve higher yields than owner-operators. Even in the larger size classes, owner-operators frequently do not exhibit any clear-cut productivity differentials relative to other tenure classes.[42] It is our impression, for example, that a careful review of land reform efforts in Southeast Asia, excluding Japan and Taiwan, would not reveal a single example of a successful land reform program when evaluated in terms of contributions to growth of productivity or production. Apparently this conclusion also applies to the post-World-War-II land reform efforts in Eastern Europe and in the developing countries which have followed the socialist agrarian reform model.[43]

[40] United Nations, *Land Reform: Defects in Agrarian Structure as Obstacles to Economic Development* (New York: United Nations, Department of Economic Affairs, 1951). Warriner indicates that most current theorizing with respect to the relationship between tenure and productivity stems from the 1951 UN Report. See Doreen Warriner, *Land Reform*, p. 371. The 1951 UN Report is more correctly viewed as a source of historical generalizations concerning the relationship between tenure and productivity.

[41] For Japan, see M. Kaihara, "On the Effects of Postwar Land Reform in Japan," *Land Tenure, Industrialization and Social Stability*, ed. Walter Froehlich (Milwaukee: The Marquette University Press, 1961), pp. 143–56; Takekazu Ogura (ed.), *Agricultural Development in Modern Japan* (Tokyo: Fuji Publishing Co., 1963), pp. 119–44, 613–77; and R. P. Dore, *Land Reform in Japan* (London: Oxford University Press, 1958). For Taiwan, see Chen Cheng, *Land Reform in Taiwan* (Taiwan: China Publishing Co., 1961), pp. 90–91; and S. C. Hsieh and T. H. Lee, *An Analytical Review of Agricultural Development in Taiwan—An Input-Output and Productivity Approach* (Taipei: Joint Commission on Rural Reconstruction, Economic Digest Series No. 12, July 1958).

[42] Vernon W. Ruttan, "Tenure and Productivity of Philippine Rice Producing Farms," *Philippine Economic Journal* 5 (First Semester 1966): 42–63.

[43] Folke Dovring, *Land and Labor in Europe, 1900–1950* (The Hague: Martinus Nijhoff, 1956), p. 350; Folke Dovring, *Economic Results of Land Reforms* (Spring Review of Land Reform) (Washington: U.S. Agency for International Development, June 1970).

Apparently, neither the empirical predictions based on logical deductions from the neoclassical theory of the firm nor the historical generalizations based on the evolution of land tenure institutions in Western Europe, North America, Japan, and Taiwan are adequate guides to modern land tenure policies in the developing economies.

The first step in achieving greater precision in understanding the productivity implications of changes in land tenure institutions and in the design of land tenure policies is to reject the assumption that there is a single optimum land tenure system. The relationship between tenure and agricultural development is reciprocal rather than direct—"while some land reforms are essential for economic development, economic development is essential for the success of many land reforms."[44]

The share tenure systems, which are now generally regarded as inconsistent with both efficient resource allocations and social equity, evolved primarily in response to economic incentives to extract a larger marketable surplus than could be achieved under feudal or precolonial systems of economic organization. Both colonial administrators and the commercially oriented indigenous elite have at times used share tenure as an effective device to force increased production from a peasant agriculture prior to the extensive monetization of economic activity in several areas. Owners of estates or haciendas have used share tenure arrangements as more effective methods of labor management than use of direct wage labor in the production of commodities, such as rice, cotton, or copra, which required close personal attention or a high degree of husbandry skill on the part of the cultivator. And, in the absence of effective credit and marketing institutions, peasant farmers have, at times, found that share tenure arrangements exposed them to less income uncertainty from price and yield fluctuations than fixed rent leasehold arrangements on a debt-encumbered owner-operatorship.

Modification of the neoclassical analysis to incorporate the dynamic effects of monetization and commercialization of agricultural production in an environment characterized by a static agricultural technology and substantial imperfections in capital, labor, and product markets would imply more rapid growth of agricultural production than under fixed-rent leasehold or owner-operator systems. This conclusion is consistent with the rapid growth of both the share tenure system and of agricultural exports in a number of tropical countries and colonial dependencies during the latter half of the nineteenth century.[45]

In advanced urban industrial economies the relationship between tenure and productivity growth in agriculture also appears to be less direct than sug-

[44] Raj Krishna, "Some Aspects of Land Reform and Economic Development in India," ed. Froehlich, *Land Tenure*, p. 223. This same point is made by Warriner, "the relationship between structure and development is a reciprocal process, early development conditioning change in structure, which itself *may* condition further development," *Land Reform*, p. 391.

[45] See, for example, the discussion of agricultural development in Burma in J. S. Furnivall, *Colonial Policy and Practice* (New York: New York University Press, 1956).

gested by either neoclassical analysis or historical generalizations.[46] In a progressive urban industrial economy, characterized by rapid technical progress in agriculture and efficient labor, land, capital, and product markets, both technical efficiency and rapid productivity growth appear to be consistent with a wide range of tenure arrangements. In such an economy, both share and fixed rent tenure arrangements make it easier for farmers to adjust the size of farm operations in response to technical change. Strong intersector labor and capital markets provide incentives for both the tenant and the land owner to develop leasing arrangements that are consistent with rapid growth in production and in factor productivity. In the dynamic environment in which agriculture has operated in the United States over the last several decades, land rental has played an important role in facilitating rapid change in farm size.[47] In the technically progressive grain and livestock producing areas of the Middle West, which account for almost half of national agricultural production, the proportion of leased and tenant operated land is higher than in other regions and is continuing to rise.

The most direct relationship between land tenure institutions and the growth of agricultural productivity is found in agrarian systems which are undergoing a transition from a relatively static subsistence structure to a technically progressive, small-scale commercial structure in economies where the rate of growth of employment in the urban industrial sector is not high enough to permit decline in the agricultural labor force. Under these conditions the conversion of tenant holdings to small-scale owner-operatorship units, as in western and southern Yugoslavia in the 1920's, Japan in the late 1940's, Taiwan in the early 1950's, and Iran in the 1960's, has clearly been consistent

[46] In 1940 T. W. Schultz, in "Capital Rationing, Uncertainty and Farm-Tenancy Reform," *Journal of Political Economy* 48 (June 1940): 309–24, pointed out that in an agriculture characterized by high levels of capital input per worker, "changing tenant farmers over to [debt] encumbered owners reduces measurably the returns of farmers who have limited assets" (p. 323). D. Gale Johnson, "Resource Allocation," develops the implications of share tenure leases for allocative efficiency when the tenant has effective alternative employment opportunities for his labor and the landlord has alternative investment opportunities for his capital. In a study sponsored by the North Central Land Tenure Research Committee, Walter G. Miller, Walter E. Chryst, and H. W. Ottoson, *Relative Efficiencies of Farm Tenure Class in Intrafirm Resource Allocation* (Ames: Iowa State College Agricultural and Home Economics Experiment Station, Research Bulletin 461, November 1958), failed to find significant differences in the marginal productivity of resources related to tenure.

[47] James O. Bray, "Farm Tenancy and Productivity in Agriculture: The Case of the United States," *Food Research Institute Studies*, vol. 4, No. 1 (1963): 25–38. According to Bray, "The most impressive development of recent years has been the persistent increase in the percentage of land in the hands of part owners. These operators generally own more land than do full owners in the same region, and, in addition, rent an acreage similar to that farmed by the average tenant. Thus they farm larger acreages than either full owners or tenants. The increasing proportion of all land in farms held by part owners suggests that this group contains some of the most successful owners who have enlarged their operations by renting, as well as successful tenants who have bought a farm but continue to rent other land" (p. 36).

with both productivity and equity objectives. The essential reason for the success of such small holding reforms is the increase in production incentives resulting from the removal of sharing arrangements and other constraints on individual decision-making. The incentive effects become particularly important where labor market alternatives are limited and existing share tenure arrangements represent, in effect, a tax on both the operator's labor inputs and on inputs purchased from the industrial sector.[48]

The primary conclusion which emerges from our review of the experience of land tenure reform is that the economic gains to be had from a radical modification in land tenure patterns will be greatest during periods when rapid technical changes are opening up new production possibilities which are inhibited by existing tenure relationships. The enclosure of open fields, which accompanied the English Agricultural Revolution of the eighteenth and early nineteenth centuries, represents one example. This shift from share tenure to more secure leaseholds, or to full owner-operator systems associated with the introduction of technical changes embodied in industrial inputs in Western Europe, North America, and East Asia, represents a second example. The search for a system of land tenure which combines the use of mechanical motive power and centralized management with high levels of labor intensity in the socialist countries has represented a relatively unsuccessful attempt to modify land tenure institutions to take advantage of new technical opportunities.[49]

In our judgment, the current simultaneous incidence of a technical revolution in grain production and an explosive rate of growth in the agricultural labor force is again opening up the possibility of economic gains from modifications of land tenure relationships that are substantially greater than in the 1950's and 1960's in many developing countries. The embodiment of the new technical potentials in new crop varieties and in industrial inputs means that tenure systems which dampen incentives to use the new inputs will reduce both the production impact and the social returns from the new biological technology. And tenure systems which discourage the evolution of more labor-intensive systems of crop and livestock production will exacerbate the labor absorption problem.

The limited impact of land tenure reform efforts during the 1950's and the 1960's seems to reflect the fact that the economic returns from changes in technical and economic opportunities in many less developed countries were

[48] In his summary of the economic results of land reforms at the 1970 US AID Spring Review, Dovring emphasizes both the labor absorptive capacity and efficiency in the use of industrial inputs under smallholder owner operator systems. He also points out that the effect of reduction in farm size on production, as a result of land reform, "is in part favorable as long as agriculture retains the bulk of residual unemployment or underemployment," Dovring, *Economic Results*, p. 12.

[49] "The usual model of the collective farm, Soviet style, is in fact a sharecropping arrangement and carries a similar handicap of disincentive to individuals as old fashioned sharecropping systems, only compounded by the administrative overheads," ibid., p. 11.

not sufficiently large to induce the necessary political effort to make the reforms effective. It seems likely that the pay-off to the tenure reforms, involving a shift from share tenure, plantation, and collective tenure systems to small holder owner-operator systems, may be greatly increased for many LDC's as a result of the simultaneous impact of newly created potential in food grain production and the acceleration in the growth of the agricultural labor force that is anticipated in the coming decade.

Market Structure Reform

Market structure reform is a second commonly accepted prerequisite for successful agricultural development.[50] As a traditional economy undergoes the transformation leading to modernization, the share of economic resources devoted to marketing of agricultural products grows. The proportion of food moving through commercial channels rises, and the flow of inputs from the industrial centers to agricultural producers increases.

As the market linkages between producers and consumers become increasingly complex there is a tendency to question the productivity of the resources devoted to the marketing function. Traders, as a group, tend to be viewed unsympathetically by both producers and consumers. The middleman is viewed as exploiting the peasant through his dual or triple capacity as marketer—moneylender—merchant.[51] Traditional marketing structures are viewed as a barrier to the achievement of both pricing and operational efficiencies in the marketing system.

Many developing countries have initiated efforts to regulate or replace traditional market structures through the organization of marketing boards, the promotion of co-operatives, or the transfer of particular marketing functions from the private to the public sector. For example, India adopted a policy in 1958 to initiate state trading to reduce the price spread between producers and consumers. State trading itself was viewed as "an interim measure to be followed by a complete co-operative marketing organization from the producer to the consumer. The policy of state trading was at first restricted to wheat and

[50] For a review of the recent literature on market structure reform see J. C. Abbott, "The Development of Marketing Institutions," Southworth and Johnston, *Agricultural Development*, pp. 364–98; Food and Agriculture Organization (FAO), "Agricultural Marketing Improvement Programmes: Some Lessons from Recent Experience," *The State of Food and Agriculture, 1969* (Rome: FAO, 1969), pp. 83–106; Kurt R. Anschel, Russell H. Brannon, and Eldon D. Smith, eds., *Agricultural Cooperatives and Markets in Developing Countries* (New York: Praeger, 1969). For a critical review of the early postwar literature on market reform see P. T. Bauer and B. S. Yamey, "The Economics of Marketing Reform," *Journal of Political Economy* 62 (June 1954): 210–35.

[51] C. R. Wharton, Jr., "Marketing, Merchandising, and Moneylending: A Note on Middleman Monopsony in Malaya," *Malayan Economic Review* 7 (October 1962): 24–44. Also Peter F. Bell and Janet Tai, "Markets, Middlemen and Technology: Agricultural Supply Response in the Dualistic Economies of Southeast Asia," ibid. 14 (April 1969): 29–47.

rice only and was gradually to be extended to other food grains. State trading was connected with the zonal system of rice and wheat distribution initiated in 1957. Zones were formed by matching surplus states with deficit states in an attempt to create self-sufficiency within each zone. . . . Any surplus in a zone was to be procured by the state and exported to other areas on a state-to-state basis."[52] Kenya provides an even more extreme example of state intervention. Since 1960, marketing has been controlled by twenty-seven agricultural marketing boards. It is illegal to move maize across district boundaries in quantities of more than sixty pounds. Even within districts, farmers can sell maize or beans only to consumers and licensed buying agents of the boards.[53]

The thrust for market reform and institutional development rests on a triple foundation. One element is the analytical insight into market behavior generated by the neoclassical theories of imperfect competition and market structure. A second element is a concern for the achievement of technical or logistical efficiency in the movement of goods from producers to consumers; a third element is a concern with the equity, or income distribution implications, of market imperfections and operational inefficiency for the returns the farmer receives from his production or for the price the consumer pays for the product.[54]

The marketing literature bearing on these concerns is mostly descriptive. A great deal of information has been generated on marketing costs, marketing margins, and the socioeconomic characteristics of peasant markets. There is also a substantial body of normative or policy-oriented literature, much of which is concerned with the elimination of inequities in the marketing system. There is remarkably little empirical evidence in the marketing literature regarding the implications of market reform for pricing efficiency, income distribution, or agricultural development. Factor markets have been almost totally ignored. Consideration of strategy—the sequencing of market development and reform in relation to other development activity—is frequently ignored.

The evidence that is available suggests that there are few economic gains to be realized by market reform efforts in the economies characterized by gradual changes in technology and demand. The possibility of substantial economic gains to resources devoted to market reform may, however, become large in situations characterized by rapid growth in domestic or international demand

[52] Uma J. Lele, "The Traders of Sholapur," *Developing Rural India; Plan and Practice*, ed. John W. Mellor et al. (Ithaca: Cornell University Press, 1968), pp. 238, 239.

[53] Vance Q. Alvis and Peter E. Temu, *Marketing Selected Staple Food-stuffs in Kenya* (Morgantown: West Virginia University, Department of Agricultural Economics and Office of International Programs, IP-25, March 1968).

[54] See Richard H. Holton, "Marketing Structure and Economic Development," *Quarterly Journal of Economics* 67 (August 1963): 344–61; also J. C. Abbott, "The Role of Marketing in the Development of Backward Agricultural Economies," *Journal of Farm Economics* 44 (May 1962): 349–62.

or in the presence of technical changes leading to rapid growth in potential output.

As quantitative studies supplement the anecdotal material that often passes for marketing research in developing economies, there is increasing evidence that traditional market systems are effective in transmitting marketing information among the different markets (producer, wholesale, and retail) in the system.[55]

It is possible to design an empirical test of the efficiency with which the marketing system transmits information among the different markets. In Southeast Asia it seems reasonable to expect that the supply of marketing services for rice and corn is relatively elastic. This stems from the fact that the physical storage facilities are relatively unspecialized and that marketing is a labor-intensive activity. In commercial channels rice and corn are typically stored in sacks in open *godowns* (warehouses) rather than in highly specialized storage facilities. A substantial share of the harvest is stored at the farm and village level in even less specialized facilities. It seems likely that scale economies are quite limited and that the marginal cost of providing marketing services is approximately horizontal over the relevant range. We hypothesize, therefore, a model in which the supply function for marketing services is highly elastic; in which the demand curve for marketing services is highly inelastic; and in which both curves shift to the right with the long-term growth in the marketed surplus.

Under these conditions a slope coefficient of a linear regression equation relating the farm to the retail price not significantly different from 1.0 would imply that the marketing margin is independent of the price, and the supply of marketing services approximates perfect elasticity. This would be inconsistent with the hypothesis that middlemen profit by widening the margin between farmers and consumers during periods when retail prices are relatively high. Since it is difficult to visualize a model of middleman monopsony behavior consistent with a constant absolute marketing margin between farm, whole-sale, and retail prices, and since constant absolute margins are consistent with the competitive market model in a situation where scale economies are limited and the marginal cost of providing the marketing services is horizontal over the relevant range, the existence of a constant or almost constant absolute marketing margin over a substantial price range for the product would represent a rather strong rejection of the middleman monopsony hypothesis.[56]

[55] This section draws heavily on Vernon W. Ruttan, "Agricultural Product and Factor Markets in Southeast Asia," *Economic Development and Cultural Change* 17 (July 1969): 501–19 (reprinted in Anschel, Brannon, and Smith, *Agricultural Cooperatives*, pp. 79–106).

[56] The perfect market model which describes price relationships among geographically separated points in space, among different points in time, and among alternative forms of a common raw product has been described by King as follows: "Prices in different geographic areas of a country will differ by not more than the cost of transfer from one point to another. Within a given market area, prices will differ exactly by transfer cost from point of

Analysis of national and regional data for rice and corn in the Philippines in the late 1950's and early 1960's indicated that the supply of marketing services between the farm and the retail levels and between the wholesale and retail levels approaches perfect elasticity.[57] An unpublished study by Geoffrey Shepherd showed essentially the same results for rice in Vietnam (prior to 1964). Similar results, using the same methodology, were also obtained by G. R. Allen for fruit and vegetables in East Pakistan.[58] Jere R. Behrman's studies of rice in Thailand[59] and Uma J. Lele's studies of sorghum in India[60] also indicated that product markets are relatively efficient in transmitting price information among geographic areas.

Thus the results of the limited empirical tests suggest that for several important commodities in five important Asian countries the product market is relatively efficient in transmitting price information and incentives between consumers and producers, and any arbitrary power to modify price behavior is of relatively short-run or local significance. The commodities traded in these markets were typically characterized by rather slow growth in production and in demand. Similar conclusions have been suggested by William O. Jones[61] in a review of the results of marketing research in Africa. It is anticipated, however, that in situations characterized by rapid progress in production technology and/or rapid expansion in market demand traditional marketing systems will not have the capacity to respond to the demands placed on them. They may find it necessary to transport, store, and market a production volume that may be several times larger than before. Under such conditions the inelastic supply of marketing services could represent a serious constraint on the response of agricultural producers to new production or marketing opportunities.

On the product market side, Robert D. Steven's analysis illustrates the im-

---

production to point of consumption. . . . Similarly, prices at one point in time will not exceed prices in a previous point in time by more than the cost of storage. . . . Finally, the price of a product will differ from the price of another product derived from the same raw product by no more than the cost of processing." R. A. King, "Product Markets and Economic Development," *Economic Development of Tropical Agriculture*, ed. W. W. McPherson (Gainesville: University of Florida Press, 1968), p. 82.

[57] See Ruttan, "Agricultural Products and Factor Markets," *Economic Development and Cultural Change*, for a detailed presentation of the empirical results.

[58] G. R. Allen, *Agricultural Marketing Policies* (Oxford: Basil Blackwell, 1959), pp. 111–40; "Short-term Variations in Retailing Margins on Fruits in East Pakistan," *Farm Economist*, vol. 9, no. 6 (1959): 259–66.

[59] Jere R. Behrman, *Supply Response in Underdeveloped Agriculture: A Case Study of Four Major Annual Crops in Thailand, 1937–1963* (Amsterdam: North Holland Publishing Co., 1968).

[60] Uma J. Lele, "Market Integration: A Study of Sorghum Prices in Western India," *Journal of Farm Economics* 49 (February 1967): 147–59. See also Lele, "Traders of Sholapur," pp. 237–94.

[61] William O. Jones, "Agricultural Marketing and Economic Development," Paper No. 13 of Cornell Workshop on *Some Emerging Issues Accompanying Recent Breakthroughs in Food Production*, March 30–April 3 (Ithaca: Cornell University, 1970).

pact of the structural transformation associated with the shift of population from rural to urban areas on the growth of demand for marketing services at different levels in the market system.[62] As development occurs, a higher and higher proportion of food flows through wholesale and retail channels. For countries starting out with a relatively low ratio of food passing through wholesale and retail channels, the rate of increase in food passing through these channels can be explosive as income rises from a per capita level of 50 to 200 dollars accompanying a sharp rise in the share of urban population. Even if the marketing margin is constant, this means a very substantial "leakage" of national resources into the marketing process. Any tendency for the marketing margin to drift upward in response to a rising demand for marketing services further magnifies the resources that must be devoted to the marketing sector in the process of economic development.

Under these conditions substantial gains may be realized from technical and institutional innovations in the marketing sector. This point is illustrated by a study in the Cauca Valley region of Colombia.[63] This area is experiencing rapid urban industrial development. The study estimated that even after allowing for relatively high internal rates of return to investment in public and private food distribution facilities it would be possible, through a program of technical assistance, to reduce food costs to consumers by approximately 10 percent over a ten to fifteen year period.

Significant amounts of resources must also be devoted to factor markets, if technical change is to occur at a sufficiently rapid rate to provide an agricultural surplus sufficient to meet the needs of rapid growth of demand in the urban industrial sector. Much of the new technology needed to raise productivity per hectare and per man is embodied in the form of mechanical or biological inputs which must be produced by and purchased from the nonagricultural sector of the economy. This requires the allocation of resources to the organization of factor markets.

The problem of organization in factor markets—the market for inputs purchased from the nonfarm sector—differs sharply from that of product market structure in most developing economies. In contrast to the product markets, which have had a long history of evolution, the organization of factor markets to supply the modern technical inputs to subsistence or peasant farmers is relatively new in most areas and is rudimentary or even nonexistent in many areas. Yet, "it is the very essence of the Green Revolution that the division of labor between farm and non-farm penetrate into the heart of the farm produc-

---

[62] Robert D. Stevens, *Elasticity of Food Consumption Associated with Changes in Income in Developing Countries* (Washington: U.S. Department of Agriculture Economic Research Service, Foreign Agricultural Economic Department, No. 23, March, 1965).

[63] Harold Riley et al., *Market Coordination in the Development of the Cauca Valley Region —Colombia*, (East Lansing: Michigan State College, Latin American Studies Center, Research Report No. 5, 1970), p. 376.

tion process itself. Where once the farmer undertook to provide seed for planting, to maintain soil fertility by composts, manure, cover crops, and crop rotation, and to control weeds, pests, and diseases as best he could, it is proposed now that he obtain these critical inputs by using improved seeds 'designed' by plant breeders, and perhaps multiplied by others, and by purchase of fertilizers, herbicides, and pesticides that are the product of the industrial sector."[64] If farmers are to employ the new biological and chemical inputs, they must have confidence that they will be available in sufficient quantity at the time when they are needed. It is also important that the prices of the new inputs vary within sufficiently narrow limits to permit reliable planning decisions.

In response to the emergence of new production potential in food cereals in the tropics the modernization of marketing systems is again emerging on the agenda of agricultural and economic development priorities (see pages 215–18). In this modernization process the potential gains from improvements in technical and logistical efficiency appear, at least initially, to be greater than from attempts to achieve structural reform.

Credit Institutions

The development of modern agricultural credit institutions as a prerequisite for agricultural development has received even more emphasis in professional literature and in official policy than land tenure and market structure reform.

The emphasis on credit as an instrument of agricultural development is based primarily on four perspectives. First is the Schumpeterian perspective, which identifies innovation as the critical element in economic development and credit as the essential organizing instrument which enables the innovator to bid resources away from other activities. A second perspective is based on a view similar to that of market reform. The farmer obtains credit and sells his output to the same middleman and is exploited in each transaction. A third perspective, closely related to the second, views public credit institutions as part of the supervised education and credit package designed to induce traditional farmers to adopt modern inputs. A fourth perspective views credit as an income transfer mechanism to remove inequities in income distribution in rural areas. Where intermediate credit institutions obtain their funds from external agencies under concessional arrangements, it is generally held that these institutions are not justified in charging the higher "market" rates in their own lending operations because of equity considerations. These several perspectives have been involved in the heavy emphasis on the development of public or quasi-public credit institutions in the agricultural development effort of the 1950's and 1960's. The weight given to each perspective has varied among

[64] Jones, "Agricultural Marketing," p. 6.

programs, but all four elements are reflected to some degree in most programs.[65]

The support of credit programs has been particularly attractive to the international aid agencies. In some areas, such as Latin America, resources for credit activities made up a large part of externally funded agricultural programs. "In the nine years 1960 to 1968 the Agency for International Development (AID), the Inter-American Development Bank (IDB), and the World Bank group (IBRD) provided assistance for agricultural credit worth in excess of 915 million dollars in Latin America. . . . In the case of AID, over half of the total direct assistance to agriculture in Latin America has gone into credit activities. In addition to this direct assistance, AID has helped channel to agricultural credit institutions substantial amounts of 'counterpart funds' and 'local currencies' resulting from Program Loans and Public Law 480 sales in several countries."[66] IBRD has stressed livestock loans. IDB has tended to support colonization and farm settlement programs. AID has emphasized technical assistance to credit institutions, supervised credit to family-size farms and general expansion of loans to agriculture.

These efforts have frequently been initiated without serious analysis of the saving and investment behavior in rural areas or theoretical analysis of the role of credit in the agricultural development process. During the mid- and late 1960's, however, data and analysis began to become available that raised serious questions concerning the assumptions on which the credit programs of the 1950's and 1960's had been based.[67]

[65] See Horace Belshaw, *Agricultural Credit in Economically Underdeveloped Countries* (Rome: FAO, Agricultural Studies, No. 46, 1959); International Conference on Agricultural and Cooperative Credit, *Proceedings*, vol. I and II (Berkeley: University of California, 1952); Wharton, "Marketing, Merchandising, and Moneylending." According to Belshaw, "Efficient systems of agricultural credit are necessary if agriculture is to make its contribution to national improvement. But credit will run to waste, or its contribution will be limited, unless it is supported within the rural sector by other measures. . . . We attach great importance to institutional reform with special emphasis on land tenure, taxation, agricultural extension and marketing" (p. 228).

[66] Dale W. Adams, *Agricultural Credit in Latin America: External Funding Policy* (Columbus: Ohio State University, Department of Agricultural Economics and Rural Sociology, Occasional Paper No. 9, April 15, 1970), p. 1.

[67] The work by Long and Bottomley in Asia and by Adams in Latin America is particularly useful. Rudolph Blitz and Millard F. Long, "The Economics of Usury Regulation," *Journal of Political Economy* 73 (December 1965): 608–19; P. Thisyamondol, V. Arromdee, and M. Long, *Agricultural Credit in Thailand* (Bangkok: Kasetsart University, 1965); Millard Long, "Interest Rates and the Structure of Agricultural Credit Markets," *Oxford Economic Papers* 20 (July 1968): 275–88; Millard F. Long, "Why Peasant Farmers Borrow," *American Journal of Agricultural Economics* 50 (November 1968): 991–1009; Anthony Bottomley, "The Costs of Administering Private Loans in Underdeveloped Rural Areas," *Oxford Economic Papers* 15, new series (July 1963): 154–63; Anthony Bottomley, "The Structure of Interest Rates in Underdeveloped Rural Areas," *Journal of Farm Economics* 46 (May 1964): 313–22; Anthony Bottomley, "The Premium for Risk as a Determinant of Interest Rates in Underdeveloped Rural Areas," *Quarterly Journal of Economics* 77 (November 1963): 637–47; Anthony Bottomley, "The Determination of Pure Rates of Interest in Underdeveloped Rural Areas," *Review of Economics and Statistics* 46 (August 1964): 301–4. The work by Adams and his associates is reviewed in Adams, *Agricultural Credit*.

The organization of credit markets in Asia apparently differs sharply from those in Latin America. Studies of credit markets in Asia indicate that informal credit systems (private individuals, money lenders, and merchants) provide a large part of the total rural credit, perhaps over 80 percent in most areas. The data for Latin America suggest a much smaller role for informal credit. Noninstitutional credit is relatively unimportant.

In spite of structural differences in credit markets there is an emerging consensus that "the high interest rate problem has been oversold." This perspective is best summarized by Long: "interest rates on agricultural loans in South and South-east Asia are high, possibly because of some monopoly in credit markets, but primarily because capital is scarce, because farm loans are costly to administer, because the uncertainties of agriculture result in considerable loss through default, and because the demand for credit is seasonal."[68] The evidence from Latin America suggests that by holding interest rates down "governments have kept the private banking system and the credit markets from providing substantial amounts of credit to agriculture."[69]

It also seems clear that there has been a tendency to grossly underestimate the elasticity of supply of savings in rural areas. Evidence is accumulating to the effect that savings and capital formation by peasant farmers varies substantially among areas and over time, in response to profitable investment opportunities. In the Philippines, for example, capital formation appears to be more rapid in areas of new settlement[70] and on farms engaged in the production of commodities where rapid growth in productivity is feasible.[71] In the early 1950's Taiwan was quite successful in mobilizing voluntary savings by raising interest rates. This experience has been repeated in Korea in the late 1960's.[72]

The most obvious effect of failure to employ efficiency prices in credit markets is the exaggeration of credit needs and the erosion of credit resources. Perhaps an even more important effect of the failure to set interest rates at levels reflecting opportunity costs is the distortion of resource-use patterns in agricultural production. This point can be illustrated by drawing on the experience of the ACAR program in Brazil.[73]

[68] Long, "Interest Rates," p. 287.

[69] Adams, *Agricultural Credit*, p. 25.

[70] Levy A. Tinidad, "Private Capital Formation in Philippine Agriculture," *Philippine Economic Journal* 3 (Second Semester 1964): 130–54. The papers in this issue of the journal were presented at a Conference on "Saving and Capital Formation in Philippine Agriculture," International Rice Research Institute, April 24–25, 1964.

[71] L. P. de Guzman, "The Effect of Productivity and Technological Change on Savings and Capital Accumulation in Philippine Agriculture," *Philippine Economic Journal* 3 (Second Semester, 1964): 169–83.

[72] Adams, *Agricultural Credit*, pp. 27, 36.

[73] This section draws heavily on Arthur T. Mosher, *Technical Co-operation in Latin-American Agriculture* (Chicago: The University of Chicago Press, 1957); and José Paulo Ribeiro and Clifton R. Wharton, Jr., "The ACAR Program in Minas Gerias, Brazil," *Subsistence Agriculture and Economic Development*, ed. Clifton R. Wharton, Jr., (Chicago: Aldine Publishing Company, 1969), pp. 424–38.

The ACAR (Associacão de Crédito e Assistencia Rural) was established in 1948 under the joint sponsorship of the state of Minas Gerias and the American International Association.[74] In 1960 ACAR became an independent solely Brazilian agency. The program of ACAR began as an experimental effort to test the conviction that a program of supervised credit similar to that developed by the U.S. Farm Security Administration would lead to both better living conditions in rural areas and increased agricultural production. The program as it evolved during the first few years included four activities: supervised credit; general farm and home extension education; medical care and health education; and distribution of materials. Approximately 80 percent of the total activity was, in the early years, accounted for by supervised credit and general extension.

A 1957 evaluation by Mosher concluded that the ACAR program was the outstanding program in Latin America when evaluated in terms of its impact on family welfare. It had exerted a substantial impact on the levels of living and the agricultural resources of the families with which it had worked. The program had not yet exerted a measurable impact on agricultural production in either Brazil, the state of Minas Gerias, or "even the Municipalities (counties) in which the program has operated."[75]

In evaluating the ACAR growth potential, Mosher emphasized the rather thin technical basis on which its production recommendations rested and the prospect that the program would quickly exhaust the contribution of prior research. The difficulty of ACAR in competing for credit resources was also identified as a potential limitation. Subsequent analysis has supported Mosher's insight.

More recent evaluations by Wharton,[76] Elisau Alves,[77] and by José P. Ribeiro and Wharton[78] have confirmed the contribution of the ACAR program to the welfare of the individual families who have participated in it. By 1964 ACAR had expanded its services to include approximately 30 percent of the farmers in the state of Minas Gerias. It has been particularly effective in reaching small farmers, and it established an enviable record for effective administration and flexibility in response to the changing needs of the farmers it served. As an example of a combined package of supervised credit and exten-

---

[74] The American International Association (AIA) is a nonprofit corporation which was organized in 1946 by Mr. Nelson A. Rockefeller to plan, organize, and operate self-help programs in underdeveloped areas. The ACAR program was only one of AIA's activities in Brazil.

[75] Mosher, *Technical Co-operation*, p. 71.

[76] Clifton R. Wharton, Jr., "The Economic Impact of Technical Assistance: A Brazilian Case Study," *Journal of Farm Economics* 42 (May 1960): 252–67.

[77] Elisau Roberto de Andrade Alves, "An Economic Evaluation of an Extension Program, Minas Gerias, Brazil" (Purdue University: Department of Agricultural Economics, January 1968), Master's thesis.

[78] Ribeiro and Wharton, "The ACAR Program."

sion, the ACAR program was clearly one of the model programs anywhere in the developing world.

At the same time the performance of the ACAR program as an instrument of agricultural development has been disappointing. Part of the difficulty in achieving a productivity or a development impact centers around the issue of subsidized credit. The interest rate charged on ACAR loans ranged from 6 to 8 percent. The annual rate of inflation in Brazil fluctuated between 15 and 25 percent in the 1950's and averaged slightly more than 30 percent during the 1960's. At such rates of inflation persons securing ACAR loans were, in effect, receiving very substantial income transfers through the credit market.[79] The interest rate subsidy helps explain the finding of Alves that non-ACAR farmers had a higher level of technical efficiency than ACAR farmers. As a result of the interest rate subsidy, ACAR farmers were "overinvesting" in capital assets. Farmers who borrowed from ACAR were presumably following a rational strategy of maximizing net worth rather than net income or productivity. The interest rate subsidy also helps to explain Wharton's earlier finding that farmers in the largely subsistence area (Corvelo) achieved greater gains in productivity than farmers in the more commercial farming area (Uba). The commercial farmers were, presumably, in a better position to follow a strategy of maximizing net worth than the subsistence farmers.

The agricultural development experience of the last several decades does provide some insight into the role of credit institutions in the agricultural development process. "Efficient agencies extending production credit to farmers can be an important accelerator of agricultural development. To produce more, farmers must *spend* more—on improved seeds, pesticides, fertilizers, and implements. Such expenditures must be financed either out of savings or by borrowing."[80] But credit can provide little leverage for development in the absence of profitable investment opportunities. In traditional agriculture new and profitable investment opportunities for farmers, in the form of more productive inputs with the capacity to generate higher income streams, have generally been lacking. Where technical change has opened up profitable new opportunities for investment, credit bottlenecks may act as real constraints on the growth of agricultural output. Under such circumstances the resources devoted to the development of credit institutions capable of mobilizing the savings generated by the new sources of income and directing these savings into productive employment in agriculture can yield relatively high returns.

[79] Ribeiro and Wharton pointed out that ". . . when the ACAR program was first set up, one of the arguments for such credit programs for small farmers was their exclusion from normal banking system, whose rates of 8 per cent were equally negative in real terms and whose loan funds were consequently totally monopolized by larger commercial farmers," Ribeiro and Wharton, ibid., p. 432.

[80] Arthur T. Mosher, *Getting Agriculture Moving: Essentials for Development and Modernization* (New York: Praeger, 1966), p. 141.

INFRASTRUCTURE DEVELOPMENT

The capacity of agricultural producers to respond to the technical and economic opportunities available to them depends significantly on the level of infrastructure development in rural areas. Although the term is used rather loosely, infrastructure is typically used to refer to those inputs and services which are organized and controlled by the community rather than by the individual producer.[81] A concept of externality and group control is usually implied. The control group may be the farmers served by the infrastructure, as in a community irrigation system, or an agency of government, as in the case of an agricultural experiment station. There is also usually a distinction made between the physical infrastructure, such as roads, rural electrification, and irrigation works, and the organizational or institutional infrastructures, such as extension education systems, disease and pest control organizations, or quality control and/or certification activities.

Infrastructure development has, along with institutional reform, typically occupied an important role in national development policy and in the programs of the international aid agencies in efforts to reverse the trend toward disequilibrium in world agriculture. In this section we give particular attention to extension education for farmers and land and water resource development. It is recognized, of course, that some of the topics discussed in the previous section might also be classified under the infrastructure rubric.

Extension Education for Farmers

Development of an effective system of disseminating information and providing production education to agricultural producers is generally accorded relatively high priority among the prerequisites for agricultural development in the less developed countries. Two major concerns that characterize discussions emphasizing the role of production education in overcoming the major barriers to the modernization of agriculture are the inherent conservatism, or the lack of response to economic incentives, and the low proficiency of peasant producers in performing production tasks and allocating resources.[82] Extension programs have been designed with the objectives of changing attitudes

---

[81] For a more detailed discussion of the infrastructure concept see Clifton R. Wharton, Jr., "The Infrastructure for Agricultural Growth," ed. Southworth and Johnston, *Agricultural Development*, pp. 107–42. See also A. T. Mosher, *Creating A Progressive Rural Structure* (New York: Agricultural Development Council, Inc., 1969).

[82] Everett M. Rogers, "Motivations, Values, and Attitudes of Subsistence Farmers: Toward a Subculture of Peasantry," ed. Wharton, *Subsistence Agriculture*, pp. 111–35. Also Everett M. Rogers (in association with Lynne Svenning), *Modernization Among Peasants* (New York: Holt, Rinehart and Winston, 1969). See also the critical review of Rogers' perspective by Gelia Castillo, "A Critical View of a Subculture of Peasantry," ed. Wharton, *Subsistence Agriculture*, pp. 136–42.

toward modernization, technical proficiency in agricultural production, and effectiveness in allocating the available resources.

Much of the literature on peasant behavior can be classified into two categories. One perspective has viewed the lack of response by peasant cultivators to economic opportunities as a rational response to the environment in which the peasant lives. In an environment characterized by poverty, limited opportunities, and lack of control over the physical environment, behavior characterized by risk aversion and a subsistence rather than a market orientation has been regarded as a functional response to the needs for survival. A second perspective places less emphasis on the rational and a greater emphasis on the traditional or psychocultural determinants of peasant behavior. Both perspectives contributed to a view that a major thrust of extension effort in traditional societies should be directed toward motivating peasants to take advantage of the economic opportunities available to them or the new opportunities that could be made available to them.

These perspectives have been used to support the view that peasant motivation represented a more serious barrier to modernization than the availability of technical and economic opportunities. This interpretation has been reinforced by observation of the wide differences in land and labor productivity among producers in peasant societies. Data such as that in Table 11-1, showing the wide differences in yield obtained by producers in the same district, combined with a "diffusion model" perspective on agricultural development (Chapter 3), has been used to support the view that the primary emphasis should be given to narrowing the productivity gap between the leading farmers and the farmers at the lower end of the productivity ladder. Since the resources and technology needed to narrow the productivity gap were presumably available and known, the major problem was frequently viewed as one of achievement motivation.

During the last decade this perspective has been eroded. Yield differentials among farmers in developed countries characterized by effective extension education programs have been shown to be as wide as the yield differences observed among cultivators in developing countries characterized by weak extension programs (compare Table 11-2 with Table 11-1).

Concurrently a substantial body of evidence has been accumulated that peasant producers are reasonably responsive to changes in relative prices in shifting area planted among competing crops.[83] Less successful attempts to detect a measurable yield response to price change do not appear to indicate the limited motivation of peasant producers, but rather to suggest that they have little means to respond (e.g., traditional crop varieties of limited fertilizer response).[84] There is also increasing evidence that in most areas peasant pro-

---

[83] Raj Krishna, "Agricultural Price Policy and Economic Development," ed. Southworth and Johnson, *Agricultural Development*, pp. 497–540.

[84] Mangahas, Recto, and Ruttan, "Price and Market Relationships."

Table 11–1. Index numbers of average yield per acre of paddy, wheat and maize in the upper
and lower two deciles in selected districts in India, crop years 1962–64* (median
yield for all farms = 100)

	Index of average yield		Index of average yield in district	Index of average yield	
	First decile	Second decile		Ninth decile	Tenth decile
Tanjore–Paddy					
Samba crop	173	140	100	70	42
Kuruvai crop	167	131	100	70	49
Thaladi crop	170	133	100	58	41
West Godavari–Paddy					
First crop	173	145	100	57	27
Second crop	168	140	100	66	41
Shahabad–Paddy	185	152	100	60	34
Raipur–Paddy	213	160	100	49	24
Ludhiana–Wheat	175	142	100	70	43
Shahabad–Wheat	219	141	100	43	30
Ludhiana–Maize	195	143	100	53	33

* Based on unpublished calculations of average yields for each of the crop years 1961–62
to 1963–64, inclusive, by Dr. W. David Hopper, Ford Foundation, New Delhi, using crop
cutting data for Intensive Agricultural Districts. The samba crop, harvested in January,
is the main rice crop in Tanjore District. This is followed by the kuruvai crop planted
in January and harvested in April or May. The kuruvai crop is followed by the thaladi
crop.

Source: F. E. Hill, "Some Viewpoints Concerning Agricultural Development." Paper
presented to the American Farm Economics Association at the Allied Social Service Association Meetings, New York, December 28, 1965, p. 7.

ducers are reasonably efficient resource allocators. The data tend to support
the thesis that the farmers in traditional agriculture are poor not because they
are irrational or incompetent but because they have few opportunities to
improve their situation.[85]

By the mid-1960's a new orthodoxy had emerged to the effect that "rapid and
substantial increases in crop yields are more likely to be the result of technological and economic changes that stimulate increased yields on the best farms
as well as on the poorer ones rather than the result of extension programs
designed to push farmers on the lower rungs of the yield 'ladder' toward the
top."[86]

[85] Theodore W. Schultz, *Transforming Traditional Agriculture* (New Haven: Yale University Press, 1964); Raymond Firth, "Social Structure and Peasant Economy: The Influence
of Social Structure upon Peasant Economies," ed. Wharton, *Subsistence Agriculture*, pp.
23–37.

[86] F. F. Hill, "Some Viewpoints Concerning Agricultural Development," paper presented
to the American Farm Economic Association at the Allied Social Science Association Meetings, New York, December 28, 1965, p. 7.

Table 11–2. **Index numbers of estimated median yields of selected crops on commercial farms in the upper and lower two deciles in New York State, 1948 and 1964* (median yield for all farms = 100)**

Crop and year	Median yield		Median yield all farms	Median yield	
	First decile	Second decile		Ninth decile	Tenth decile
Wheat					
1948	154	135	100	69	46
1964	148	128	100	74	57
Shelled corn					
1948	180	145	100	50	30
1964	167	142	100	72	50
Hay					
1948	187	147	100	67	53
1964	176	138	100	71	57
Potatoes					
1948	166	141	100	62	43
1964	139	124	100	76	61
Cabbage					
1948	200	167	100	56	22
1964	188	156	100	56	44
Apples					
1948	191	154	100	59	37
1964	159	141	100	65	53

* From "Farm Business Charts" prepared by Professor S. W. Warren of Cornell University and printed for classroom and extension use in December, 1948 and February, 1964. No special studies were made for the purpose of gathering data for these charts. Available data from a number of sources were used including farm management surveys, New York farm cost accounts, extension account club records, the New York Crop Reporting Service, and the United States Census of Agriculture. When data from different sources did not agree precisely, judgment was used in deciding what figures best represented all New York commercial farms. The figures represent estimated yields during the two or three years preceding 1948 and 1964 on commercial farms under normal weather conditions using existing production technology.

Source: F. E. Hill, "Some Viewpoints Concerning Agricultural Development." Paper presented to the American Farm Economics Association at the Allied Social Service Association Meetings, New York, December 28, 1965, p. 8.

The perspective that had emerged by the mid-1960's is summarized in the report of the President's Science Advisory Committee on *The World Food Problem.* "General cultural influences . . . affect primarily each farmer's *degree of freedom of action.* They determine whether he is under pressure to adhere to traditional ways or is free to innovate. In general, traditions and values are not subject to direct manipulation; instead they change under the impact of new opportunities and new pressures."[87] In the view of the panel, agricultural

[87] President's Science Advisory Committee, Report of the Panel on the World Food Supply, *The World Food Problem*, vol. 2 (Washington: U.S. Government Printing Office, May 1967), p. 504.

development programs should place more attention on activities designed to create opportunities for farmers to adopt more productive methods. New profit opportunities were regarded as a prerequisite for the success of efforts aimed more directly at influencing the decisions of farmers.

It seems appropriate, therefore, to view the contribution of extension education to agricultural development within the broader context of the role of the total education process. What are the particular characteristics of agricultural development that generate an increase in the demand for production education in agriculture? And what are the implications of growth in demand for extension education?

It appears useful to consider separately the impacts of production education on task proficiency—the proficiency of farmers in performing individual tasks, such as transplanting rice or driving a tractor—and allocative proficiency—the ability to choose which rice variety to plant or which commodities to produce; the decision to use or not use fertilizer or how much fertilizer to apply; the decision to shift from the use of animal to mechanical power.

In a subsistence or traditional agricultural society characterized by a static technology, farmers can attain through experience the proficiency in task performance and resource allocation which has been customary for generations. In an environment characterized by modest growth in technical opportunities and modest growth in the demand for farm products it seems reasonable to hypothesize that production education would have very little to contribute to either the task proficiency or the allocative efficiency of the worker. On the other hand, in a fully dynamic agriculture characterized by a continuous stream of new technical and economic opportunities the return to increased capacity to make allocative decisions is hypothesized to be very high.

This perspective is supported by the recent analysis of the returns to investment in education generally[88] and of investment in extension education in U.S. agriculture.[89] Finis Welch finds that increases in the level of research activity, leading to a flow of new inputs, have the effect of enhancing the differential productivity of college graduates relative to lower levels of education. At the same time increases in the level of extension activity, leading to a flow of information about new inputs, reduces the relative productivity advantage of college graduates. In interpreting his quantitative results Welch argues that a major production effect of education is to enhance the ability of a producer to acquire or decode information about the productive characteristics of new inputs. Therefore, the more rapid the flow of new inputs the greater will be the productivity differential associated with additional education. In contrast, the activity of information dissemination, such as extension, reduces the cost of

[88] For a review of recent literature see Theodore W. Schultz, *Economic Growth and Agriculture*, pp. 109–71.

[89] F. Welch, "Education in Production," *Journal of Political Economy* 78 (January–February 1970): 35–59.

acquiring information and the level of education required to interpret information. Extension education represents, therefore, a method of overcoming the disadvantages associated with inadequate education in a situation where rapid technical development is increasing the value of improvements in both the task proficiency and allocative efficiency of the individual producer.

In this view, the major factor limiting the contribution of extension programs to agricultural growth in many developing economies is that the advances in technology have not been sufficiently rapid to produce high returns to improvements in the capacity to acquire and interpret new information.

Land and Water Resource Development

The major category of public investment expenditure in most developing countries is typically for physical infrastructure development. Physical infrastructure investments have been large for several reasons.

The fundamental economic rationale for public investment in social overhead capital is that marginal public benefits exceed private benefits by such a wide margin that only the public sector can afford to undertake them. Spillover or secondary development impacts which are not captured in the form of price or user charges for the services provided result in public returns that substantially exceed private returns. From the apparent scarcity of social overhead capital in the less developed countries, returns to physical infrastructure investment were considered very high.

There is a strong presumption that such investments in transportation, communication, power, irrigation, and related facilities are a necessary precondition for economic growth. There is a view that until these facilities are constructed to a "critical minimum" level the payoff to private economic activity would be inadequate to induce the investment necessary for sustained growth. This argument has been buttressed by the political appeal of "monumental" infrastructure investments, such as big dams and superhighways.

A further reason for the large share of external development funds allocated to physical infrastructure investment is that highways, railroads, and irrigation can be planned and developed in "project units" which are amenable to the algebra of conventional cost-benefit calculations. This contrasts with investments in such activities as research and education which present, at both the conceptual and empirical level, more difficult problems for cost-benefit or cost-effectiveness calculations.

We have argued, in the previous section, that the failure to correctly analyze the linkages between technology and institutions has been responsible for the disappointing results from a number of technical assistance efforts in the area of institutional reform. It appears that the same failure applies to physical infrastructure development. Imbalance between investments designed to generate technological advances in agriculture and to build physical infrastructure, typically land and water development, has resulted in low returns to the physical infrastructure investment. And failure to invest in infrastructure development has, at times, limited the return to investments in the development of new crop varieties or in the production of education for farmers.

Labor-intensive land and water resource development has, in the past, been one of the most important sources of growth in land productivity and of agricultural output (Chapter 3). There is, typically, a high degree of complementarity between technical advances embodied in new biological, chemical, and mechanical inputs and improvements in the precision of environmental control made possible by investments in land leveling, drainage, and irrigation. This complementarity is particularly strong in the wet rice cultivation areas of Asia.[90]

Since the last century advances in engineering have sharply lowered the costs of land clearing, leveling, and drainage and of water storage, delivery, and pumping.[91] The effect has been to increase the economic advantage of lands on which such practices are technically and economically feasible relative to other areas for agricultural production. Land and water resource development programs have induced major shifts in the geographic concentration of production, as, for example, the shift in cotton production from the southeast to the southwest in the United States. Progress in drainage and irrigation technology has enabled new areas, such as the delta regions of Thailand and Burma and the Gezira area of Sudan, to move into intensive systems of cultivation. It has also made major contributions to the development of intensive-cropping systems, as in Taiwan.

During the 1950's and 1960's land and water resource development projects have absorbed a significant share of the resources devoted to agricultural development in the less developed countries by the international aid agencies. By the end of 1967, for example, the World Bank (IBRD) had financed approximately fifty irrigation projects.[92] These developments have been primarily of three types. The most dramatic development efforts have been the "big dam" gravity irrigation projects. Among those which have received major attention and have absorbed substantial resources are: the Gezira scheme in the Sudan; the Aswan High Dam in Egypt; the Indus River Plain salinity problem in Pakistan; the Lower Mekong River scheme involving Thailand, Cambodia,

---

[90] See for example Shigeru Ishikawa, *Economic Development in Asian Perspective* (Tokyo: Kinokuniya Bookstore, 1967), pp. 57–214; Clifford Geertz, *Agricultural Involution; The Process of Ecological Change in Indonesia* (Berkeley: University of California Press, 1966).

[91] Edward A. Ackerman and George O. G. Löf, *Technology in American Water Development* (Baltimore: The Johns Hopkins University Press, 1959). For a careful review of the effect of declining cost per acre foot of lift and rising pumping depths on the cost per acre foot of water, see William E. Martin and Thomas Archer, "The Cost of Pumping Irrigation Water in Arizona: 1891 to 1967," *Water Resources Research* (forthcoming, 1971).

[92] A. Otten and S. Reutlinger, *Performance Evaluation of Eight Ongoing Irrigation Projects* (Washington: International Bank For Reconstruction and Development, International Development Section, March 28, 1969, Economics Department Working Paper No. 40), p. 3.

Laos, and Vietnam; and the Bhakra Nangal project in the Punjab, India. These projects have all involved public sector investment with major foreign assistance.

There has also been substantial interest and investment in the opening up of new lands for settlement. Such projects have often been conceived as methods of reducing the population pressure in settled areas by the transmigration of peasants to frontier areas. In Peru development of the interior areas on the eastern slope has been undertaken to reduce the population pressure on the Andean highlands. In Indonesia transmigration to the outer islands was undertaken to reduce the population pressure on Java. Such projects have also frequently involved substantial commitment of foreign aid and credit and technical assistance.

The third pattern of land and water resource development has involved intensification of production on lands already being cultivated. This has meant investment at the individual farm or local community level in land leveling, drainage, pump irrigation, and other improvements leading to more effective soil and water management. The pattern represents, in many respects, an extension of the traditional forms of land and water resource developments induced by technical advances in earth moving, pumping, drainage, and other equipment. This pattern of development may be highly capital-intensive in some economies and highly labor-intensive in others.

In several countries the development of "big dam" gravity irrigation systems has been of major importance as a source of growth in agricultural output.[93] In Mexico, for example, the expansion of irrigated acreage from 1.5 million hectares in 1926 to approximately 3.5 million hectares in the late 1960's set the stage for the rapid diffusion of technical change in wheat and maize production. Reed Hertford has estimated that in the absence of irrigation the annual increase in demand for purchased inputs by Mexican farmers would have risen at less than 3.5 percent, rather than at the annual rate of 9.2 percent.[94]

Yet the more typical experience with gravity irrigation projects has been disappointing. Costs per-man-year of additional employment and per unit increase in output have been high. A recent review of the performance of eight ongoing irrigation projects indicated that project execution has been more expensive than anticipated in the original studies. In most cases, however, the revised rates of return remained positive. Even after revision, the projected rates of return were between 15 and 20 percent for four projects and slightly

---

[93] Reed Hertford, "Sources of Change in Mexican Agricultural Production, 1940–65" (Chicago: The University of Chicago, Department of Economics, March 1970), Ph.D. dissertation; Reed Hertford, "Mexico: Its Sources of Increased Agricultural Output," *Economic Progress of Agriculture in Developing Nations, 1958–1968* (Washington: U.S. Department of Agriculture, Economics Research Service, May 1970), pp. 90–104.

[94] Hertford, ibid., p. 100.

higher for two others.[95] In recent years, however, it has become increasingly difficult to find such projects that meet even the "soft" cost-benefit criteria employed by the international lending agencies and the national programs of development assistance.[96]

The experience with new settlement projects has also been highly unsatisfactory. An analysis of the performance of twenty-four new land development schemes in Latin America concludes: "Few spheres of economic development have a history or reputation for failure to match that of government sponsored colonization in humid tropical zones."[97] There is a record of consistent discrepancy between initial projections and results. Internal rates of return have been grossly overestimated. In Africa, where land settlement schemes have frequently been coupled with tractor mechanization schemes, there has also been a consistent record of failure.[98]

The third pattern of development, involving intensification of production on lands already cultivated and greater scope for local and farm level planning and decision-making, has been relatively more successful. A particularly interesting example of such development has been the rapid expansion of tube-well irrigation in both East (Indian) and West (Pakistan) Punjab.[99] Initially the tube-well development proceeded less rapidly in East Punjab than in West Punjab, because of constraints on the drilling of tube wells in canal command areas. When these restraints were lifted and policy was directed toward a system of co-ordinated groundwater-surfacewater development, there was a rapid growth of tube wells in East Pakistan. Walter P. Falcon and Carl H. Gotsch estimate that the additional water accounted for about half of the increased output in West Punjab and more than one-third of the increase in crop output in East Punjab between 1953/54 and 1965/66. Since 1966, growth in output in both East and West Pakistan rose even more rapidly as a result of the introduction of new fertilizer-responsive wheat and maize varieties.

Two important conclusions have been drawn from the Punjab experience:

[95] Otten and Reutlinger, *Performance Evaluation*, pp. 5, 6.

[96] President's Science Advisory Committee, *World Food Problem*, pp. 460–69. Data are presented on capital costs for an inventory of projects under construction or in various stages of planning. The lowest costs among major projects were for ground water developments in West Pakistan to make available supplemental irrigation for lands privately irrigated. See also Colin Clark, *The Economics of Irrigation* (Oxford: Pergamon Press Ltd., 1967), pp. 41–65 for a review of irrigation cost estimates.

[97] Michael Nelson, *Public Policy for New Land Development in the Humid Tropics of Latin America* (Washington: Resources for the Future, Inc., and Santiago, Chile: The Latin American Institute for Economic and Social Planning, March 1970), mimeo.

[98] Carl Eicher, Thomas Zalla, James Kocher, Fred Winch, *Employment Generation in African Agriculture* (East Lansing: Michigan State University, Institute of International Agriculture, College of Agriculture and Natural Resources, Research Report No. 9, July 1970), pp. 20–29.

[99] Walter P. Falcon and Carl H. Gotsch, *Agricultural Policy and Performance in the Punjab: A Comparative Study of India and Pakistan* (Cambridge: Harvard University, Development Advisory Service and Project for Quantitative Research in Economic Development, Economic Development Report No. 96, May 1968).

"The first and foremost lesson has involved the response to economic stimuli demonstrated by Punjab cultivators on both sides of the border. When prices have changed to favor the production of certain crops, the farmers have reacted; when cost-price relationships have improved for inputs, they have used larger quantities; when a new and profitable technology has become available, they have innovated."[100] The second conclusion centers around the similarity of the input package and the dissimilarity of the policies that have been used in East and West Punjab. In spite of the policy differences the growth rates of crop output were essentially similar. "However, in terms of the *inputs* that were stressed . . . there is a great similarity: fertilizer, controlled water supplies and improved varieties. . . . These successes also lend support to the recent approaches to agricultural development which have emphasized the role of technology embodied in new inputs, and which have placed relatively less emphasis on the role of direct technical assistance to individual farmers."[101]

A conclusion which we would stress, perhaps more strongly than Falcon and Gotsch, is the strategic role of technical change in making use of the new inputs profitable to Punjabi farmers. Advances in the technology of tube well irrigation and in the technology of fertilizer manufacture sharply reduced the costs of these two strategic inputs. And more recently the development of fertilizer-responsive crop varieties has further increased the rate of return to irrigation investment and fertilizer use.

TOWARD EQUILIBRIUM IN WORLD AGRICULTURE

In this chapter we have reviewed the forces that have contributed to greater disequilibrium in world agriculture and the attempts that have been made by the developing countries and the international aid agencies to reverse the trend toward greater disequilibrium. We suggest that the limited success of these programs has been based on four analytical errors.

An initial error was the failure to anticipate the effects on domestic production and innovation behavior of the specific distortions in economic incentives associated with nationalist economic policies. The nationalist ambitions of the indigenous political elites in new states, the methodology of economic planning and management transferred to the developing economies from advanced countries, and the constraints on use of resources imposed by both the bilateral aid programs and the international lending institutions have resulted in a bias toward autarkic development. These policies, together with the protectionist policies of the developed countries, have raised the cost of growth to the poor countries.

[100] Ibid., p. 43.
[101] Ibid., p. 45.

A second error was the stress on equity rather than productivity considerations in the design of institutional innovations and reforms. This led to a series of institutional reforms which did not generate sufficiently high rates of return to achieve the degree of economic viability necessary to support the equity goals of the reform programs.

The third error of analysis was a failure to recognize the role of economic incentives in directing the flow of both public and private economic activity. The autarkic development policies and the reforms designed to remove the inequities of traditional land tenure, market organizations, and credit institutions frequently failed to generate the incentives, at either the level of program administration or among producers, to make the new programs economically viable. Innovations in economic institutions occur because it appears profitable for individuals or groups in society to undertake such changes.

The fourth error was a failure to develop a strategy of institutional innovation which fully considered the close articulation between institutional, technological, and economic change. Even in the case of productivity-oriented extension programs there was frequently failure to take into consideration the importance of simultaneous investment in the generation of new technical knowledge and the development of new inputs.

This does not imply that the programs that were implemented in the 1950's and the 1960's will not make important contributions to the growth of agricultural output during the 1970's and 1980's. As a result of the recent advances in cereal production technology in the tropics, some of the programs should now be given a relatively high priority in national development strategies. It seems likely that increasingly high priorities will be placed on policies designed to achieve consistency between equity and productivity considerations in the diffusion and use of the new technology. In retrospect, however, it appears that more careful attention to the sequencing and timing of these programs in relation to the investments needed to advance agricultural science and technology could have resulted in a larger contribution by the agricultural sector to the total development process. In other cases the limited impact of the programs initiated in the 1950's and 1960's might be viewed in the same perspective as the investments in the development of the land grant colleges and the federal-state experiment stations in the United States during the nineteenth century (Chapter 7); a fairly long gestation period is required before institutional innovations begin producing economic returns.

CHAPTER TWELVE

Agricultural Transformation and

Economic Growth

In the previous chapter we attempted to answer the question—
Why was the record of agricultural development in the less developed countries of the world so poor during most of the 1950's and 1960's? During the late 1960's a new perspective has emerged on the prospects for agricultural development in the poor countries. Many of the same analysts who saw only the prospect of continued stagnation in world agriculture are now heralding a "green revolution."[1] The pendulum has swung from a fear of scarcity toward concern with abundance and from skepticism with respect to the potential acceptance of new agricultural technology to a concern with the social and political implications of the differential impact of the new technology among regions and within rural communities.[2]

The optimism of the late 1960's may be just as exaggerated as the earlier predictions of world famine in the 1970's. Nevertheless, the "green revolution" does point the direction toward a reversal of the trend toward a widening agricultural productivity gap between the developed and the less developed countries. It was the result of a direct attack on the basic cause of the widening productivity gap—the inability of the less developed countries to shift rapidly from a natural resource-based agriculture to a science-based agriculture.

[1] Compare, for example, Lester R. Brown, "The Agricultural Revolution in Asia," *Foreign Affairs* 46 (July 1968): 688–98, with *Man, Land, and Food; Looking Ahead at World Food Needs* (Washington: U.S. Department of Agriculture, Economic Research Service, Regional Analysis Division, Foreign Agricultural Report No. 11, November 1963). For the more extreme views on the world food situation during the late 1960's see William and Paul Paddock, *Famine—1975!* (Boston: Little, Brown, 1967). Also, Paul R. Ehrlich, *The Population Bomb* (New York: Ballantine Books, 1968); and *Food for Freedom* (Washington: U.S. Department of State Bulletin, vol. 54, no. 1392, February 1966), pp. 336–41. For a more balanced view see President's Science Advisory Committee, *The World Food Problem*, Vol. I and Vol. II, (Washington: U.S. Government Printing Office, May 1967). Also Martin E. Abel and Anthony S. Rojko, *The World Food Situation: Prospects for World Grain Production, Consumption and Trade* (Washington: U.S. Department of Agriculture, Economic Research Service, Foreign Agricultural Economics Report No. 35, August 1967).

[2] Clifton R. Wharton, Jr., "The Green Revolution: Cornucopia or Pandora's Box?," *Foreign Affairs* 47 (April 1969): 464–76.

285

The new seed-fertilizer technology has involved the diffusion of experiment station capacity and the application of scientific methodology to tropical agriculture. This was made possible by the institutional innovations designed to mobilize scientific and technical manpower internationally for this purpose (Chapters 8 and 9), thereby reducing the constraints imposed by the limited domestic capacity for scientific research and development in the less developed countries. The impact of these efforts is not confined to the high-yielding cereal varieties developed for tropical agriculture. Even more important is a recognition by the political leadership and the development planners and administrators in many developing countries of the relatively high returns to be had from investment in the experiment station capacity to produce a new biological and chemical technology that is ecologically adapted and economically viable, and the capacity to produce the industrial inputs in which the new agricultural technology is embodied. Agricultural development is viewed not only as a necessary condition for meeting food requirements but also as a productive source of economic growth.

In this chapter we explore the conditions necessary to maintain the momentum for over-all economic growth.

NEW PROSPECTS FOR AGRICULTURAL GROWTH IN THE LDC'S

The performance of world agriculture during the 1950's and 1960's was poor primarily in relation to the growth in aggregate demand and in terms of the growing imbalance in the rates of growth of production and demand among countries. However, compared to the historical performance of the presently developed countries, or with historical growth rates in the less developed countries, performance was not bad. It just was not good enough. Total production of food on a world-wide basis increased at a rate of 2.8 percent per year in the 1950's and at approximately the same rate throughout the 1960's. This compares to an annual increase in the growth of world population of approximately 1.9 percent per year during the 1950's and slightly more than 2.0 percent per year in the 1960's. Total demand, reflecting both the effects of population growth and rising incomes, was probably growing at slightly more than 3.0 percent per year during the 1960's. Thus, during the period when concern with the world food problem was becoming more intense, per capita availability of food in the world actually increased—although not as fast as the food demand.[3]

The mounting concern with the world food situation was based primarily on two factors. In the aggregate, the rate of growth of food production

[3] Willard W. Cochrane, *The World Food Problem: A Guardedly Optimistic View* (New York: Crowell, 1969); John H. Sanders and Richard C. Hoyt, "The World Food Problem: Four Recent Empirical Studies," *American Journal of Agricultural Economics* 52 (February 1970): 132–35.

remained relatively constant while the rate of growth in demand, from population and income growth, was rising. Furthermore, the rate of growth in demand was expanding most rapidly in the LDC's, while the growth of production was expanding most rapidly in the developed countries. In India and Pakistan per capita food production declined between the early and mid-1960's, and in Africa per capita food production has declined since the mid-1950's, although it should be recognized that per capita production in India and Pakistan has increased importantly since 1966 (Table 12–1).

At a more sophisticated level than the simple food-population balance there was concern that growth in the agricultural sector was not occurring in a manner consistent with a balanced contribution of the agricultural sector to national economic growth. Much of the growth that was occurring was still based on the old conservation model. It was expensive in terms of resource use and in terms of its demand on labor. The shift from a resource-based to a science-based agriculture was not occurring at a sufficiently rapid rate to generate the larger income streams necessary to support advances in the quality of life—in housing, education, health, and the other dimensions of economic development.

By the late 1960's a new perspective on the possibilities of agricultural development in the less developed countries had emerged. This perspective was the direct result of extending the impact of advances in biological technology from the temperate zone countries to the tropics and subtropics in Latin America, Asia, and Africa through adaptive research and development. This revolution had, by the late 1960's, extended to the major cereal crops—wheat, rice, and, to a lesser extent, maize. Its measurable impact on national average yields and total output was limited to a few countries, primarily Mexico, the Philippines, India, Pakistan, and Turkey. Nevertheless, the impact was sufficiently great to largely reverse the former pessimism at national policy levels with respect to the potential contribution of the agricultural sector to national economic growth.

The opportunities for agricultural development that now seem apparent will not be easily secured in most developing countries. Our analysis, and the experience of the 1950's and 1960's, strongly supports an emerging consensus that agricultural research designed to produce and continuously improve an economically viable and ecologically adaptable technology represents a critical missing link in the agricultural development process in many countries. There is a growing agreement that much agricultural research is highly location-specific. In order to produce viable results it must be conducted in an environment in which both ecological and socioeconomic conditions approximate those where the innovation will be employed. Lack of a sufficient stock of scientific and technical manpower in the tropical and subtropical countries, which is essential to the conduct of location-specific research, imposes a severe constraint on the exploitation of the new technical opportunities for growth.

Table 12–1. Indices of world food production (excluding Communist Asia), per capita 1954–70 (1957–59 = 100)*

Country or region	1954	1955	1956	1957	1958	1959	1960	1961	1962	1963	1964	1965	1966	1967	1968	1969	1970
World[a]	95	97	100	98	101	101	102	102	103	103	105	103	106	108	109	108	109
Developed countries[b]	92	97	98	97	101	101	103	103	106	105	108	107	114	116	119	117	117
Less developed countries	99	98	100	97	101	100	102	102	102	104	104	101	100	104	104	106	107
India	97	100	101	96	102	103	106	108	102	103	103	94	91	96	101	105	108
Pakistan	104	93	104	99	95	106	108	106	101	112	109	107	100	110	113	118	117
Other Asia[c]	99	96	100	98	102	100	100	101	103	102	104	102	105	107	107	107	105
Africa[d]	100	98	100	99	100	101	102	96	101	101	99	98	96	96	95	97	95
Latin America[e]	99	99	101	100	101	99	99	102	103	105	106	107	106	108	107	106	109

* 1961–70 computed on 1961–65 base and shifted to 1957–59 = 100.
[a] Excluding Communist Asia.
[b] U.S., Canada, Europe, U.S.S.R., Japan, Republic of South Africa, Australia, and New Zealand.
[c] Excluding India, Pakistan, Communist Asia, and Japan.
[d] Excluding Republic of South Africa.
[e] Excluding Cuba.

Source: Data prepared by Foreign Regional Analysis Division, Economic Research Service, U.S. Department of Agriculture.

Thus, how to manage science or to organize agricultural research so as to utilize most effectively the scarce limiting factor—scientific and technical manpower—is a critical factor in the agenda for agricultural development.

MANAGING SCIENCE FOR TECHNICAL PROGRESS

In spite of an initial dramatic impact, the scientific and technical basis on which the recent advances in grain yields in the tropics have been based is extremely thin in most developing countries. If the momentum of the green revolution is to be maintained, substantial investments will have to be made in agricultural experiment station capacity, together with investments in industrial capacity, irrigation, and other physical infrastructure, and in the education of agricultural producers.

For that purpose it is not sufficient to simply build new agricultural research stations. In many developing countries existing research facilities are not employed at full capacity because they are staffed with research workers with limited scientific and technical training, because of inadequate financial and logistical support, because of isolation from the main currents of scientific and technical innovation, and because of failure to develop a research strategy which relates research activity to the potential economic value of the new knowledge it generates.

The body of knowledge relating to the organization and management of agricultural research is, if anything, even weaker than the body of research results available to agricultural producers in the less developed countries.[4] There are, however, a number of principles which do seem to have a substantial grounding in research that represent, as a minimum, constraints that strongly condition the productivity of research investment.

The results of agricultural research tend to be relatively location-specific. Furthermore, the results tend to become more location-specific as the sophistication of the research and the production technology advance. Although this principle applies to advances in both mechanical and biological technology, it is more obvious in the case of biological technology. The location-specific character of agricultural technology is a function of variations in the physical, biological, and socioeconomic environments in which agricultural activities are conducted. This means that much of agricultural research must

---

[4] Among the useful references are Walter L. Fishel, ed., *Resource Allocation in Agricultural Research* (Minneapolis: University of Minnesota Press, 1971), forthcoming; Melvin G. Blase, ed., *Institutions in Agricultural Development* (Ames: Iowa State University Press, 1971), forthcoming; Albert H. Moseman, ed., *Agricultural Sciences for the Developing Nations* (Washington: American Association for the Advancement of Science, Publication No. 76, 1964); Albert H. Moseman, *Building Agricultural Research Systems in the Developing Nations* (New York: Agricultural Development Council, Inc., 1970).

be conducted and the results analyzed, tested, interpreted, and applied within a relatively decentralized system (see discussions in Chapters 3 and 7).

There are scale economies in agricultural research. Analysis by Evenson, based on thirty-nine state experiment stations in the United States, indicates that the marginal returns per research dollar were generally higher in stations with more scientists, more graduate students, higher staff salaries, and higher levels of staff training.[5] There was also a tendency for smaller experiment stations to produce a relatively higher proportion of final products (such as agronomic knowledge) to intermediate products (such as advances in genetics). Also smaller stations are likely to produce fewer new material inputs in which new knowledge is embodied. While there may be some question regarding the greater productivity of the largest stations as compared to the typical station, there can be no question that in the United States, and in many developing countries, experiment stations are frequently too small and too poorly financed to provide the library, professional communication, and logistical support to be productive.

The production of location-specific research results by a research system in which the individual units experience scale economies imposes severe strains on the organization of agricultural research. Most national or state research administrations are faced with continuous pressure both for greater decentralization, to bring the research capacity to bear on the specific problems of regions and localities, and for strengthening of central experiment station staffs, in order to create viable centers of professional excellence.

Effective information linkages among the units of a decentralized system are essential to achieve optimum system, in contrast to individual station, productivity. Both the Japanese and the U.S. agricultural research systems have been characterized by the capacity to mobilize research resources to respond to problems of regional and national significance, while retaining sufficient autonomy to respond to local priorities (Chapter 7).

An essential feature of both the Japanese and the U.S. research systems was the establishment of effective communication linkages among the units of the national research system and across national boundaries. The international linkages have involved intensive efforts to collect and adapt crop varieties and livestock breeds from other regions. This is in contrast to the approaches followed in some developing countries in which there is a nationalistic bias against "exotic" genetic materials.

The success of the international centers for wheat and maize research in Mexico (CIMMYT) and for rice research in the Philippines (IRRI) was facilitated by close professional and institutional linkages with related agricultural research centers in the United States, Japan, and elsewhere. These centers have, in turn, become major institutional linkages in the flow of scientific and

[5] Robert E. Evenson, "Economic Aspects of the Organization of Agricultural Research," ed. Fishel, *Resource Allocation.*

technical information relating to wheat, maize, and rice research among the agricultural research community in the developing countries.[6]

A final characteristic of a viable agricultural research system is integral involvement in education and training for research. Development of scientific and technical manpower by education and training is essential for removing the scientific manpower constraints that limit the capacity of the less developed countries to shift toward a science-based agriculture. Such education is most effective when it occurs in association with a significant research program. Moreover, the presence of students and trainees encourages a continuous interchange and flow of new ideas. Indeed the dialectic interaction among students and teachers is the major source of scientific advance.

It is probably an overstatement to argue that "a national research center that is not an integral part of a major research-oriented university is, under present conditions, an inefficient location for such research."[7] Nevertheless, even the new international commodity-research centers, which were not established as part of the universities, have established close linkages to local educational institutions and have effectively utilized nonacademic training programs and visiting scholar arrangements.

The principles of research organization outlined above do not impose any specific optimum pattern for organizing professional and institutional resources to produce new technical knowledge in agriculture. The research institute and the university represent alternative methods of organizing resources to induce change. In developed societies, characterized by a highly articulated infrastructure linking the university to other public and private institutions involved in technical, social, and economic change, research within the university may represent an effective link in the total system devoted to the production, application, and dissemination of new knowledge. When a single component is transplanted separately into societies where such institutional infrastructure does not exist, it rarely performs as an effective instrument of technical change.[8]

In our judgment, this is one of the major factors responsible for the substantial frustration involved in attempting to utilize the "land grant university" model as an instrument to generate and disseminate technical change in agriculture in many developing countries.[9] Moseman has pointed out that a major

[6] A. H. Moseman, "Building Research Systems in the Developing Nations," ed. Blase, *Institutions in Agricultural Development.*

[7] Theodore W. Schultz, "The Allocation of Resources to Research," ed. Fishel, *Resource Allocation.*

[8] See Vernon W. Ruttan, "Research Institutions: The Organization Questions," ed. Blase, *Institutions in Agricultural Development.*

[9] This point has been vigorously argued by Guy Hunter, *Modernizing Peasant Societies* (London: Oxford University Press, 1969). "Certainly in India this allocation of [extension] responsibility to the new Agricultural Universities, with their strong Land Grant College flavour, has caused much confusion. ... If ever there was a thoughtless transfer of inapplicable experience from one civilization to another, this is one" (pp. 184–85).

difficulty in the understanding of the integrated agricultural research system in the United States has been failure to recognize the active role of the USDA in regional and national research.[10] The result has been a serious provincialism in attempting to guide the development of effective national systems of agricultural research in co-operating developing nations. Localized and fragmented research continues to present one of the most serious obstacles in the strengthening of effective systems for agricultural science and technology in the developing nations. The frequent result of transplanting one component of a developed country research system into a developing country, in the absence of effective linkages into a national or international system, is to burden the developing country with an over-extended academic bureaucracy or a collection of relatively sterile back-country research stations of little real economic value.

If developing areas are to overcome the technical and institutional limitations that separate the performance of the world's high and low income economies, they must make efficient use of the professional competence which represents their single most limiting resource in the generation of more productive inputs for agriculture. This implies a pragmatic search for patterns of institutional organization which permit a nation to effectively utilize the scarce scientific and technical manpower available to it. The international research training institutes which have evolved for corn and wheat research in Mexico and for rice research in the Philippines are an example of one pattern that has been exceptionally effective in situations where the institutional infrastructure linking science to the rest of the economy is lacking.

We do not hold this model, or the models followed in Japan and the United States, as idealized forms which should be transferred intact to other developing economies. Rather, it is illustrative of the desirability of a pragmatic rather than an ideological search for institutions consistent with the endowments of both human and nonhuman resources in the developing economies.

GUIDING TECHNOLOGY AND INSTITUTIONS FOR AGRICULTURAL TRANSFORMATION

For a new technology to be an effective instrument for agricultural development it must be consistent with changes in the conditions of factor supply and product demand in the economy. Research on staple cereal production in the tropics was successful not only because institutional innovations facilitate the effective transfer and utilization of scientific manpower but also because it was responsive to shifts in factor supplies and in product demand. The new technology has released the constraint on increased output per unit of the limiting factor (land) by increasing the capacity to substitute fertilizer, which became

[10] Moseman, *Building Agricultural Research Systems.*

relatively more abundant, for land (Chapter 9). Changes in the conditions of factor supply and product demand are, therefore, critical considerations in designing research for agricultural and economic development.

In this context, the implications of the acceleration in the growth in the labor force, which is expected to occur in the less developed countries in the 1970's following the acceleration of population growth rates during the 1950's and 1960's, must be given a high priority in designing an agricultural development strategy for the 1970's and 1980's.[11] A calculation by Bruce Johnston indicates that, if the labor force grows at an annual compound rate of 3 percent, in an economy which starts from an initial condition in which labor engaged in agriculture occupies 80 percent of the total labor force, the agricultural labor force will double in less than forty years even if nonagricultural employment increases as rapidly as 4.5 percent per year. And it will double within thirty years if nonagricultural employment grows at only 3 percent.[12]

The population growth rates in the less developed economies in the past decades have typically been in the range of 2.5 to 3.0 percent. In a few countries population growth rates have approximated 3.5 percent per year. These are now being converted into labor force growth rates of roughly the same magnitude. Historically it has been difficult to achieve sustained growth rates in productive employment outside of agriculture of over 5 percent per year. Thus Johnston's calculations imply that in the coming decades labor will press very strongly against land in these economies, especially in those of already densely populated areas. Even in more sparsely populated countries, such as Brazil, it is unlikely that the arable land area will be doubled within three or four decades without causing undue strain on public resources. Therefore, in most less developed countries labor will increasingly be more abundant relative to land. From a national resource allocation standpoint, the development of a system of agricultural technology and institutions, which are consistent with the growth in the labor force relative to land, should have a high pay-off.[13]

From the historical experience of Japan, Taiwan, and Korea it appears that the new seed-fertilizer technology is both neutral in the use of labor and in scale (Chapter 9). Yet rapid progress in tractorization among larger holdings following the spread of high-yielding varieties, particularly in the wheat areas in the Indo-Pakistan subcontinent, suggests the possibility that the new tech-

[11] Bruce F. Johnston and John Cownie, "The Seed-Fertilizer Revolution and Labor Force Absorption," *American Economic Review* 59, part I (September 1969): 569–82. Also Carl Eicher, Thomas Zalla, James Kocher, Fred Winch, *Employment Generation in Agriculture* (East Lansing: Michigan State University, IIA Research Report No. 9, July 1970).

[12] Bruce F. Johnston, "Agriculture and Economic Development: The Relevance of the Japanese Experience," *Food Research Institute Studies*, vol. 6, no. 3 (1966): 251–312.

[13] Kusum Nair, *The Lonely Furrow: Farming in the United States, Japan, and India* (Ann Arbor: The University of Michigan Press, 1969).

nology has contributed to the displacement of agricultural workers and to a bimodel distribution of farm income and of farm size.[14]

Whether or not the production function of the new technology has the properties of labor-saving bias and increasing returns to scale is yet to be established. It does appear that existing credit, extension, and related rural institutions are biased with respect to scale in many countries and are directing the new technology toward a labor-saving pattern of economic organization in rural areas. In the absence of adequate institutions to facilitate co-operation among small farmers, irrigation, which is vital for the introduction of new technology, tends to be monopolized by larger-scale farmers who can build tube wells. The larger farmers have better access to new knowledge and low interest rate loans available from co-operative or government credit agencies, which lowers the cost of capital investment and encourages mechanization. The small farmers are, on the other hand, subject to severe capital rationing.

[14] The evidence with respect to the differential impact of the new cereals technology on income distribution among farmers, within rural communities, and among regions is still, at this time (1971), clouded by more emotion than empirical evidence. In Mexico evidence to the effect that the new wheat and corn technology had been adopted primarily by the larger farmers leads Bruce Johnston to contrast the "Mexican" and "Japanese models" of agricultural development. Bruce F. Johnston, "Agriculture and Economic Development," ". . . the contrast between the Japanese and Mexican approaches to agricultural development lies in the fact that the increase in farm output and productivity in Japan resulted from the widespread adoption of improved techniques by the great majority of the nation's farmers, whereas in Mexico a major part of the impressive increases in agricultural output in the postwar period have been the result of extremely large increases in production by a very small number of large-scale, highly commercial farm operators" (p. 286). There is a presumption among many observers that the Mexican model is characteristic of the pattern of agricultural development in Latin America. More recent examination of the Mexican data does not confirm the view that the large-scale mechanized farms have represented the primary source of growth in agricultural production. See Folke Dovring, *Land Reform in Mexico* (Washington: Agency for International Development, AID Spring Review Country Paper, June 1970); Reed Hertford, "Sources of Change in Mexican Agricultural Production, 1940–65" (Chicago: University of Chicago, Ph.D. thesis, March 1970); Marnie W. Mueller, "Changing Patterns of Agricultural Output and Productivity in the Private and Land Reform Sectors in Mexico, 1940–60," *Economic Development and Cultural Change* 18 (January 1970): 252–66.

In the Philippines diffusion of the new rice varieties appears to be consistent with the Japanese model. Robert E. Huke and James Duncan, "Spatial Aspects of HYV Diffusion," *Seminar-Workshop on the Economics of Rice Production* (Los Baños: International Rice Research Institute, December 1969), pp. 2–1 to 2–40. The study by Huke and Duncan indicates that in the municipality of Gapan, Nueva Ecija, almost 60 percent of the farmers in the entire municipality had adopted the new varieties by 1969, four years after initial introduction. In the barrios where the new varieties were initially introduced, the adoption rate exceeded 95 percent. Tenure status was not a significant factor affecting the rate of adoption. See also Mahar Mangahas, "An Economic Analyses of the Diffusion of New Rice Varieties in Central Luzon" (Chicago: University of Chicago, Ph.D. thesis, April 1970).

In the wheat producing areas of India and Pakistan, particularly in West and East Punjab, it is reported that rapid diffusion of the new wheat varieties has been accompanied by large-scale mechanization along the lines of the Mexican model. See Hiromitsu Kaneda, "Economic Implications of the 'Green Revolution' and the Strategy of Agricultural Development in West Pakistan," *Pakistan Development Review* 9 (Summer 1969): 111–43. In the rice-producing areas initial experience with diffusion of the new rice varieties appears to be more consistent with the Japanese model.

In contrast, traditional village communes in Japan (and the *pao-cha* system in Taiwan) were effective means of diffusing new knowledge and of mobilizing communal labor for the construction of irrigation facilities, small waterways and reservoirs, and the building of other forms of social capital such as roads and schools. The village communal system provided the basis for the development of water-utilization and marketing co-operatives, and for agricultural associations which promoted extension services through the national-prefectural-local networks (Chapter 7).

If the new seed-fertilizer technology is to be guided in an optimum direction, in terms of national resource allocation and rural welfare, new institutions have to be developed or existing institutions reformed to reverse the present institutional bias in favor of larger farms and toward the substitution of capital for labor. The institutional innovations should in turn be complemented by research to generate technical changes, which raises the returns to institutional innovation at the community and farm levels.

Another major consideration is the change in demand and supply of agricultural commodities in the coming decade. If the new seed-fertilizer technology continues to advance and diffuse at the rate observed during the late 1960's, the shift in the aggregate supply of staple cereals could exceed the shift in aggregate demand by a wide margin. The result would be a continued decline in the price of cereals in both international and domestic markets and a possible decline in the income of cereal producers, particularly the cereal producers located in regions in which the new grain production technology is not fully adapted (Chapter 10).

Diversion of resources from the staple cereal sector to the production of commodities with higher income elasticities will become indispensable for maintaining incentives for the use of resources in agricultural production. New patterns of product combination and resource use, which are drastically different from traditional cereal grain monoculture, have to be developed. The new patterns should also be consistent with the changes in factor endowments—implicit in the rapid growth of population in rural areas. It is desirable that product diversification contribute to greater intensity in labor use.[15]

The diversification will be particularly profitable both for private producers and the national economy if it is designed to utilize seasonally slack resources in agriculture. In some areas the new high-yielding cereal varieties are contributing to a fuller utilization of land and labor. Where adequate irrigation is available, their nonphoto-period-sensitive character permits double and in some cases, triple cropping a year. Still, the underemployment of agricultural labor between seasonal peaks often represents the single most important slack in the resources in the less developed economies today, particularly in the

---

[15] For a survey of recent literature on diversification see Dana G. Dalrymple, *The Diversification of Agricultural Production in Less Developed Nations* (Washington: U.S. Department of Agriculture, International Agricultural Development Service, August 1968).

countries where adequate institutions are not established to mobilize this slack labor for the construction of social overhead capital.[16]

The changes in the demand and supply of products and factors expected for the 1970's and 1980's will require a major agricultural transformation in the less developed economies in the tropics (the term *agricultural transformation* is defined here as a significant change in the pattern of product combination, production sequences, and resource use in agriculture). Both technological and institutional changes will represent critical elements in the agricultural transformation, if they can be utilized to develop new patterns of agricultural production consistent with changes in factor and product markets.

It is useful to review several examples of such transformations, drawing on the historical experiences of Great Britain, Denmark, and Japan.

British Experience

Britain experienced two major agricultural transformations in the mid-eighteenth and the mid-nineteenth centuries.

We have already reviewed, in Chapter 3, the transformation in eighteenth-century Britain, which is commonly called the Agricultural Revolution. The technical basis for the eighteenth-century Agricultural Revolution was the Norfolk crop rotation system integrating crop production with livestock production. This system intensified the recycling of nutrients among plants, livestock, and soil, thus permitting a rise in output per unit of land area, while maintaining soil fertility. The institutional basis was the enclosure—the consolidation of communal pasture and farm land into single private units—which facilitated the introduction of an integrated system of crop-livestock production.

The technology associated with the Agricultural Revolution was consistent with the conditions of demand and supply of factors and products. The increase in population since the second quarter of the eighteenth century expanded the demand for food and raised the price of food grains. The increase in population was followed by increases in the labor force. Both food demand and labor supply pressed against land. It was both technically feasible and economically profitable to adopt an intensive integrated crop-livestock system of agricultural production.

The second classical example of agricultural transformation in Britain occurred following the repeal of the Corn Laws and the Navigation Acts (see Chapter 10). Confronted with the competition of foreign grains, British agriculture successfully transformed itself by specializing in livestock production, increasing the share of area planted in fodder crops, and diverting arable land to permanent pasture. This involved the substitution of land for labor, which

[16] Shigeru Ishikawa, *Economic Development in Asian Perspective* (Tokyo: Kinokuniya, 1967).

was consistent with the rapid absorption of labor by manufacturing industries in "the Workshop of the World."

In contrast to the pattern developed in the Agricultural Revolution, in which the primary value of livestock was the dung it produced for restoring soil fertility, livestock produce such as meat and milk became the major value of agricultural production in "high farming" in the mid-nineteenth century. This, of course, represented a rational response to the rising animal food prices relative to cereal prices in this period.

The high farming was supported technically by advances in soil conservation techniques, including underground drainage, application of guano and commercial fertilizers, and the traditional excellence of British livestock breeding techniques which produced numerous improved breeds. Institutionally, the establishment of an entrepreneurial tenant farming system based on the Common Law conventions of the compensation by landlords for tenant's investment, including soil improvements, facilitated the rational adjustment of agriculture to the changing economic environment.

These British experiences represent the two classical "ideal types" of agricultural transformation. Except as an illustration of effective response of technology to economic opportunities, the British experience is, however, of limited value to the developing countries today, because of the extreme differences in the economic environment and technological possibilities as compared to eighteenth- and nineteenth-century Great Britain. The Agricultural Revolution in the eighteenth century occurred in an environment in which agriculture was a relatively self-contained system. The linkage of industry to agriculture through the supply of industrially produced inputs was not yet established. The agricultural transformation of the nineteenth century occurred at a time when the labor supply to agriculture was contracting. The British experience is more relevant to Japan and other developed countries than to most developing countries.

The Danish agricultural transformation experience, particularly the developments associated with the invention of the cream separator and the establishment of co-operative creameries, and the Japanese experience of development in sericulture are more relevant cases.

Danish Experience[17]

Agricultural development in Denmark during the last quarter of the nineteenth century and the first quarter of this century represents a case of remarkable transformation of agriculture in response to changes in product and

---

[17] This section draws heavily on Einer Jensen, *Danish Agriculture—Its Economic Development* (Copenhagen: J. H. Schultz Forlag, 1937); C. P. Kindleberger, "Group Behavior and International Trade," *Journal of Political Economy* 50 (February 1951): 30–46; and Bruce F. Johnston, "Agricultural Development and Economic Transformation: A Comparative Study of the Japanese Experience," *Food Research Institute Studies* 3 (November 1962): 223–76.

Table 12-2. Farm receipts and cash expenses of a representative farm[a] in Denmark: 1881, 1901, and 1929

	1881		1901		1929	
	Kroner	Percent	Kroner	Percent	Kroner	Percent
Receipts	3,481	100	5,112	100	17,400	100
Crops	1,613	46	711	14	2,820	16
Cereals	1,509	43	645	13	2,206	13
Others[b]	104	3	66	1	614	3
Livestock	2,168	62	4,401	86	14,580	84
Butter	761	22	2,101	41	6,161	35
Pork	448	13	1,199	23	5,852	34
Others[c]	959	27	1,101	22	2,567	15
Expenses	2,310	100	3,620	100	12,042	100
Feed	228	9	511	14	4,077	34
Fertilizer	12	1	38	1	700	6
Machine repairs	100	4	200	6	500	4
Hired labor	615	27	836	23	3,425	28
Others[d]	1,355	59	2,035	56	3,340	28
Net spendable income[e] (current prices)	1,471		1,492		5,358	
Net spendable income[f] (1881 prices)	1,471		1,812		3,995	

[a] A hypothetical farm of 28 hectare located in the island of Sjaelland, Denmark, which is supposedly representative of farms in the whole east-Danish loam section.

[b] Peas, potatoes, and seed.

[c] Beef, lambs, wool, eggs, and horses.

[d] Seed, building repairs, veterinary care, insurance, light and power, real estate tax, and mortgage interest.

[e] Receipt minus expense.

[f] Income in current prices deflated by general price index (Statistical Index).

Source: Einer Jensen, Danish Agriculture—Its Economic Development (Copenhagen: J. H. Schultz Forlag, 1937), pp. 258, 262, and 385.

factor market conditions. Denmark was traditionally a grain exporter to the British market. When a large quantity of grains began to be imported into Britain from the new continents and the grain prices fell the traditional economic base of Danish agriculture came under severe pressure. In response to this challenge, Denmark successfully transformed itself into a major exporter of butter and bacon. An important point is that this transformation was carried out while the agricultural labor force was expanding. The absolute size of the agricultural labor force in Denmark did not begin to decline until the late 1920's.

The process of transformation can be illustrated by the farm earnings and expenses of a representative farm calculated by Einer Jensen (Table 12-2). The Jensen calculation indicates that cereals were still a major item in the farm sales in Denmark in 1881, when the agricultural transformation began. In this pattern of production, labor use "was highly seasonal."[18]

[18] Jensen, Danish Agriculture, p. 261.

A dramatic change can be observed for 1901 as compared with 1881. The relative importance of livestock greatly increased, and butter replaced cereals as the most important item in the farm receipts. This was clearly a rational response to a decline in the price of wheat by more than 40 percent and a decline in the price of butter of only 15 percent during this period. Because of this transformation, the representative farmer was able to increase his income in real terms in spite of the decline in the prices of agricultural products in Europe during this period (see the last row of Table 12–2).

In 1929 pork (for bacon) became as important an item as butter in farm receipts. The purchase of feed exceeded the sale of crops over a wide margin. The new pattern of agricultural production in Denmark was then clearly established. Through this transformation, Danish agriculture not only absorbed a growing labor force but also achieved a more efficient utilization of labor by reducing the peaks and troughs of labor use.

A number of technological advances facilitated the transformation of Danish agriculture. These included tile drainage, increases in the application of fertilizer and lime (see Table 12–2), and improvements in seed and livestock varieties. The innovations that were most critical to the agricultural transformation were the invention and diffusion of the cream separator and the co-operative creamery system. The success of these innovations was, in turn, related to a favorable land tenure system and a high level of education among Danish farmers,[19] and without them the modern agricultural production pattern in Denmark could hardly have been established.

Practically usable centrifugal cream separators were developed by the Danish inventor L. C. Nielsen in 1878 and the Swedish physicist G. deLaval in 1879. Both were immediately utilized in production, and by 1881 there were eighty separators operating in Denmark.[20] Prior to this invention the production of butter was dominated by large farms or manors which could build a "skimming hall," a large ventilated room where milk was kept fresh twenty-two to forty-six hours while the cream was rising. Small farmers who could not afford such a large capital investment were unable to participate in the profitable butter production; therefore the expansion of dairy production was limited.

The invention of the cream separator removed this constraint. A remarkable aspect was that the new potential which emerged from this technical invention was exploited by an institutional innovation—the co-operative creamery. With this combination of technical and institutional innovations "the profitableness of milk production was raised on middle-sized farms and even on small-holdings, to the level of the big farms."[21]

---

[19] "The development of the co-operative in response to a technological need ... was the product of the prevalence of the freehold in Danish land tenure, together with the high degree of education in Danish farmers," Kindleberger, "Group Behavior," p. 45.

[20] Jensen, *Danish Agriculture*, p. 174.

[21] Ibid., p. 176.

This innovation also contributed to the integration of dairy and hog operations. Large quantities of skim milk, a by-product of butter production, provided cheap feed for hogs. Production of lightly cured bacon based on this integrated system was developed in Denmark, and its exports to Britain came to exceed the export of bacon to Britain from the United States; "this is an outstanding example of an 'old' agricultural country entering a market fully occupied by the new over-seas competitors."[22]

The Danish experience demonstrates the critical role of technical and institutional innovations for agricultural transformation.[23] This experience is relevant to the less developed countries today because the technology and institutions were so developed as to absorb a larger number of workers in agriculture and to utilize the farm labor more fully by reducing the seasonality of agricultural production.

Development of Sericulture in Japan[24]

An even more relevant example for the agricultural transformation in the less developed countries may be drawn from the development of sericulture in the early period of modern Japanese economic growth. There is some question whether the development of sericulture in Japan can be correctly referred to as an agricultural transformation. It has been argued that modern agricultural development in Japan since the Meiji period is characterized by the persistence of traditional production patterns.[25] Apart from issues of terminology, however, it is clear that the development of sericulture made a critical contribution to agricultural and economic growth by raising the utilization of labor, land, and capital.

From the 1870's to the 1920's cocoon production increased ten-fold from the level of 35 thousand metric tons to 350 thousand tons; and the share of sericultural production in the total value of agricultural production rose from about 5 percent to about 15 percent. This development was vital for Japanese economic growth because silk was the major source of foreign exchange earnings. It accounted for nearly 50 percent of foreign exchange earnings throughout the nineteenth century, and as much as 30 percent even in the 1920's.

---

[22] Ibid., p. 191.

[23] Kindleberger, "Group Behavior."

[24] This section is based on Takekazu Ogura, ed., *Agricultural Development in Modern Japan* (Tokyo: Fuji Publishing Co., 1963), pp. 541–65; Nogyo Hattatsushi Chosakai, ed., *Nihon Nogyo Hattatsushi* (History of Japanese Agricultural Development), vol. 5 (Tokyo: Chuokoronsha, 1955), pp. 134–85; Japan, Ministry of Agriculture and Forestry, Division of Statistical Research, *Yosan Ruinen Tokeihyo* (Historical Statistics of Sericulture) (Tokyo: Norin Tokei Kyokai, 1961).

[25] For example see Kazushi Ohkawa and Henry Rosovsky, "The Role of Agriculture in Modern Japanese Economic Development," *Economic Development and Cultural Change* 9, part 2 (October 1960): 43–67.

There is an argument that attributes this development to luck. For example, Martin Bronfenbrenner attributed the development of Japanese sericulture, in addition to the existence of the world silk market, to special conditions, such as the spread of a silkworm disease in Italy and Spain and to the Taipei Rebellion in China, which coincided with the opening of Japan to the West.[26] This view is untenable because it does not explain why Japanese silk continued to increase in its share of the world silk market after the elimination of the silkworm disease in Europe due to the efforts of Louis Pasteur and after the Taipei Rebellion in China.

The basic element in the Japanese dominance over its competitors was the progress of technology, both in sericulture and in the silk reeling industry, supported by a number of institutional innovations. Most critical, and particularly relevant in the present context, is the development of summer-fall rearing of cocoons. Traditionally, spring—April to June—is the period of sericultural production. However, this period coincides with the peak of the labor requirement for rice and other crop production and is hence competitive in its demand for labor.

Summer-fall culture, using the nonhibernating bivoltine varieties, had been practiced on a very small scale before the Meiji period. It was only after the discovery in 1875 by Mototada Otaka, a manager of the Tomioka Silk Reeling Mill, of a method of postponing the hatching of hibernating varieties by storing the silkworm eggs in cool caves that the summer-fall culture became practical for many farmers. Later a method of artificial hatching by chemical processing was developed. Finally, a hydrochloric acid processing method was established in 1912–13 at the Aichi Prefectural Egg Multiplication Station.

The summer-fall culture was greatly facilitated by the development of F_1 hybrid varieties (originally by Kametaro Toyama in 1906). The hybrids proved much more vigorous, resulting in a dramatic improvement in the survival rate of summer-fall reared silkworms.

There are a number of advantages of the summer-fall rearing in the use of resources. It increased the efficiency of capital use for farmers because it enabled the use of rearing equipment and utensils more than once in a year. Also, reelers could economize on the use of circulating capital, because they were able to divide payments for cocoons between the spring and summer-fall seasons. It reduced the risk of frost on mulberry leaves, which often damaged early spring culture. The most critical contribution, however, was the increase in the efficiency of labor utilization by providing employment for seasonally idle labor.

Cocoon production from summer-fall culture rose from a negligible level at the beginning of the Meiji period (1868) to 12 thousand tons in 1890, about 25 percent of the total production, and to 119 thousand tons in 1920, about half

[26] Martin Bronfenbrenner, "The Japanese 'Howdunit'," *Transaction* 6 (January 1969): 32–36.

of the total production. This development in the summer-fall culture represents the innovation which enabled the Japanese sericulture industry to surpass France, Italy, and China. This was made possible by a technical innovation which encouraged more efficient utilization of those resources, such as labor, for which the supply was relatively elastic.

This technical innovation was supported by a number of institutional innovations, including the establishment of silk inspection stations (1895), national and prefectural silkworm egg multiplication stations (1910–11), and sericultural colleges in Tokyo (1896), Kyoto (1899), and Ueda (1920). In addition to these government institutions, the development of sericulture co-operatives was a crucial element. Their activities ranged from the transmission of technical information and the co-operative rearing of young worms, to the management of co-operative silk reeling mills and even the training centers.

This experience in the development of the Japanese sericulture industry is of particular interest for the less developed countries as an illustration of how technological change and institutional development have been employed to achieve economic diversification in agriculture.

We do not imply, of course, that there are direct transfer possibilities, either at the technological or institution level, in the experience of Great Britain, Denmark, or Japan. Nor are these the only experiences on which we might have drawn. The significance of these cases is the development of "location-specific" technological and institutional innovations adapted to changes in resource endowments and in product demand of a particular country or region at a particular time in economic history. These innovations occurred in response to economic possibilities rather than in response to efforts to distort the impact of economic change in the domestic and world economies.

MOBILIZING AGRICULTURAL GROWTH FOR OVER-ALL DEVELOPMENT

A continuous sequence of technical and institutional innovations to create and evolve a pattern of agricultural production consistent with changes in product demand and factor supply conditions can sharply reduce the cost of increased income streams generated by the agricultural sector.

What are the implications of these higher income streams for economic development? It has become a generally accepted tenet of development theory that the diversion of the increments in agricultural income for the support of the emerging nonfarm section is essential for rapid economic development (Chapter 2). In this perspective a central question of general development theory has been: "How can peasants be encouraged to produce a cumulative surplus of food and fibers over and above their own consumption, and how can this surplus largely be channeled to investment activity in the nonfarm sector without requiring in exchange an equivalent transfer of productive value to the farm sector?"[27]

Alternative approaches to the diversion of income streams generated and the resources released from agricultural production have been employed by colonialist (or plantation), socialist, and decentralized market economic systems. Our analysis supports the proposition that the market system, combined with a highly decentralized family-operated structure of agricultural production, represents an effective guide to the public and private sector activities engaged in the generation of the new technical knowledge and the more productive inputs which are the sources of the new income streams generated by the agricultural sector. Such a system "provides a framework within which increased agricultural production, . . . can be rendered essentially automatic and almost a direct function of public investment in agricultural research and rural education and of the adequacy of complementary rural financial institutions and farmer's financial reserves."[28]

The market system is not only effective in inducing increased streams of output. The product market also represents an effective device for the transfer of the gains of productivity growth to other sectors of the economy. The market mechanism is, of course, not the only effective device for achieving intersectoral income transfers. Some socialist countries have been successful in designing effective intersector transfer through direct taxation or compulsory delivery. These more direct requisition or "command" systems have typically not been as successful in generating comparable rates of output and productivity growth as is true of market systems characterized by autonomous production units.[29]

Under the colonial systems, the intersectoral income transfers were used to purchase growth in the metropolitan rather than the colonial economy. A large share of the growth in income streams from agriculture was transferred abroad through the remittances of "foreign factors"—foreign capital, entrepreneurs, management, and technical personnel.[30] Also, a significant portion of income was spent for foreign consumer goods by a cluster of "luxury importers," who developed a taste for foreign goods, rather than spilling over into demand for domestic manufactures. Furthermore, agricultural product

---

[27] Wyn F. Owen, "The Double Developmental Squeeze on Agriculture," *American Economic Review* 56 (March 1966): 43–44.

[28] Ibid., p. 53.

[29] Hla Myint, "Market Mechanism and Planning—The Functional Aspect," *The Structure and Development of Asian Economics* (Tokyo: The Japan Economic Research Center, December 1968), pp. 282–313.

[30] Jonathan V. Levin, *The Export Economies: Their Pattern of Development in Historical Perspective* (Cambridge: Harvard University Press, 1960). Also, see Robert E. Baldwin, "Patterns of Development in Newly Settled Regions," *Manchester School of Economic and Social Studies* 24 (May 1956): 161–79; and Melville H. Watkins, "A Staple Theory of Economic Growth," *Canadian Journal of Economics and Political Science* 29 (May 1963): 141–58.

processing and input manufacturing were monopolized by metropolitan countries, thereby reducing the critical forward and backward linkage effects. In contrasting the economic history of Java and Japan, Geertz insists that, "the real tragedy of colonial history in Java after 1830 is not that the peasantry suffered. It suffered worse elsewhere, ... The tragedy is that it suffered for nothing."[31]

This pattern is still persisting in the export-based tropical economies today, particularly in the plantation economies.[32] Policies to promote the substitution of foreign factors by domestic factors, particularly through the training and education of native people for administrative, technical, and engineering work, are essential for redirecting the transfer of agricultural income to the purchase of domestic growth.

Yet an abrupt break from the traditional pattern based on ideological appeal, rather than rational economic calculation, would not contribute to economic growth. It is not the specialization in primary production for export, but rather the lack of "an ability to shift resources at the dictates of the market . . . resource flexibility and innovation sufficient to permit shifts into new export lines or into production for the domestic market,"[33] which are responsible for the underdevelopment of tropical export economies. Efforts to transform the structure and pattern of the economy, without solving this basic problem by education and by institutional and technological innovations, will continue to be unproductive.

The income streams generated in the agricultural sector have in many developing countries been used to purchase a nonviable industrial sector or a nonproductive military and administrative bureaucracy. It has been an article of faith in development thought that it is easier for a poor country to purchase a modern steel industry than a modern agriculture. The experience of the last several decades indicates that while it may be easy for poor countries to acquire an industrial sector, particularly an industrial sector that produces manufactured products that were formerly imported, it is difficult to purchase an industrial sector that is capable of making a sustained contribution to income streams comparable to those generated by the agricultural sector.

If the intersector income transfers resulting from technical change in agriculture are to result in a cumulative contribution to economic growth, the new sectors purchased by these transfers must also be capable of generating intersector transfers. They must be capable of producing the industrial materials needed to sustain the process of agricultural development. They must be

---

[31] Clifford Geertz, *Agricultural Involution; The Process of Ecological Change In Indonesia* (Berkeley: University of California Press, 1966), p. 143.

[32] George Beckford, "Toward an Appropriate Theoretical Framework for Agricultural Development Planning and Policy," *Social and Economic Studies* 17 (September 1968): 233–42; George L. Beckford, "The Economics of Agricultural Resource Use and Development in Plantation Economies," ibid. (forthcoming, 1971).

[33] Watkins, "A Staple Theory," p. 149.

organized to increase the demand for labor in the industrial sector, and the impact must be transferred back to the agricultural sector or through the intersector labor market. And they must be capable of sustaining the necessary investment in education and in urban sector public infrastructure.

During the next several decades the development test will be two-fold. Will the developing economies fully utilize the relatively inexpensive sources of growth that can be obtained by the transformation of agriculture from a traditional to a modern science-based sector? Furthermore, will the dividends from such investments be used to purchase a modern urban industrial sector that is in turn an inexpensive source of economic growth?

INDUCED DEVELOPMENT AND AGRICULTURAL DEVELOPMENT POLICY

The single most significant conclusion that emerges from our analysis of the agricultural development experience of Japan and the United States, and of contemporary development processes in the LDC's, is the powerful role of economic forces in inducing both technical and institutional change.

Our analysis reinforces the view that relative factor and product prices exert a pervasive impact on the direction of both the innovative and production activity of farmers and of the firms that supply the industrial inputs used in agricultural production. The analysis of "induced innovation" has been extended to include the behavior of public sector institutions. Although the theory of induced innovation on the part of the public sector is not complete, it is developed sufficiently to guide us in seeing that in the U.S. and Japan the public sector research and education institutions serving agriculture have responded effectively to economic forces in releasing the constraints on agricultural growth imposed by inelastic factor supplies. The evolution of agricultural research capacity in the LDC's, first in the export crop sectors and recently in the food crop sectors, is also consistent with the induced development hypothesis.

The pervasive role of economic forces in the resource allocation decisions of both private sector firms and public sector institutions places a major burden on the efficiency of the pricing system. Our analysis suggests that where price relationships have been distorted, through either market imperfections or government intervention in market processes, both the innovative behavior and production behavior of private sector firms and public institutions have been distorted. The distortion of prices in both domestic and international factor and product markets and the restrictions on resource mobility and product movements, which have been imposed in pursuit of national development policies, have clearly contributed to the widening disequilibrium in world agriculture during the interwar period and through much of the period since World War II.

In most developing economies the market systems are relatively under-developed. A major challenge facing these countries in their planning is the development of a well-articulated market system capable of accurately reflecting the effects of changes in supply, demand, and production relationships. An important element in the development of a more efficient market system is the removal of the rigidities and distortions resulting from government policy itself—including the maintenance of overvalued currencies, artificially low rates of interest, and unfavorable factor and product price policies for agriculture.[34]

The strategy of attempting to protect agriculture from the impact of economic forces rather than investing in institutions that would improve the capacity of the agricultural sector to respond to economic change has, in many countries, resulted in wide disparities in the economic welfare of the urban and rural population and has severely restricted agriculture's capacity to contribute toward national economic growth. In contrast, investments in public institutions which have increased the capacity of the agricultural sector to respond to economic forces have been critical to the success of agricultural development in countries such as Japan, the United States, and Denmark. The capacity to move from a natural-resource-based to a science-based agriculture—to generate a continuous stream of technical innovations that are responsive to the supply of factors and product demand—depends in most developing countries on substantial investment in experiment station capacity. Equally important is the capacity of the country to undertake the institutional innovations and reforms necessary for agricultural producers to respond to the new technical opportunities which become available to them. Institutional innovations which permit firms and institutions to internalize the benefits of innovative activity become particularly important in creating the incentives for both innovative and productive behavior.

The microeconomic approach to the analysis of the agricultural development process and to the design of agricultural development policies stands in sharp contrast to the macrodevelopment perspective that has characterized both the growth stage and dual economy perspectives. If the perspective we have outlined is relevant to the total development process, and not simply to that of agricultural development, it represents a serious challenge to much of the doctrine and ideology that has dominated recent development theory and development policy.

The "macroplanning" perspective that has dominated postwar development thought was largely evolved out of an attempt to provide an intellectual inter-

---

[34] Hla Myint, "Market Mechanism and Planning": "the more important source of the artificial distortions and rigidities in the economy is not the old fashioned private monopoly power but government policy promoting and sheltering monopolistic firms under a network of direct controls necessitated by inappropriate pricing policies in the key sectors of the economy" (p. 292).

pretation of the traumatic economic and political convulsions of the 1930's and 1940's. Development would occur, it was believed, if a country would (a) utilize national economic planning not only to guide but to replace market forces; (b) achieve a sufficiently high rate of savings and capital accumulation to achieve rapid industrialization; and (c) reduce its dependence on primary production. It was anticipated that "a critical minimum effort" would permit a "take-off" into "cumulative" or "self-sustained" growth. A flow of external resources to eliminate the savings-investment gap and the export-import gap has been regarded as of critical importance to a successful development effort.[35]

The initial enthusiasm with which the success of a few countries, which had followed policies based on the macroplanning perspectives, was being heralded has been greatly dampened in recent years. A number of the examples which appeared so promising in the late 1950's and mid-1960's no longer represent useful "success examples." In retrospect, the macroplanning perspective has resulted in policies leading to an excessively high cost route to economic development. This has been the direct result of the neglect of investment in indigenous capacity to generate technical change and of the failure to invest in the accumulation of labor, managerial, technical, and scientific skill. There has also been a failure to introduce the institutional changes necessary to effectively channel incentives for both innovative and production activities to individuals, private firms, and public institutions.

[35] Perhaps the most skillful single example of analysis conducted within the macroplanning framework outlined above is Hollis B. Chenery and Alan M. Strout, "Foreign Assistance and Economic Development," *American Economic Review* 56, part 1 (September 1966): 679–733. According to Chenery and Strout, "the achievement of a high rate of growth, even if it has to be initially supported by large amounts of external capital, is likely to be the most important element in the long-term effectiveness of assistance. The substantial increases in internal savings ratios that have been achieved in a single decade of strong growth ... demonstrate the speed with which aid-sustained growth can be transformed into self-sustained growth once rapid development has taken hold" (p. 725).

APPENDIX A

Intercountry Cross-Section Data[1]

In this appendix we explain the data used for the intercountry cross-section analysis in Part II (Chapters 4 and 5).

Data were collected for forty-three countries for 1955, 1960, and 1965. In principle the data for flow variables, such as agricultural output and fertilizer input, were measured, respectively, as 1952–56 averages, 1957–62 averages, and 1962–66 averages; and those for stock variables, such as agricultural land area and the number of farm workers, were measured as of 1955, 1960, and 1965. The periods for averaging flow variables were determined in consideration of data availability; the 1957–62 period was adopted for 1960, because the seed and feed data are so documented in the original source; and 1952–56 and 1962–66 averages were adopted for 1955 and 1965, respectively, because 1966 was the latest year for which data were available when this study was initiated. The major intercountry cross-section statistical series are presented in Table A–5 (Series K1–K31).

Agricultural Output (K1–K3)

The output variable employed in this study is specified as gross agricultural output, net of agricultural intermediate products such as seed and feed. The series of 1957–62 average agricultural outputs (K2) was estimated by the procedures described below, and the series of 1952–56 outputs (K1) and 1962–66 average outputs (K3) were extrapolated from the 1957–62 data using the Food and Agricultural Organization's (FAO) indices of agricultural production (FAO, Production Yearbook) for the respective countries.

The series of 1957–62 average outputs was estimated using the following steps: (a) deducting the seed, feed (including imported feed), eggs for hatching, and milk for calf-rearing, from the quantities of individual agricultural commodities produced; (b) aggregating the quantities of the three sets of wheat-

---

[1] More detailed explanations on the intercountry cross-section data are available in Yujiro Hayami in association with Barbara B. Miller, William W. Wade, and Sachiko Yamashita, *An International Comparison of Agricultural Production and Productivities* (St. Paul: University of Minnesota Agricultural Experiment Station Technical Bulletin 277, March 1971).

relative prices derived from the farm-gate prices (or the import prices of commodities not produced domestically) for the U.S.A., Japan, and India to produce three aggregate output series; and (c) combining these three series into a single composite series by taking their geometrical means. Denoting quantity produced of the jth commodity in the ith country by q_{ij}, the corresponding quantity to be deduced by d_{ij}, and the wheat-relative price of the U.S.A., Japan, and India by w_{Uj}, w_{Jj}, and w_{Ij} respectively, our composite series of gross output, Y_i's, may be expressed as:

$$Y_i = \sqrt[3]{Y_{Ui}\, Y_{Ji}\, Y_{Ii}},$$

where

$$Y_{Ui} = \sum_j w_{Uj}(q_{ij} - d_{ij}); \quad Y_{Ji} = \sum_j w_{Jj}(q_{ij} - d_{ij});$$

$$\text{and} \quad Y_{Ii} = \sum_j w_{Ij}(q_{ij} - d_{ij}).$$

The underlying assumptions of the above aggregations procedures are: (a) there exist three types of relative price structures characteristic of the three stages of economic development, which may be called "advanced stage," "mid-way stage," and "initial stage"; (b) these three stages may be represented by the U.S.A., Japan, and India, respectively; and (c) any bias arising from aggregating commodities by the prices of one of these representative countries will be cancelled out by the determination of the geometrical means of three such series. Needless to say, it is arbitrary to assume three stages (why not four?) and to represent the three stages by the U.S.A., Japan, and India. The availability of data rather than theory led us to the selection of the above criteria for our analysis.

Data on the quantities produced were taken from FAO's *Production Yearbook*, various issues, and data for the deduction of seed and feed from FAO's *Food Balance Sheets 1957–59 Average* and *1960–62 Average*. It is the availability of pertinent data in the latter publications which limited the number of countries to forty-three. Because of the lack of necessary information, capital formation and stock changes, especially in the form of livestock and perennial plants, are not counted in computing output. Only the products of agriculture are included in agricultural output, which excludes the products of fishery and forestry. However, the aggregate output of the primary sector, including fishery and forestry, was estimated with the price weights of Japan for the deduction of fishery and forestry workers, as explained later. In principle, quantities produced are measured in farm-gate forms, i.e., sugar cane or cocoon instead of sugar or silk. Major exceptions to this rule are meat products, where the availability of data in the form of meat is much greater than it is in the form of livestock.

Farm-gate prices were taken from the various sources of the three governments. Import prices into the three countries were obtained from the FAO *Trade Yearbook 1965.* Where the imports do not exist in farm-gate forms (e.g., imports of cocoon to the U.S.A.), the import prices in manufactured forms (e.g., silk) were multiplied by the ratios between the prices of the manufactured goods and their source as raw materials in the exporting country (e.g., the price of cocoon relative to the price of silk in Japan).

Prices at farm-gate or at port thus obtained are shown in Table A–1 as they are converted to wheat-relative prices. The results of applying the aggregation procedures, as described above, with the weighing systems in Table A–1, to determine agricultural output are presented in Table A–2.

Value Added in Agriculture (K4)

For the estimation of value added in agriculture it is necessary to estimate agricultural inputs supplied from nonagricultural sectors. It is close to impossible, however, to estimate such inputs directly for all forty-three countries. Social account studies of agricultural sectors, which provide information on the ratios of value added to gross output, are limited to a handful of nations. In order to estimate value added in agriculture for the forty-three countries with any comparability we are limited to a very rough method with bold assumptions.

In this study we established the following assumptions: (a) agricultural inputs supplied from nonagricultural sectors can be classified into two major categories, land-substitutes and labor-substitutes and (b) the input of land-substitutes is proportional to fertilizer input and the input of labor-substitutes is proportional to farm machinery input. With these assumptions we estimated the values of agricultural inputs supplied from nonagricultural sectors, using the U.S.A. and Japan as the bases of aggregation, in order to: (a) construct the indices of fertilizer input and farm machinery input with the inputs in the base countries being set equal to 1; (b) allocate the total values of the agricultural inputs in the base countries to the two major categories of inputs, land-substitutes and labor-substitutes; and (c) sum the inputs of land-substitutes and of labor-substitutes estimated by multiplying the fertilizer index by the value of land-substituting inputs in the base countries and the machinery index by the value of labor-substituting inputs. These two series of agricultural inputs, either with U.S. weights or Japanese weights, were deducted from the corresponding series of gross agricultural output, net of seed and feed, estimated in the previous section, to produce the two series of value added in agriculture. The two series of value-added ratios calculated on such data of gross output and value added were averaged geometrically so as to cancel out any bias which may arise from the specific input structure of the U.S.A. or Japan. The above procedures are inconsistent with those for gross output, because the aggregation using Indian weights was not attempted. This inconsistency was unavoidable, because of the lack of appropriate data for agricultural inputs in Indian agriculture.

If we denote the input of fertilizer in the ith country by F_i, the input of farm machinery by M_i, the input values of land-substitutes in the U.S.A. and Japan by f_U and f_J, respectively, and the input values of labor-substitutes in the U.S.A. and Japan by m_U and m_J, the final series of value added in the ith country, V_i, can be expressed as:

$$V_i = Y_i \sqrt{r_{Ui} \, r_{Ji}},$$

where

$$r_{Ui} = \frac{1}{Y_{Ui}} \left[Y_{Ui} - \left(f_U \frac{F_i}{F_U} + m_U \frac{M_i}{M_U} \right) \right]$$

and

$$r_{Ji} = \frac{1}{Y_{Ji}} \left[Y_{Ji} - \left(f_J \frac{F_i}{F_J} + m_J \frac{M_i}{M_J} \right) \right]$$

Data for fertilizer and farm machinery used for those calculations are the series K16 and K19 in Table A–5. Table A–3 summarizes the estimation of the values of the agricultural inputs which are supplied from nonagriculture for these major categories in the U.S.A. and Japan.

The two series of value-added ratios and the final estimates of the value added are presented in Table A–4. At a glance one would wonder if the value-added ratios in some of the advanced countries, especially the Scandinavian countries, might not be estimated too low. The tendency to overestimate the value-added ratios in the industrialized countries seems inherent to our estimation procedures. For example, our fertilizer and machine series may not adequately represent the two major categories of inputs. More importantly, representing the input of labor-substitutes by tractor horsepower is likely to lead to underestimation of the input levels of labor-substitutes in less-developed countries, where farmers are equipped primarily with animal plows and/or hand hoes. Furthermore, in the highly industrialized countries, the inputs of industrial origin, such as fertilizers and tractors, are supplied to farmers more cheaply relative to farm-product prices, leading to the implication that value-added ratios in these countries are relatively higher for their levels of inputs of such factors. The extremely low value-added ratios estimated for the Scandinavian countries (Finland, Norway, and Sweden) seem to indicate that the relative prices of inputs and outputs are especially favorable for their farmers, rather than that their income is very low relative to gross sales.

Number of Farms (K5)

Data for the number of farms (agricultural holdings) were collected mainly from the FAO report on the 1960 World Census of Agriculture, supplemented by several other governmental and private publications: "Chile—Committee on Inter-American Development," *Land Tenancy and Socioeconomic Development* (Santiago 1966), p. 42; "France—Interpolated from 1955 and 1963 Data," in Ministere de l'agriculture, *Enqûete communautaire sur la structure des exploitations agricole en 1967* (1968), p. 7; "India—Directorate of Economics and Statistics," Ministry of Food, Agriculture, Community Development and Cooperation, *Indian Agriculture in Brief* (1967), p. 65; "Israel and Syria," Marion Clawson and others, *Agricultural Potential of the Middle East*, Parts I and II (Resources for the Future, Inc. [mimeo.] 1969), pp. 8–16; "Mauritius—Number of Sugar Planters," in J. E. Mead, *The Economic and Social Structure of Mauritius* (London, 1961), p. 75; "Switzerland—Extrapolated from 1950 and 1955 data," in *Dritter Bericht der Bundesversammlung über die Lage der Schweizerischen Landwirtschaft und die Agrarpolitik des Bundes* (Berne, 1965), p. 6; "UAR," M. M. El-Kammash, *Economic Development in Egypt* (New York, 1968), p. 260.

Number of Male Workers in Agriculture (K6–K8)

The number of male workers in agriculture was estimated from the data of the economically active male population in agricultural occupations (agriculture, forestry, hunting, and fishing), published in the *Yearbook of Labor Statistics* (various issues) by the International Labor Organization (ILO).

A deduction for the number of forestry and fishery workers (excluding hunters) from the ILO's labor population in agricultural occupations was made by multiplying the population by the ratio of the gross output in agriculture to the gross output of agriculture, forestry, and fishing combined, both aggregated with Japan's wheat-relative prices. That is, the economically active male population in agriculture in country i, L_i, can be estimated from that in agricultural occupations, L_i', as

$$L_i = L_i' \frac{Y_{Ji}}{Y_{Ji}'} \text{ (see } Y_{Ji} \text{ and } Y_{Ji}' \text{ in Table A–2).}$$

This method is based on the assumption that labor productivities are equal between these agricultural occupations.

In order to preserve the international comparability of data, only males are counted. In countries where original data are unavailable for specified years (or nearby years), extrapolations or interpolations were conducted by using the growth rates.

Agricultural Land Area (K9–K11)

The area of agricultural land, including permanent meadows and pastures, of the year as reported in FAO's *Production Yearbook* (various issues) was used as the land variable. There have been several attempts to aggregate arable land and unimproved pasture land using appropriate weights. Such attempts are bound to be arbitrary. The proportion of arable land to total agricultural land area can be considered as a variable which farmers can, in the very long run, manipulate by changing the method of farming and the intensity of cultivation. We preferred, therefore, to use as the land variable the unweighted sum of arable land and pasture land areas, partly to avoid arbitrariness and partly to enable the making of comparisons of the equilibrium reached when the adjustments in land utilization resulting from changes in the demand for agricultural land are completed. This procedure, however, tends to overestimate the endowment of agricultural land in newly settled countries, such as Australia, primarily engaged in pastoral farming, leading to a serious underestimation of land productivity for these countries.

Using the growth rates of the original data, land areas for specified years were estimated by extrapolations and interpolations.

Livestock (K12–K14)

Data for the numbers of livestock animals existing on farms are available in FAO, *Production Yearbook* (various issues). We have aggregated the various kinds of animals in terms of livestock units. The weights for aggregation are: camels, 1.1; buffalo, horses, and mules, 1.0; cattle and asses, 0.8; pigs, 0.2; sheep and goats, 0.1; poultry, 0.01.

Fertilizer Consumption (K15–K17)

The data on fertilizer input in terms of total physical weights of N, P_2O_5 and K_2O contained in commercial fertilizers consumed are taken from FAO, *Fertilizer Annual Review* (various issues).

Tractor Horsepower (K18–K20)

Tractor horsepower data were obtained for the countries which belong to the Organization for Economic Cooperation and Development (OECD) from OECD, *Evolution de la motorization de l'agriculture et de la consommation et des prix des carburant dans les pays membres, June 1963*. For countries outside of OECD, tractor horsepower was estimated from the number of farm tractors by assuming that the average horsepower of farm tractors and garden tractors was 30 and 5, respectively. Data for the number of tractors were taken from the FAO, *Production Yearbook* (various issues). Differences between the specified years and the reporting years were adjusted by using the growth rates.

Literacy Ratio (K21)

The data for literacy ratios are the medians of interval estimates of literacy ratios in United Nations Educational, Scientific, and Cultural Organization (UNESCO), *World Illiteracy at Mid-Century*, 1957.

School Enrollment Ratio (K22–K24)

The school enrollment ratio relates the actual total of the number enrolled in the first and second levels of education to the population of potential enrollment. Adjustments were made to minimize the effects of differences in the school system among countries. The data were taken from UNESCO, *Basic Facts and Figures* and UNESCO, *Statistical Yearbook* (various issues).

The school enrollment ratio represents the increase in the level of general education, primary and secondary, more adequately than the level of education itself. In order to convert the enrollment ratio into a measure of the stock of education, we averaged the data for three specified years at five-year intervals, i.e., averaged 1945, 1950, and 1955 to obtain the 1955 series (K15); averaged 1950, 1955, and 1960 to obtain the 1960 series (K16); and averaged 1955, 1960, and 1965 to obtain the 1965 series (K17).

Number of Graduates from Agricultural Colleges per 10,000 Male Farm Workers (K25–K27)

As a proxy variable for the level of advanced technical education in agriculture, we prepared a series of the number of graduates from agricultural colleges, the third level of education, per 10,000 male workers in agriculture. Sources of the data for the number of graduates are the same as for the school enrollment ratio. To reduce the effect of annual fluctuations in the number of graduates, the five-year averages (1953–57, 1958–62, and 1963–67 averages) were adopted to be related to the number of male workers in agriculture (K6–K8). Extrapolations and interpolations were extensively utilized to estimate the number of graduates for the specified years.

Ratio of Nonagricultural Labor (K28)

As an indicator of industrialization, the ratios of male workers engaged in nonagricultural occupations (other than agriculture, forestry, hunting, and fishing) to the total number of male workers in the economy were calculated for respective countries from the data published in ILO, *Yearbook of Labor Statistics 1965*, pp. 39–131.

Farm Wage Rate (K29–K31)

The farm wage rate is here defined as the wage received by a male farm worker per day, including board. The original source of data is FAO, *Production Yearbook* (various issues). Monthly, weekly, and hourly wages are converted into daily wages by assuming, respectively: (a) twenty-two work days in a month, (b) 5 work days in a week and (c) 8 work hours in a day; and (c) an addition of 10 percent of cash wages to the data which exclude board.

Table A-1. Weights for aggregating agricultural products: wheat-relative prices per metric ton, 1957–62*

Commodity	U.S.A. (w_U)	Japan (w_J)	India (w_I)
Grains			
Wheat	1.00	1.00	1.00
Barley	0.61	1.00	0.69
Buckwheat	0.74	1.24	0.84
Maize	0.63	0.72	0.78
Millet	0.68	0.74	0.87
Oats	0.63	0.70	0.69
Rice (rough)	1.58	1.61	0.94
Rye	0.58	0.77	0.69
Sorghum	0.55	0.81	0.81
Mixed grain	0.61	0.74	0.69
Starchy roots			
Cassava	0.16	0.11	0.58
Potatoes	0.57	0.27	0.58
Sweet potatoes	0.81	0.22	0.58
Sugar			
Beets, not processed	0.19	0.15	0.15
Cane, not processed	0.12	0.18	0.10
Pulses and oil crops			
Copra	0.84	0.48	3.10
Cottonseed	0.75	0.83	0.78
Groundnuts	3.39	2.55	1.21
Linseed	1.30	0.66	1.50
Olives	1.66	1.31	1.13
Palm kernels	1.13	1.44	3.10
Pulses (all)	2.12	1.94	0.84
Rapeseed	0.87	1.45	1.91
Sesame seed	4.56	3.98	2.07
Soybeans	1.16	1.50	1.22
Sunflower seed	2.50	1.17	1.11
Nuts			
Unshelled	13.14	2.31	5.24
Fruits			
Bananas	0.65	1.52	0.63
Citrus	0.98	1.15	1.40
Dates	2.05	0.55	3.33
Other fresh	1.27	0.94	1.79
Unspecified	1.13	1.05	1.79
Vegetables			
All	0.83	0.42	1.31

Table A-1—(Continued)

Commodity	U.S.A. (w_U)	Japan (w_J)	India (w_I)
Livestock products			
Beef and veal	12.36	9.99	5.00
Mutton and lamb	12.58	5.03	5.00
Pork	9.51	7.36	5.00
Poultry	6.47	5.15	2.98
Eggs	7.35	5.12	5.24
Milk	1.36	0.76	1.21
Fibers			
Abaca	5.77	3.88	4.12
Cotton	10.30	6.06	2.17
Flax	5.50	3.37	6.27
Hemp	6.94	6.29	1.70
Henequen	2.54	2.30	2.41
Jute	3.11	2.30	1.93
Silk, cocoon basis	17.32	12.86	18.88
Sisal	2.54	2.30	2.41
Wool, greasy basis	14.44	13.52	14.58
Miscellaneous			
Cocoa	8.27	6.30	6.16
Coffee	10.84	7.82	8.21
Rubber	9.33	6.74	7.14
Tea	15.70	3.44	8.88
Tobacco	19.47	8.56	4.63
Timber	—	0.15[a]	—
Marine products			
Fish	—	1.44	—
Whale	—	13.96[b]	—

* Farm-gate values of 1 metric ton of wheat in native currencies were: 67.6 dollars in the U.S.A.; 36,072 yen in Japan; and 46.4 rupees in India. See sources and estimation procedures in the main text.

[a] Per cubic meter of round wood.

[b] Per whale.

Table A–2. Agricultural output, 1957–62, averages of 43 countries, in 1,000 wheat units

Country	U.S.A. weights (Y_U)	Japan weights		India weights (Y_I)	Composite $(Y = \sqrt[3]{Y_U Y_J Y_I})$
		Agriculture (Y_J)	Agriculture, forestry, fishery (Y_J')		
Argentina	63,698	49,814	51,748	43,378	51,626
Australia	49,800	38,451	40,853	38,841	42,054
Austria	11,414	7,908	9,635	9,260	9,419
Belgium (and Luxemburg)	14,312	9,392	9,852	10,911	11,361
Brazil	96,753	80,409	97,277	71,317	82,162
Canada	43,960	33,340	48,538	33,554	36,633
Ceylon	6,617	3,483	3,608	5,124	4,906
Chile	7,605	5,658	7,064	6,705	6,607
Colombia	19,973	16,310	19,526	14,030	16,594
Denmark	18,411	12,528	13,713	12,889	14,378
Finland	7,145	4,578	11,439	5,832	5,756
France	101,537	71,462	78,595	87,972	86,093
Germany, Fed. Rep.	70,189	48,047	52,866	54,999	57,023
Greece	13,222	8,813	9,428	11,150	10,911
India	216,477	193,272	197,107	153,821	185,986
Ireland	9,117	6,193	6,290	6,562	7,182
Israel	2,412	1,940	1,964	2,368	2,229
Italy	72,348	49,281	52,461	69,189	62,709
Japan	60,770	47,646	66,771	49,828	52,436
Libya	599	338	495	533	476
Mauritius	630	834	846	534	655
Mexico	32,811	26,572	27,541	23,483	27,354
Netherlands	21,250	13,021	13,651	16,866	16,709
New Zealand	20,724	13,149	13,968	14,702	15,882
Norway	4,118	2,496	6,338	3,174	3,195
Pakistan	56,317	40,345	42,445	40,454	45,125
Paraguay	1,215	1,066	1,340	1,183	1,153
Peru	9,046	7,100	12,547	7,252	7,751
Philippines	16,057	14,133	15,698	14,715	14,946
Portugal	9,020	6,306	7,865	8,794	7,937
South Africa	19,218	15,294	16,631	15,414	16,547
Spain	45,107	28,507	31,764	38,539	36,727
Surinam	258	206	258	162	205
Sweden	12,177	8,378	15,183	9,721	9,971
Switzerland	8,346	5,355	5,905	7,121	6,827
Syria	5,334	4,027	4,032	4,256	4,504
Taiwan	10,122	8,507	9,049	8,493	9,009
Turkey	37,213	25,300	26,642	34,347	31,856
U.A.R.	20,890	15,986	16,331	16,714	17,737
U.K.	49,882	32,493	34,511	35,510	38,605
U.S.	435,480	330,953	380,166	304,332	352,619
Venezuela	5,960	5,694	6,522	4,738	5,437
Yugoslavia	20,133	14,475	16,986	17,087	17,075

Table A–3. **Agricultural inputs supplied from the nonagricultural sector, United States and Japan, 1957–62 averages***

Country	Unit	Land substitutes	Labor substitutes
U.S.	Dollars (in millions)	1,845	8,906
	Wheat units (in thousands)	27,299 ($= f_U$)	137,747 ($= m_U$)
Japan	Yen (in billions)	2,162	1,698
	Wheat units (in thousands)	5,895 ($= f_J$)	4,708 ($= m_J$)

* Agricultural inputs supplied from the nonagricultural sector are divided into "land substitutes," "labor substitutes," and "unclassifiable." The value of "unclassifiable" inputs are allocated to "land substitutes" and "labor substitutes" according to the proportions of inputs of both categories. The classification of items and the sources of data are:

Sources:

    U.S.: U.S. Department of Agriculture, *Agricultural Statistics, 1964.*

        Land substitutes: Fertilizer and lime.

        Labor substitutes: Repairs and operation of motor vehicle and machinery, depreciation of motor vehicle, other machinery and implements.

        Unclassifiable: Repairs and operation of farm buildings, miscellaneous current farm expenses, depreciation of farm buildings, accidental damage of farm capital.

    Japan: Ministry of Agriculture and Forestry, *Nogyo oyobi Noka no Shakai Kanjo (Social Accounts of Agriculture and Farm Households) 1967.*

        Land substitutes: Fertilizer.

        Labor substitutes: Light and power, small equipment, repairs of machinery and implements, depreciation of machinery and implements.

        Unclassifiable: Agricultural medicines, repairs of farm buildings, depreciation of farm buildings, miscellaneous materials, miscellaneous expenses.

Table A–4. Estimation of value added in agriculture, 1957–62, averages of 43 countries

Country	Value-added ratio			Value added (1,000 WU) $(V = r_Y)$
	U.S. weights (r_U)	Japan weights (r_J)	Composite $(r = \sqrt{r_U r_J})$	
Argentina	0.953	0.936	0.944	48,753
Australia	0.822	0.762	0.791	33,265
Austria	0.760	0.640	0.698	6,571
Belgium (and Luxemburg)	0.817	0.715	0.765	8,687
Brazil	0.975	0.969	0.972	79,875
Canada	0.648	0.510	0.575	21,076
Ceylon	0.966	0.935	0.951	4,663
Chile	0.909	0.874	0.891	5,889
Colombia	0.961	0.950	0.956	15,862
Denmark	0.772	0.653	0.710	10,210
Finland	0.615	0.374	0.479	2,759
France	0.760	0.647	0.701	60,367
Germany, Fed. Rep.	0.681	0.518	0.594	33,849
Greece	0.906	0.855	0.880	9,606
India	0.991	0.990	0.991	184,274
Ireland	0.813	0.715	0.762	5,473
Israel	0.874	0.839	0.856	1,909
Italy	0.869	0.801	0.834	52,310
Japan	0.829	0.777	0.803	42,106
Libya	0.878	0.772	0.823	392
Mauritius	0.879	0.910	0.895	586
Mexico	0.947	0.932	0.939	25,692
Netherlands	0.843	0.738	0.788	13,175
New Zealand	0.852	0.757	0.803	12,753
Norway	0.545	0.218	0.345	1,102
Pakistan	0.995	0.993	0.994	44,855
Paraguay	0.988	0.986	0.987	1,138
Peru	0.949	0.935	0.942	7,303
Philippines	0.978	0.974	0.976	14,588
Portugal	0.920	0.883	0.901	7,154
South Africa	0.859	0.816	0.837	13,850
Spain	0.921	0.873	0.897	32,937
Surinam	0.938	0.917	0.928	190
Sweden	0.586	0.370	0.465	4,641
Switzerland	0.889	0.821	0.854	5,833
Syria	0.974	0.964	0.969	4,366
Taiwan	0.933	0.920	0.926	8,346
Turkey	0.964	0.944	0.954	30,398
U.A.R.	0.954	0.940	0.947	16,797
U.K.	0.705	0.527	0.610	23,535
U.S.	0.635	0.496	0.561	197,788
Venezuela	0.946	0.941	0.944	5,131
Yugoslavia	0.905	0.864	0.884	15,100

Table A-5. Major intercountry cross-section statistical series

Country	Agricultural output			Value added 1960 (K4)
	1955 (K1)	1960 (K2)	1965 (K3)	
	1,000 wheat units			
Argentina	49,003	51,626	57,253	48,753
Australia	34,947	42,054	49,279	33,265
Austria	7,825	9,419	10,472	6,571
Belgium (and Luxemburg)	10,281	11,361	12,501	8,687
Brazil	60,964	82,162	92,842	79,875
Canada	36,705	36,633	48,414	21,076
Ceylon	4,261	4,906	5,698	4,663
Chile	5,800	6,607	7,118	5,889
Colombia	14,201	16,594	17,590	15,862
Denmark	12,468	14,378	15,219	10,210
Finland	4,956	5,756	6,598	2,759
France	74,402	86,093	100,195	60,367
Germany, Fed. Rep.	50,761	57,023	63,147	33,849
Greece	8,585	10,911	13,283	9,606
India	158,609	185,986	200,046	184,274
Ireland	6,432	7,182	7,695	5,473
Israel	1,332	2,229	3,108	1,909
Italy	55,171	62,709	67,751	52,310
Japan	44,088	52,436	57,921	42,106
Libya	346	476	596	392
Mauritius	n.a.	655	n.a.	586
Mexico	19,432	27,354	32,743	25,692
Netherlands	14,260	16,709	18,681	13,175
New Zealand	13,264	15,882	18,128	12,753
Norway	3,108	3,195	3,176	1,102
Pakistan	39,980	45,125	50,621	44,855
Paraguay	n.a.	1,153	n.a.	1,138
Peru	6,487	7,751	8,815	7,303
Philippines	12,346	14,946	17,242	14,588
Portugal	7,688	7,937	8,981	7,154
South Africa	13,436	16,547	18,804	13,850
Spain	32,728	36,727	42,092	32,937
Surinam	n.a.	205	n.a.	190
Sweden	10,041	9,971	10,061	4,641
Switzerland	6,237	6,827	6,909	5,833
Syria	3,944	4,504	5,675	4,366
Taiwan	7,323	9,009	10,737	8,346
Turkey	25,791	31,856	37,097	30,398
U.A.R.	14,647	17,737	20,699	16,797
U.K.	32,905	38,605	45,731	23,535
U.S.	326,384	352,619	381,252	197,788
Venezuela	4,263	5,437	7,291	5,131
Yugoslavia	12,106	17,075	18,820	15,100

Table A–5—(Continued)

Country	Number of farms 1960 (K5)	Number of male workers in agriculture		
		1955 (K6)	1960 (K7)	1965 (K8)
		1,000's		
Argentina	472	1,411	1,295	1,334
Australia	252	433	395	392
Austria	402	369	297	267
Belgium (and Luxemburg)	269	266	215	174
Brazil	3,350	7,566	8,698	8,911
Canada	481	625	484	420
Ceylon	1,174	1,131	1,263	1,255
Chile	174	496	512	533
Colombia	1,210	1,704	1,612	1,957
Denmark	197	338	303	273
Finland	388	201	187	173
France	1,994	2,969	2,395	2,205
Germany, Fed. Rep.	1,678	1,780	1,477	1,273
Greece	1,156	1,083	1,101	1,096
India	48,882	66,165	86,847	91,339
Ireland	360	393	343	316
Israel	70	90	77	80
Italy	4,294	5,129	3,898	3,364
Japan	6,057	5,745	4,897	4,405
Libya	146	n.a.	n.a.	n.a.
Mauritius	22	55	56	57
Mexico	1,365	4,778	5,287	5,998
Netherlands	77	451	387	351
New Zealand	301	117	112	109
Norway	434	118	103	95
Pakistan	12,155	17,233	18,464	23,206
Paraguay	161	191	231	248
Peru	870	711	758	797
Philippines	1,639	3,305	3,959	4,183
Portugal	n.a.	1,060	1,075	1,047
South Africa	110	1,351	1,415	1,493
Spain	3,008	3,868	3,023	3,442
Surinam	16	n.a.	12	n.a.
Sweden	265	274	225	201
Switzerland	185	267	233	219
Syria	418	420	477	508
Taiwan	808	1,095	1,116	1,320
Turkey	3,410	4,122	4,469	4,907
U.A.R.	2,946	3,960	4,046	4,509
U.K.	396	961	877	799
U.S.	3,711	4,584	3,542	3,088
Venezuela	320	616	650	685
Yugoslavia	2,624	n.a.	n.a.	n.a.

Table A-5—(Continued)

Country	Agricultural land area		
	1955 (K9)	1960 (K10)	1965 (K11)
	1,000 hectares		
Argentina	139,287	137,829	136,386
Australia	385,442	468,135	485,837
Austria	4,080	4,050	3,984
Belgium (and Luxemburg)	1,870	1,857	1,791
Brazil	126,728	137,034	148,178
Canada	62,291	62,848	64,170
Ceylon	1,710	1,723	1,889
Chile	12,964	13,742	14,594
Colombia	17,751	19,653	21,759
Denmark	3,117	3,127	3,033
Finland	2,863	2,849	2,883
France	33,668	34,539	34,001
Germany, Fed. Rep.	14,251	14,254	14,059
Greece	8,698	8,911	8,678
India	169,496	176,036	177,243
Ireland	4,705	4,560	4,709
Israel	564	1,210	1,223
Italy	20,904	20,930	20,440
Japan	6,276	7,020	7,683
Libya	9,800	11,285	11,988
Mauritius	129	123	124
Mexico	94,045	102,909	112,608
Netherlands	2,307	2,317	2,255
New Zealand	13,125	13,341	13,634
Norway	1,033	1,033	1,008
Pakistan	24,404	n.a.	28,071
Paraguay	1,246	1,222	1,615
Peru	13,730	13,956	14,701
Philippines	7,588	7,954	11,318
Portugal	4,828	n.a.	4,918
South Africa	97,340	101,170	107,824
Spain	29,633	33,880	34,769
Surinam	39	46	55
Sweden	4,495	4,282	3,735
Switzerland	2,173	2,161	3,179
Syria	10,391	12,566	13,057
Taiwan	933	880	901
Turkey	53,827	54,018	54,378
U.A.R.	2,713	2,569	2,767
U.K.	19,404	19,894	19,623
U.S.	443,831	439,941	439,800
Venezuela	17,800	19,178	25,193
Yugoslavia	14,752	14,923	14,756

Table A-5—(Continued)

Country	Livestock			Fertilizer consumption $(N + P_2O_5 + K_2O)$		
	1955 (K12)	1960 (K13)	1965 (K14)	1955 (K15)	1960 (K16)	1965 (K17)
	1,000 livestock units			1,000 metric tons		
Argentina	50,412	46,043	48,270	17	14	24
Australia	28,274	30,223	31,220	433	605	819
Austria	2,846	2,794	2,720	108	221	304
Belgium (and Luxemburg)	2,751	3,030	3,216	333	377	452
Brazil	75,358	87,705	107,713	71	191	228
Canada	10,605	10,963	11,689	237	324	527
Ceylon	2,032	2,093	2,417	33	57	71
Chile	3,525	3,906	4,030	51	77	102
Colombia	12,646	15,194	14,522	24	38	116
Denmark	4,009	4,746	4,610	319	386	455
Finland	1,972	2,074	2,023	148	216	283
France	19,840	20,949	21,360	1,312	2,183	2,816
Germany, Fed. Rep.	14,106	14,939	15,789	1,699	2,307	2,627
Greece	3,410	3,595	3,271	78	144	214
India	186,441	207,240	224,483	121	340	599
Ireland	4,652	4,695	5,480	88	174	224
Israel	202	267	336	27	32	36
Italy	10,806	11,762	11,704	624	816	931
Japan	4,276	4,558	4,801	1,018	1,577	1,780
Libya	575	694	787	2	3	4
Mauritius	40	38	49	10	18	25
Mexico	29,060	37,599	41,716	43	188	266
Netherlands	3,451	4,202	4,590	440	467	531
New Zealand	9,056	10,284	11,781	192	263	373
Norway	1,390	1,398	1,280	119	145	158
Pakistan	35,742	40,023	41,607	9	48	103
Paraguay	4,250	4,352	5,314	n.a.	n.a.	1
Peru	6,029	6,656	7,006	75	76	94
Philippines	6,225	6,305	7,307	42	66	109
Portugal	2,061	2,256	2,367	114	123	158
South Africa	15,029	15,523	15,949	141	213	270
Spain	8,001	9,277	7,803	426	659	755
Surinam	32	38	42	<1	1	1
Sweden	2,636	2,797	2,367	253	286	343
Switzerland	1,764	1,864	1,903	65	99	122
Syria	1,566	1,110	1,404	4	9	18
Taiwan	1,072	1,180	1,131	115	173	196
Turkey	17,682	20,255	20,555	20	45	100
U.A.R.	4,222	5,322	4,709	125	204	280
U.K.	13,387	14,971	15,635	824	984	1,464
U.S.	99,987	100,834	107,238	5,444	7,225	9,380
Venezuela	6,808	6,544	7,130	7	13	30
Yugoslavia	8,039	8,541	8,146	46	253	391

Table A–5—(Continued)

Country	Tractor horsepower			Literacy ratio	School enrollment ratio		
	1955 (K18)	1960 (K19)	1965 (K20)	1960 (K21)	1955 (K22)	1960 (K23)	1965 (K24)
	1,000 hp.			percent	percent		
Argentina	969	3,485	5,634	87.5	64	69	73
Australia	6,235	7,782	9,491	98.5	83	89	91
Austria	1,263	2,247	3,922	98.5	76	72	70
Belgium (and Luxemburg)	796	1,405	2,217	96.5	84	92	99
Brazil	1,353	1,972	2,364	47.5	30	39	50
Canada	15,435	16,800	24,549	97.5	71	77	81
Ceylon	6	13	51	62.5	68	67	77
Chile	472	473	734	77.5	62	68	74
Colombia	519	741	940	52.5	31	40	51
Denmark	1,687	3,227	4,861	98.5	80	86	88
Finland	1,152	2,288	3,819	98.5	76	82	83
France	8,282	18,996	25,934	96.5	78	80	91
Germany, Fed. Rep.	9,212	16,173	23,782	98.5	91	87	86
Greece	331	818	1,467	72.5	70	70	72
India	314	686	1,587	17.5	21	26	33
Ireland	821	1,243	1,895	98.5	100	98	95
Israel	120	214	317	92.5	74	85	88
Italy	4,839	7,536	13,055	87.5	53	56	60
Japan	473	5,234	29,431	97.5	86	90	89
Libya	6	71	243	7.5	13	25	40
Mauritius	7	9	8	52.5	53	52	78
Mexico	961	1,229	1,738	62.5	40	44	59
Netherlands	954	1,857	2,234	98.5	85	90	91
New Zealand	2,099	2,452	2,967	98.5	88	97	91
Norway	987	1,568	2,250	98.5	77	85	88
Pakistan	30	117	50	17.5	20	23	27
Paraguay	n.a.	17	n.a.	67.5	51	57	62
Peru	208	204	300	47.5	46	49	57
Philippines	169	128	163	62.5	80	76	75
Portugal	146	309	489	57.5	41	52	61
South Africa	1,760	2,250	4,008	42.5	49	58	70
Spain	798	1,273	4,546	82.5	53	61	67
Surinam	8	17	25	72.5	68	73	80
Sweden	3,403	4,682	6,985	98.5	75	79	79
Switzerland	590	652	1,438	98.5	64	72	66
Syria	56	123	241	27.5	35	39	42
Taiwan	15	37	61	47.5	48	59	70
Turkey	1,379	1,375	1,590	32.5	33	39	46
U.A.R.	215	220	221	22.5	26	35	43
U.K.	12,491	12,989	13,037	98.5	75	79	85
U.S.	140,410	155,540	195,625	96.5	100	100	100
Venezuela	292	320	467	52.5	41	56	70
Yugoslavia	378	1,134	1,403	72.5	n.a.	63	n.a.

Table A-5—(Continued)

Country	Number of graduates from agricultural colleges per 10,000 farm workers			Ratio of nonagriculture labor	Farm wage rate per day		
	1955 (K25)	1960 (K26)	1965 (K27)	1960 (K28)	1955 (K29)	1960 (K30)	1965 (K31)
	number			percent	U.S. dollars		
Argentina	2.11	1.82	2.18	77.1	n.a.	n.a.	n.a.
Australia	3.12	9.02	24.72	86.7	n.a.	n.a.	n.a.
Austria	3.80	5.79	8.46	82.0	1.79	2.51	3.53
Belgium (and Luxemburg)	9.65	11.77	12.03	91.6	3.17	3.69	4.92
Brazil	0.45	0.60	0.90	34.2	n.a.	n.a.	n.a.
Canada	7.10	11.40	15.61	85.1	6.40	7.36	7.80
Ceylon	0.08	0.03	n.a.	49.4	0.52	0.57	0.59
Chile	0.46	2.21	5.48	65.6	n.a.	n.a.	n.a.
Colombia	0.13	0.39	1.01	36.8	n.a.	n.a.	n.a.
Denmark	5.03	5.20	7.13	77.1	3.36	4.47	6.47
Finland	5.66	7.81	10.44	62.2	3.12	3.04	4.16
France	1.60	2.46	3.75	79.9	1.53	2.01	2.77
Germany, Fed. Rep.	5.86	7.62	8.65	90.4	2.20	3.43	5.47
Greece	0.90	0.97	2.05	51.8	n.a.	n.a.	n.a.
India	0.27	0.41	0.99	31.4	0.25	0.26	0.40
Ireland	2.98	4.64	4.80	57.7	2.38	2.98	4.00
Israel	2.45	8.05	11.25	85.9	n.a.	n.a.	n.a.
Italy	1.85	1.50	1.65	72.4	n.a.	n.a.	n.a.
Japan	8.77	14.24	20.54	74.4	0.85	1.21	2.28
Libya	n.a.	n.a.	n.a.	n.a.	n.a.	n.a.	n.a.
Mauritius	3.90	5.34	6.72	62.7	0.67	0.97	1.56
Mexico	0.07	0.15	0.20	41.1	0.58	0.75	1.11
Netherlands	8.49	11.15	13.73	87.5	n.a.	n.a.	n.a.
New Zealand	11.48	19.23	24.09	82.3	5.08	5.76	5.86
Norway	7.54	10.06	13.09	75.9	3.78	5.13	6.77
Pakistan	0.32	0.26	0.13	26.6	n.a.	n.a.	n.a.
Paraguay	n.a.	n.a.	n.a.	38.7	n.a.	n.a.	n.a.
Peru	1.94	1.66	4.59	45.2	0.78	1.09	n.a.
Philippines	1.39	1.60	1.15	30.8	1.02	0.97	n.a.
Portugal	0.60	1.64	0.42	52.4	0.71	0.87	1.31
South Africa	1.29	1.57	2.50	65.0	n.a.	n.a.	n.a.
Spain	1.36	0.93	0.77	63.6	n.a.	n.a.	n.a.
Surinam	n.a.	n.a.	n.a.	74.9	n.a.	n.a.	n.a.
Sweden	4.49	6.89	8.20	82.1	4.48	6.40	9.28
Switzerland	n.a.	5.27	n.a.	85.3	n.a.	n.a.	n.a.
Syria	2.76	2.43	2.22	46.8	n.a.	n.a.	n.a.
Taiwan	3.91	6.18	7.25	50.8	n.a.	n.a.	n.a.
Turkey	0.34	1.15	1.51	38.9	0.80	1.23	n.a.
U.A.R.	1.33	3.66	5.51	42.2	n.a.	n.a.	n.a.
U.K.	6.10	7.40	8.51	93.5	4.29	6.36	7.26
U.S.	18.76	21.82	29.78	91.4	5.36	6.40	7.33
Venezuela	0.31	0.83	0.91	62.0	n.a.	n.a.	n.a.
Yugoslavia	n.a.	n.a.	n.a.	n.a.	n.a.	n.a.	n.a.

APPENDIX B

Time-Series Data of Labor and Land Productivities
of Five Selected Countries, 1880–1960

Historical time-series data of agricultural output per male farm worker and per hectare of agricultural land for selected countries (The United States, Japan, Denmark, France, and The United Kingdom) in wheat units are compiled so that they are comparable with the cross-country data; these are the data for Figures 4–5, 4–6, and 4–7 in Chapter 4. The procedures are: (a) the index of agricultural output net of inputs supplied from the agricultural sector is divided by indices of the number of male farm workers and of agricultural land area to produce the indices of output per worker and per hectare; and (b) these indices are spliced to the cross-country outputs per worker and per hectare for 1957–62 (Table 4–1, Chapter 4) in wheat units. These procedures are adopted to adjust for the differences between the time-series labor force and land area data that are collected for intertemporal comparability and the cross-country data that are collected for international comparability. The sources of data and the estimation procedures are summarized in Tables B–1 to B–5.

In principle, data for a flow variable (agricultural output) is the average for the five years centering on the years shown, and those for stock variables (labor force and land area) are measured in the years shown.

Table B–1. Time-series data for the United States, 1880–1960

Year	Index 1960 = 100							Percent of male workers in nonagri-culture (US 8)
	Agricultural output (US 1)	Number of male workers (US 2)	Agricultural land (US 3)	Output per male worker (US 4)	Output per hectare (US 5)	Output per male worker (US 6)	Output per hectare (US 7)	
	percent					WU	WU	percent
1880	29	200	46	15	63	14.6	0.5	45
1885	32	214	50	15	64	15.0	0.5	
1890	35	230	54	15	65	15.1	0.5	52
1895	40	238	64	17	63	16.8	0.5	
1900	46	248	73	18	62	18.2	0.5	57
1905	47	254	75	19	63	18.4	0.5	
1910	48	260	77	19	63	18.4	0.5	64
1915	51	259	80	20	64	19.6	0.5	
1920	53	256	83	21	63	20.6	0.5	69
1925	56	246	80	23	70	22.8	0.6	
1930	60	236	88	25	69	25.3	0.5	74
1935	56	224	94	25	59	24.8	0.5	
1940	68	214	94	32	72	31.7	0.6	78
1945	78	186	102	42	76	41.5	0.6	
1950	84	160	104	52	81	52.1	0.6	85
1955	90	130	104	69	87	68.9	0.7	
1960	100	100	100	100	100	99.5	0.8	91

(US 1) Index calculated from Series U1 in Table C–2, Appendix C.
(US 2) Index calculated from Series U4 in Table C–2, Appendix C.
(US 3) Index calculated from Series U5 in Table C–2, Appendix C.
(US 4) (US 1)/(US 2).
(US 5) (US 1)/(US 3).
(US 6) Index in column (US 4) spliced with intercountry cross-section series of output per worker for 1957–62(Table 4–1, Chapter 4).
(US 7) Index in column (US 5) spliced with intercountry cross-section series of output per hectare for 1957–62 (Table 4–1, Chapter 4).
(US 8) *Sources:* Same as the source for (US 2); see Appendix C.

Table B–2. Time-series data for Japan, 1880–1960

	Index 1960 = 100							Percent of male workers in nonagriculture (JA 8)
Year	Agricultural output (JA 1)	Number of male workers (JA 2)	Agricultural land (JA 3)	Output per male worker (JA 4)	Output per hectare (JA 5)	Output per male worker (JA 6)	Output per hectare (JA 7)	
			percent			WU	WU	percent
1880	28	126	78	22	36	2.4	2.7	21
1885	32	125	79	25	40	2.7	3.0	24
1890	35	109	81	28	43	3.0	3.2	28
1895	37	124	83	29	44	3.1	3.3	31
1900	42	123	86	34	49	3.6	3.7	35
1905	46	122	87	38	53	4.1	4.0	38
1910	53	122	92	43	57	4.6	4.3	43
1915	60	122	95	49	63	5.2	4.7	47
1920	65	122	99	53	66	5.6	5.0	52
1925	65	122	97	53	66	5.6	5.0	55
1930	69	122	98	57	71	6.1	5.3	57
1935	73	112	101	66	73	7.1	5.5	61
1940	73	102	101	72	73	7.7	5.5	64
1945	63	98	95	64	67	6.8	5.0	62
1950	71	124	96	57	73	6.1	5.5	60
1955	83	118	99	70	84	7.5	6.3	66
1960	100	100	100	100	100	10.7	7.5	74

(JA 1) Index calculated from Series J 1 in Table C–3, Appendix C.
(JA 2) Index calculated from Series J 4 in Table C–3, Appendix C.
(JA 3) Index calculated from Series J 6 in Table C–3, Appendix C.
(JA 4) (JA 1)/(JA 2).
(JA 5) (JA 1)/(JA 3).
(JA 6) Index in column (JA 4) spliced to intercountry cross-section series of output per worker for 1957–62 (Table 4–1, Chapter 4).
(JA 7) Index in column (JA 5) spliced with intercountry cross-section series of output per hectare for 1957–62 (Table 4–1, Chapter 4).
(JA 8) Percentages calculated from the population census data for census years; linear interpolations for intercensus; and the percentage in 1920 (the first census year) multiplied by the ratios on the number of gainful workers in agriculture to the total number of gainful workers in Kazushi Ohkawa et al., *The Growth Rate of Japanese Economy* (Tokyo: 1957).

Table B–3. Time-series data for Denmark, 1880–1960

Year	Index 1960 = 100					Output per male worker (DE 6)	Output per hectare (DE 7)	Percent of male workers in nonagriculture (DE 8)
	Agricultural output (DE 1)	Number of male workers (DE 2)	Agricultural land (DE 3)	Output per male worker (DE 4)	Output per hectare (DE 5)			
			percent			WU	WU	percent
1880	24	107	92	22	26	10.5	1.2	46
1885	25	107	93	23	26	10.9	1.2	
1890	27	108	94	26	29	11.9	1.3	49
1895	29	108	94	27	31	12.6	1.4	
1900	31	103	94	30	33	14.1	1.5	53
1905	35	111	94	31	37	14.8	1.7	
1910	41	114	93	36	44	16.9	2.0	55
1915	43	118	93	36	46	17.1	2.1	
1920	44	130	103	34	43	16.1	2.0	58
1925	48	133	104	36	46	16.9	2.1	
1930	66	131	104	51	64	23.9	2.9	62
1935	69	129	105	53	65	25.2	3.0	
1940	63	129	104	49	60	23.0	2.8	67
1945	60	122	103	49	59	23.4	2.7	
1950	76	113	102	67	75	31.9	3.4	77
1955	90	111	101	81	81	38.4	3.7	74
1960	100	100	100	100	100	47.4	4.6	77

(DE 1) Index of gross agricultural output net of intermediate goods produced in agriculture. *Sources:* Kjeld Bjerke and Niels Ussing, *Studier Over Danmarks National Produkt, 1870–1950*, p. 144; USDA, *Indices of Agricultural Production in Western Europe, 1950–1968*, ERS-Foreign 266, July 1969, pp. 25–26.

(DE 2) Index calculated from the data of the economically active males in agriculture excluding fishing, hunting, and forestry. Males in agriculture are estimated as a percentage of the total agricultural labor force given by Bjerke with data from Dovring of males in agriculture for 1900, 1930, and 1950. *Sources:* Bjerke and Ussing, *Studier Over Danmarks National Produkt*, p. 142; Folke Dovring, *Land and Labor in Europe in the Twentieth Century* (3rd ed.; Hague: Martines Nijhoff, 1965), p. 63.

(DE 3) Index calculated from the data of agricultural land including temporary fallow and grass plus permanent pasture. *Sources:* Einar Jensen, *Danish Agriculture* (Copenhagen: J. H. Schultz Forlag, 1937), p. 389; Danmarks Statistik, *Land Brusstatistik, 1900–1965* (Copenhagen: 1968), pp. 8–9.

(DE 4) (DE 1)/(DE 2).

(DE 5) (DE 1)/(DE 3).

(DE 6) Index in column (DE 4) spliced with intercountry cross-section series of output per worker for 1957–62 (Table 4–1, Chapter 4).

(DE 7) Index in column (DE 5) spliced with intercountry cross-section series of output per hectare for 1957–62 (Table 4–1, Chapter 4).

(DE 8) Percentage of males economically active in nonagriculture estimated from percentage of labor force in nonagriculture given by Bjerke by splicing ILO data of males in nonagriculture at 1950, 1955 average. *Source:* Bjerke and Ussing, *Studier Over Danmarks National Produkt*, p. 142.

Table B-4. Time-series data for France, 1880-1960

	Index 1960 = 100							Percent of male workers in nonagriculture (FR 8)
Year	Agricultural output (FR 1)	Number of male workers (FR 2)	Agricultural land (FR 3)	Output per male worker (FR 4)	Output per hectare (FR 5)	Output per male worker (FR 6)	Output per hectare (FR 7)	
	percent					WU	WU	percent
1880	43	193	100	22	43	7.9	1.1	51
1885	43	183	100	24	43	8.5	1.1	
1890	44	178	99	25	45	8.9	1.1	55
1895	46	200	100	23	46	8.2	1.1	
1900	47	195	101	24	47	8.7	1.2	56
1905	50	192	104	26	48	9.4	1.2	
1910	53	190	106	28	50	10.0	1.2	60
1915	53	183	106	29	50	10.5	1.3	
1920	54	176	104	31	52	10.9	1.3	60
1925	58	166	105	35	55	12.5	1.4	
1930	62	157	103	40	60	14.2	1.5	67
1935	62	150	101	41	61	14.8	1.5	
1940	n.a.	n.a.	n.a.	n.a.	n.a.	n.a.	n.a.	
1945	52	149	93	35	56	12.5	1.4	67
1950	60	128	97	47	62	16.7	1.5	
1955	71	115	97	61	73	22.0	1.8	75
1960	100	100	100	100	100	35.9	2.5	80

(FR 1) Index of gross agricultural output net of intermediate goods produced in agriculture. *Source:* J. C. Toutain, "Le produit de l'Agriculture Francaise de 1700 a 1958"; II: *La Croissance, Histoire Quantitative de l'Economie Francaise*, Vol. 2, (Paris: I.S.E.A., 1961), pp. 6, 128–29 (lumber deducted from Table 110, pp. 128–29); EEC, *Agrarstatistik* 4 (1968): 26–27.

(FR 2) Index calculated from the data of the economically active males in agriculture excluding fishing, hunting, and forestry. *Source:* Toutain, "Le produit de l'Agriculture Francaise," pp. 200–1.

(FR 3) Index calculated from the data of agricultural land comprised of arable land including temporary fallow and grass plus permanent pastures. *Source:* Ministére de l'Economie et des Finances, *Annuaire Statistique de la France, Resume Retrospectif*, p. 177.

(FR 4) (FR 1)/(FR 2).

(FR 5) (FR 1)/(FR 3).

(FR 6) Index in column (FR 4) spliced with intercountry cross-section series of output per worker for 1957–62 (Table 4–1, Chapter 4).

(FR 7) Index in column (FR 5) spliced with intercountry cross-section series of output per hectare for 1957–62 (Table 4–1, Chapter 4).

(FR 8) Same as (FR 2).

Table B-5. Time-series data for the United Kingdom, 1880-1960

Year	Index 1960 = 100							Percent of male workers in nonagri- culture (UK 8)
	Agricul- tural output (UK 1)	Number of male workers (UK 2)	Agricul- tural land (UK 3)	Output per male worker (UK 4)	Output per hectare (UK 5)	Output per male worker (UK 6)	Output per hectare (UK 7)	
	percent					WU	WU	percent
1880	54	151	95	36	57	15.7	1.1	84
1885	55	148	96	37	57	16.4	1.1	
1890	56	145	97	39	58	17.0	1.1	86
1895	56	142	98	39	57	17.2	1.1	
1900	55	138	99	40	55	17.4	1.1	88
1905	56	140	98	40	57	17.5	1.1	
1910	56	143	98	39	57	17.3	1.1	88
1915	56	141	97	40	58	17.6	1.1	
1920	56	135	96	42	58	18.3	1.1	89
1925	57	140	100	41	57	17.8	1.1	
1930	60	134	99	45	61	19.7	1.2	90
1935	64	132	98	49	66	21.6	1.3	
1940	71	126	98	56	72	24.7	1.4	
1945	76	121	98	63	78	27.7	1.5	
1950	82	115	98	71	83	31.2	1.6	91
1955	85	109	98	78	88	34.5	1.7	92
1960	100	100	100	100	100	44.0	1.9	94

(UK 1) Index of gross agricultural output, net of intermediate goods produced in agricul-
ture. *Sources:* Colin Clark, *The Conditions of Economic Progress* (3rd ed.; London:
Macmillan & Co., 1957), p. 267. Minister of Agriculture, Fisheries and Food, *A
Century of Agricultural Statistics Great Britain, 1866-1966* (London: HMSO,
1968), pp. 76-77. E. M. Ojala, *Agriculture and Economic Progress* (London:
Goeffrey Cumberlege, 1952), p. 210.

(UK 2) Index calculated from data of the economically active males in agriculture, excluding fishing, hunting, and forestry. *Source:* Clark, *Conditions of Economic
Progress*, p. 264; FAO, *Production Yearbook*, various issues.

(UK 3) Index calculated from the data of agricultural land area including temporary
fallow and grass plus permanent pasture. *Source:* Central Statistics Office, *Annual
Abstract of Statistics* (London: HMSO), various issues.

(UK 4) (UK 1)/(UK 2).

(UK 5) (UK 1)/(UK 3).

(UK 6) Index in column (UK 4) spliced with intercountry cross-section series of output
per worker for 1957-62 (Table 4-1, Chapter 4).

(UK 7) Index in column (UK 5) spliced with intercountry cross-section series of output
per hectare for 1957-62 (Table 4-1, Chapter 4).

(UK 8) Percentage of males economically active in nonagriculture is estimated from percentage of labor force in nonagriculture given by Deane & Cole by splicing ILO
data of males in nonagriculture at 1950-55 average. *Source:* Phyllis Deane and
W. A. Cole, *British Economic Growth, 1688-1959* (Cambridge: Cambridge University Press, 1967), p. 142. ILO, *Annual Yearbook*, various issues.

APPENDIX C

Time-Series Data for U.S. and Japanese Agricultural Development, 1880–1960

In this section we explain the data which were primarily used for the analysis in Part III (Chapters 6–8).

The observations are quinquennial: Stock variables, such as land and labor, are measured at five-year intervals starting at 1880, and flow variables, such as fertilizer input, are five-year averages centering the year specified. Prices are measured as the average of five years ending the year specified. This is to enable consideration of the expectation and adjustment lag effects. In addition, five-year averages centering the year specified were prepared for the prices of flow variables. The price data of Japan for 1945 and 1950 are omitted because they were subject to the violent disturbances of World War II.

Output

Data for agricultural output are in terms of gross output net of intermediate agricultural products (seed, feed, etc.). Value added was not used in order to include such current inputs as fertilizer in our analysis. The crop output index was prepared for supplementary purposes.

Labor

Two series of labor are prepared: the number of male farm workers and the number of farm workers including females. The former seems to overestimate the agricultural labor force in the United States relative to Japan and the latter to underestimate it, because about half of the farm workers in Japan are female while in the United States female workers occupy only a small fraction. Man-hour data are not used, primarily because of the lack of availability.

Land

Two series of area of land used in agriculture are compiled: arable land area and agricultural land area, which includes arable land and permanent pasture land. For the United States, arable land is identified as crop land and agricultural land is identified as land in the farm according to the census definition (with minor modifications). For Japan the statistics for permanent pasture land are available only after World War II. Pasture land is of minor importance in Japanese agriculture, however, comprising only about 10 percent of the arable land area. Since there is no reason to assume this ratio has changed significantly over time, in cases where the figure for agricultural land area is needed it was estimated on the basis of the ratio between arable land and agricultural land areas in the 1960 Census. For the consideration of the importance and the special nature of paddy fields in Japan, we used the paddy field area to obtain supplementary information. A major defect of our land statistics is that they do not incorporate quality changes due to the depletion of soil fertility or due to irrigation construction and land improvement projects. Harvested area or planted area are not used because the objective of our analysis includes the process of increases in the intensity of land use (due to increases in double cropping, etc.), which we regard as an innovational process.

Power and Machinery

Two series of nonhuman power at the farm are prepared: the number of work animals (horses, mules, and work cattle) and the tractor horsepower. Movements in these two series represent two major innovation processes: horse mechanization and tractorization. Their substitution processes are of great interest. Work animals of all ages are included. Deduction of the animals under working age was not attempted because no information was available for Japan. One underlying assumption of our analysis is that the services of machinery moved proportionally to the increase in both animal and tractor power.

Fertilizer

Our fertilizer data are the simple sums, in terms of their physical weights, of the N, P_2O_5, and K_2O included in commercial fertilizers.

Prices

Our price data are somewhat inconsistent. Only the data of factor prices as the costs of factor services for labor and fertilizer were obtainable. Land prices in the United States as reported are (a) the average value of farm land and buildings per hectare of farm land and (b) the index of farm real estate value. In those cases where the average value of arable land was needed for comparison purposes, total value of farm land and buildings was divided by the crop land area. This, of course, overestimates per-hectare arable land value, as it includes the values of pasture land and buildings. For the purpose of comparison with Japan, however, this procedure may have some merit by compensating for the overestimation of land value in Japan, where the large irrigation capital tied to paddy fields is included. The price of power and machinery presents the most serious problem, where only the conventional price index of farm machinery is available, although we attempted to adjust quality changes in machinery (see Appendix C–2). Before World War II even the conventional price index is not available for farm machinery, and it was necessary to substitute the general machinery price index.

Fertilizer prices are the unit price obtained by dividing the total value of fertilizer consumed by the total weight of plant nutrients contained therein.

C–1. ON THE AGGREGATION OF WORK STOCK AND TRACTOR HORSEPOWER

In this study we constructed the series of power on the farm by aggregating work stock and tractors in terms of the horsepower (HP) they would generate. For this aggregation we assumed one work animal is equivalent to one HP on the following reasoning: One HP is a unit of power equal to that required to raise 33,000 ft.-lbs. at the rate of one foot per minute. Two strong horses can pull a 14 inch walking plow with a 6 inch depth through soil weighing 6 lbs. per square inch at the rate of 2 miles per hour. This implies that 2 horses can pull 88,704 ft.-lbs. per minute (14 in. $\times$ 6 in. $\times$ 6 lbs. $\times$ 5,280 ft. $\times$ 2 $\div$ 60 minutes). If the above assumptions hold, one horse is equivalent to 1.344 HP (88,704 ft.-lbs. $\div$ 33,000 ft.-lb. $\div$ 2 horses). This figure is not inconsistent with the estimates that "a 1000-lb. horse can develop 0.67 HP, a 1200-lb. horse, 0.80 to 1.00 HP, and a 1600-lb. horse, 1.07 to 1.33 HP," F. R. Jones, *Farm Gas Engines and Tractors* (2nd ed.; New York: McGraw-Hill, 1938), p. 8. Neither does it seem out of the range of the experiments conducted by James Watt as reported in Ponnell Hunt, *Farm Tractor and Machinery Management* (Ames: Iowa State University Press, 1964), p. 23.

Considering the nature of the above calculation, it is reasonable to omit the fraction and adopt one HP per horse as the factor for aggregation. We assumed mules and oxen are equivalent to horses. In any case our power series is affected little by trying fractions ranging 0.5 to 1 for mules and oxen.

One may argue against the adoption of the aggregation factor of one HP per horse, considering the nature of our data. Our work-stock data include horses, mules, and oxen of all ages on farms. The average power per head could be smaller than the power of a "representative working horse" used in the previous example. On the other hand, our tractor horsepower series does not include the power of trucks and other prime movers on the farm, which, to some extent, substituted for the work hours of horse and mules. For such considerations we estimated a factor from our aggregate data. For 1920–60 in

Table C-1. The results of regression computations to determine the value of k

k	Case 1		Case 2		Case 3		Case 4	
	β	R^2	β	R^2	β	R^2	β	R^2
0.5	0.368	0.9884	0.283	0.9618	0.367	0.9908	0.282	0.9723
0.6	0.382	0.9910	0.294	0.9676	0.382	0.9926	0.293	0.9768
0.7	0.396	0.9927	0.306	0.9723	0.395	0.9934	0.304	0.9802
0.8	0.409	0.9936	0.316	0.9761	0.409	0.9936*	0.315	0.9829
0.9	0.422	0.9940	0.327	0.9792	0.421	0.9934	0.325	0.9850
1.0	0.435	0.9940*	0.337	0.9817	0.434	0.9928	0.335	0.9865
2.0	0.547	0.9807	0.428	0.9893*	0.546	0.9762	0.425	0.9879*
3.0	0.648	0.9577	0.512	0.9819	0.649	0.9523	0.509	0.9773
4.0	0.746	0.9299	0.593	0.9670	0.749	0.9248	0.592	0.9607
5.0	0.843	0.8981	0.675	0.9464	0.850	0.8941	0.675	0.9395
6.0	0.939	0.8622	0.756	0.9205	0.951	0.8600	0.759	0.9137
7.0	1.034	0.8218	0.838	0.8890	1.052	0.8217	0.845	0.8829
8.0	1.126	0.7762	0.919	0.8516	1.152	0.7785	0.931	0.8466
9.0	1.212	0.7249	0.997	0.8074	1.250	0.7297	1.016	0.8039
10.0	1.290	0.6673	1.070	0.7561	1.340	0.6744	1.097	0.8683

* The highest R^2.

Source: Data from Table C–2.

H = U 7
W = U 8

L = U 4 in Case 1 and Case 2
  = U 3 in Case 3 and Case 4

A = U 5 in Case 1 and Case 3
  = U 6 in Case 2 and Case 4

the United States, when the substitution of tractors for horses was started and completed, we ran the following regression:

$$\log \left(\frac{A}{L}\right) = \alpha + \beta \log \left(\frac{W + kH}{L}\right),$$

where A, L, W, H, and k are respectively land area, labor force, tractor horsepower, work stock, and the factor for work stock in aggregation. The above equation expresses the relation that the area utilized or cultivated per worker is constrained by the amount of power per worker.

The equation can also be considered a production function, a relation of production of "land area cultivated" as an intermediate good for the input of power. We computed the regressions by changing k parametrically from 0.5 to 10.0 and determined the value of k giving the highest fit. The results are as summarized in Table C-1. The value of k which yields the highest fit differs depending on the data used, but in all cases it is close to one. These results, together with the previous reasoning, provide the basis for adopting one HP for the factor of aggregating work stock.

C-2. COMPUTATIONAL PROCEDURES OF QUALITY ADJUSTMENT FACTORS FOR THE FARM MACHINERY PRICE INDEX

Quality adjustment factors for the farm machinery price index (USDA index of prices paid) were calculated for 1915-60 on the basis of L. P. Fettig, "Adjusting Farm Tractor Prices for Quality Change, 1950-1962," *Journal of Farm Economics* 45 (August 1963); 599-611. The adjustment factors we calculated are originally for tractor prices, but not for the prices of farm machinery in general. The basic assumption we have to make in order to use those factors for farm machinery prices is that the quality improvement in farm machinery can be represented by or is parallel with the quality improvement in wheel tractors.

The basic approach used by Fettig to construct the quality adjusted index of farm tractors for 1950-62 is (a) to estimate the regression of tractor price on the two quality variables (average horsepower per tractor and a dummy variable for diesel engine) on cross-section data and (b) to discount the price changes due to the changes in these quality variables from the actual changes in tractor prices by the estimated regression equations.

Our quality adjustment factors for 1955-60 are based on the ratios of change in Fettig's quality adjusted index (Fettig, ibid., Column 4, Table 6, p. 609) to changes in the USDA index (average of columns 1-3, Table 6). The ratios calculated are 0.99 from 1950 to 1955, and 0.94 from 1950 to 1960.

For 1915-50 we calculated the adjustment factors using Fettig's linear regression equation on 1950 cross-section data (Fettig, ibid., p. 606). Since the numbers of diesel-powered tractors are negligible before 1950, and also data are unavailable, the diesel dummy was dropped from the equation. The equation used is:

$$Y_t = 176.02 + 43.81 \ X_t,$$

where X_t is the average horsepower per tractor and Y_t is the estimate of tractor price (1950 U.S. dollars) for the corresponding horsepower in year t. Y_t divided by Y_{1915} can be interpreted as the degree of quality improvement in tractors from 1915 to year t. The inverse of (Y_t/Y_{1915}) is the quality adjustment factor (k_t).

Year	X_t	Y_t	k_t
	(HP)	(dollars)	$(1008/Y_t)$
1915	19	1,008	1.00
1920	20	1,052	0.96
1925	22	1,140	0.88
1930	24	1,227	0.82
1935	25	1,271	0.79
1940	27	1,359	0.74
1945	27	1,359	0.74
1950	27	1,359	0.74
1955			0.73
1960			0.70

k's for 1955 and 1960 are calculated by multiplying k for 1950 by the ratios of Fettig's index to the USDA index (0.99 and 0.94), as explained previously.

Data for average horsepower per tractor are calculated from U.S. Dept. of Agriculture, ERS, *Farm Cost Situation*, 36, Nov. 1965, p. 14, for 1940–60; and Austin Fox, *Demand for Farm Tractors in the United States*, Agricultural Economic Report No. 103 (1966), p. 33, for 1925–35. For 1915–20, the average horsepower is extrapolated from the 1925 value by a quinquennial growth rate of 7 percent (average rate for 1925 to 1940).

C–3. MAJOR STATISTICAL SERIES

In principle, the data for the United States are for 48 coterminous states and the data for Japan are for Japan proper, including Okinawa before 1945 but not since 1945.

The following notations are adopted:

    a. Values for the year shown,

   b. Values for the five-year average centering the year shown,
   c. Values for the five-year average ending the year shown.
Values estimated by simple linear interpolation are shown in parentheses.
   The following abbreviations are used in the explanations for the individual columns which follows:

Agricul. Statistics: U.S. Dept. of Agriculture, *Agricultural Statistics*

Century of Agriculture: ———, *A Century of Agriculture in Charts and Tables*, Agriculture Handbook No. 318, 1966.

Production and Efficiency: ———, *Changes in Farm Production and Efficiency*, Statistical Bulletin No. 233, 1964.

Major Stat. Series: ———, *Major Statistical Series of the U.S. Department of Agriculture*, Agriculture Handbook No. 118, 1957.

Historical Statistics: U.S. Dept. of Commerce, *Historical Statistics of the United States, Colonial Times to 1957*, 1967.

LTES: Kazushi Ohkawa, Miyohei Shinohara, and Mataji Umemura (eds.) *Long Term Economic Statistics of Japan since 1868*, 13 vol. Toyokeizai-shimposha, 1965.

Table C–2. **Major time series, United States***

Year	Agricultural production (1880 = 100)		Labor (thousand)		Land (million ha.)	
	All commodities b (U 1)	All crops b (U 2)	All workers a (U 3)	Male workers a (U 4)	Agricultural land a (U 5)	Arable land a (U 6)
1880	100	100	8,585	7,959	202	76
1885	(110)	112	(9,261)	(8,551)	(219)	(88)
1890	119	130	9,938	9,142	235	100
1895	(137)	139	(10,413)	9,511	(277)	(115)
1900	155	161	10,888	9,880	318	129
1905	(160)	177	(11,211)	(10,120)	(325)	(146)
1910	164	182	11,533	10,359	333	163
1915	174	209	(11,462)	(10,290)	(348)	(176)
1920	180	217	11,390	10,221	363	189
1925	192	221	(10,856)	(9,818)	350	184
1930	204	228	10,321	9,414	381	194
1935	190	204	(9,658)	(8,950)	409	195
1940	232	247	8,995	8,487	411	187
1945	264	267	(7,974)	(7,419)	444	188
1950	285	288	6,953	6,352	451	193
1955	306	292	(5,684)	(5,163)	454	188
1960	340	329	4,415	3,973	435	181

Table C–2—(Continued)

Year	Power (thousand) Work stocks a (U 7)	Tractor horsepower a (U 8)	Fertilizer $N + P_2O_5 + K_2O$ (thousand m. tons) b (U 9)	Corn yield per harvested acre (bushels) b (U 10)	Percentage of total corn area planted with hybrid corn b (U 11)	Total inputs (1880 = 100) b (U 12)
1880	13,775		116	25.6		100
1885	15,858		(165)	25.4		(110)
1890	19,171		214	27.0		119
1895	21,595		280	25.5		(228)
1900	21,964		425	25.9		138
1905	22,877		602	29.0		(147)
1910	24,851	18	824	26.9		155
1915	26,998	475	895	25.4		166
1920	26,112	4,920	941	26.9		173
1925	22,754	11,968	1,185	25.9		179
1930	19,124	21,804	1,289	24.7		182
1935	16,683	26,410	1,241	22.6	2.5	169
1940	14,478	42,300	1,776	30.6	30.7	181
1945	11,950	63,600	2,776	32.9	63.5	188
1950	7,781	91,600	4,312	39.6	79.7	192
1955	4,309	130,400	6,017	43.6	89.4	191
1960	3,089	159,300	7,536	57.3	95.9	190

* Values in parentheses are simple linear interpolations.

Table C–2—(Continued)

	Agricultural price (1910–14 = 100)				Farm wage	
	All farm commodities		All crops		Daily wage rate ($/day)	Composite index (1910–14 = 100)
Year	b (U 13)	c (U 14)	b (U 15)	c (U 16)	a (U 17)	c (U 18)
1880	82	80	81	79	0.90	59
1885	76	85	75	85	0.95	64
1890	71	70	70	69	0.95	67
1895	62	68	62	68	0.85	64
1900	71	63	70	62	1.00	67
1905	81	79	81	78	1.30	75
1910	97	91	96	90	1.35	94
1915	120	99	120	98	1.40	102
1920	178	186	188	199	3.30	175
1925	145	139	150	147	2.35	170
1930	115	141	105	133	2.15	183
1935	101	84	100	81	1.35	106
1940	115	106	101	96	1.60	128
1945	222	176	216	168	4.35	267
1950	277	261	249	241	4.50	426
1955	242	267	236	251	5.30	507
1960	242	239	225	225	6.60	583

Table C–2—(Continued)

	Land price		Machinery price (1910–14 = 100)		Fertilizer price, average value of plant nutrient ($/m. ton)	
	Average value of arable land ($/ha.)	Index of real estate value (1910–14 = 100)	Quality adjusted	Unad-justed		
	a	c	c	c	b	c
Year	(U 19)	(U 20)	(U 21)	(U 22)	(U 23)	(U 24)
1880	163	46	146	146	212	228
1885	147	55	138	138	179	204
1890	132	52	119	119	170	173
1895	114	52	117	117	166	173
1900	129	48	94	94	156	152
1905	165	79	105	105	168	165
1910	213	95	110	110	175	173
1915	225	103	101	101	177	212
1920	352	138	136	142	309	310
1925	269	143	134	152	240	221
1930	247	120	126	154	202	175
1935	170	84	114	144	142	149
1940	180	84	114	154	153	153
1945	287	103	124	168	177	192
1950	389	167	174	235	202	205
1955	519	222	226	309	196	183
1960	711	268	249	356	168	163

Table C–3. Major time series, Japan

	Agricultural production (1880 = 100)		Labor (thousand)		Land (thousand ha.)	
	All com-modities	All crops	All workers	Male workers	Paddy field	Arable land
	b	b	a	a	a	a
Year	(J 1)	(J 2)	(J 3)	(J 4)	(J 5)	(J 6)
1880	100	100	14,655	7,842	2,801	4,748
1885	113	111	14,481	7,766	2,824	4,814
1890	126	120	14,279	7,677	2,858	4,922
1895	131	121	14,185	7,651	2,877	5,034
1900	149	134	14,211	7,680	2,905	5,200
1905	165	144	14,069	7,617	2,936	5,300
1910	188	159	14,020	7,606	3,007	5,579
1915	214	176	13,942	7,585	3,072	5,778
1920	232	182	13,939	7,593	3,136	5,997
1925	231	179	13,941	7,586	3,199	5,914
1930	249	185	13,944	7,579	3,274	5,961
1935	263	198	13,750	6,972	3,290	6,103
1940	264	202	13,549	6,365	3,276	6,121
1945	226	182	13,760	6,130	3,153	5,741
1950	253	205	15,990	7,720	3,231	5,858
1955	297	237	15,410	7,350	3,302	5,981
1960	358	282	13,390	6,230	3,382	6,071

Table C–3—(Continued)

Year	Power (thousand)		Fertilizer $N + P_2O_5 + K_2O$ (thousand m. ton)	Paddy rice yield per unit area planted (ton/ha.)	Percentage of rice area planted with improved varieties	Total inputs (1880 = 100)
	Work-stocks a (J 7)	Tractor horsepower a (J 8)	b (J 9)	b (J 10)	a (J 11)	b (J 12)
1880	1,152		63	1.95	0.2	100
1885	1,078		61	2.09	0.7	100
1890	1,048		61	2.18	1.6	101
1895	1,127		69	2.07	4.1	102
1900	1,204		86	2.30	13.9	105
1905	1,088		128	2.46	29.5	107
1910	1,258		224	2.62	35.9	112
1915	1,261		286	2.78	39.5	116
1920	1,256	0.05	378	2.92	42.0	119
1925	1,327	0.18	468	2.84	41.5	121
1930	1,348	0.45	576	2.89	55.5	125
1935	1,518	1.1	640	3.04	56.0	127
1940	1,853	19.5	705	3.08	60.0	127
1945	1,827	38.1	328	2.95	57.0	116
1950	2,234	92.1	764	3.27	67.4	134
1955	2,719	460	1,344	3.40	75.0	147
1960	2,313	3,957	1,579	3.93	70.0	156

Table C–3—(Continued)

Year	Agricultural price (1934–36 = 100)				Farm wage	
	All farm commodities		All crops		Daily wage rate (yen/day)	Index (1934–36 = 100)
	b (J 13)	c (J 14)	b (J 15)	c (J 16)	a (J 17)	c (J 18)
1880	30.9	24.8	32.9	28.8	0.22	18.3
1885	21.3	26.9	33.1	33.6	0.16	21.4
1890	24.7	22.2	39.6	35.8	0.17	19.3
1895	32.9	28.4	52.8	47.3	0.19	25.9
1900	43.8	41.6	64.5	62.2	0.31	40.3
1905	51.9	47.1	86.6	72.9	0.31	44.9
1910	59.6	53.4	85.5	92.0	0.41	49.5
1915	61.7	63.3	86.7	82.6	0.46	61.9
1920	136.3	113.7	175.3	136.8	1.39	127.3
1925	126.2	128.6	171.5	179.0	1.65	172.9
1930	83.6	103.8	120.0	151.6	1.12	156.5
1935	99.4	83.5	101.1	93.1	0.91	96.9
1940	156.1	138.0	173.9	148.3	1.90	154.2
1945						
1950						
1955	39,300	36,800	45,300	43,700	357	36,000
1960	42,000	39,200	50,400	47,000	440	46,600

Table C–3—(Continued)

	Land price				
	Average value of arable land (yen/ha.)	Arable land price index (1934–36 = 100)	Machinery price (1934–36 = 100)	Fertilizer price (yen/m. ton)	
	a	c	c	b	c
Year	(J 19)	(J 20)	(J 21)	(J 22)	(J 23)
1880	343	10.5	65.6	402	383
1885	373	12.4	55.3	260	319
1890	444	14.6	54.0	354	318
1895	615	21.7	55.2	399	374
1900	917	31.5	70.6	328	452
1905	998	34.5	77.0	472	445
1910	1,583	46.9	81.9	420	429
1915	1,613	63.0	85.7	471	429
1920	3,882	109.7	160.2	850	825
1925	3,711	140.3	135.0	660	672
1930	3,388	132.4	103.3	432	532
1935	2,783	97.1	95.7	396	381
1940	4,709	131.1	137.8	620	552
1945					
1950					
1955	868,000	19,700	30,000	90,200	95,300
1960	1,415,000	45,900	37,000	82,100	83,800

Explanations for the Individual Columns in Tables C–2 and C–3

U 1   Gross farm output net of intermediate goods supplied within agriculture.

SOURCE: *Production and Efficiency*, p. 50.

U 2   1910–60: USDA crop production index. 1880–1909: Series of production of wheat, rye, corn, oats, barley, potatoes, tobacco, cotton, and buckwheat aggregated by using 1910–14 average prices as weights and linked to USDA crop production index by multiplying by the 1910–14 average ratio.

SOURCE: USDA crop production index—*Production and Efficiency*, pp. 7–8; individual commodity production—*Century of Agriculture*, pp. 25–34; price weights—*Major Stat. Series*, pp. 24–34.

U 3–4   1900–60: Economically active population (population census data adjusted by Kaplan and Casey). 1880–90: Number of gainful workers (population census data adjusted by Edwards).

SOURCE: A. M. Edwards, *Comparative Occupational Statistics for the United States, 1870–1940*, U.S. Department of Commerce, 1943, p. 100; D. L. Kaplan and M. C. Casey, *Occupational Trends in the United States 1900 to 1950*, U.S. Bureau of Census Working

Report No. 5, 1958, p. 6; U.S. Bureau of Census, *U.S. Census of Population 1960 U.S. Summary*, Final Report PC(1)–ID, 1960, p. 563.

U 5 Land in farm (excluding farmstead and road area) in the U.S. Census of Agriculture. 1955 and 1960 figures are of 1954 and 1959 censuses.

SOURCE: *Agricul. Statistics*, 1967, p. 512, and *Major Stat. Series*, p. 4.

U 6 Cropland in the U.S. Census of Agriculture. Areas of cropland used for pasture for 1920–40 are estimated by multiplying the areas of "cropland used for crops and idle or in cover crops," by 0.16 (1945–60 average ratio), 1955 and 1960 figures are of 1954 and 1959 censuses.

SOURCE: Same as column U 5.

U 7 Number of horses, mules, and oxen on farms on January 1. Horses include colts.

SOURCE: *Century of Agriculture*, p. 38; W. M. Hurst and L. M. Church, *Power and Machinery in Agriculture*, U.S.D.A. Miscellaneous Publication No. 157, 1933, p. 12.

U 8 Horsepower on farm on January 1, 1910–20 figures are estimated by multiplying the number of farm tractors by the average horsepower per tractor which is extrapolated from 1925 average horsepower with the quinquennial growth rate of 7 percent.

SOURCE: U.S. Department of Agriculture, *Farm Cost Situation 36*, 1965, p. 14; Austin Fox, *Demand for Farm Tractors in the United States*, U.S. Department of Agriculture, ERS, Agricultural Economic Report No. 103, 1966, p. 33.

U 9 In terms of principal plant nutrients ($N + P_2O_5 + K_2O$). 1910–60; USDA data. 1880–1909: Series of quantity of commercial fertilizer consumed in *Historical Statistics* linked to USDA plant nutrient series by multiplying by 1910–14 average ratio.

SOURCE: *Production and Efficiency*, pp. 21–22; *Historical Statistics* Series K160, p. 285.

U 10 Yield per harvested acre.

SOURCE: *Century of Agriculture*, p. 27.

U 11 SOURCE: *Agricul. Statistics*, 1963, p. 41.

U 12 SOURCE: *Production and Efficiency*, p. 50.

U 13–16 1910–60: USDA indexes of prices received by farmers. 1880–1909: BLS and Warren–Pearson wholesale price indexes of farm commodities linked to USDA indexes by multiplying by 1911–15 average ratio.

SOURCE: *Agricul. Statistics*, 1957, p. 571; *Agricul. Statistics*, 1967, p. 563; *Historical Statistics*, Series E1 and E13, pp. 115–17.

U 17 Farm wage per day without board. 1880, 1885, 1895, 1900, and 1905 figures are respectively of 1879 or 1880, 1884 or 1885, 1889 or 1890, 1899, and 1906.

SOURCE: *Historical Statistics*, series K80, pp. 280–81; *Agricul. Statistics*, 1967, p. 530.

U 18 Composite index of farm wage rates. 1880, 1885, 1980, 1900, 1905, and 1910 figures are respectively the averages of 1877–80, 1881–84, 1887–89, 1891–95, 1898–99, 1902–10, and 1906–09.

SOURCE: *Historical Statistics*, Series K76, pp. 280–81; *Agricul. Statistics*, 1967, p. 530.

U 19 Total value of farm land and buildings (from the Census of Agriculture) divided by total area of arable land (from column U 6). 1885, 1895, and 1905 figures are interpolated by use of agricultural price index (from column U 14).

SOURCE: *Historical Statistics*, Series K4, p. 279; *Agricul. Statistics*, 1967, p. 510.

U 20 1912–60: Index of average value of farm real estate, March 1. 1880–1911: Series of average value of farm land and building per acre of land in farm linked to the index of average farm real estate value by multiplying by the 1912–14 average ratio. Intercensus years are interpolated by use of the agricultural price index (from column U 14).

SOURCE: *Historical Statistics*, Series K5 and K7, p. 278; *Agricul. Statistics*, 1967, p. 517.

U 21 Farm machinery price index adjusted for the quality changes of machinery. Column 22 multiplied by the quality adjustment factors in Appendix C–2.

U 22 1915–60: USDA index of farm machinery price paid by farmers. 1895–1910: BLS wholesale price index of metal and metal products linked to USDA index by multiplying by the 1911–15 average ratio. 1880–1990: Warren–Pearson wholesale price index of metal and metal products spliced to the BLS index at 1890.

SOURCE: *Agricul. Statistics*, 1957, p. 572; *Agricul. Statistics*, 1967, p. 564; *Historical Statistics*, Series E 7 and 20, pp. 115–17.

U 23–24 1910–60: Current farm expense for fertilizer divided by quantity of principal plant nutrients consumed. 1885–1909: Fertilizer price index is constructed from the data of Vail by simply averaging the indexes of organic fertilizer and mineral fertilizer. Those two indexes are the simple averages of the indexes of the prices of cottonseed meal, castor pomace, ground fish, and tankage in the case of organic fertilizer, and of nitrate of soda, sulfate of soda, superphosphate and muriate of potash in the case of mineral fertilizer on the Connecticut market. The fertilizer price index thus calculated is linked to the unit plant nutrient price by multiplying by the 1911–15 average ratio. 1875–84: Warren–Pearson wholesale price index of chemicals and drugs linked to the fertilizer price index by multiplying by 1881–85 average ratio.

SOURCE: farm expense for fertilizer—U.S. Dept. of Agriculture, *Farm Income Situation*, FIS-207, 1967, p. 56; annual data for 1910–19 are furnished from Economic Research Service; consumption of plant nutrients—*Production and Efficiency*, 1964, pp. 21–22; Connecticut fertilizer prices—E. E. Vail, *Retail Prices of Fertilizer Materials and Mixed Fertilizers*, Ithaca: N.Y. (Cornell) Agricul. Exp. Stat. Bulletin 545, 1932; wholesale price index of chemicals and drugs—*Historical Statistics*, Series E9, pp. 115–16.

J 1 Gross agricultural output net of intermediate goods supplied within agriculture. The index of gross agricultural production (linked index) multiplied by (1 − the ratio of agricultural intermediate goods) calculated from 1934–36 constant price aggregates of gross agricultural production and of agricultural intermediate goods.

SOURCE: The index of gross agricultural production—*LTES*, vol. 9, series 10, Table 35, pp. 222–23; 1934–36 price aggregates—*LTES*, vol. 9, series 14, Table 4, pp. 152–53, and Series 6–7, Table 16, pp. 186–87.

J 2 SOURCE: *LTES*, vol. 9, series 10, pp. 152–53.

J 3–4 Number of gainful workers.
SOURCE: *LTES*, vol. 9, series 1 and 3, Tables 33, pp. 218–19.

J 5–6 SOURCE: *LTES*, vol. 9, series 13 and 14, Table 32, pp. 216–17.

J 7 Horses and draft cattle of all ages at the end of the year.
SOURCE: *LTES*, vol. 3, pp. 166–67.

J 8 Estimated from the number of tractors (garden tractors or cultivators) by assuming that the average horsepower is five. Figures on farm at the end of the year.
SOURCE: *LTES*, vol. 3, p. 172.

J 9 In terms of principal plant nutrients ($N + P_2O_5 + K_2O$).
SOURCE: *LTES*, vol. 9, series 1, Tables 20–22, pp. 196–203.

J 10   In terms of husked brown (not milled) basis.

SOURCE: *LTES*, vol. 9, p. 37; Ministry of Agriculture and Forestry, *Norinsho Ruinen Tokei-hyo* (Historical Statistics of the Ministry of Agriculture and Forestry), 1955, p. 24.

J 11   Estimated by interpolation from Hayami–Yamada data.

SOURCE: Yujiro Hayami and Saburo Yamada, *Technological Progress in Agriculture* in L. R. Klein and Kazushi Ohkawa (ed.), *Economic Growth: The Japanese Experience since the Meiji Era*, Homewood, Illinois: Irwin, 1968, pp. 135–61.

J 12   SOURCE: *LTES*, vol. 9, series 4, Table 36, pp. 224–25.

J 13–16 SOURCE: *LTES*, vol. 8, series 5–6, Table 10, p. 165.

J 17   Wage of male daily contract workers. 1890 figure is of 1892.

SOURCE: *LTES*, vol. 8, series 24, Table 25, p. 245; *LTES*, vol. 9, series 3, Table 34, pp. 220–21.

J 18   Index of male daily contract workers' wage. Data not available in *LTES* are estimated by interpolation or extrapolation on the basis of the agricultural price index (column J 14).

SOURCE: *LTES*, vol. 9, series 3, Table 34, pp. 220–21.

J 19   Weighted average of the prices of the paddy field and the upland field, using the area as weights. In case of the paddy field, the 1885 price is extrapolated by the rent data and the 1880 and 1895 prices are extrapolated and interpolated by the rice price. In the case of the upland field, the 1885 price is extrapolated by the rent data, and the 1880 and 1895 prices are extrapolated and interpolated by the price index of crops except rice.

SOURCE: prices of paddy and upland field—*LTES*, vol. 9, series 9–10, Table 34, pp. 220–21; rent—*LTES*, vol. 9, series 9–10, Table 34, pp. 220–21; rice and other crop price index, *LTES*, vol. 8, pp. 168–71.

J 20   Simple average of the paddy field price index and the upland field price index. 1880–1905 figures are of the years shown. 1885 figures are extrapolated by the rent data. 1880–95 figures are extrapolated and interpolated by the rice price and other crop price indexes.

SOURCE: same as column J 19.

J 21   1950–60: the index of farm machinery price (price received by farmers) of the Ministry of Agriculture and Forestry. 1880–1940: the index of machinery price linked to the index of farm machinery price by multiplying by the 1951–55 average ratio.

SOURCE: *LTES*, vol. 8, series 21, Table 8, pp. 160–63; Bank of Japan, *Hundred-year Statistics of the Japanese Economy*, p. 83.

J 22–23 Current farm expense for fertilizer divided by the total quantity of principal nutrients consumed. 1940 figure in column J 22 is of the 1938–41 average. 1880 and 1955 figures in column J 23 are of the 1878–80 average and the 1952–55 average.

SOURCE: *LTES*, vol. 9, pp. 194–201.

APPENDIX D

Index of Rice Seed Improvement in Japan[1]

The index of rice seed improvement in Japan used for the analysis in Chapter 10 (S in Table 10–2) is constructed by aggregating the areas planted in various varieties using as weights the standard yields of these varieties, which are fixed by two major regions (Eastern prefectures and Western prefectures).

The Eastern prefectures include: Aomori, Iwate, Miyagi, Akita, Yamagata, Fukushima, Ibaragi, Tochigi, Gunma, Chiba, Saitama, Tokyo, Kanagawa, Niigata, Nagano, Yamanashi, Shizuoka, Aichi. The Western prefectures include: Toyama, Ishikawa, Fukui, Gifu, Mie, Shiga, Kyoto, Osaka, Hyogo, Nara, Wakayama, Tottori, Shimane, Okayama, Hiroshima, Yamaguchi, Tokushima, Kagawa, Ehime, Kochi, Fukuoka, Saga, Nagasaki, Kumamoto, Oita, Miyazaki, Kagoshima.

Areas planted in individual varieties in the original data are grouped into the specified varieties by prefectures, which are in turn aggregated into Eastern and Western Regions (Tables D–1 and D–2). Original area data are available only since 1907. The planted area data before 1907 were extrapolated by connecting linearly the areas in 1907 with the areas (assumed zero) in the years of selection by individual varieties.

The standard yields were determined on the basis of the results of yield tests conducted by various experiment stations (Tables D–3 and D–4). In general we adopted as the standard yield the median of experiment yield data collected for each variety. However, there is a tendency for the median to underestimate the yield capacity of the varieties which were tested widely in many prefectures over the nation, because the samples of the test results of these varieties tend to include those conducted under unsuited environmental conditions. Therefore, we adopted as the standard yields the upper quartiles in the collected samples for those widely tested varieties.

Linear interpolations were used to obtain the index for the years shown in Table 10–2 after constructing the index for the years shown in Tables D–1 and D–2.

[1] This appendix draws from Yujiro Hayami and Saburo Yamada, "Agricultural Productivity at the Beginning of Industrialization," *Agriculture and Economic Growth: Japan's Experience*, ed. Kazushi Ohkawa, Bruce F. Johnston, and Hiromitsu Kaneda (Tokyo: University of Tokyo Press, 1969), pp. 105–35.

348

Rōnō varieties are the improved varieties selected by the *Rōnō* (veteran farmers). The *Rōnō* varieties in the following tables include those which were improved by experiment stations after selection by farmers. Traditional varieties include improved varieties which cannot be specified here.

Sources of data are: Japan Ministry of Agriculture and Forestry, *Suitōhinshu no Hensen to Ikuseihinshu no Tokusei Narabini Fukyūjōkyō no Gaiyō* (Summary Report on Changes in Rice Varieties and the Characteristics and Diffusions of Improved Varieties), 1953; *Suitōhinshubetsu Sakuzuke Menseki Chōsasho, 1951* (Survey Report on Area planted in Respective Rice Varieties in 1951), 1952; *Ine Mugi Hinshu no Tokuseihyō* (Tables of Characteristics of Rice, Wheat, Barley and Naked Barley), 1955; *Suirikuto Mugirui Shōreihinshu Tokuseihyō* (Tables of Characteristics of Selected Rice, Wheat, Barley and Naked Barley), 1964; *Suitō oyobi Rikutō Koshu Yōkō* (Report on Rice Cultivation), 1936; *Nōgyō Hattatsushi Chōsakai, Meijiikōni okeru Suitōhinshu no Hensen* (Changes in Rice Varieties since the Meiji Era), 1955.

Table D–1.   Areas planted in rice by varieties: Eastern prefectures   (unit: 1,000 chō)*

	1875	1880	1885	1890	1895	1900	1907	1910	1919	1928	1932	1936	1939	1946	1951	1956	1963
Rōnō varieties																	
Aikoku					4	23	143	142	176	253	249	221	197	97	149		
Asahi									1	38	73	95	111	152	123	17	
Kameno-o							17	52	133	121	70	21	12	6	3		
Omachi							1	3									
Shinriki					2	27	80	82	110	63	34	28	22	7			
Others																	
Bōzu					3	22	67	66	61	131	203	209	148	28	31		
Gin-bōzu										35	72	92	81	29	37		
Ishiziro					1	5	15	17	25	15	12	3	2	17	14		
Oba							4	4	5	4	3						
Takenari			1	3	7	19	37	29	5								
Experiment station varieties																	
Prewar selection																	
Nōrin numbers											11	73	179	370	383	276	55
Rikuu-132											121	212	210	62	63	19	
Others											5	15	55	54	47	222	64
Postwar selection																	
Nōrin numbers														18	157	462	740
Others															28	217	274
Major improved varieties total			1	3	17	96	364	395	516	660	853	969	1,017	840	1,035	1,213	1,133
Traditional varieties	1,150	1,187	1,192	1,228	1,224	1,152	922	923	858	826	696	558	436	547	451	389	556
Total	1,150	1,187	1,193	1,231	1,241	1,248	1,286	1,318	1,374	1,486	1,549	1,527	1,453	1,387	1,486	1,602	1,689

* 1 chō equals 0.99174 hectare.

Table D-2. Areas planted in rice by varieties: Western prefectures

(unit: 1,000 cho)*

	1875	1880	1885	1890	1895	1900	1907	1910	1919	1928	1932	1936	1939	1946	1951	1956	1963
Rōnō varieties																	
Aikoku									21	54	86	86	79	38	62		
Asahi									12	81	296	435	481	285	296	40	
Omachi	1	3	5	7	12	41	122	113	96	40	28	17	9		3		
Shinriki		1	10	28	72	211	440	441	500	318	171	68	49	28	30		
Others																	
Gin-bōzu			1	4	7	14	25	19	6	28	62	80	57	29	23		
Ishiziro								3	13	15	16	14	15	10			
Kameji									21	26	37	29	24	7	9		
Oba					2	18	45	51	52	29	22	5	2				
Takenari					1	3	14	7	8								
Experiment station varieties																	
Prewar selection																	
Nōrin numbers												42	79	330	394	320	125
Rikuu-132													1	1	8		
Others														5	46	321	142
Postwar selection																	
Nōrin numbers														1	104	338	475
Others															14	144	176
Major improved varieties total	1	4	16	39	94	287	646	634	729	591	718	776	796	734	989	1,163	918
Traditional varieties	1,338	1,378	1,364	1,442	1,390	1,213	888	918	836	953	824	734	679	598	426	320	552
Total	1,339	1,382	1,380	1,481	1,484	1,500	1,534	1,552	1,565	1,544	1,542	1,510	1,475	1,332	1,415	1,483	1,470

* 1 chō equals 0.99174 hectare.

351

Table D-3. Rice yields per tan* by varieties in experiments: Eastern prefectures (unit: koku)**

		Parameters			Standard yields adopted	Remarks on the standard yields
	Number of experiments	Arith. mean	Median	Upper quartile		
Rōnō varieties						
Aikoku	43	2.83	2.8	3.0	3.0	Upper quartile
Asahi	17	2.71	2.7	2.8	2.7	Median
Kameno-o	16	2.82	2.8	3.1	2.8	Median
Omachi	—	—	—	—	2.9	Same as Western Prefectures
Shinriki	37	3.04	3.0	3.5	3.0	Median
Others						
Bōzu	16	2.54	2.6	2.9	2.6	Median
Gin-bōzu	11	2.75	2.8	3.0	2.8	Median
Ishiziro	4	2.79	2.7	2.7	2.7	Median
Oba	—	—	—	—	2.7	Same as Ishiziro
Takenari	—	—	—	—	2.8	Same as Gin-bōzu
Experiment station varieties						
Prewar selection						
Nōrin numbers	81	2.71	2.7	3.0	3.0	Upper quartile
Rikuu-132	13	3.00	2.9	3.3	2.9	Median
Others	13	2.80	2.8	2.9	2.9	Upper quartile
Postwar selection						
Nōrin numbers	60	2.91	2.9	3.2	3.2	Upper quartile
Others	14	3.15	3.2	3.2	3.2	Upper quartile
Traditional varieties	71	2.28	2.4	2.6	2.4	Median

* 1 tan = 0.1 chō.
** 1 koko of brown rice weighs 150 kilograms.

Table D-4. Rice yields per tan* by varieties in experiments: Western prefectures   (unit: koku)**

	Number of experiments	Parameters			Standard yields adopted	Remarks on the standard yields
		Arith. mean	Median	Upper quartile		
Rōnō varieties						
Aikoku	26	2.90	2.9	3.1	2.9	Median
Asahi	70	2.92	2.9	3.1	3.1	Upper quartile
Omachi	19	2.97	2.9	3.2	2.9	Median
Shinriki	31	3.17	3.1	3.5	3.1	Median
Others						
Gin-bōzu	11	2.93	2.9	3.2	2.9	Median
Ishiziro	—	—	—	—	2.7	Same as Eastern Prefectures
Kameji	9	2.93	2.9	3.0	2.9	Median
Oba	2	3.08	3.1	—	3.1	Median
Takenari	—	—	—	—	2.8	Same as Eastern Prefectures
Experiment station varieties						
Prewar selection						
Nōrin numbers	101	2.72	2.8	3.0	3.0	Upper quartile
Rikuu-132	—	—	—	—	2.9	Same as Eastern Prefectures
Others	19	2.84	2.8	3.1	3.1	Upper quartile
Postwar selection						
Nōrin numbers	81	2.87	3.0	3.2	3.2	Upper quartile
Others	7	2.99	3.0	3.2	3.2	Upper quartile
Traditional varieties	84	2.73	2.7	3.0	2.7	Median

* 1 tan = 0.1 chō.
** 1 koku of brown rice weighs 150 kilograms.

Index

355